THE ARMIES OF GEORGE S. PATTON

THE ARMIES OF GEORGE S. PATTON

George Forty

ARMS AND
ARMOUR

THIS BOOK IS DEDICATED TO
THE PATTON MUSEUM OF CAVALRY AND ARMOR,
FORT KNOX, KENTUCKY

Arms and Armour Press
A Cassell Imprint
Wellington House, 125 Strand, London WC2R OBB.

Distributed in the USA by Sterling Publishing Co. Inc.,
387 Park Avenue South, New York, NY 10016-8810.

First published in paperback 1998
Reprinted 1999

British Library Cataloguing-in-Publication Data: a catalogue record for this book is available from the British Library

ISBN 1-85409-484-X

Designed and edited by DAG Publications Ltd.
Designed by David Gibbons; edited by Michael Boxall;
printed and bound in Great Britain by
MPG Books Ltd, Bodmin, Cornwall.

Jacket illustrations
Front: Major General George S. Patton, Jr, Commanding General US 2nd Armored Division, photographed in front of his tank during the Louisiana manoeuvres of autumn 1941; inset, portrait of Patton painted by Boguslav Czedekowski in September 1945; US Army Photo courtesy of the Patton Museum, Fort Knox, Kentucky.
Back, from top: sets of commemorative stamps featuring Patton (courtesy of Mike Province); one of the last photographs of Patton, taken in the summer of 1945 and showing him wearing most of his decorations; and the 'Pyramid of Power' – the symbol of American Armor (see page 74).

All photographs in this book are US Army Photographs which have mainly been supplied courtesy of the Patton Museum, Fort Knox, Kentucky, USA, except where indicated otherwise.

Contents

Acknowledgements

As always I have many people to thank for their help with the preparation of this book, first and foremost Mrs Katie Talbot, the Librarian of the Patton Museum of Cavalry and Armor, for her generous, unstinting and continued support. She has provided me with a constant stream of information and advice, not to mention allowing me to borrow many of the Museum's photographs and, most importantly, a copy of the massive After Action Report in which all Third Army's wartime operations are recorded. I have dedicated this book to the Patton Museum, the living symbol of GSP's sparkling career, so as to record formally my thanks to her, to John Purdy the Museum Director and to all his staff. Next I must thank Mike Province, President and Founder of the George Smith Patton, Jr Historical Society for his usual generous help. He is due to visit England this autumn, so I will be able to thank him in person. As well as all those who have allowed me to quote from their works on Third Army, both published and unpublished, I must also thank the Tank Museum, the Ministry of Defence Library, the US Army Center of Military History and the US Army Military History Institute for their invaluable assistance. Finally I must thank Colonel Owsley Costlow, Colonel Haynes Dugan and Colonel James Leach, DSC, all US Armor Retd, also Colonel David Higgins, US Armor, who is currently Deputy Commander of the RAC Gunnery School. Thank you all for your help and kindness.

George Forty
Bryantspuddle, Dorset
August 1995

Introduction

Some years ago I had the privilege of being asked to write an illustrated history of the exploits of the US Third Army in the Second World War. I found it a stimulating experience, not just because of their incredible war record – they went farther, faster than any other army had done in history; not just because of their great commander whom I had always rated as being one of the best armour commanders ever; but mainly because of the large number of ex-Third Army GIs with whom I had the pleasure of corresponding – and still do in a number of cases. From them I believe I was able to get a far truer picture of GSP and all he achieved, than from the myriad of books that have been written about him since the war ended. Everyone nowadays seems to delight in trying to prove that our war heroes had feet of clay, so someone as flamboyant as Patton is a perfect target. He was no politician, that is for certain, but he was a highly successful soldier, and it is on his undoubted success in his chosen field of endeavour, namely as a military commander, that we should judge him.

Patton was the only senior armour commander of the Second World War who had fought in tanks during the Great War at a sufficiently high level as to be able fully to appreciate their true worth, yet had not become hidebound by the semi-static tactics of that battlefield. GSP handled tanks the way they should be handled – with *élan*, but at the same time with common sense and expertise. One can criticise him for his use of colourful bad language – but his soldiers loved it; for his lack of tact off the battlefield – but as he once said, he wasn't trying to be the 'Shah of Persia'; for his flamboyant dress – but his soldiers were smarter than any other GIs; or even for his penchant for carrying two pistols – although he was an expert shot and did kill at least two men with them; but one cannot fault him for his generalship of armour.

However, this book is not meant to be just another biography of Patton, but rather a 'nuts and bolts' primer on the armies he commanded – and what a fascinating collection they were! In 1918 he led the *first* US tank brigade in its *first* tank action, having formed and trained it virtually from scratch. At the beginning of the Second World War he was in command of the 2nd Armored Division, training it to perfection and ensuring that it would live up to its reputation and never lose the fighting spirit which he had so imbued into all his 'Hell on Wheelers'.

Commanding the Western Task Force of Operation 'Torch' gave him the chance to get into the war earlier than most other American tank commanders and his subsequent revitalisation of US I Corps after the débâcle at Kasserine Pass in Tunisia deserves far more space than I have been able to give it. Commanding the US Seventh Army in the Allied assault on Sicily, GSP quickly restored Americans' pride in their soldiers' abilities and fighting spirit, with his bold, intelligent and highly successful handling of the American part of the campaign. So it is all the more extraordinary that he should have almost lost his chance for senior command in North-west Europe over the ridiculous slapping incident, which was blown up out of all proportion by the American media, only days after they had been praising him to the heavens for killing and maiming the enemy on the battlefield. No wonder the Germans were hoodwinked by Operation 'Fortitude', the D-Day cover plan. To their logical military minds, would the Allies really sacrifice their best armour general just because he slapped a malingerer? Obviously, they reasoned, GSP was being kept for greater things, namely to lead the real Allied assault in the Pas de Calais area.

Eisenhower was probably correct in keeping Patton at Army Command level, where he was close to the 'sharp end' and could exert his influence on the battle almost minute by minute. He would inevitably have been a complete disaster as an Army Group commander, not least because of the antagonism which had existed since Sicily, between GSP and that other brilliant, but just as difficult to manage, British general – Montgomery. Patton was entirely in his element commanding Third Army, as his spectacular successes show.

As soon as the fighting was over and warfare was replaced by diplomacy, it was not long before Patton found himself in trouble yet again, this time basically for his outspoken views on Communism, although anti-Semitism and even that he was a Nazi sympathiser were charges also levelled against him. How anyone who described Hitler as: a 'paper-hanging son of a bitch' and who told his troops that 'the Nazis are the enemy' encouraging them to 'Wade into them – Spill their blood – Shoot them in the belly!' could ever be described as a Nazi sympathiser is beyond me, but then who can always understand the true motives behind newspaper headlines?

His last command, US Fifteenth Army, was a strange, but interesting organisation and GSP injected his own speed of working into their task which was in danger of becoming moribund. His energy and enthusiasm were still there despite everything. However, he was clearly reaching boiling-point and there must have been a fair number of politicians and senior officers who were not looking forward to his return to the USA. Sadly we shall never know what might have been, a needless traffic accident ending his life, instead of, as he had wished, the last bullet of the last battle of the war.

There has been a great deal to cover in this book and, of necessity, I have devoted much of the space to describing the organisation and equipment of US Third Army, one of the best organised, armed and equipped armies the world has ever seen, while its fighting spirit, epitomised by its fighting general, is plain for all to see. However, I have tried also to cover in sufficient detail his Great War and early Second World War commands, so I hope the resulting 'mix' will be of interest and value.

PART I

THE MAKING OF AN ARMOUR COMMANDER

1
The Making of an Armour Commander (Part One)

SECTION 1: THE EARLY YEARS (1885–1917)

George Smith Patton, Junior, was born on his maternal grandfather's working ranch in San Gabriel, California, on 11 November 1885. His grandfather, Benjamin Davis Wilson, who had died in 1875, was a famous pioneer from Wilson County, Tennessee, nicknamed 'Don Benito', and had built the ranch house in about 1830. The cattle ranch had then extended from Redlands to Los Angeles and he is reputed to have given away gratis part of his cattle pens as the site for the city of Pasadena, in order to encourage people to come out west to settle. He was a 'larger-than-life' character, who had fought hostile Indians, been savaged by a wounded bear and captured by bandits in his adventurous life. His own grandfather had been a hero of the Revolutionary War, Congress giving him 2,000 acres of wilderness in what later became the state of Tennessee, as a reward. Patton's paternal grandfather was a Civil War hero, killed in 1864 while commanding the Confederate division which had faced Sheridan's historic charge at Winchester. The family could also claim to be direct descendants of John Washington, who came to Virginia in 1657 and was the grandfather of the great George Washington. These are but a few examples of the abundance of colourful characters who made up the Patton ancestry on both sides of his family tree, so it is understandable that the young Patton would wish to follow in their martial footsteps and fight for his beloved country. His daughter, Mrs Ruth Ellen Patton Totten, once told me that from the age of five her father had always wanted to be a soldier – up until then he had favoured the fire brigade!

Despite this plethora of warlike and adventurous forebears, Patton's immediate family were sober, professional men, lawyers and the like, men of substance and good breeding. His father, for example, always dressed for dinner and GSP inherited this trait for immaculate attire, which was to become one of his hallmarks in the army. Not only did he dress to perfection, but he quickly realised that smartly dressed soldiers, who had something special in their uniform which took them out of the 'common herd', were invariably well-motivated soldiers with a high morale. His family thus had breeding and a certain amount of money, but it was his wife to be, Beatrice Ayer, who had the enormous wealth that gave the Pattons that indispensable attribute – financial independence – so that they need not be hidebound by any of the petty rules and regulations which often stifle army family life. Beatrice brought a great deal more to the marriage than mere dollars, however. Indeed Patton's incomparable biographer, Martin Blumenson, goes so far as to aver that Patton was ' ... as man and legend, to a large degree, the creation of his wife'.[1]

Initially he did not have an easy schooling, not learning to read or write until he was twelve years old, mainly because he was kept at home, one result being that he never fully mastered spelling or punctuation, although Beatrice did her best to help him later on. At school he made steady but not spectacular progress, first at the 'Classical School for Boys' in Pasadena and then at the Virginia Military Institute. He developed a taste for history, especially military history, and for poetry. The former was of enormous use to him in his military career, as he quickly realised how much could be learnt from the past. 'A picture without a background,' he once wrote, 'is both uninteresting and misleading. Hence, in order to paint you an intelligent picture ... as it exists today, we must provide an historical background.' The latter taste, which perhaps seems out of place in such a warlike character, continued throughout his life and he wrote many poems, some of which have fortunately been saved for posterity.[2]

West Point. In 1904 he managed, with the help of his father, to gain selection for West Point, but initially did not do as well as might have been expected. He was 'turned back' at the end of his first year (the 'plebe' year), but fortunately not discharged and merely had to repeat the year all over again. Patton was undoubtedly what we would now call a 'late developer', so this extra year was perhaps a blessing in disguise, giving him the extra time he needed to mature. Through hard work and diligence he eventually made good, although graduating in the middle of his class (46th out of 103). Nevertheless, he achieved the rank of Class Adjutant, excelled at 'Drill Regulations', won an 'A' for athletics (track and field), and was a member of the riding, fencing and shooting teams. He also played football in the West Point squad, in four of his last five years there, breaking both arms, his nose (three times) and dislocating his shoulder! Of course, he also had his bad points – being inclined towards boastfulness and having an almost obsessive concern for future glory, which did not earn him many friends. He was a handsome, loyal, hard-working young man, immaculate in dress and appearance, with a fine military bearing and a pleasant personality, in short the perfect cadet, who would undoubtedly make a splendid young officer.

Joining the Cavalry. 'Georgie', as he was listed in the 1909 edition of the Academy Yearbook, *Howitzer*, was commissioned into the US Cavalry, his first appointment being with 'K' Troop of the 15th Cavalry at Fort Sheridan, Illinois. Already an expert horseman, sabreur and pistol shot, the cavalry had been the obvious choice for him and he soon immersed himself in the everyday life of a military post, impressing his Troop Commander, Captain Francis C. Marshall, as being 'a young officer of especial promise' and earning a reputation with the enlisted men for 'guts', after stoically continuing to drill with his squad, having been injured by a bucking horse and bleeding like a 'stuck pig'.

GSP clearly had other matters on his mind as well as soldiering, because in the following summer he and Beatrice married – a grand society wedding, covered in great detail in all the Boston newspapers. After a month honeymooning in Europe, the couple returned to her family home in Boston and thence to Fort Sheridan. Their first child was born in 1911 and Patton took temporary command of 'K' Troop in the absence of Captain Marshall. That year he also wrote his first military papers: one entitled: 'Saddle Drill' for his troop, the other a treatise entitled 'National Defense' for his own amusement. The former showed his innate grasp of the basic cavalry teachings, many of which were to colour his philosophy on the handling of tanks in the future. The latter, although unfinished, contained a phrase which encapsulates Patton's approach to battle: 'Attack, push forward, attack again until the end.' He would go on to write many articles in the *Cavalry Journal*, and Beatrice, who spoke French fluently, helped him by translating writings from French military journals. Another theme from a different paper written by GSP at about this same time, which he would also continue to follow throughout his career, concerned his regard for the men he commanded, viz., 'We children of a mechanical age are interested and impressed by machines to such an extent that we forget that no machine is better than its operator.' Patton never did forget that his soldiers were individuals and not just 'cannon-fodder' and, despite such aberrations as the notorious 'slapping incident' in Sicily in 1943, he constantly showed them respect and affection, which was undoubtedly reciprocated. It was this rapport which made the men of his great Third Army in the Second World War refer to themselves, with both pride and delight, as being 'Georgie's Boys'.

The Olympics. In December 1911 the Pattons moved with 15th Cavalry to Fort Myer, Virginia, and the following June they sailed for Stockholm, where GSP would represent the USA in the Modern Pentathlon at the Olympic Games. He had trained hard for all six events – he even swam in a water-filled wooden tank aboard the ship on passage to Europe! There were 47 competitors, but GSP was the only American, the other two, both civilians, having dropped out. He finished third in the fencing, third in the riding, sixth in the swimming and third in the running – collapsing over the finishing line, having given his all. That just left his best event, the pistol shooting, in which he had already broken the Olympic record in practice, gaining 197 points out of a possible

200. Disaster struck, when two of his shots were adjudged to have missed the target, so he dropped to 21st and was placed fifth in the overall competition, thus outside the medals. It seems possible that the two shots went through other bullet holes on the target, but without the type of accurate measuring instruments we have today, this could not be proved. Patton made no complaint or excuse.

Saumur. After the Olympics the Pattons went to the French Armour School at Saumur for two weeks, where he was given private lessons by the Master of Arms, who was the professional fencing champion of Europe. This later resulted in GSP being picked to go to Saumur in July 1913, to study swordsmanship, after being selected for a posting to the Mounted Service School at Fort Riley for duty as 'Master of the Sword', which involved re-writing the sabre manual for the US Army. It is perhaps once again prophetic that GSP adjudged the entire French system for using the sabre while mounted, as being based upon just one word – Attack!

Mexico. Patton continued to prosper in the cavalry as one might have expected, becoming Squadron Adjutant soon after joining 'D' Troop, 8th Cavalry at Fort Bliss on leaving the Mounted Service School. In March 1916 he was detached to the Headquarters of a Punitive Expedition, sent to Mexico to hunt for Pancho Villa and his gang, who had been attacking towns in New Mexico. The expedition was led by Brigadier General John J. 'Black Jack' Pershing. Patton had the temerity to 'volunteer' his services to Pershing, who after initially turning him away, agreed that the pushy young subaltern could become his acting aide-de-camp and HQ Commandant. GSP was determined not to spend his time on camp administration and had the good fortune or natural cunning to be commanding the patrol which tracked one of Villa's guerrilla bands to their isolated ranch house lair. He had already started to wear two pistols – something that would become another of his famous 'trademarks' during the Second World War. A party of bandits rode up and opened fire. GSP returned their fire and in a brief gun battle shot dead two of them – one of them was 'General' Julio Cardenas, Pancho Villa's personal bodyguard. He brought the two corpses back to Pershing's HQ, strapped on the front mudguards of his open touring car! He was later 'mentioned in dispatches' by Pershing, who rated him as 'an efficient young officer, very enthusiastic in his work'. This was high praise indeed from the highly efficient 'Black Jack' and would result in GSP being selected to command the Headquarters Troop of the American Expeditionary Force (AEF), which Pershing took to France in May 1917, some eight weeks after the USA had declared war on Germany. The time for training and 'playing at soldiers' was past. Now the young George Smith Patton, Junior, was about to embark upon real warfare – and he could not wait to be at it!

SECTION 2: 'TREAT 'EM ROUGH!'

The Move to Tanks

'There is a lot of talk about "Tanks" here now and I am interested as I can see no future to my present job.... It will be a long time yet before we have any [tanks] so don't get worried.... I love you too much to try to get killed but also too much to be willing to sit on my tail and do nothing.'

That is how GSP wrote to Beatrice on 19 September 1917, from General Pershing's headquarters at Chaumont in France, and it is clear from this and other correspondence that the euphoria he had originally felt on being chosen to command the Headquarters Troop and then on being shipped to Europe only ten days later had now disappeared and he was thirsting for real action. Fortunately, both for GSP and equally, it has to be said, for the embryo US Tank Corps, he was accepted and selected quite quickly to organise, train and command the light tank element of the new force. This apparently haphazard choice was primarily due to the fact that Lieutenant Colonel Roy Eltinge, who had been chosen by Pershing to take charge of all tank matters for the HQ AEF, was Patton's old troop commander and clearly knew that he would put his heart and soul into the new project. GSP was now 31, very slim, erect and youthful, 6 feet 1 inch in height and weighing 165 pounds; not only an expert horseman and fencer, but also having a specialist knowledge of petrol engines and navigation, which would stand him in good stead in the new Corps. He could rightly claim from his days in Mexico (and did so in his application to join the tanks) that he was the only serving American officer to have ever made an attack in a motor vehicle! In addition, he was reasonably fluent in reading, writing and speaking French, which made him an ideal choice to be given the task of finding out everything possible about the little 6-ton, Renault FT 17 light tank, which had been chosen by the Americans to equip a major part of their tank force.[3]

Patton was promoted to major and sent off to Langres, some twenty miles from Chaumont, to open the first US Army Light Tank Center, where tank commanding and tactics would be taught. A few weeks later, he also opened the 302nd Light Tank Center at Bourg, a village near to Langres, where tank driving and maintenance would take place. Patton had to command, organise and run both these establishments; however, before getting down to the 'nitty gritty' of his command, he spent time at both the British and French tank centres, learning all he could. His subsequent report on the Renault light tank to the Chief of the Tank Service not only showed his rapid grasp of all things mechanical, but also his innate practical ability, in that it contains no fewer than 26 proposed improvements to the original model of the Renault, which he advocated for the 1,200 FT 17 'copies' which the AEF had ordered, so as to make them more suitable for US use. It is true to say that this report was extremely important in that it provided a firm foundation for building the American tank effort in France, and Patton was rightly very proud of it. Years later, when he was arranging his files, he wrote at the top of the report: 'This paper was and is the Basis of the US Tank Corps. I think it is the best Technical Paper I ever wrote. GSP Jr.'

By the time that he had been promoted to lieutenant colonel and had organised and been selected to command the 304th Tank Brigade,[4] GSP was undoubtedly the leading tank expert in the AEF. In one of his many memoranda, he wrote about the essential qualities required by tanks. In it he shows a more far-sighted approach to tank warfare than most of his contemporaries who were obsessed only with making it possible for a tank to cross wider and wider trenches by adding to its length (this could be done very easily by the addition of a 'tail'). He felt this would negate many of the features which he believed were desirable for the tank and to which he assigned the following priorities:

1. Mobility of strategic employment
2. Speed and radius of action on the battlefield
3. Ease and cheapness of construction
4. Command for the guns and vision
5. Ability to cross trenches.

Clearly Patton already placed mobility above everything else, explaining that he thought the ideal tank would be one that was able to travel on its own wheels on the roads leading to the scene of combat, then in his own words: '... to mount itself on caterpillars on entering battle' – much as Walter J. Christie's revolutionary 'fast tanks' would do in the 1920s and 1930s, which then became the basis of the Soviet BT medium tank series and led on to the T 34, one of the most successful tanks ever produced.

Despite his enthusiasm and new-found knowledge, it was not all plain sailing for GSP, especially when he discovered that another cavalryman was to be appointed as Chief of the AEF's Tank Service, over him. This was Colonel Samuel Dickerson Rockenbach, who was then serving in the Quartermaster Corps. They never really got on well, GSP describing his Chief as being 'the most contrary old cuss I ever worked with'. But Rockenbach clearly recognised Patton's ability, recommended him for promotion and gave him a relatively free hand.

Esprit de Corps

As well as ensuring that his newly recruited 'tankers' were taught how to drive, maintain and fight their tanks, Patton also imbued them with a tremendous *esprit de corps*, which was vital for a newly formed unit such as the Tank Corps. He was a strict disciplinarian and had already gained a reputation for this at HQ AEF, so the students of his two schools had to follow the highest standards of dress and behaviour – a 'George Patton', for example, was the nickname given to a really smart salute throughout the entire AEF! GSP was also determined to give his soldiers that little extra something, a unifying symbol, much in the same way that Swinton had done for the British Tank Corps with his 'tank arm badge'. In the US Tank Corps it was to be a new shoulder patch and Patton set all the officers of the tank centre the task of designing one. The result, a tricoloured 'pyramid of power', indicated that the tanks had the firepower of artillery (red), the mobility of cavalry (yellow) and the ability to protect territory held by infantry (blue). Patton was delighted and paid out of his own pocket to have sufficient sets made up locally for all his men. Later the triangular patch was further embellished by the addition of an endless track, a cannon and a lightning bolt. 'Georgie's Boys' were already different from the rest of the AEF!

Organising the Tanks

In addition to establishing the training schools, GSP's paper on light tanks also laid out his ideas as to how the US tank battalions should be organised and staffed. The organisation which he proposed is shown here, and it was approved by Pershing on 23 September 1917 and brought into effect with only very minor amendments. He wrote: 'The highest tactical and administrative unit should be a battalion of three companies with a repair unit and perhaps an attached transport truck company.' He went on to describe the organisation in detail, which, in summary, is shown overleaf.

He goes on to suggest that it might be better to group more of the trucks together, namely to take the five ammunition and two gas trucks from each company, making a total of 21 trucks, and to place them with Bn HQ and just leave tank companies with their baggage truck and kitchen truck. If a tank company were detached, it should take its full complement of trucks carrying all its supplies. In the same way, the twelve mechanics of the three companies should be available, when necessary, to assist at the battalion repair shop. But he felt it that it was also vital to have a separate large repair shop in some semi-permanent or permanent location where badly damaged tanks and other vehicles could be sent for major repairs or a thorough overhaul. He also foresaw the need of a system of replacing major components, such as tank engines, via this semi-permanent centre.

So far as mobility was concerned, he considered it essential that the tank battalion have the means of moving long distances, but not on its tracks. One way would be to attach 77 trucks, each able to pull a tank on a trailer or to carry it fully laden, but this would tie down the trucks if they were kept with the battalion permanently; and if they were used for other duties they would seldom be available when required urgently. A second way would be to have 27 large, specially built trucks, each

ORGANISATION OF THE TANK BATTALION

(as described in Patton's report on light tanks)
(Total strength: 18 officers, 331 enlisted men, 77 tanks and 42 vehicles including motorcycles)

Battalion HQ

[2 tanks (1 for CO, 1 signal), 3 trucks (1x5-ton machine truck with trailer, 2x5-ton with trailers for spares), 1 automobile and 2 motorcycles]

Tank Company — Tank Company — Tank Company

(each 5 officers, 96 enlisted men, 25 tanks and 12 vehicles)

Company HQ

[10 tanks (1 for OC, 1 signal, 8 for supply, training and reserve), 9 trucks (5 for ammunition, 2 for gas & oil, 1 with trailer for baggage, 1 kitchen, with rolling kitchen trailer), 1 automobile (Ford) and 2 motorcycles]

Tank Platoon — Tank Platoon — Tank Platoon

5 tanks
(1 tank with 3in gun
2 tanks with 6pdr gun
2 tanks with machine-guns)

Personnel

BATTALION HQ
1 major commanding
1 lieutenant, adjutant
1 lieutenant, quartermaster
1 sergeant major
1 sergeant quartermaster
1 sergeant signal
2 corporals (tank drivers)
20 privates, helpers
10 mechanics (6 regular mechanics, 2 blacksmiths, 2 welders)
2 motorcyclists
4 chauffeurs (3 for trucks, 1 for automobile)
2 cooks
Total: 3 officers and 43 enlisted men

COMPANY HQ
1 captain commanding
1 lieutenant, reconnaissance and ordnance officer
1 first sergeant
1 supply sergeant
1 mess sergeant
1 signal sergeant
1 corporal clerk
20 privates, helpers
1 mechanic
2 motorcyclists
10 chauffeurs (9 for trucks and 1 for automobile)
3 cooks
Total: 2 officers and 41 enlisted men

PLATOON
1 lieutenant, chief of platoon, 3in gun tank
2 sergeants, 6pr gun tanks
2 corporals, machine gun tanks
5 private first class, drivers
5 private helpers
1 mechanic
Total: 1 officer and 15 enlisted men

capable of carrying one tank and pulling another on a trailer. But these would be large and heavy, would need to be carefully designed, and would require two round trips to move all the 53 fighting tanks, plus one reserve.

His third solution was to utilise the 27 transport trucks already with the battalion, by ensuring that they were all 'short-couple trucks' like the Knox or Hewiet, which carried no load themselves, but towed large trailers ('The load is carried on the trailer,' he wrote, 'and traction to the driving wheels of the truck is given by the weight of the trailer.'). This meant that they could be used for both jobs and be capable of moving the entire battalion, plus all its ammunition and baggage in three round trips.

GSP then goes on to itemise all the tools and extras which should be carried by each tank and by the battalion repair unit, in minute detail. This shows his remarkable eye for detail, his ability to improvise and, of course, his determination to ensure that the US tank battalions would always be highly mobile wherever they had to operate, all of which would stand him in good stead in future years.

The 'Treat-'em Rough Boys'

Back in the USA, another young captain, destined to become the most famous American soldier of the Second World War, had been given the task of creating the first Tank Corps Training Center. This was Captain Dwight D. Eisenhower. Camp Colt at Gettysburg, Pennsylvania, was the chosen location where the volunteers would come in their thousands. In May 1918, a camp newspaper called *Treat 'em Rough* was begun and the name soon became synonymous with the new tankmen.

The men who were to crew the light tanks were, as far as GSP was concerned, 'heavily armored infantry soldiers', rather than, as in the French Army, artillerymen. He also proposed that those selected to attend the tank centre should have either experience in driving automobiles or motorcycles, or the mechanical skills associated with blacksmiths, foundry hands or gas fitters. On arrival they would undergo a four-weeks' training programme, then, in the fifth week, would act as instructors to the next batch of recruits and so on, until the necessary two battalions had been fully trained. As Dale E. Wilson explains in his history of the birth of American armour: 'Patton claimed that this system, in addition to turning out fully trained units, would give the fledgling tankers the opportunity to practice the principles just learned. It would also enhance unit cohesiveness by allowing the officers and men to become accustomed to each other and to each other's methods.' In the event this system had to be modified somewhat because of a shortage of available tanks on which to train, at least six men having to be assigned to train on a single two-man vehicle. The first companies were not formed until sufficient tanks were available. In the meantime, the men were sent to other schools to learn about gunnery (machine-guns or small cannon); the tank centre held on to the best-qualified 'graduates' to serve as assistant instructors for the next batch of students.

So far as uniform was concerned, these early tankers wore a one-piece overall, which appears from wartime photographs to have been in various shades of brown or khaki. They wore the normal overseas side-cap, or in some cases when mounted, an odd-looking leather helmet. They wore khaki puttees with laced brown boots; officers wore puttees, knee-length buckled brown leather gaiters or brown riding boots. Normal service uniform was also worn with or without the overalls on top, in many cases still with the wearer's original branch insignia (e.g., coloured piping on officers' caps). The AEF Tank Corps patch came in, as already explained, but no evidence is available that it was ever worn in action.

First Blood

Having organised, trained and equipped the first American light tank units, it was only fitting that Patton should lead them into their first battle. This was to be in support of the American First Army attack at St-Mihiel in September 1918. The tanks being built in the USA were not ready,[5] so the French provided sufficient of their little Renaults to equip GSP's two fully trained battalions. The plan was to reduce the enemy salient by two simultaneous attacks – one from the north and one from the south. The French 505th Tank Brigade would also support the attack, making a total of some 260-plus tanks, to accompany sixteen US infantry divisions, the French II Colonial Corps, 3,000-plus artillery pieces and 1,500 aircraft. Patton had of course been in on the detailed planning, typically fuming at one inflexible staff officer, who told him that he could not add in his request for smoke shells because the stencil had already been cut – 'The biggest fool remark I ever heard,' he commented in his diary. Clearly the paramount need for flexibility in any armoured plans would become another GSP maxim.

Patton wrote special instructions to his men which included such exhortations as: 'No tank is to be surrendered or abandoned to the enemy. If you are left alone in the midst of the enemy keep shooting. If your gun is disabled use your pistols and squash the enemy with your tracks. By quick changes of direction cut them with the tail of your tank. If your motor is stalled and your gun broken still the infantry cannot hurt. You hang on, help will come.... You must establish the fact that AMERICAN TANKS DO NOT SURRENDER.... As long as one tank is able to move it must go forward, its presence will save the lives of hundreds of infantry and kill many Germans. Finally, this is our BIG CHANCE; WHAT WE HAVE WORKED FOR.... MAKE IT WORTHWHILE.'

With GSP at its head, the 304th went into the attack at 0500 hours on 12 September. Initially the 345th Tank Battalion followed behind the 42nd Infantry Division until it had passed the Tranches d'Houblons and then the tanks took over the lead. Despite thick mud and heavy shellfire, they overran many enemy machine-gun posts, destroyed a complete battalion of artillery and took some prisoners. The 344th Tank Battalion was operating with the 1st Infantry Division and they managed to get through the enemy wire and silence a number of machine-gun posts around the Bois de Rate. Although he had little to do once battle was joined, Patton remained in the thick of action, mainly on foot, although he did ride on the outside of a tank for part of the time, taking risks, showing himself to his soldiers and 'leading from the front', which was, as he rightly surmised, the correct place for any armour commander. It didn't save him from getting a thorough dressing-down from Rockenbach at the end of the battle, who had been trying for hours to find out what was happening! GSP later wrote to Beatrice: 'Gen R gave me hell for going up (with the forward elements) but it had to be done. At least I will not sit in a dug-out and have my men out in the fighting.'

He was to go on in this vein, be awarded both the Distinguished Service Cross and the Distinguished Service Medal, be promoted to Colonel, get himself seriously wounded, and build the solid platform on which much of his future greatness would be based. It is worth remembering that in the Second World War Patton was the only senior tank officer of any nation who had taken part in tank action and commanded tanks at a high level towards the end of the Great War.

Notes to Chapter 1

1. Blumenson, Martin. *The Patton Papers 1885–1940.*
2. See, for example: Province, Charles M. *The Unknown Patton.*
3. Pershing had decided, on Eltinge's advice, to order both British heavy tanks and French light tanks to equip the US Tank Corps, which would consist of five heavy tank battalions (later doubled) and twenty light tank battalions.
4. This was the first US tank brigade to be formed and comprised the 1st and 2nd Light Tank Battalions, both of which GSP had organised and commanded from their inception.
5. An enormous number of heavy and light tanks – 23,405 in total – were ordered, but there were many delays for a wide variety of reasons, so only 80 (one Heavy Mk VIII, fifteen Ford two-man and 64 Renault) had been completed by the Armistice, so the US Tank Corps had to rely on equipping with British and French tanks.

2
The Making of an Armour Commander (Part Two)

SECTION 1: BACK TO THE CAVALRY (1920–1940)

Peacetime Reductions

When the Great War ended, the US Tank Corps comprised more than 20,000 officers and enlisted men of whom some 12,000 were in France, the rest being still under training in the USA. By May 1919 most of these had been demobilised and all that remained were 300 officers and 5,000 enlisted men, in three tank brigades, the Tank Centre (with repair and depot companies) and the Tank Corps GHQ. A few months later, Congress fixed the size of the new corps at just 154 officers and 2,508 men. Fewer than 800 AFVs were available to this tiny force – and were an incongruous mix of foreign and home-built light and heavy models.[1] Rockenbach was appointed Commandant of the Tank Corps, a disappointing choice as he had neither the enthusiasm nor drive that Patton would have brought to the job. As it was, the infant Tank Corps did not last long, being abolished by Congress in 1920, all tank matters then coming under the general supervision of the Chief of Infantry. All existing tank units were broken up and assigned on the basis of one company per infantry division. Furthermore, it was decided that for the future there would be just two types of tank: light (under 5 tons) and medium (under 15 tons), so that the lights could be carried by truck, and that both types could be carried by rail and be able to use all existing road bridges and pontoons.

Rockenbach protested but to no avail. He was demoted to colonel, and GSP went down to captain on 30 June 1920, but was promoted to major the following day. Shrewdly appreciating that there was going to be no future in the emasculated 'Infantry (Tanks)', however, he relinquished command of 304th Tank Brigade and returned to the cavalry, joining 3rd Cavalry at Fort Meyer, Virginia, on 3 October, being appointed as CO of 3rd Squadron. This does not mean that he had entirely lost interest in the new weapon system, and he was to devote much time and thought to the subject of tank warfare during the inter-war years, despite being heavily involved in cavalry matters.

Immersing himself in the work and pleasures of peacetime regimental soldiering, which included, in addition to normal military pursuits, riding, playing polo and hunting, GSP also took full advantage of the splendid facilities offered to a rich, popular, bemedalled army officer with a heroic war record. He could easily have spent all his time enjoying himself without a thought for the future, but such was not Patton's approach to life. Of course he played a full part in all recreational activities, but he also kept his seat on the Tank Development Board, maintained his acquaintance with such armoured gurus as the irascible inventor Walter J. Christie, read all the articles about tanks in European military magazines and wrote many articles on the future of armoured warfare for the *Cavalry Journal* and other military magazines. One of his articles, 'Tanks in Future Wars', which appeared in the *Cavalry Journal* in May 1920, advocated that tank units be kept as a separate corps (just as Fuller in the UK was saying to anyone who would listen), working together with the infantry, artillery, engineers and cavalry, but not supplanting any of them. In another article he tactfully contended that cavalry and tanks could work together, the tanks providing the main frontal thrust in an attack, whilst the cavalry swept around the flanks. Some of his articles found favour, others did not, but all kept GSP's name alive in the armoured field, which would bode well for the future.

Patton did not neglect his career either in the cavalry or in the army as a whole. He attended the Field Officers' Course and the Command and General Staff College Course in 1923, passing out as an 'Honor Graduate' from the latter in June 1924. Staff appointments followed in Boston and Hawaii, then in 1928 he joined the Office of the Chief of Cavalry in Washington, where he was responsible for rewriting the army manual on the pistol. Three years later he attended the Army War College, then returned to 3rd Cavalry at Fort Meyer as Executive Officer. Promoted to Lieutenant Colonel on 1 March 1934, he went back to Hawaii where he was assigned to G–2 Hawaiian Department. While there he wrote several more papers on mechanisation, including one in which he predicted the advent of self-propelled artillery. He also developed an abiding interest in amphibious warfare, accurately forecasting both Allied and Axis use of this doctrine and including in his study of the Japanese how they would, of necessity, bomb Pearl Harbor. His personal confidential reports of the period graded him as 'excellent' and said that he was 'ambitious, progressive, original, professionally studious, conscientious in the performance of his duties – fine appearing – the most physically active officer I have ever known ... of very high general value to the service.'

In June 1937, he left Honolulu in his yacht *Arcturus*, arriving in Los Angeles on 12 July. Later, after some time on sick leave when his right leg had been broken by a kick from a horse, he was posted to the 9th Cavalry, promoted to colonel on 1 July 1938 and selected to command the 5th Cavalry at Fort Clark in Texas. He was now over 50 and clearly thinking ahead to retirement, because he bought a farm in South Hamilton, near Boston. However, probably much to his relief, the 'quiet life' was to elude him and, as war clouds grew in Europe, Patton was posted from Fort Clark to Fort Meyer in Virginia, to command the post and the 3rd Cavalry who were stationed there. His biographer, Martin Blumenson, feels, realistically, that this move was because Patton had a private income and was thus able to cope with the social obligations required in commanding 'a show place' like Fort Meyer, which had, for example, to provide all the escorts and guards of honour for such visiting dignitaries (in Patton's time there) as HM King George VI and Queen Elizabeth in June 1939, the first ever visit to the USA by a reigning British monarch.

By now Patton had received two recommendations for promotion to brigadier general, but so far the promotion had eluded him. Then, in the spring of 1940, various events occurred which would change his career dramatically.

The first of these was the holding of the Third Army manoeuvres in April and May, during which General Adna A. Chaffee's 7th Mechanised Cavalry Brigade from Fort Knox and the Provisional Motorised Tank Brigade from Fort Benning so dominated events as to convince GSP, who was acting as an umpire, that horsed cavalry had now, once and for all, been superseded by mechanisation. This prompted him to write to Chaffee, to congratulate him on his success in the manoeuvres and on being selected to command the new Armored Force which was about to come into being at Fort Knox. He may well have indicated that he wished that he could be a part of the new force, but the letter is lost, so this is pure speculation. Whatever was said, however, it had the desired result, Chaffee telling GSP in his reply that he had put him down on his 'preferred list' as an armoured brigade commander and commenting: 'I think it is a job which you could do to the queen's taste, and I need just such a man of your experience in command of an armored brigade. With two light armored regiments and a regiment of tanks employed in a mobile way, I think you could go to town.'

At about the same time another old friend of Patton's, Henry L. Stimson, was appointed Secretary of War by President Roosevelt, so GSP wrote congratulating him on his new appointment. Stimson wrote back thanking him and in all probability must have wondered why such a competent armoured soldier – one of the few serving officers with wartime battle experience in tanks – was still serving in the cavalry. Perhaps he mentioned the fact to General George C Marshall,[2] yet another friend of GSP's, who was now Army Chief of Staff. This is really all supposition; most people had long forgotten Patton's past tank experience and knew him only as a highly competent, rich and accomplished senior cavalryman.

The outcome was inevitable; Patton was assigned to the 2nd Armored Division at Fort Benning, Georgia, to take over command of the 2nd Armored Brigade on 27 July 1940. This was exactly what he wanted and he must have realised that he was once again on the road to fame, provided he could get a 'piece of the action'!

SECTION 2: GOODBYE TO BOOTS AND SADDLES! (1940–2)

'Vaguely at first you hear a hundred giant cog-wheels rolling unclad down an iron road. Then they become a battalion, a battalion of ancient Trojan chariots, their wheels pounding the stony plain. In the early dawn you wake up to remember that your are at Ft Benning, Georgia. It is August 1940. There is an aura of urgency in the frightful racket. You crawl out of your bunk and feel your way to the window. Now the gnashing of steel sprockets blends with the roar of motors. As they pass, you can see each man's head in the cupola of each tank, each wearing a rubber-haloed crash helmet. The faces are serious, cavalry men riding out on a mission. Can it be that this great noise is their way of proclaiming their superiority over the soldiers still asleep in the barracks?'[3]

Organisation. The 'Trojan chariots' were of course Patton's armoured brigade, the 'iron fist' of the 2nd Armored Division. Organised from the Provisional Tank Brigade, it comprised two light armoured regiments (66th and 68th) and one medium armoured regiment (67th). Each regiment comprised three tank battalions. When it was activated on 15 July 1940, the full 2nd Armored Division establishment was:

2ND ARMORED DIVISION
- CG Major General Charles L. Scott
- Div HQ and HQ Company (Coy)
- Div Service Coy
- 48th Signal Coy

2ND ARMORED BRIGADE
- Commander Brigadier General George S. Patton, Jr.
- 66th Armored Regiment (light)
- 67th Armored Regt (medium)
- 68th Armored Regt (light)

DIVISION CONTROL
- 41st Armored Infantry Regiment
- 14th Field Artillery Regiment
- 78th Field Artillery Battalion
- 2nd Reconnaissance Battalion (including an attached air observation squadron)
- 17th Engineer Battalion (Armored)
- 17th Ordnance Battalion
- 14th Quartermaster Battalion (Armored)
- 48th Medical Battalion.

Equipment. The tanks of 1940 were manned by converted infantry and cavalrymen, the light tanks being a mix of M2A2 and M2A3 infantry light tanks, together with the M1 and M2 combat cars of the cavalry. All were basically the same vehicle, the simplest way of distinguishing them being that the light tanks had twin turrets (earning themselves the nickname 'Mae Wests' for obvious anatomical reasons), while the combat cars had single turrets. Both types were armed only with machine-guns – .50 and .30 calibre. They weighed 8 to 9 tons, had a crew of four and were very fast – 65mph without the governors, according to one driver!

The medium tanks were also a mix, mainly of M2 and M2A1 mediums, but there could well have been other older models still being used for training. For example, there were eighteen obsolete M1 convertible tanks at Fort Benning in 1940.

All units were entirely motorised, the troops riding in some 3,000 vehicles and on 810 motorcycles (this was long before jeeps arrived). It was estimated that the division needed 80 miles of road space on a non-tactical march, taking three to four hours to pass a given point! Patton was to test their ability to move long distances, and at the same time, give the American public the opportunity to see their armoured forces at first hand, when he later moved a major portion of 2nd Armored Division from Columbus to Panama City, Florida, and back – a round trip of more than 400 miles – in mid-December 1940. A total of 1,100 vehicles took part, including 101 light and 24 medium tanks. The exercise certainly hit the newspapers: 'Gen Patton of the Cavalry sets fast pace for the Tank Corps – Army knows his name as synonym for daring action!' so read the headlines in the Washington *Sunday Star* on 15 December 1940.

Of course 2nd Armored Division was only a part of Chaffee's Armored Force, which now comprised I Armored Corps, consisting of 1st and 2nd Armored Divisions; one non-divisional tank battalion, the 70th, stationed at Fort Meade; the Armored Force Board; the Armored Force School and Replacement Training Center. As the US Army grew in size so the number of armoured corps and divisions increased, II Armored Corps coming into existence in February 1942. Eventually there would be a total of sixteen armoured divisions activated. At the same time, US industry was gearing itself to build the mass of armoured fighting vehicles needed to equip not only this force, but many other Allied nations' tank forces. In the end, a staggering 88,410 tanks of all types would be built in America, more than 50% of them being the ubiquitous M4 Medium Sherman.

Uniform. In 1940, US Armor officers wore cavalry jodhpurs and boots, but they were soon found to be impracticable for wear in tanks. In the field some officers wore leather flying-jackets although these were frowned upon by 'higher authority'. Inside the tank, crews wore either

Specifications of Light Tanks and Combat Cars

Specifications	*Combat Car M1 (Light Tank M1A1)*	*Cavalry Combat Car M2 (Light Tank M1A2)*	*Infantry Light Tank M2A2*	*Light Tank M2A3*
Crew	All had a crew of four, commander, driver, co-driver and gunner			
Combat Weight	19,644lb	19,644lb	19,100 lb	20,050 lb
Length	13ft 7in	13ft 7in	13ft 7in	14ft 6½in
Height	7ft 9in	7 ft 9in	7ft 9in	7ft 9in
Width	7ft 10in	7 ft 10in	7ft 10in	8ft 2in
Armament and Mountings	All had one .50-cal. MG and three .30-cal. MG Single turret with all round traverse		Double turrets with limited traverse	
	All had one .30 MG in hull and one for AA defence			
Armour thickness max/min	15min /6.25mm	15mm /6.25mm	15mm /6.25mm	17.5mm /6.25mm
Max Speed	45mph	45mph	30mph	40mph
Radius of action	140ml	140ml	130ml	130ml

Specifications of Medium Tanks

Specification	*M2*	*M2A1*
Date of manufacture	1939	1940
No built	18	94*a
Combat Weight	38,020lb	41,315lb
Length	17 ft 8 in	17 ft 8 in
Height	9 ft 4 in	9 ft
Width	8 ft 7 in	8 ft 7 in
Armament	1 x 37mm gun, plus eight x MGs (4 x in sponsons, 2 x front glacis, 2 x AA)	
Armour thickness	up to 25mm	up to 32mm
Engine	350hp Wright radial	400hp Wright radial
Top speed	26mph	26mph
Radius of action	130ml	130ml

(*a. Originally 1,000 were ordered, however, once it was realised that German medium tanks were equipped with a 75mm gun, it was decided to stop building M2A1s and to concentrate on the M3 medium (see later). They were only ever used for training in USA or as testbeds for the development of the M3).

the old dome-shaped leather crash helmet or the modified 'doughnut' type with a thick ring of padding all round.[4] The standard issue steel helmet fitted over the crash helmet and was recommended to be used outside the tank or by commanders when standing in the turret. Armour troops wore grey-green coveralls, laced ankle boots (or shoes) and side-caps when not wearing crash helmets. Off duty or in barracks, they wore the normal GI uniform, the most important item being, of course, the Divisional Shoulder Patch, the 'armored triangle of power' having the numeral '2' at the apex of the triangle, and the division's nickname: 'HELL ON WHEELS' on an embroidered strip below.

Personal equipment was usually limited to a webbing belt, a brown leather pistol holster (for officers, containing their .45 automatic pistol), webbing ammunition pouch, first-aid pouch (small) and a canteen. Commanders of course also had binoculars, map board, whistle, message book, 'grease' (chinagraph) pencils, etc., which they would stow in the tank or wear about their person.

Expansion Brings Promotion

In the middle of September, the Commanding General (CG) of 2nd Armored Division, Major General Charles L. Scott, was moved to Fort Knox to assist General Chaffee, who was starting to show signs of ill health (he was to die of cancer a year later), and Patton took over as acting divisional commander. A few days later, on 1 October, his promotion to the permanent rank of brigadier general was promulgated. Scott would not return, and although he would command I Corps, he would not be selected to replace Chaffee, this job going to Jacob L. Devers, a West Point classmate of Patton's and another enthusiastic polo player. GSP himself was promoted to major general on 4 April 1941 and assigned as Commanding General, 2nd Armored Division seven days later.

In the meantime he was in his element, busily moulding 2nd Armored Division into a highly effective and efficient fighting force, as they ably demonstrated on the Louisiana and Texas manoeuvres of 1941. 'I was constantly impressed', wrote Lieutenant General Walter Krueger, Third Army commander, in a letter to GSP after the manoeuvres were over, 'by the high morale, technical proficiency and devotion to duty of the personnel of the 2nd Armored Division....Your leadership has produced a fighting organization.'

'How he worked those civilians in uniform!', wrote Alden Hatch in his book: *George Patton, General in Spurs*. 'They sweated out forced marches through the blazing Georgia summer, and froze in winter in what shelter they could find ... they manoeuvered all over the Southern states. Patton was everywhere. When he could not get around fast enough in a jeep, he brushed up on his piloting and bought a little Stinson plane. Nobody in 2nd Armored Division ever knew when the Commanding General would skim over the treetops and drop in, screaming, "Hurry up!".... Between the marches are manoeuvres – even during them – the troops polished equipment and boots and helmets; pressed uniforms, washed linen; shaved every day – and cursed the General who made them do it.'

Patton had the ability to get swiftly to the heart of any problem, to lay aside all the verbiage and to express himself in simple terms which any soldier could understand: 'Fire and Manoeuvre' became 'Grab 'em by the nose and kick 'em in the ass!' 'you young lieutenants have got to realise that your platoon is like a piece of spaghetti,' he told his junior officers. 'You can't push it, you've got to get out in front and pull it. I expect every one of you to return a conqueror or a corpse.... Make damn sure you're in control at all times and that you know what's going on. Ninety per cent of being in command is nothing more than making sure orders are followed and that the mission is accomplished. Once you've issued an order, get the hell out of the way of the people doing the job – but – make sure they know you're in charge, that you expect them to bring the mission to full fruition, and that they are responsible for its completion.' Some of his short, pithy statements: 'A pint of sweat will save a gallon of blood'; 'A good solution applied with vigour now is better than a perfect solution applied ten minutes later'; 'Do everything you ask of those you command', and, perhaps the one which encapsulates the Patton philosophy in five short words: 'In case of doubt, attack!', all bear the hallmark of his brilliance and his ability, not only to see complicated matters in simple terms, but also to be able to pass this clarity of mind down to his subordinates. However, one should not get the impression that he slavishly followed the American trend of striving to promote apparent equality between officers and soldiers, as epitomised by, for example, the single field cookhouse and 'one chow line for all'. Here Patton distanced himself, and his immaculate attire was undoubtedly due to the excellence of his soldier servants – or batmen as we call them in the British Army – rather than his own prowess with a can of Brasso and a button stick! Nevertheless, there are ample examples of his being the first to take his coat off and help in an emergency, such as with a broken down or bogged vehicle. He also undoubtedly had a 'nose' for trouble and did not 'suffer fools gladly'. As one sergeant is reported to have commented: 'You're all right if you do exactly what you're told, and you don't have to be too brilliant doing it. But don't lay an egg in front of him. He don't like it.'[5]

Corps Command and the Desert Training Center

On 7 December 1941, the Japanese attack on Pearl Harbor brought America into the war and, just over a month later, on 15 January, Patton was assigned as CG, I Armored Corps. He was naturally elated by this promotion, but saddened at having to leave his beloved division.

His personal message to all ranks read: 'I desire to express to all ranks my sincere appreciation of your magnificent performance. Your untiring effort on training has made you a great division. When you meet the enemy, the same spirit of devotion will make you feared and famous. I shall be very proud of you.' Patton was replaced by Brigadier General Willis D. Crittenberger. GSP had planned to depart with as little fuss as possible, but as Donald E. Houston relates in his history of the division entitled *Hell on Wheels*, some of his men heard that he was leaving and 'they lined the streets, waving and cheering; some saw tears in Patton's eyes. Perhaps because it was the first and only division he ever commanded, perhaps because of the send-off, or possibly because of its later accomplishments, 2nd Armored Division was always Patton's favorite heavy armored division.' Alden Hatch also comments about the 'civilian soldiers' who had cursed their general for working them so hard and now 'tore the shirts of their backs and waved them at the stern, bespangled figure of their general. The car passed so quickly that they could not see that the fraudulent old softy was crying.'

Patton was not given very long to settle down to his new job as an armoured corps commander, because less than two months later, on 26 March, he was detailed to organise and command the newly forming Desert Training Center, a requirement clearly considered vitally important, because the only theatre in which the British were successfully engaged at the time was the Western Desert. If and when American troops were sent to join in battle against the Axis, the desert of North Africa was considered to be one of the most obvious places, so they clearly had to learn everything about living and fighting in the desert. Not that GSP knew anything about it himself at this stage, but he quickly wrote to a friend in the War Department, asking him to send 'any and all information, pamphlets and what-not, you may have on the minutiae of desert fighting'. He then made, as his most immediate task, a detailed reconnaissance of the proposed training area, some 12 million acres, which included parts of California, Nevada and Arizona – 'a vast wasteland half the size of Pennsylvania'. Most of the area was uninhabited, although there were a handful of small towns (Indio, Needles, Blythe and Yuma) around the edges and the area was served by three railway lines.

Patton was delighted with the area and immediately decided that the troops coming to the training centre would live in spartan conditions, namely in tents, without electricity, sheets for their beds, heat or hot water. Any buildings for use by the permanent administrative staff would be simple single-storey wooden structures, the base camp being twenty miles east of Indio, with divisional campsites being near Desert Center, Iron Mountain and Needles. He wrote enthusiastically that the area was the best he had ever seen for training, not only because it was so like Libya, both in terrain and climate, but because there was so much empty space. The troops who first used the centre called it 'the place that God forgot'! In these surroundings much of what was being learnt about desert living by British tank crews in the Western Desert was similarly being found out the hard way by the American tankers. For example, in North Africa, tank crews invariably employed a form of cooking, using petrol to fuel what was known as a 'Benghazi'. This had its US equivalent in the 'Patton desert stove'.

Patton naturally lived under the same conditions as his men, no doubt supported by his new young aide Captain Richard N. Jenson, whose family had known the Pattons for many years. In addition, GSP, as a major general, was entitled to a second aide, so he chose one of his old tankers, Lieutenant Alexander C. Stiller, who had been a sergeant with him in France. He would serve him principally as a bodyguard. Also joining him at the Desert Training Center was his Negro orderly, Sergeant (later Master Sergeant) George Meeks, who would remain with GSP for the rest of his life, finally helping to carry Patton's coffin at his funeral.

Mission of the Desert Training Center. In an article published in the *Cavalry Journal*, GSP stated that the tactical mission of the Desert Training Center had been to 'devise formations for marching and fighting which, while affording control and concentrated firepower, at the same time do not present lucrative air targets. It is felt that these ends have been accomplished. Formations now in use can move cross country, followed by the combat train, and without halting can deploy into the attack formation and execute an attack, and at no time present any target worthy of bombardment.'[6] He went on to explain that they had also developed methods for going into bivouac so as to guard against night attacks and air bombardment, yet still be capable of quickly forming a rapid formation for combat or for march. Everyone had learnt how to live on a gallon of water a day for all purposes, even when operating under temperatures of 130 degrees in the sun for three days (GSP adds drily: 'The temperature in the shade is not mentioned because there was no shade.')

Armoured Division Organisation

By early 1942 the armoured divisions of I Armored Corps had been reorganised into what were then known as 'Heavy armored divisions'. Each had five major headquarters: Division HQ, Combat Command 'A and Combat Command 'B' (each equivalent to a British Brigade HQ), Division Artillery and Division Trains. In the two tank regiments the emphasis on light and medium tanks had been completely reversed, so there were now two medium battalions and only one light. The infantry regiment had three battalions, as did the artillery, while each artillery battalion had three batteries. The reconnaissance battalion lost its integral infantry company, but now had three reconnaissance companies and a light tank company, while the engineer battalion had four companies and a bridging company. Total strength was 14,620 all ranks, and the principal weapons included 232 medium tanks, 158 light tanks, 54 self-propelled 105mm howitzers, 79 armoured cars, 773 half-tracks and scout cars, together with 2,146 other vehicles and trailers.

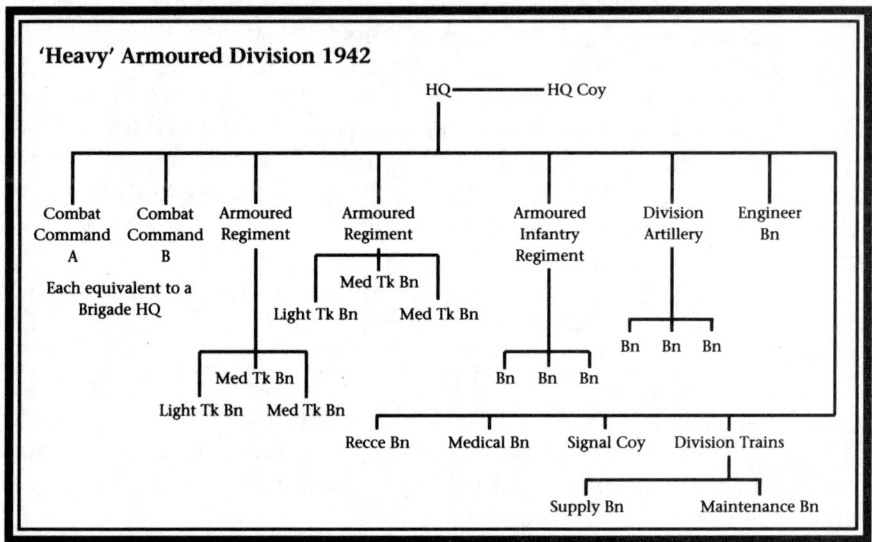

During training, divisions had experimented with methods of employing the Army Air Corps directly in support. A Forward Air Controller (then called a Bomber Demand Unit) was attached to the recon battalion and to each of the mission forces. However, it was not very successful because of the length of time it took to pass requests – anything up to three hours! The tankers decided that the best method would be to use radio communications and that is of course what eventually happened.

On the Move Again

Ever since America had entered the war, Patton had been champing at the bit, wondering if and when he would manage to get into action. Now, stuck out in the middle of nowhere, he was fretting even more, because he was certain that he would be overlooked. He needn't have worried. On 29 July he received the news that, while drawing up a schedule for the move of certain divisions overseas, Lieutenant General Lesley J. McNair, General Marshall's Chief of Staff, had selected Patton and his headquarters to be in command of those tank troops at the top of the overseas list, so he would have the honour of leading the first contingent of combat troops to leave the USA. Later he would discover that these troops would be part of the Western Task Force scheduled to land in North Africa in Operation 'Torch' on 8 November 1942. This time he left so hurriedly that he was unable to say a personal goodbye to the staff of the Center, so he sent Major General Alvan G. Gillem, who replaced him there, a message thanking them for all they had done for him, which closed with the words: 'Having shared your labors I know the extreme difficulties under which we worked and I also know how splendidly and self-sacrificingly you did your full duty. I thank you and congratulate you – it was an unparalleled honor to have commanded such men.'

George Patton was off to battle once again. He was supremely confident of his own abilities, writing in his diary on 22 October 1942, while visiting the UK and having spent some time watching part of the Task Force load for Operation 'Torch': 'When I think of the greatness of my job and realise I am what I am, I am amazed, but on reflection, who is as good as I am? I know of no one.'

Notes to Chapter 2

1. There were: 218 Renault FT 17s and 450 American-built copies, 28 British Heavy Mk Vs and 100 Heavy Mk VIIIs (also called the International, which was to have been built in large numbers by UK, USA and France), making a grand total of 796.
2. In his 'little black book' Marshall wrote: 'George will take a unit through hell and high water.' Beneath that note, however, he had written: 'But keep a tight rope round his neck,' and beneath that: 'Give him an armored corps when one becomes available.' (As quoted in Leonard Mosley's biography of Marshall.)
3. *Roll Again Second Armored* by Majors N. H. Perkins and M. E. Rogers.
4. Patton did of course design his own 'Green Hornet' tanker's uniform made of green gabardine, which included a helmet rather similar in design to those used by American Football players (reputedly painted gold). It appeared in many newspapers (modelled by GSP), but was never adopted!
5. Quoted in *The Biography of General George S. Patton* by Ian V. Hogg.
6. Taken from 'The Desert Training Corps', an article by Major General George S. Patton, Jr, which appeared in the *Cavalry Journal*, September–October 1942.

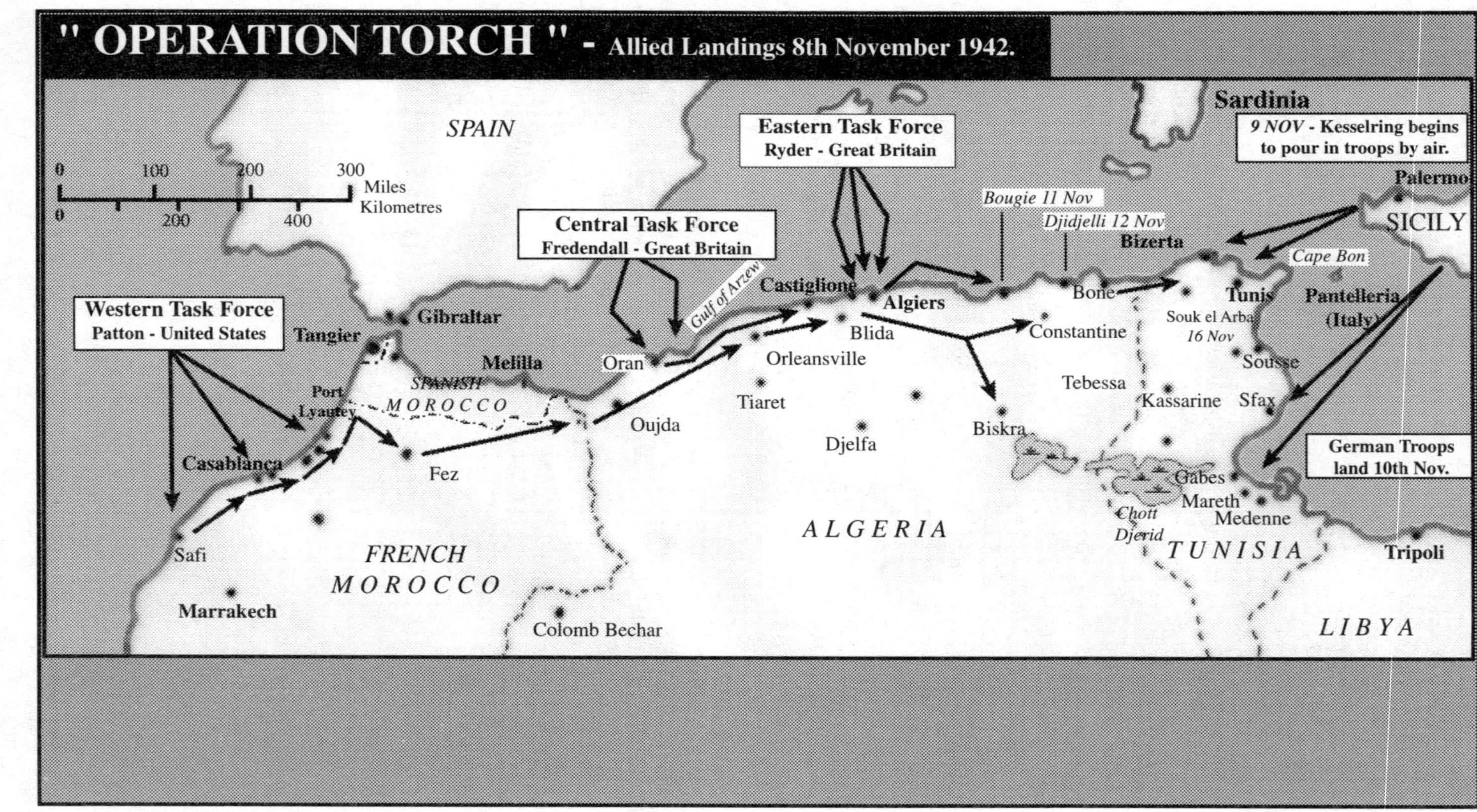
" OPERATION TORCH " - Allied Landings 8th November 1942.
SPAIN
0 100 200 300 Miles
0 200 400 Kilometres
Western Task Force
Patton - United States
Central Task Force
Fredendall - Great Britain
Eastern Task Force
Ryder - Great Britain
Sardinia
9 NOV - Kesselring begins to pour in troops by air.
Palermo
SICILY
Bougie 11 Nov
Djidjelli 12 Nov
Bizerta
Cape Bon
Gibraltar
Tangier
Melilla
Gulf of Arzew
Oran
Castiglione
Algiers
Blida
Orleansville
Bone
Constantine
Tunis
Souk el Arba
16 Nov
Pantelleria
(Italy)
Sousse
SPANISH
MOROCCO
Port
Lyautey
Casablanca
Fez
Oujda
Tiaret
Djelfa
Biskra
Tebessa
Kassarine
Sfax
German Troops land 10th Nov.
Gabes
Mareth
Medenne
Chott
Djerid
Safi
FRENCH
MOROCCO
Marrakech
Colomb Bechar
ALGERIA
TUNISIA
Tripoli
LIBYA

3
Higher Command

SECTION 1: OPERATION 'TORCH' AND II CORPS

The Landings.

'I am sending this back by Captain Gordon Hutchins of this ship, the *Augusta*. By the time it reaches home, everything that happened will be in the papers. We left Norfolk at 8:10 am of the 24th and the sortie was remarkable for its orderly, and apparently faultless, efficiency. We moved in column through the minefields and out the swept and buoyed channel, where we joined a line of five columns with the *Augusta* leading.' That is how GSP let Beatrice know that he had embarked for North Africa in a letter dated 29 October 1942.

Operation 'Torch' was a combined American and British operation, which took place on 8 November and involved landing three Task Forces on the coast of French North Africa, the Centre and Western being American, the Eastern British. General Dwight D. Eisenhower was overall CinC for 'Torch', with Admiral Sir Andrew Cunningham as Allied Naval Commander. General Patton was to command the Western Task Force. It had been hoped to arrange a cease-fire with the Vichy French forces, so that the landings would not be opposed, but unfortunately this did not happen. Landing difficulties delayed the attacks on Casablanca and Mehdia (Patton's Western Task Force), there was heavy fighting at Oran, and two destroyers were lost off Algiers. By 10 November, however, a cease-fire had been agreed. The major drawback to the Allied plans was that Tunisia could not be occupied immediately and this allowed the Germans time to react, which they did with commendable speed, swiftly flying in troops and pushing out a perimeter to protect Rommel's rear. It would take several months of hard fighting before the long-term aims of 'Torch' could be realised.

Patton wrote home somewhat sombrely on 6 November: 'In forty hours I shall be in battle ... it seems that my whole life has been pointed to this moment. When this job is done, I presume I will be pointed to the next step in the ladder of destiny. If I do my full duty, the rest will take care of itself.'

Western Task Force

Patton had divided his task force into three groups (see **Annex 'A'** to this chapter for full details): the northern one under Major General

Lucian K. Truscott was to land near Mehdia and capture Port Lyautey; the centre, under Major General Jonathan W. Anderson, and the southern, under Major General Ernest A. Harmon, would land at Fedala and Safi respectively, then converge and take Casablanca from the landward side.

Patton had arranged to go ashore at 0800 hrs, by which time it was expected that the first objectives would have been taken. He enjoyed witnessing the naval battle that began just prior to the landing, but cannot have been best pleased when the first blast of gunfire from the *Augusta* blew his landing craft (which had been on deck and about to be launched) 'to hell' and he lost all his kit, except for his precious pistols which fortunately he had just got his orderly, Sergeant George Meeks, to fetch from his baggage! GSP then had to remain a virtual prisoner on board, no doubt fretting about what was going on ashore, as virtually no information was reaching him. When he eventually landed at about 1320 hrs, there was still quite a fight going on, but no bullets came his way. After spending the night ashore at his headquarters, which had been set up in the Hotel Miramar in Fedala, Patton was up before dawn and went to see Major General Anderson, whom he found still in bed. GSP was not best pleased and even more incensed when he looked around the beach and harbour. 'The beach was a mess and the officers were doing nothing,' he wrote in his diary. 'As a whole the men were poor, the officers worse; no drive. It is very sad. I saw one lieutenant let his men hesitate to jump into the water. I gave him hell. I hit another man who was too lazy to push a boat. We also kicked a lot of Arabs.' This was typical of GSP, to get to the nub of the problem and to deal with it in the way he felt would be the most effective. Some might argue that it was wrong for a General to do the job of a Master Sergeant and 'kick butts', but that is what the situation demanded, so that is exactly what he did – and it worked!

But it was not all bad news and by that evening the airport at Lyautey in the north had been captured by Truscott, while Harmon's southern landing force had defeated an enemy column, destroying nineteen trucks and six tanks, and was marching on Casablanca: 'All this shows that we should push on. God favors the bold, victory is to the audacious,' wrote GSP in his diary.

Next day, GSP received orders from Eisenhower which read: 'Algiers has been ours for two days. Oran defenses crumbling rapidly with shore batteries surrendering. Only tough nut to crack is in your hands. Crack it open quickly and ask for what you want.' At the same time as he sent this signal to GSP, Ike had sent one back to his Chief of Staff at Allied Forces Headquarters saying : 'Reports from Patton still meager but ... information indicates he is progressing steadily. If he captures Casablanca by noon tomorrow, I will recommend both him and Fredenhall for third stars.' In fact, GSP was actively engaged in 'cracking the nut', but had wisely decided that H-Hour for the final attack on Casablanca should be delayed until 0730 hrs, to give Anderson's green troops time to form up in daylight, and for his ultimatum to the French to negotiate an armistice, time to work. Fortunately, although he admitted later that 'the hours between 7.30 and 11 were the longest in my life', all went smoothly and the Casablanca garrison surrendered without a shot being fired.

'I Wish I Could Get Out and Kill Someone.'

There now followed a period of three months in which GSP was out of the real action, his task being a political one, namely to establish good relations with the erstwhile enemy, the French, and with the Sultan of Morocco. Despite the fact that this was not what he really wanted to do and, let's face it, he was no politician, he began extremely well. His love of France, combined with his generous, honest nature, came to the fore and he quickly smoothed any ruffled feathers there might have been *chez* General Nogues and his staff, making promises which were perhaps not his to make and finally inviting them to join him in a glass of champagne. As General Essame said in his study of Patton: 'Not surprisingly, the conference ended in an atmosphere of profound relief on the part of the French and of mutual cordiality and esteem. As an impromptu theatrical display of military magnanimity in the grand manner of Napoleon it was magnificent: to describe it as a politically ham performance would be an understatement.'[1] Unfortunately, Nogues was playing a double game, keeping in touch with both Vichy France and the Germans, while appearing to be the friend of the Allies, but the politically naïve Patton took him at face value.

This is not the place to dissect GSP's abilities as a politician, but it has to be said that he quickly found himself out of his depth and, although he made the best of it, spent the period until early March watching from the sidelines as the conflict in Tunisia turned sour and the situation for the Americans got worse and worse. 'You have probably read in the papers and seen on the movie screen that for the last ten days we have been very busy entertaining the leading lights of the world,' he wrote in a letter to Washington. 'It was very amusing but was not war. Personally, I wish I could get out and kill someone.' In fact, GSP did not spend the entire time on political junketing. He and his staff had transformed all aspects of the administrative 'tail' that was required in order properly to support the American forces that were now operational. The ports were cleared and put back into full working order; airfields were modernised, road and rail communications developed and the fighting troops not at the front smartened up and put under rigorous training. Patton's usual edicts on dress and turnout were rigorously enforced, as was proper saluting. 'A pint of sweat will save a gallon of blood' was one of Patton's favourite maxims, which he had incorporated into his message to all his troops before embarking on 'Torch', and now they would begin to understand what he meant!

Patton personally was 'saved by the bell' through two related happenings. The first was the arrival on the scene of the 'Desert Fox', the redoubtable Field-Marshal Erwin Rommel, whose troops staged a come-back in the north, in particular around the vital Kasserine Pass area; the second was the continued poor performance of the then commander of II Corps, Major General Lloyd R. Fredenhall, whose HQ had been sent by Eisenhower to take command of operations in Tunisia. When Ike was told that Fredenhall was losing his grip on the situation, he did not send Patton in immediately to replace him, but rather gave Major General Ernie Harmon, the gravel-voiced commander of 2nd Armored Division (who had led GSP's southern landing force), the strange task of going to the front, taking command not of the Corps or of 1st Armored Division who were heavily embroiled, but rather of the American forces 'in the battle'. At the same time he was tasked to investigate British complaints of bad leadership at II Corps HQ. Harmon did so, reporting bluntly that he considered Fredenhall to be both a 'physical and moral coward'.

Eisenhower was more diplomatic and said that he was replacing Fredenhall with GSP, because, to use Patton's words, the fighting in Tunisia was 'primarily a tank show and I know more about tanks'. But GSP was also left in no doubt that Fredenhall's relations with the British had been bad and that had to stop. The British overall commander, Alexander – ever the diplomat – told Patton when they met, that II (US) Corps would no longer be under First (British) Army command, but would come directly under Alexander's 18th Army Group, so that Patton would have an entirely separate all-American sector. GSP was very taken by Alexander and later told Beatrice that he had impressed him a lot and was 'very quiet and good looking'.

On 6 March 1943 Patton was assigned as Commanding General II Corps and he hit them like 'Moses descending from Mount Ararat'. But instead of the Ten Commandments he brought his own personal text of severe, unrelenting discipline. He motored around all the units, down to battalion level, escorted by siren-screeching scout cars and half-tracks, all bristling with weapons and covered in the largest stars his aides could produce. No unit was spared from his blistering speeches, and such regulations as wearing ties, leggings, helmets and sidearms, and shaving every day were rigorously enforced. 'At this point Patton was probably the most unpopular commander in American history. But something happened to II Corps. It became, in spite of itself, a Patton army – the first one – tough and bitter and proud; capable of doing the impossible, and then going out next day and doing it again.'[2]

Of course, as with the landings, this was the visible face of GSP, dishing out the medicine he knew the 'patient' needed and doing it in his own inimitable way. What the troops on the ground did not see were the long hours he spent running his staff ragged, making them get all the supplies the Corps needed, such as new tanks, vehicles, equipment, uniforms and rations. Part of his genius was being able to ensure that everything was available exactly when and where it was needed and he was materially assisted in this task in Tunisia by Major General Omar N. Bradley, whom Eisenhower had appointed to be his deputy. Field Marshal Alexander said of them that both were good soldiers but 'Patton was a thruster, prepared to take any risks; Bradley was more cautious.'

In many ways, when the battle began, the opposing commanders, Rommel and Patton, were almost mirror-images of each other. Eisenhower and Alexander had the utmost difficulty in stopping GSP from continually leading his troops from the front, and in my book, *Tank Commanders*, I quoted an example of Patton's actions on 7 April 1943, when he discovered that one of his tank/infantry battle-groups was held up by a minefield and that the commander was reluctant to move forward. After berating him on the radio without success, GSP drove forward and personally led the way through the minefield and on until they were only 45 miles from Gabes. After ordering the commander to 'keep going for a fight or a bath', GSP reluctantly returned to his headquarters. On the 'other side of the hill' Rommel was behaving in much the same way. 'You should have seen their eyes light up when he suddenly appeared,' Rommel's aide wrote to Frau Rommel. 'It was just like the old days, among the very foremost infantry and tanks, in the midst of their attack, he hit the dirt just like the riflemen when the enemy's artillery opened up! What other commander is there who can call on such respect!' Rommel did of course have to leave the battlefield before Patton, flying back to Germany in late March, to beg for his gallant army to be evacuated. Hitler not only refused, but would not allow Rommel to return.

II (US) Corps

In Tunisia, II Corps was composed of three infantry divisions and one armoured division. It was supported by 13th Field Artillery Brigade, together with the requisite number of supporting units such as Signal, Ordnance, Medical, Engineers, etc. Senior commanders were as follows:

1st Infantry Division:	Major General Terry de la M. Allen
9th Infantry Division:	Major General Manton C. Eddy
34th Infantry Division:	Major General Charles W. Ryder
1st Armored Division:	Major General Orlando Ward (replaced by Major General Ernest A. Harmon on 5 April 1943)
13th Field Artillery Brigade:	Brigadier General John A. Crane.

Infantry Divisions

Taking 1st Infantry Division ('The Big Red One') as an example, the basic divisional organisation was:

HQ and HQ Company (Coy)

INFANTRY: 16th, 18th, 26th Infantry Regiments (each three battalions, plus Service Coy, Cannon Coy and Anti-tank Coy)

ARTILLERY: 5th, 7th, 32nd, 33rd Field Artillery Battalions

SPECIAL TROOPS: 1st Engineer Combat Bn, 1st Medical Bn, 1st Reconnaissance Troop, 1st Quartermaster Coy, 1st Ordnance (Light Maintenance) Coy, 1st Signal Coy and a Military Police Platoon.

According to T/O 7 and allied tables dated 1 August 1942, the strength of an infantry division was 15,514 all ranks, of which 9,999 made up the three infantry regiments. The main weaponry consisted of:

Rifles .30:	6,233
Automatic rifles, .30:	567
MGs, .30:	147
MGs, .50:	133
Mortars 60mm:	81
Mortars 81mm:	57
Anti-tank guns 37mm:	109
Howitzers 75mm SP:	18
Howitzers 105mm:	36
Howitzers 105mm SP:	6
Howitzers 155mm:	12

In total, there were 2,149 vehicles of all types.

As far as the 'Torch' landings had been concerned, 1st Infantry Division had formed the bulk of the Centre Task Force, which had captured Oran. For their operations in Tunisia 'The Big Red' One had the following units attached (20 November 1942 – 30 May 1943):

105th Coast Artillery Battalion
1st Bn 6th Armored Regiment
1st Bn 13th Armored Regiment
601st Tank Destroyer Battalion
701st Tank Destroyer Battalion
2624 Signal Service Battalion
56th (British) Reconnaissance Regiment
(less one squadron)
1st Ranger Battalion.

Dress and equipment. When the British saw the Americans for the first time in North Africa, they were on the whole, most impressed. The war correspondent Alan Moorehead wrote at the time: 'They were hardly more than boys, most of them, but wonderfully tall and well proportioned, looking very forbidding under their Nazi-like helmets. Unlike the British battledress and equipment which tends to hold a man stiffly upright, these boys were in a uniform which gave them plenty of free movement. The short and formless weatherproof jacket was scarcely a garment of beauty, but it allowed the men to walk in the easy stooping way to which they were accustomed.

'Most of the American stuff was first class and even as good as or better than the German. Their mess-tins, water-bottles, rubber-soled boots, woollen underclothes, and windbreakers were superior to the British equivalents and their uniforms in general were made of finer stuff. The Garand rifle (M1) and officer's carbine were already regarded by many veterans as the best small arms on the front.'[3] However, they didn't get everything right. The Pentagon had not supplied the Tunisian force with any rain wear or cold weather gear. The nights in Tunisia, once the sun had gone down, were bitterly cold so everyone wore whatever they could find – sweaters, knitted caps, gloves and, where possible, greatcoats. The GIs also rapidly adopted the casual dress of the British in the desert, so, for example, when not directly under fire, helmets were never worn; instead just the olive drab wool cap, known as the 'beanie' and designed to be worn only under the steel helmet, became the most favoured headgear.

One can imagine how GSP reacted to this sloppy dressing, the dreaded 'beanie' becoming the symbol of slovenly discipline in II Corps. I have already mentioned his dress orders which were enforced rigorously within the entire corps area and they were coupled with a uniform system of fines that went up to $50 for officers and $25 for enlisted men. 'When you hit their pocketbooks,' he used to say, 'you get a quick response!'

1st Armored Division

Before leaving the USA for UK as part of the build-up for 'Torch', 'The Old Ironsides' had been re-organised into T/O 17 of 1 March 1942, making it into what was known as a 'heavy armored division'. The armored brigade organisation had disappeared together with one of the armored regiments and in their place were two combat commands (CCA and CCB) and two armored regiments. The combat commands, which were in essence 'mini-operational HQs' had both intelligence and operations capabilities, but depended upon division for logistics and administration. The total strength of the division was 14,620 all ranks. The major units were:

HQ and HQ Coy (inc CCA and CCB)
1st Armored Regiment (two bns of medium tanks and one bn of light tanks)
13th Armored Regiment (ditto)
6th Armored Infantry Regiment
27th Armored Field Artillery Battalion
68th Armored (FA) Battalion
91st Armored (FA) Battalion
81st Reconnaissance Battalion (Armored)

16th Engineer Battalion (Armored)
141st Signal Company (Armored)
19th Ordnance Company (Medium Maintenance, Armored)
13th Quartermaster Battalion (Armored)
47th Medical Battalion (Armored)
Attached, 701st Tank Destroyer Battalion

Only CCB of the 1st Armored Division took part in the 'Torch' landings; the bulk of the division remained in the UK, then followed up in December. This meant that when they went into battle in Tunisia, they had a mixture of light and medium tanks, viz. two battalions of M3 light tanks, armed with 37mm guns, making a total of 158 light tanks; three battalions of M3 medium Grant tanks with the low-velocity 75mm in a sponson mount and a 37mm in the turret, plus one battalion of early model Sherman medium tanks which they had picked up in the UK, making a total of 232 mediums. Anti-tank weapons comprised 37mm anti-tank guns mounted in small trucks or towed, and 75mm (French 1897 type) mounted on trucks/half-tracks. The artillery battalions had been issued with the self-propelled 105mm howitzers.

Dress and equipment. The standard tankers' uniform in North Africa was the one-piece, light grey-green overall, worn with the zippered windcheater jacket (much sought after!), brown, laced ankle boots, leather crash helmet and personal webbing. An interesting list of personal 'impedimenta' packed by an officer going to Tunisia included: a water-resistant canvas bedroll and valpack, shelter-halves, topcoat and rain gear (sensible chap!), musette bag for toilet articles (these included a shaver which ran on a small 90v Signal Corps battery, insect repellent and malaria pills), steel helmet and liner, tank helmet and field cap, web belt with pistol holster, compass, canvas-covered canteen and ammunition clips, .45 cal automatic pistol and Tommy-gun, mess kit, flashlight, whistle, field-glasses, message book, rainproof map-case with crayons, pens, pencils, protractor and ruler, and a foot-locker for uniforms, field manuals, other training literature, camera and miscellaneous. Fortunately it could be distributed between his tank, half-track and supply truck.[4]

Just 43 Days in Command

Eisenhower had never intended that Patton should stay long with II Corps, because he had already been earmarked to command the US Seventh Army for the coming operation in Sicily, which was scheduled as the first stage of the Allied assault on *'Festung Europa'*, so it was vital that he return to Morocco to continue planning Operation 'Husky', as the landings would be code-named. Patton's task was to get II Corps back on track after their disastrous showing at Kasserine Pass, where 1st Armored Division in particular had taken a pasting. Under him, their next battle at Gafsa was a different matter entirely; they took the initiative and won. The success restored their confidence and proved once again GSP's ability to succeed. The capture of Gafsa received wide publicity in the American press, which undoubtedly lessened the shock of Kasserine.

The magic of Lieutenant General George Patton (he had received his third star on 12 March) was also made to work in the munitions factories back home, where large posters had been printed bearing the legend:

'Old Blood & Guts attacks Rommel
"Go Forward!
"Always go forward!
"Go until the last shot is fired and the last drop of
gasoline is gone and then go forward on foot!"
– Lieut General George S. Patton, Jr
Dare we working here do less?'

Back to Morocco

On 15 April 1943 GSP was relieved of the operational command of II Corps, handed over to his deputy Omar Bradley and returned to Rabat and his planning staff. He wrote to Beatrice: 'Darling B. Well the campaign or battle or whatever they call it lasted 43 days and I am back where I was and will be here and hereabouts for a while.'

It would not be long before he was off to war again, as the invasion of Sicily was now planned for 10 July, just a few short weeks away. Patton naturally did not like leaving II Corps, with the job still not yet finished and victory still some weeks away. However, like the good soldier he was, he fully realised that he must follow orders as he was needed to help co-ordinate the final planning for 'Husky'. His farewell message to the soldiers of II Corps was full of praise for their 'valor, loyalty and unfaltering endurance', and he hoped that he would have the opportunity to command some or all of them again. General Marshall sent him a telegram which read: 'You did a fine job and further strengthened confidence in your leadership.' GSP had undoubtedly done well and had completed the task he had been set with great panache, so he could be well pleased with his 43 days of operational duty. And, in any case, Bradley had shown that he could cope, so there were no real worries. Besides, with his third star now firmly on his shoulder, GSP knew that he was destined for greater things; 'If I do my duty,' he wrote, 'I will be paid in the end.'

SECTION 2: OPERATION 'HUSKY' AND US SEVENTH ARMY

Background Planning

The detailed planning of the Sicilian operation was carried out by Patton's I Armored Corps (Reinforced), which was made up of what remained of the Western Task Force Headquarters after it had provided

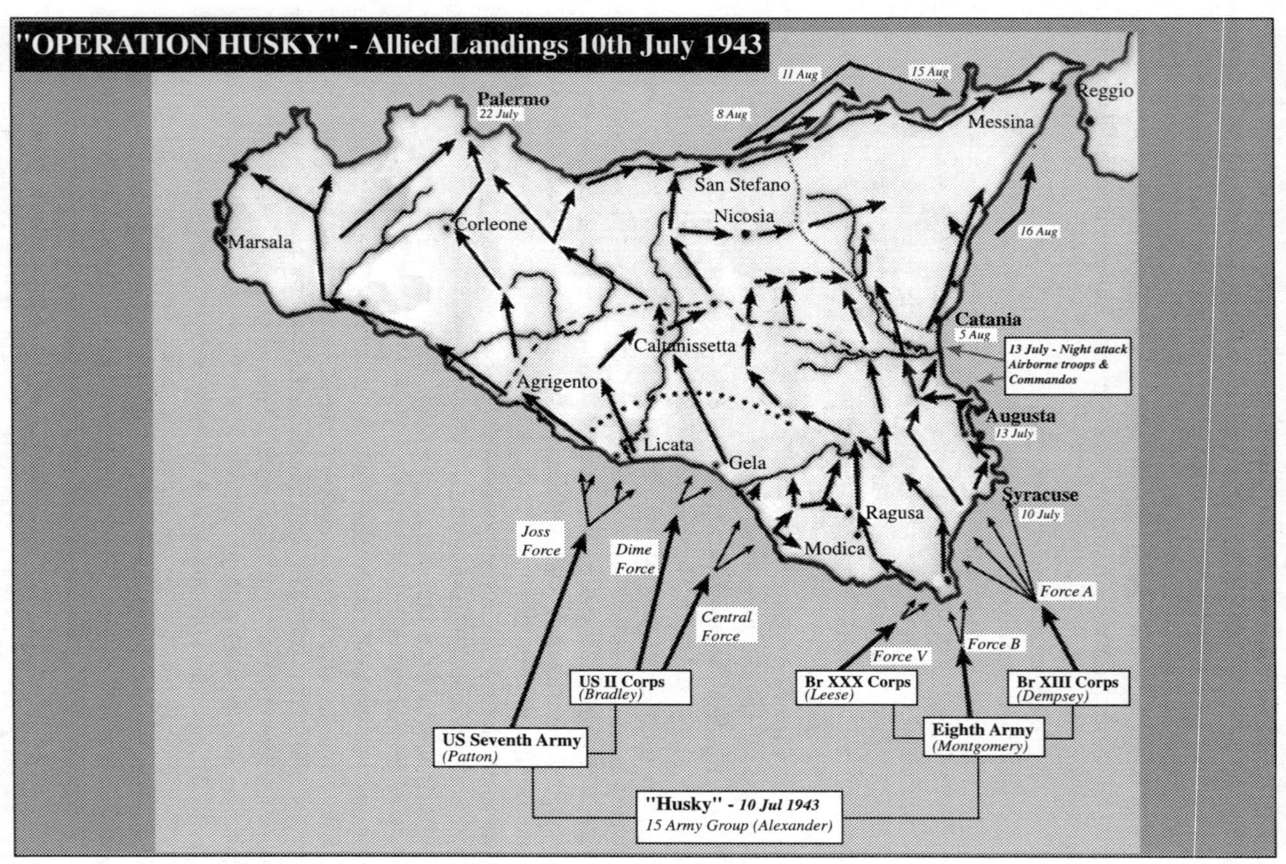
"OPERATION HUSKY" - Allied Landings 10th July 1943
Palermo
22 July
Marsala
Corleone
Agrigento
Caltanissetta
Licata
Gela
San Stefano
Nicosia
8 Aug
11 Aug
15 Aug
Messina
Reggio
16 Aug
Catania
5 Aug
13 July - Night attack Airborne troops & Commandos
Augusta
13 July
Syracuse
10 July
Ragusa
Modica
Joss Force
Dime Force
Central Force
Force V
Force B
Force A
US II Corps
(Bradley)
US Seventh Army
(Patton)
Br XXX Corps
(Leese)
Br XIII Corps
(Dempsey)
Eighth Army
(Montgomery)
"Husky" - 10 Jul 1943
15 Army Group (Alexander)

officers and enlisted men for the newly created Fifth Army.[5] To prevent confusion this planning HQ was known as 'Force 343' and then on D-Day became HQ US Seventh Army. In brief, the troops allocated to Operation 'Husky' comprised two Task Forces – a Western Task Force comprised of the US Seventh Army and an Eastern Task Force of the British Eighth Army. General Eisenhower would be in overall command, with Alexander as his deputy, Admiral Sir Andrew Cunningham as Allied Naval Commander and Air Chief Marshal Tedder as Allied Air Commander. As far as the Task Forces were concerned, Lieutenant General Patton was to command US Seventh Army, with Vice Admiral Hewitt, USN, in charge of the naval side and Colonel T. J. Hickey, USAAF, the air support. Montgomery – then also a lieutenant general – was commanding his already famous Eighth Army, with Admiral Sir Bertram Ramsay and Air Vice Marshal Broadhurst. Deputy Army Commander under Patton would be Major General Geoffrey Keyes.

After a considerable number of proposed plans had been put forward and amended, the following plan was finally chosen: there would be a combined assault by the Americans and the British on the south-eastern corner of the island, as the map shows.

D-Day was chosen as 10 July 1943, with H-Hour fixed for 0245 hrs, when there would be no moonlight to illuminate the seaborne troops. Airborne forces, who would be taken in by glider and launched to capture certain strategic targets, would land at 0600 hrs, so that they would have about 30 minutes of moonlight before moonset. Taking a number of airfields early was an essential part of the plan, so that air support could be switched from North Africa as quickly as possible.

Organisation

Patton's US Seventh Army comprised HQ II Corps, under Major General Omar N. Bradley, and six divisions, four infantry (one as follow-up force), one armored and one airborne:

1st Inf Div: Major General Terry de la M. Allen
3rd Inf Div: Major General Lucien K. Truscott
9th Inf Div: Major General Manton C. Eddy
45th Inf Div: Major General Troy Middleton
2nd Armd Div: Major General Hugh A. Gaffey
82nd Ab Div: Major General Matthew B. Ridgway
Three Ranger Battalions (1st, 3rd, 4th) Colonel William Darby.

As will be seen from the map, there were three assault areas and objectives in Seventh Army's 70-mile sector. Reading from west to east these were:

SECTOR JOSS – 3rd Division's task was to land and capture a 5-mile stretch of beachhead each side of Licata, plus the Licata airfield.

SECTOR DIME – 1st Division's task was to land at Gela and capture the local and Ponte Olivo airfields.

SECTOR CENT – 45th Division's task was to land and capture a 15-mile stretch of beachhead near Scoglitti and capture Comiso and Biscari airfields.

Supporting these three assaults would be a floating reserve comprising 2nd Armored Division, less any attachments; 9th Division was in reserve. A full ORBAT of these forces is given in Annex 'B' to this chapter.

Of the established divisions, 1st Infantry, 2nd Armored, 3rd Infantry and 9th Infantry had all taken part in the North Africa campaign, either as part of the 'Torch' landing forces and/or later in the bitter fighting in Tunisia, so they had all been 'blooded'. Only 45th Infantry Division had to date seen no combat, having sailed from the USA in June 1943. It was an Oklahoma National Guard unit that had been federalised in 1940 and was considered to be one of the best-trained divisions in the American Army. The 'new boys' were the men of 82nd Airborne Division which had yet to celebrate its first birthday, having only been formed in August 1942. But they had been training hard, first in the USA, then in North Africa, having arrived there in May. Of the three special Ranger battalions, two had been recently activated in North Africa, but the 1st Battalion, under Lieutenant Colonel William Darby, had already gained an enviable reputation in the Tunisia fighting.

Special Units and Equipment

In addition to the Airborne and Rangers was a specialised motorised chemical battalion, equipped with the 4.2in mortar, an extremely accurate weapon with a rifled bore, designed originally to fire smoke or gas shells, although capable of firing both HE and white phosphorus rounds. Attached to 3rd Infantry Division was a battalion-sized unit, the 4th Moroccan Tabor of Goums, who were equipped with 117 horses and 126 mules.

On the vehicle side, an intriguing newcomer was the DUKW, or to give its full title: the Truck Amphibious 2-ton 6x6, which was equally at home on land or in water. It was able to carry 25 fully equipped soldiers, 5,000 pounds of general cargo, or twelve loaded stretchers. In total some 21,000 DUKWs would eventually be built, but this was to be its debut and upon it rested much of the responsibility for keeping the Seventh Army supplied over the beaches.

The Landings

While still at sea Patton had sent a message to his men, urging them to greater glory and containing such phrases as: 'We are indeed honored to have been selected for ... this new and greater attack against the Axis. ...When we land we will meet German and Italian soldiers whom it is our honor and privilege to attack and destroy.... The glory of American arms, the honor of our country, the future of the world rests in your individual hands.' One of the last things he did, on 9 July, was to have the Chaplain in after supper to say a prayer, but it did not have the desired effect as the weather deteriorated and as H-Hour approached so did a Force 7 gale! Most of the soldiers were soaked by the time they reached the beaches, but they managed to land successfully and without much opposition. The unfortunate airborne troops were badly affected by the weather and were scattered across the Sicilian countryside, well away from their scheduled DZs. Although they managed to regroup, and did a good job in continually harassing the enemy behind his lines, they did not achieve their proper missions.

After champing at the bit throughout the first day, Patton went ashore on the 11th and was soon in his element, dodging shells, almost running into German tanks, and personally laying 4.2in mortars on to enemy infantry some 900 yards away. He remarked in his diary how effective the mortars were and how the white phosphorus terrified the Italians and Germans; '... and I personally do not blame them,' he wrote. He concluded this diary entry: 'This is the first day in this campaign that I think I earned my pay. I am well satisfied with my command today. God certainly watched over me today.'

A Clash of Personalities

Patton had been made to accept a number of major changes to the original plans, which were intended to let the more experienced Eighth Army do most of the fighting, while the Americans merely protected their left flank. It was clear from the start that GSP objected to this secondary role and was determined to show what he and his troops could do, should the opportunity present itself – and this is exactly what happened.

Space does not permit a detailed account of the campaign, but the overall plan was for Montgomery to drive up from the south-east, direct for Messina in the north-east corner of the island, while GSP cleared the west of the island and protected his left flank. But the British were soon held up by fierce resistance at Catania, only halfway to Messina. Patton meanwhile was sweeping triumphantly through western Sicily and took Palermo on 22 July. He then began advancing along the northern coast road, closing the jaws of the trap around Messina. His advance was materially assisted by a number of small-scale amphibious operations, but hindered by the fact that Montgomery was apparently able to get priority for everything. Events reached boiling-point when GSP decided to broaden his advance by creating a Provisional Corps HQ, under General Keyes, and bringing it up parallel with Bradley's II Corps, thus making continuous re-supply even more vital. To his chagrin, he discovered that Alexander had given the British priority over a central route which had already been allocated to the Americans. This was the last straw and GSP flew back to see him, protesting violently that he must be allowed to operate more freely. Alexander at last realised the strength of the American anger, retracted, and from then on almost took a back seat, letting the two 'prima donnas' slug it out!

The End in Sicily

Eventually it became a race to see who could reach Messina first, the British taking Catania on 5 August and then pressing hard northwards towards Messina, whilst the Americans were pushing equally hard from the west. Meanwhile, the enemy opposition was disintegrating, on both fronts the Italians either surrendering or crossing over the Strait of Messina to temporary safety in Italy, followed later by the Germans, who had fought a dogged campaign. By 17 August it was all over. Both army commanders emerged with glory, Patton rating himself 'the best damn ass-kicker in the whole US Army!' The campaign had, once again, shown his ability in battle, and if only he could have left it there all would have been well. Sadly, his impetuosity and quick temper led to the notorious 'slapping incident', which put a blight on the whole brilliant campaign and almost got him sacked. Much has been written on this subject and I do not intend to waste space on the rights and wrongs of what happened. As always, the press latched on to the scandal avidly, using it to pillory GSP, just days after they had lionised him for raising the morale of the whole country with his triumph in Sicily. As GSP put it in his diary: 'My command has so far disposed of 177,000 Germans, Italians and French – killed, wounded and prisoner, of which they have killed and wounded 21,000. Our average loss has been one man for 13½ of the enemy. It would be a national calamity to lose an Army commander with such a record.' Fortunately, Eisenhower felt likewise and, although he would keep a strict eye on GSP in future and not allow him to rise above Army Commander, he knew that Patton was, without doubt, one of the best, if not the best, field commanders in the entire US Army. They could ill-afford to be without his talents in the next and most important battle against the Germans.

Annex 'A' to Chapter 3
Operation 'Torch'
Composition of Western Task Force

This Task Force sailed direct from the USA in US Naval vessels under the command of Rear Admiral H. Kent Hewitt, USN. Landing area, coast of Morocco (7/8 November 1942).

CG:	Major General George S. Patton, Jr
Deputy CG:	Major General Geoffrey Keyes
Chief of Staff:	Colonel Hobart R. Gay*
Deputy COS:	Lieutenant Colonel Paul D. Harkins*

G-1 (Personnel):	Colonel Hugh Fitzgerald
G-2 (Intelligence):	Colonel Percy Black
G-3 (Plans and Training):	Colonel Kent C. Lambert
G-4 (Supply):	Colonel Walter J. Muller*
Adjutant General:	Colonel R. E. Cummings*
Artillery:	Colonel J. J. B. Williams
Engineers:	Colonel John Conklin**
Ordnance:	Colonel Thomas H. Nixon*
Signal Officer:	Colonel Elton H. Hammond*
Medical Officer:	Colonel Albert Kenner
NORTHERN LANDING FORCE	
Comd:	Major General Lucien K. Truscott
60th Inf Regt, 9th Inf Div:	Colonel F. J. de Rohan
Armd Task Force, from 2nd Armd Div:	Colonel Harry H. Semmes***
Supporting troops	
CENTRAL LANDING FORCE	
Comd:	Major General Jonathan W. Anderson
3rd Inf Div:	General Anderson
Armd Task Force, from 2nd Armd Div:	Lieutenant Colonel Richard Nelson
Supporting troops	
SOUTHERN LANDING FORCE	
Comd (also CG 2nd Armd Div):	Major General Ernest A. Harmon
47th Inf Regt, 9th Inf Div:	Colonel E. H. Rangle
Armd Task Force, from 2nd Armd Div:	Brigadier General Hugh A. Gaffey
Supporting troops	
Total: 31,000 troops.	

*With Patton throughout the war.
**Went to USA in 1943, returned with Third Army.
***Served with Patton in both world wars (holder of three Distinguished Service Crosses).

Annex 'B' to Chapter 3
Sicily – Composition of US Forces on D-Day, 10 July 1943

3RD INF DIVISION
7TH INF REGT
10th FA Bn
Coy 'G', 66th Armd Regt
one bn, 36th Combat Engr Regt
3rd Ranger Bn
2nd Bn, 15th Inf Regt
one pl, Cannon Coy, 15th Inf Regt
Coy 'B', 3rd Chem Bn
Bty 'B', 39th Fd Arty Bn
one bn, 36th Engr Combat Regt
15TH INF REGT
1st, 3rd Bns

Coy 'H', 66th Armd Regt
39th FA Bn
30TH INF REGT
41st Fd Arty Bn
Coy 'I', 66th Armd Regt
Coy 'C', 3rd Chem Bn
one bn, 36th Engr Combat Regt
FLOATING RESERVE: CCA, 2ND ARMD DIV
66th Armd Regt (3rd Bn)
41st Armd Inf Regt (1st Bn)
Coy 'B', 82nd Recon Sqn
14th Armd FA Bn
1ST INF DIVISION

FORCE X
1st Ranger Bn
4th Ranger Bn
1st Bn, 39th Combat Engrs
three coys, 83rd Chem Bn
one bn, 51st Engr Shore Regt
26TH COMBAT TEAM
26th Inf Regt
5th FA Bn
33rd FA Bn
six btys AA arty
one bn, 531st Engr Shore Regt
one med tank pl, 67th Armd Regt
16TH COMBAT TEAM
16th Inf Regt
7th FA Bn
six btys AA arty
one bn, 51st Engr Shore Regt
one med tank pl, 67th Armd Regt

45TH INF DIVISION
180TH INF REGT
171st FA Bn
Coy 'C', 2nd Chem Bn
2nd Bn, 40th Engrs
179TH INF REGT
160th FA Bn + one bty SP hows
Coys 'A' and 'B', 2nd Chem Bn
3rd Bn, 40th Engrs
157TH INF REGT
158th FA Bn + one bty SP hows
753rd Med Tank Bn
five btys AA arty
1st Bn, 40th Engrs

SEVENTH ARMY FLOATING RESERVE
2ND ARMD DIVISION
CCB
67th Armd Regt (-)
82nd Recon Sqn (-)
17th Armd Engr Bn
78th Armd FA Bn
92nd Armd FA Bn
1st Bn, 41st Armd Inf Regt
18TH INF REGT
32nd FA Bn
one Engr coy
540th Engrs
two AAA bns

Source: Appendix 'A' to 'Sicily and the surrender of Italy' in the *US ARMY in World War II* series.

Notes to Chapter 3

1. *Patton the Commander* by Major General H. Essame.
2. *George Patton, General in Spurs* by Alden Hatch.
3. As quoted in *The US Army 1941–45* by Philip Katcher.
4. Listed in *Roll Again Second Armored* by Majors Norris H. Perkins and Michael E. Rogers.
5. US Fifth Army was activated at Oudijda, French Morocco, on 5 January 1943 and at that time comprised: I Armored Corps, II Corps and XII Air Support Command. Its first Commanding General was Lieutenant General Mark Wayne Clark. It would be used for the invasion of Italy at Salerno.

Part II

Patton's Third Army

4
US Third Army, the Basics

'Well, I have an Army and it is up to me.'

After Patton's humiliation in Sicily, he was kept on tenterhooks worrying whether or not he would get the appointment he desired so much, namely to command the American invasion forces in Normandy. Although this was now out of his grasp, he would not be totally neglected because Eisenhower, as already explained, had chosen to stand by his friend despite all the pressures from above. 'I believe that he is cured,' he wrote to General Marshall, 'not only because of his great personal loyalty to you and me, but mainly because he is so avid for recognition as a great military commander that he will ruthlessly suppress any habit of his own that will tend to jeopardise it.'[1] But Ike was not prepared to go the whole hog and put GSP in total command, perhaps because he considered, with some justification, that Army command level was GSP's ceiling. In any event, an active service 'hands on' command suited Patton's temperament far better than the more senior appointment in which tact and co-operation with the British was so important. Bradley would also get an Army command and, eventually, overtake his erstwhile 'boss', to finish up above him as his Army Group commander. That was still well in the future, but it has to be said that Patton never held a grudge against Bradley and always loyally supported him, a measure of his generous spirit.

Patton arrived at Prestwick on the morning of 26 January 1944 and went immediately to London, where he was told by Eisenhower that he would get command of the Third Army when it arrived in the UK. It had only been transferred to combat status on 31 December 1943 – 'all novices' is the way GSP described them in his diary, explaining that they would be in support of Bradley's First Army – '... not such a good job, but better than nothing'. In typical style he closes this diary entry: 'Well, I have an Army and it is up to me. God show the right. As far as I can remember, this is my twenty-seventh start from zero since entering the US Army. Each time I have made a success of it, and this one must be the biggest.'

Third Army's Early Years

US Third Army first came into existence on 15 November 1918, at Ligny-en-Barrois in France, four days after the Great War had ended. It moved to Germany two days later as an army of occupation, with its

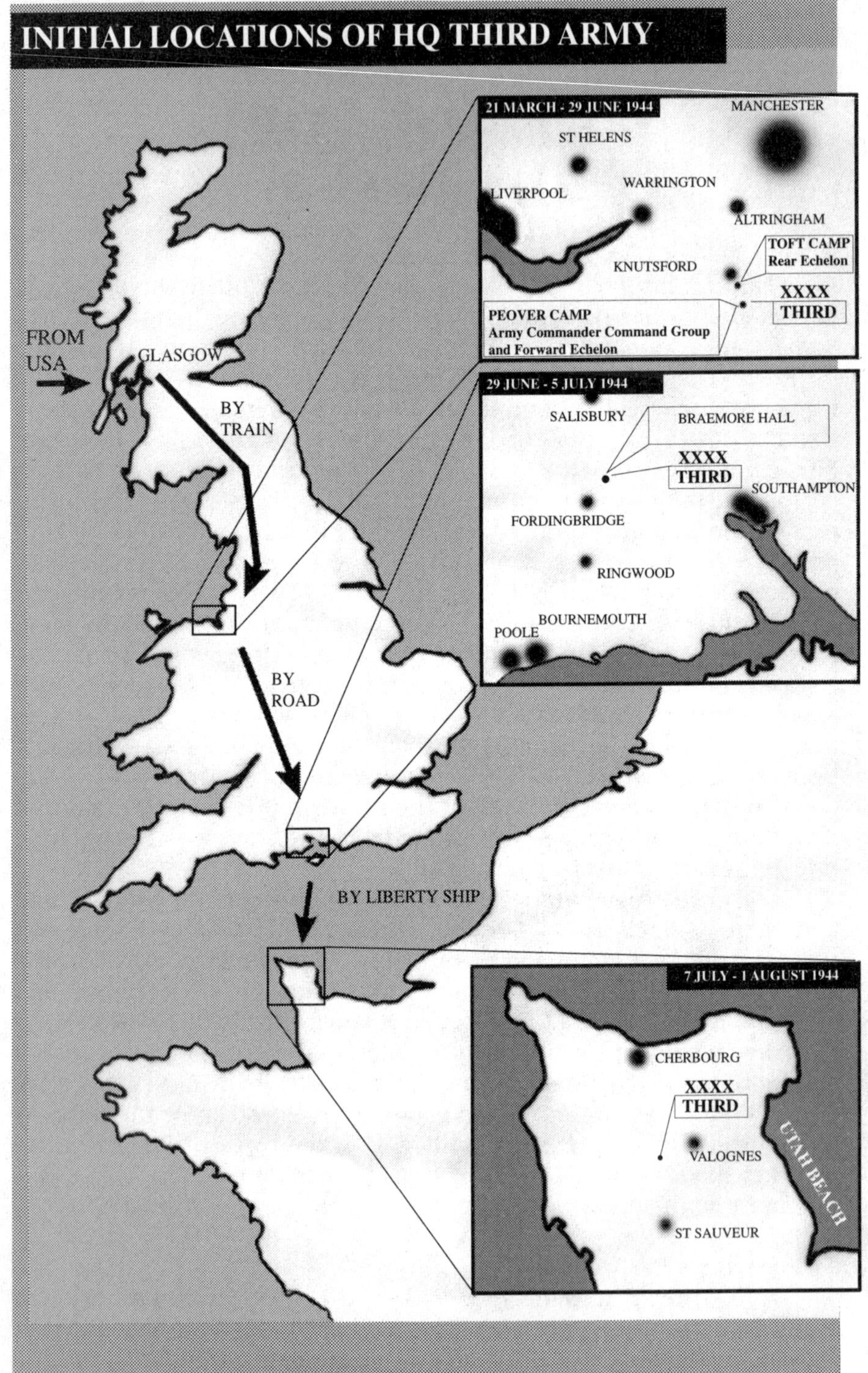
INITIAL LOCATIONS OF HQ THIRD ARMY
21 MARCH - 29 JUNE 1944
MANCHESTER
ST HELENS
LIVERPOOL
WARRINGTON
ALTRINGHAM
TOFT CAMP
Rear Echelon
KNUTSFORD
XXXX
THIRD
PEOVER CAMP
Army Commander Command Group
and Forward Echelon
FROM
USA
GLASGOW
BY
TRAIN
29 JUNE - 5 JULY 1944
SALISBURY
BRAEMORE HALL
XXXX
THIRD
SOUTHAMPTON
FORDINGBRIDGE
RINGWOOD
BOURNEMOUTH
POOLE
BY
ROAD
BY LIBERTY SHIP
7 JULY - 1 AUGUST 1944
CHERBOURG
XXXX
THIRD
VALOGNES
UTAH BEACH
ST SAUVEUR

headquarters at Koblenz. The now world-famous shoulder patch of the Third Army owes its existence to these early days, being a red 'O' encircling a white 'A', on a blue background, signifying 'Army of Occupation'. On 2 July 1919, Third Army was de-activated and its units and personnel renamed 'American Forces Germany'. Thirteen years later it was re-activated, when the continental United States was divided into four sections, with one army to each section. The Third Army was allocated the south-east section, its headquarters alternating between Atlanta, Georgia, and Fort Sam Houston, Texas.

When the USA declared war in 1941, Third Army was being commanded by Lieutenant General Walter Krueger, an old soldier, who had served in the ranks before being commissioned in 1901. A tough, gritty commander, with combat experience during the Great War, Krueger was both admired and respected by his troops; Third Army had an enviable reputation thanks to his tireless energy and drive. He handed over to Lieutenant General Courtney H. Hodges in 1943. Hodges had also risen from the ranks to become a general officer and was commanding one of the corps in Third Army under Krueger, assuming army command when the 64-year-old Krueger, who had been thirsting for an operational appointment, left to command the US Sixth Army in the Pacific Theatre – a remarkable achievement for a man of his age. Hodges was the exact opposite of his predecessor, being shy, quiet and inarticulate. He did not like administration or talking 'on his feet', so was far more inclined to leave decision-making to his subordinates. Despite this obvious change of style, Third Army continued to be the premier training and manoeuvring army in the country, being responsible, for example, for training the three Negro divisions (92nd and 93rd Infantry and 2nd Cavalry), while the vast Louisiana manoeuvre area lay within its boundaries. Much of their training success was due to Colonel John C. Macdonald, an outstanding infantryman, who was responsible for the manoeuvre area.

General Hodges was not destined to command Third Army in the field and left before it moved overseas. It is not clear why this happened because at the time no reason was given for his being relieved. However, he went on to command the US First Army most successfully in the European Theatre of Operations, although never with the same panache that his successor to be would bring to Third Army.

A New Commander

Third Army officially changed from a training army to a combat army on 31 December 1943 and was ordered to prepare to go overseas to the ETO on the following day. At the time, although Hodges' absence caused some comment within the headquarters, there was as yet no suspicion of command. However, as Colonel Robert Allen says in his book *Lucky Forward*, '... a week later the Headquarters Commandant experienced a startling jolt. In a bundle of mail he found a letter addressed to

"Lt Gen George S. Patton, Jr, CG Third US Army, APO 403, Postmaster, New York NY". The return address was that of Mrs George S. Patton, Jr.'

The news was kept secret as far as possible, but the advance party of thirteen officers and 26 enlisted men, who arrived at Glasgow aboard RMS *Queen Mary* on 29 January 1944, were met by GSP '... a-glitter in gleaming brass and boots.... 'I am your new commander,' he said. 'I'm glad to see you. I hope it's mutual.'

The main body of headquarters troops, who travelled across, packed like sardines, in the *Ile de France*, arrived in the Firth of Clyde on 21 March and made their way to Peover Hall, an 11th-century manor house, near Knutsford in Cheshire. The Chief of Staff and most of the general staff officers who had served with Hodges found posting orders awaiting them as they got off the boat, being replaced by 'Patton men', who had served with him in North Africa and Sicily. This 'purge' was not out of the ordinary; senior commanders in most armies during the Second World War invariably managed to keep key members of their staff with them when they moved 'up the chain'. It did not affect subordinate officers. Practically all of GSP's section chiefs were cavalrymen, a number being veterans of his first divisional command (2nd Armored), so riding-breeches and riding-boots became common attire, plus, as Robert Allen wryly points out, it was the only headquarters where every officer always wore a tie. 'Hot or cold, rain, snow or sunshine, in the lines or in the CP, every officer on Patton's staff always wore a necktie. Also, shaved every day. And a HQ Third Army area always was instantly recognisable by the unfailing and snappy saluting.'

Patton's Address to His Troops

During the period from March until going over to Normandy in July, there was a massive amount of detailed preparation and planning to be done. Patton made personal inspections of his troops throughout the UK, visiting all the principal units, talking to the officers and enlisted men – quite an undertaking when one considers that the personnel strength of Third Army by 31 May 1944 was more than 250,000 men! He would arrive immaculately dressed, in a well-tailored, form-fitting, brass-buttoned battle jacket, studded with four rows of campaign ribbons and decorations, pink whipcord riding-breeches and gleaming riding-boots. Around his waist was a hand-tooled leather belt, with a shiny brass buckle. On his shoulders, shirt collar and helmet were a total of fifteen large stars and in his hand a long riding-whip. In the majority of locations he made his 'off the cuff' speech, which naturally varied from place to place, although the gist always remained the same. I believe that it is well worth quoting one version here in full, as it sets the scene for Patton's greatest command. And 'Georgie's Boys' loved it!

'I want you men to remember that no bastard ever won a war by dying for his country. He won it by making the other dumb bastard die for his country. All this stuff you've heard about America not wanting to fight, wanting to stay out of this war, is a lot of horseshit. Americans love to fight. All real Americans love the sting of battle. When you were kids you all admired the champion marble shooter, the fastest runner, the big league ball players and the toughest boxers. Americans love a winner and will not tolerate a loser. Americans play to win all the time. I wouldn't give a hoot in Hell for a man who lost and laughed. That's why Americans have never lost and never will lose a war. The very thought of losing is hateful to Americans. An army is a team. It lives, eats, sleeps and fights as a team. This individuality stuff is a bunch of bullshit. The bastards who write it for the *Saturday Evening Post*, don't know any more about real battle than they do about fucking. We have the finest food and equipment, the best spirit, and the best men in the world. I pity those poor bastards we're going up against. We're not just going to shoot the bastards, we're going to rip out their living God-damned guts and use them to grease the treads of our tanks. We're going to murder those lousy Hun bastards by the bushel basket.

'Some of you men are wondering whether or not you'll chicken out under fire. Don't worry about it. I can assure you that you'll all do your duty. The Nazis are the enemy. Wade into them. Spill their blood. Shoot them in the belly. When you put your hand into a bunch of goo, that a moment before was your best friend's face, you'll know what to do. There's another thing I want you to remember. I don't want any messages saying we're holding our position. We're advancing constantly and we're not interested in holding onto anything except the enemy. We're going to hold onto him by his balls and kick the hell out of him all the time. We're going through him like crap through a goose.

'There's one thing you men will be able to say when you get back home. Thirty years from now, when you're sitting by your fireside, with your grandson on your knee and he asks: "What did you do in the great World War Two?" You won't have to shift him to the other knee, cough and say, "Well I shovelled shit in Louisiana."

'I'm not supposed to be commanding this Army. I'm not even supposed to be in England. Let the first bastards to find out be the God-damn Germans. I want them to look up and howl, "Ach! It's the God-damn Third Army and that son-of-a-bitch Patton again!"

'All right you sons of bitches, you know how I feel. I'll be proud to lead you wonderful guys into battle anywhere, anytime. That's all.'

Operation 'Fortitude'

Patton's comment: 'I'm not even supposed to be in England' was a veiled reference concerning his part in a huge, well-organised deception plan code-named Operation 'Fortitude', which was supposed to convince the Germans that the actual main Allied landings would take place in the Pas de Calais area, opposite Dover, at the narrowest part of the English Channel. GSP was an integral part of this deception plan, because of his considerable reputation with the Germans. They rated him by far the best Allied field commander, and since Sicily he had apparently disappeared, only to re-appear in England, where the Fortitude plan had him commanding a mythical Army Group in south-east England, with its headquarters in Kent, supposedly getting ready for the major assault on the Pas de Calais. A network of dummy radio traffic was transmitted constantly in the Kent area, and there were dummy camps, vehicle parks, storage depots, etc., all to hoodwink the small number of enemy reconnaissance aircraft which managed to fly over. The plan worked and the Germans stationed a large force along the coast in the area of Calais and kept them there even when the Allies had landed in Normandy. Therefore it was sensible for Patton to remain out of the limelight.

The Knutsford Incident. The 'shit hit the fan', therefore, when GSP suddenly found himself in the middle of yet another press onslaught after attending the seemingly innocent opening of a 'Welcome Club' for American officers in Knutsford. He was asked to make an impromptu speech and did so, including in it the following words: 'I feel that such Clubs as this are of very real value, because, I believe with Mr Bernard Shaw, I think it was he, that the British and Americans are two people separated by a common language, and since it is the evident destiny of the British and the Americans, and, of course the Russians, to rule the world, the better we know each other, the better job we will do.' His speech was correctly reported in the British press but deliberately misquoted in America, where the phrase 'and of course the Russians' was left out, and GSP was accused of snubbing the USSR. Such a minor matter should have blown over immediately, but the resulting storm once again almost cost Patton his job. And once again he had Eisenhower to thank for deciding to take no action other than to restrain him from making any more speeches – even to his own troops! Nevertheless, as various historians have since pointed out, by admitting that Patton was an indispensable factor in the success of 'Overlord', General Eisenhower could not have paid him a finer compliment!

The 'Hub'. During the preparatory stage in UK a great deal of coordination was required with higher headquarters, so a small HQ cell was established in Bryanston Square, London, under the Deputy Chief of Staff (Tactical) who acted in a liaison capacity. But the 'hub of activity' was Patton's War Room at Peover Hall. GSP's personal accommodation was in the Hall and immediately opposite the War Room. This is where all Third Army's invasion planning took place and where GSP held his war councils and briefings for Corps and Divisional commanders. He had brought sixteen officers with him from HQ Seventh Army who were absorbed into the existing establishment.[2] The strength of the HQ was approximately 450 officers and 1,000 enlisted men, and Patton always ensured that these figures were never exceeded, arguing that on operations too large a staff impaired the headquarters' mobility and deprived lower units of important personnel. (For full details HQ Third Army's staff including GSP's personal staff, see Chapters 5 and 6.)

Peover Hall was reasonably comfortable. One of GSP's ADCs told me: 'Although the furnishings were sparse, each room had a fireplace, bed and chair and each of us had a private room with large shower and bath on each floor. I'm afraid we used too much coal for our fireplaces during those cold winter nights.'[3] There was not enough room for all the headquarters staff in the Hall; only the Army Commander, Command Group and Forward Echelon were there, the Rear Echelon being at nearby Toft Camp. The Corps and Divisional Headquarters and all their units were of course spread over a very much larger area, one or other of them being constantly on the move, as they carried out their final battle training and manoeuvres. When the time approached for them to move over to Normandy, it was first necessary to get the headquarters nearer to the embarkation ports and this meant relocating at Breamore Hall, near Fordingbridge, some 90 miles south-west of London and only nineteen miles from Southampton. At the same time as this move was made, the troops began to practise waterproofing vehicles and made last preparations for the voyage across the Channel. The headquarters moved down to Breamore by road on 29 June, but an advanced detachment had already left for France on the 23rd, together with VIII Corps, in order to maintain liaison with US First Army and to establish a new headquarters site 'in the field' – which was to be in an apple orchard near Nehou on the Cotentin Peninsula.

As Colonel Brenton G. Wallace explained in his book, *Patton and His Third Army*, the headquarters move started with a short speech from their Army Commander on the evening of 3 June: 'Late in the afternoon of 3 June, we got word that there would be a staff meeting of Section Chiefs of the headquarters at 1730 hours. It was an unusual time for a staff meeting. We assembled quietly. There was little of the usual talk as we waited for General Patton. Exactly at the appointed time of 1730, General Patton strode quickly but quietly in and took his place before us. For just a moment his glance roved over the ranks of his staff, the men who would be carrying out and putting into effect his battle orders. Then he spoke: "Gentlemen, the moment for which we have been working and training so long has at last arrived. Tomorrow we go to war! I congratulate you. And I prophesy that your names and the name of the Third Army will go down in history – or they will go down in the records of the Graves Registration Bureau. Thank you. Good night!" The Third Army was on the roll!

Third Army, Initial Organisation of Corps and Divisions

Although a total of six Corps and forty-two divisions served under US Third Army during the period 1 August 1944 to 8 May 1945 (a full list is given in Appendix I at the end of this book), the following was the initial organisation of Third Army (the date shown being when the division was first assigned in 1944):

XV Corps
5th Inf Div: 2 January
8th Inf Div: 2 January
4th Armd Div: 1 February
35th Inf Div: 26 April

VIII Corps
79th Inf Div: 4 April
83rd Inf Div: 4 April

XX Corps
5th Armd Div: 3 March
6th Armd Div: 3 March
90th Inf Div: 5 March*
28th Inf Div: 14 April
7th Armd Div: 26 April

XII Corps
French 2nd Armd Div: 21 April
80th Inf Div: 11 June

*Attached to First Army 27 March–30 July.
See Annex 'A' to this chapter for details of corps and divisional nicknames and shoulder patches.

Organic Components of Activated Divisions initially in Third Army

Infantry Divisions

Div	*Inf Regts*			*Fd Arty Bns*				*Special Tps Sig Coy*	*Ord Coy*	*QM Coy*	*Recon Tp*	*Engr Bn*	*Med Bn*
5	2	10	11	19	21	46	50	5	705	5	5	7	5
8	13	28	121	28	43	45	56	8	708	8	8	12	8
28	109	110	112	107	108	109	229	28	728	28	28	103	103
35	134	137	320	127	161	216	219	35	735	35	35	60	110
79	313	314	315	310	311	312	904	79	779	79	79	304	304
80	317	318	319	313	314	315	905	80	780	80	80	305	305
83	329	330	331	322	323	324	908	83	783	83	83	308	308
90	357	358	359	343	344	345	915	90	790	90	90	315	315

Armored Divisions*

Div	*Armd Inf Bns*			*Tk Bns*			*Armd Fd Arty Bns*			*Cav Recon Sqn*	*Armd Engr Bn*	*Armd Med Bn*	*Armd Ord Bn*	*Armd Sig Coy*
4	10	51	53	8	35	37	22	66	94	25	24	4	126	144
5	15	46	47	10	34	81	47	71	95	85	22	75	127	145
6	9	44	50	15	68	69	128	212	231	86	25	76	128	146
7	23	38	48	17	31	40	434	440	489	87	33	77	129	147

*All Divs also had Combat Commands A, B, R

The Basic Divisions

In his book, *War As I Knew It*, Patton lays down his priorities for the running of a successful army: 'First, it must fight. Second it must eat. Third it must be capable of rapid movement. And last but not least, it must be equipped with all essentials necessary to the accomplishment of its mission. In reality, an army provides most of the necessities of life found in a community of equal size.' He then goes on to explain the function of the corps headquarters and the infantry and armoured divisions 'which do the fighting, and many supporting troops which help them to accomplish their missions. These supporting troops are made up of fighting units; such as Cavalry, Artillery, Engineers, Anti-Aircraft Artillery, Tank Destroyer and Chemical Warfare Units.' It is relevant, therefore, as an essential preliminary, to look at the detailed organisation of the two basic divisions of the US Army – infantry and armoured – *circa* 1944.

The division was the smallest composite unit capable of operating completely independently, and of the 89 divisions[4] in existence at the end of the war the vast majority were either infantry or armoured. Their organisation was laid down in special Tables of Organisation and Equipment (T/O & Es), which prescribed the standard form of units no matter where they were stationed. Although it was clearly necessary to have such basic organisations, it was also essential to be able to modify them to suit the theatre of war in which they were operating and theatre commanders were authorised to modify the tactical organisation to suit any particular set of circumstances, as were unit commanders at a lower level. T/O & Es were amended from time to time in the light of battle experience.

The Infantry Division

'During World War II new terrains, new climates, strange weapons and unfamiliar peoples acted upon the American infantrymen. These destroyed thousands of men, put a lifelong mark on others, and changed somewhat the techniques of fighting on foot; nevertheless, in spite of everything, the basic characteristics of the infantry hardly shifted. Foot soldiers continued to be the only carriers of weapons who, in theory, were never exhausted, could always go another mile, and could be counted upon to move across any terrain in every quarter of the globe.' (US Army Lineage Series, *The Infantry*.)

The main feature of the Second World War US infantry division* was its triangular organisation, brought about by eliminating the brigade level of command, the adaptation of the division to modern, open warfare and the extensive use of motor vehicles. All these had been urged since the 1920s, but did not take on a solid shape until General Marshall took command of the US Army. Initially the infantry division organisation contained approximately 15,500 men, including a minimum of organic artillery and other support elements. There were readjustments in both 1942 and 1943 which reduced the divisional strength but did not change the overall structure, the 1943 re-organisation bringing the total strength down to 14,253. There were no perma-

* See overleaf for the basic organisation of the US infantry division and also Annex 'B' to this chapter for further details.

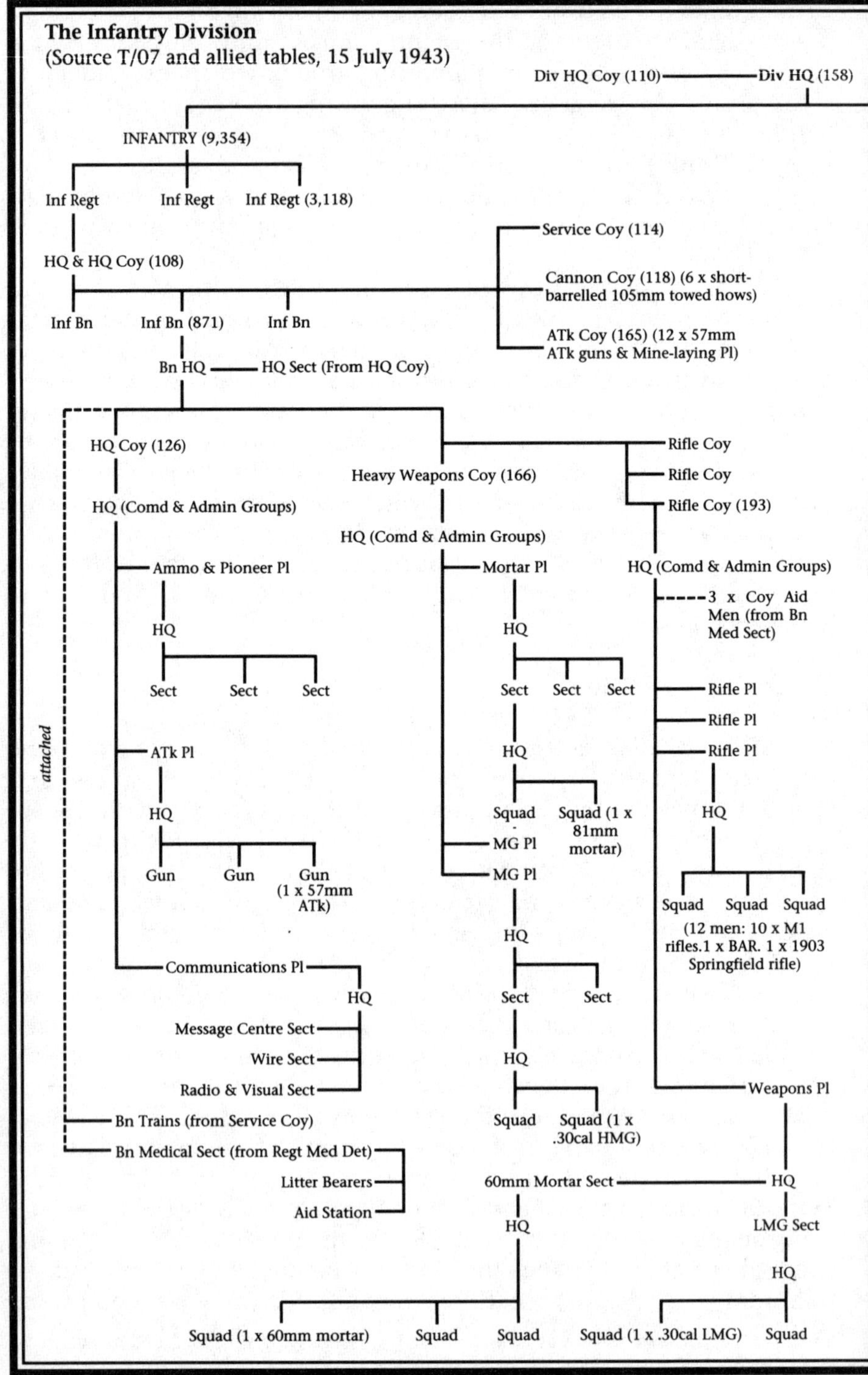
The Infantry Division
(Source T/07 and allied tables, 15 July 1943)
Div HQ Coy (110)
Div HQ (158)
INFANTRY (9,354)
Inf Regt
Inf Regt
Inf Regt (3,118)
Service Coy (114)
HQ & HQ Coy (108)
Cannon Coy (118) (6 x short-barrelled 105mm towed hows)
Inf Bn
Inf Bn (871)
Inf Bn
ATk Coy (165) (12 x 57mm ATk guns & Mine-laying Pl)
Bn HQ
HQ Sect (From HQ Coy)
HQ Coy (126)
Rifle Coy
Heavy Weapons Coy (166)
Rifle Coy
HQ (Comd & Admin Groups)
Rifle Coy (193)
HQ (Comd & Admin Groups)
Ammo & Pioneer Pl
Mortar Pl
HQ (Comd & Admin Groups)
3 x Coy Aid Men (from Bn Med Sect)
HQ
HQ
Sect
Sect
Sect
Sect
Sect
Sect
Rifle Pl
Rifle Pl
attached
ATk Pl
HQ
Rifle Pl
HQ
Squad
Squad (1 x 81mm mortar)
HQ
MG Pl
Gun
Gun
Gun (1 x 57mm ATk)
MG Pl
Squad
Squad
Squad
HQ
(12 men: 10 x M1 rifles.1 x BAR. 1 x 1903 Springfield rifle)
Communications Pl
HQ
Sect
Sect
Message Centre Sect
Wire Sect
HQ
Radio & Visual Sect
Weapons Pl
Bn Trains (from Service Coy)
Squad
Squad (1 x .30cal HMG)
Bn Medical Sect (from Regt Med Det)
Litter Bearers
60mm Mortar Sect
HQ
Aid Station
HQ
LMG Sect
HQ
Squad (1 x 60mm mortar)
Squad
Squad
Squad (1 x .30cal LMG)
Squad

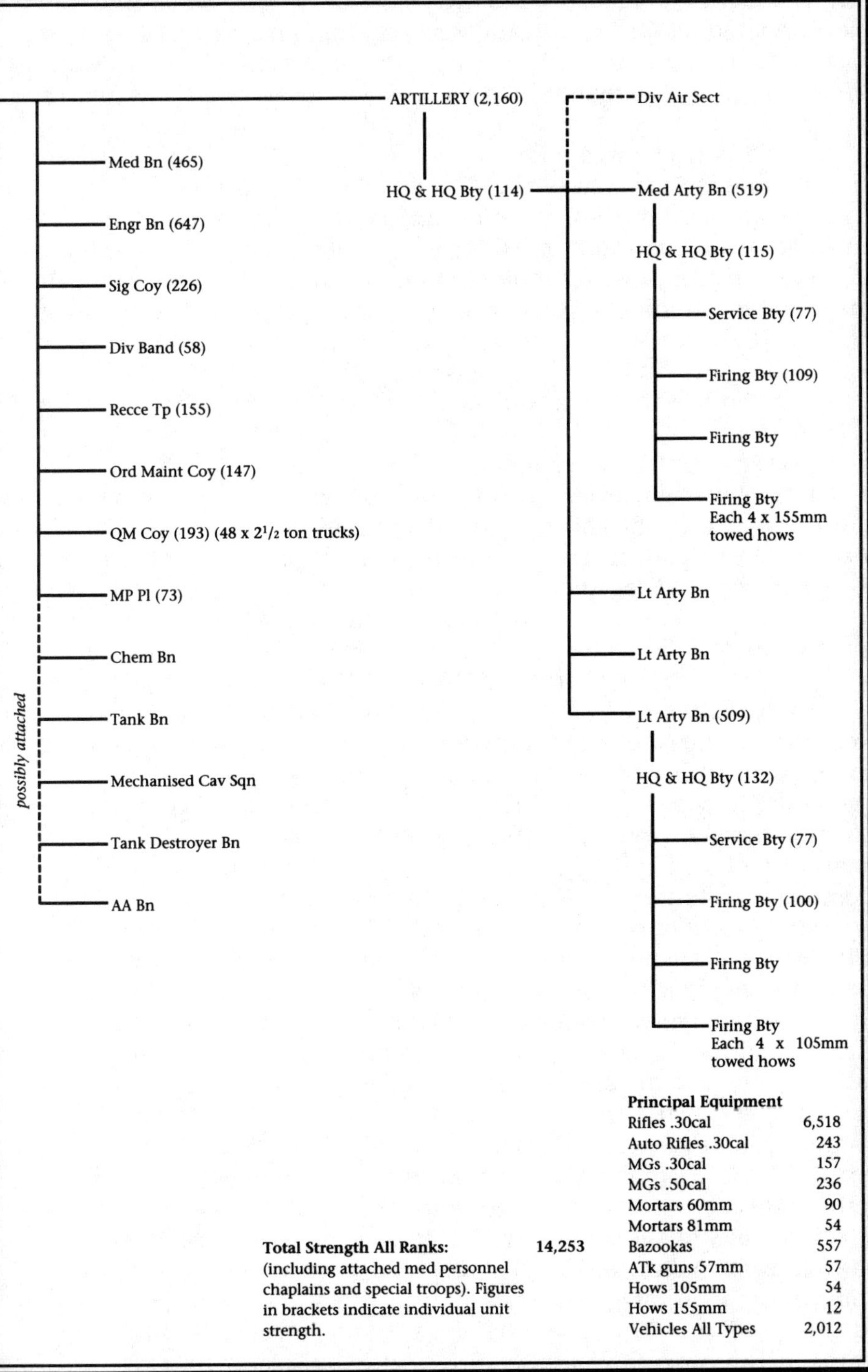

Total Strength All Ranks: **14,253**
(including attached med personnel chaplains and special troops). Figures in brackets indicate individual unit strength.

Principal Equipment	
Rifles .30cal	6,518
Auto Rifles .30cal	243
MGs .30cal	157
MGs .50cal	236
Mortars 60mm	90
Mortars 81mm	54
Bazookas	557
ATk guns 57mm	57
Hows 105mm	54
Hows 155mm	12
Vehicles All Types	2,012

nent Combat Command Headquarters (e.g., CCA and CCB) as found in the armoured division; instead, when a combined arms team was formed for a particular mission, one of the three Regimental Headquarters was used to command them and the groups were called 'Combat Teams'.

Weapon changes made in step with the 1943 re-organisation included the replacement of the 37mm anti-tank gun by the 57mm in both the anti-tank platoon at rifle company level and within the anti-tank company. The 75mm howitzer was dropped and the towed short-barrelled 105mm howitzer took the place of the self-propelled type in the restored cannon company. The M1 (Garand) became the principal rifle, the bazooka was introduced in large numbers (557 per battalion), while more jeeps and trailers were prescribed. The 2½-ton truck – generally known as the 'Deuce-and-a-half' – regained preference over the 1½-tonner.

Within infantry regiments the smallest sub-unit was the rifle squad – twelve men, armed with ten M1 (Garand) rifles, one Browning automatic rifle (BAR) and one M1903 Springfield rifle. Three squads made up a rifle platoon and three rifle platoons plus one weapons platoon were grouped together to form a rifle company. The weapons platoon had two .30 cal LMGs, three 60mm mortars, three anti-tank rocket-launchers (Bazookas) and one .50 cal Heavy MG, primarily for air defence. Total strength of a rifle company was 193 all ranks. The infantry battalion consisted of three such rifle companies, plus a heavy weapons company of six 81mm mortars, eight .30 cal LMGs, seven Bazookas and three .50 cal HMGs. Headquarters Company contained an anti-tank platoon of three 57mm anti-tank guns. Total strength of the infantry battalion was 871. There were three such battalions in an infantry regiment, plus the following regimental units: HQ and HQ Company; a cannon company of six short-barrelled 105mm howitzers (towed); an anti-tank company of twelve 57mm anti-tank guns and a mine-laying platoon. There were three infantry regiments in the division, thus giving a 'bayonet strength' of 9,354 infantrymen. Next came the supporting field artillery, which had its HQ and HQ Battery to command the divisional artillery which comprised three light artillery battalions and one medium artillery battalion. Each of the former contained an HQ battery, a service battery and three firing batteries each of four 105mm towed howitzers, making 36 guns in total. The medium battalion had a similar organisation but was equipped with 155mm towed howitzers. Total artillery manpower was 2,160. Next came the auxiliary units in the division which included a reconnaissance troop, an engineer battalion, medical battalion, quartermaster company, signal company and military police platoon. Together with attached personnel such as medical sections and chaplains with the units, the total strength of the division was 14,253 men.

For a specific operation an infantry division might be reinforced with a mechanised cavalry squadron, by one or more field artillery battalions of any appropriate calibre, by a chemical battalion manning 4.2in mortars, by tank, tank destroyer or anti-aircraft artillery units. These attachments became the 'norm' when combat developed on a large scale, the result being that an infantry divisional commander normally had well over 15,000 men.

The Armoured Division

'Armor as the ground arm of mobility, emerged from WWII with a lion's share of the credit for the Allied victory. Indeed, armor enthusiasts at that time regarded the tank as being the main weapon of the land army.' (US Army Lineage Series, *Armor-Cavalry*)

In 1943, like the infantry division, the armoured division underwent a thorough re-organisation, as well as being reduced in manpower by over 3,600 men. Light tank strength was halved (from 158 to 77) and the armored infantry element increased. Service elements were trimmed, thus increasing their mobility, while unnecessary command echelons (such as the tank regimental level) were eliminated. The new streamlined division had five commands under divisional control: Combat Command 'A' (CCA), Combat Command 'B' (CCB), Reserve Command (Res Cmd), Artillery Command (Divarty), and Trains Command (Tns Cmd). Each command headquarters consisted of a headquarters and an HQ company or detachment. It was designed to control whatever subordinate units were assigned to it for a particular mission. CCA and CCB, the strike forces, were set up to control a number of combat units (battalions or companies) and/or support units. The major units of the division were three tank battalions, each comprising an HQ and HQ company, three medium tank companies, one light tank company and a service company. Total manpower for the tank battalion was 729. Each tank company (medium or light) contained 17 tanks – three platoons of five tanks each and two in Coy HQ. Towards the end of the war an extra M4 medium tank, mounting a close-support 105mm howitzer instead of its normal 75mm or 76mm main armament, was added to each Coy HQ, increasing the medium tank strength in the division to 195.

Balancing these three tank battalion were three armoured infantry battalions, each comprising an HQ + HQ Coy, a service company and three rifle companies. Total battalion manpower was 1,001. The tanks and armoured infantry were supported by three armoured field artillery battalions, each equipped with eighteen 105mm SP howitzers (M7). Auxiliary units, such as divisional recce squadron, attached medical personnel and unit chaplains, brought the armoured divisional strength to 10,937. In addition, tank destroyer and/or AA artillery battalions were usually permanently attached.

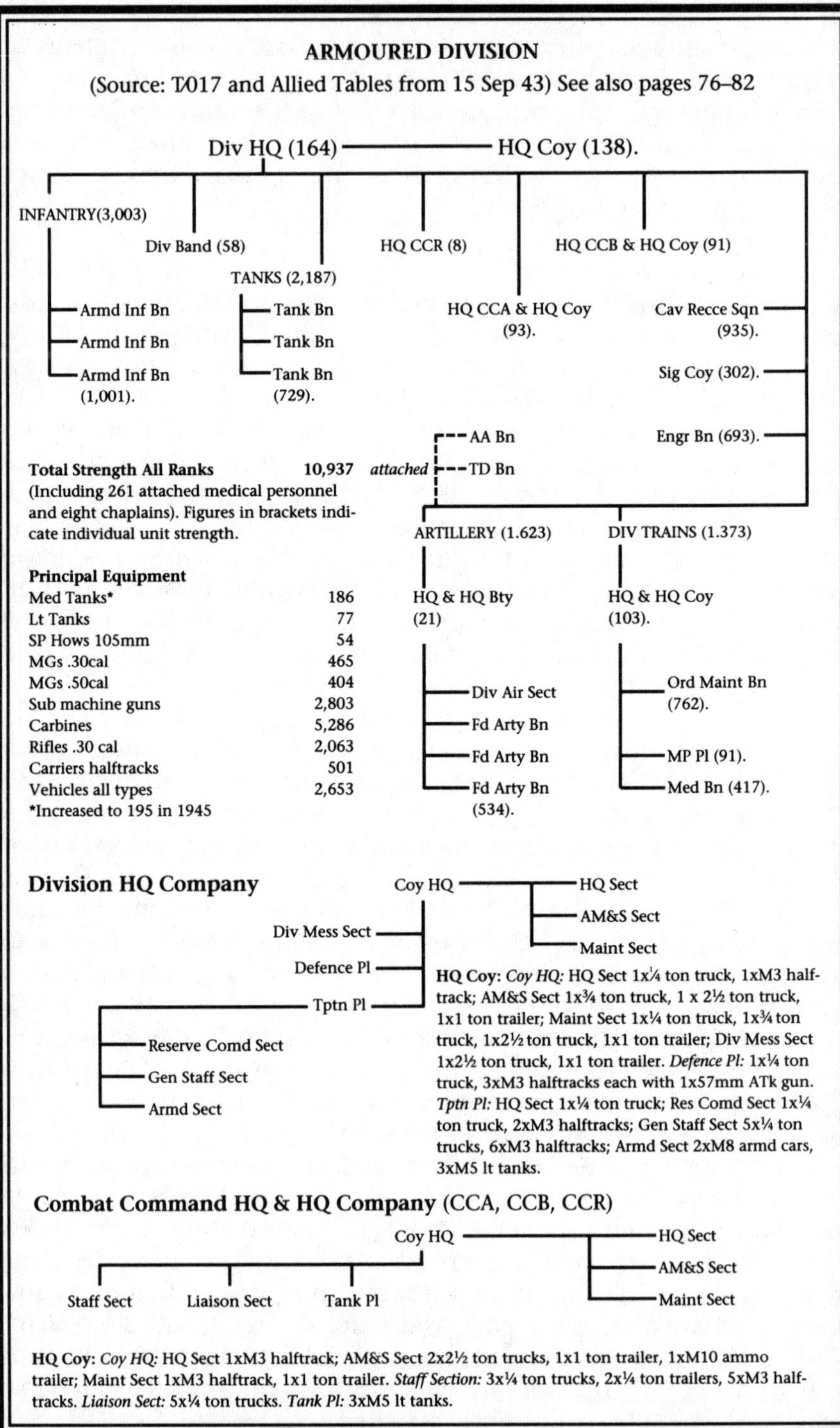
ARMOURED DIVISION
(Source: T/017 and Allied Tables from 15 Sep 43) See also pages 76–82
Div HQ (164)
HQ Coy (138).
INFANTRY(3,003)
Div Band (58)
TANKS (2,187)
HQ CCR (8)
HQ CCB & HQ Coy (91)
Armd Inf Bn
Armd Inf Bn
Armd Inf Bn
(1,001).
Tank Bn
Tank Bn
Tank Bn
(729).
HQ CCA & HQ Coy
(93).
Cav Recce Sqn
(935).
Sig Coy (302).
Engr Bn (693).
AA Bn
attached
TD Bn
Total Strength All Ranks 10,937
(Including 261 attached medical personnel and eight chaplains). Figures in brackets indicate individual unit strength.
ARTILLERY (1.623)
DIV TRAINS (1.373)
Principal Equipment
Med Tanks* 186
Lt Tanks 77
SP Hows 105mm 54
MGs .30cal 465
MGs .50cal 404
Sub machine guns 2,803
Carbines 5,286
Rifles .30 cal 2,063
Carriers halftracks 501
Vehicles all types 2,653
*Increased to 195 in 1945
HQ & HQ Bty
(21)
Div Air Sect
Fd Arty Bn
Fd Arty Bn
Fd Arty Bn
(534).
HQ & HQ Coy
(103).
Ord Maint Bn
(762).
MP Pl (91).
Med Bn (417).
Division HQ Company
Coy HQ
HQ Sect
AM&S Sect
Maint Sect
Div Mess Sect
Defence Pl
Tptn Pl
Reserve Comd Sect
Gen Staff Sect
Armd Sect
HQ Coy: Coy HQ: HQ Sect 1x¼ ton truck, 1xM3 halftrack; AM&S Sect 1x¾ ton truck, 1 x 2½ ton truck, 1x1 ton trailer; Maint Sect 1x¼ ton truck, 1x¾ ton truck, 1x2½ ton truck, 1x1 ton trailer; Div Mess Sect 1x2½ ton truck, 1x1 ton trailer. Defence Pl: 1x¼ ton truck, 3xM3 halftracks each with 1x57mm ATk gun. Tptn Pl: HQ Sect 1x¼ ton truck; Res Comd Sect 1x¼ ton truck, 2xM3 halftracks; Gen Staff Sect 5x¼ ton trucks, 6xM3 halftracks; Armd Sect 2xM8 armd cars, 3xM5 lt tanks.
Combat Command HQ & HQ Company (CCA, CCB, CCR)
Coy HQ
HQ Sect
AM&S Sect
Maint Sect
Staff Sect
Liaison Sect
Tank Pl
HQ Coy: Coy HQ: HQ Sect 1xM3 halftrack; AM&S Sect 2x2½ ton trucks, 1x1 ton trailer, 1xM10 ammo trailer; Maint Sect 1xM3 halftrack, 1x1 ton trailer. Staff Section: 3x¼ ton trucks, 2x¼ ton trailers, 5xM3 halftracks. Liaison Sect: 5x¼ ton trucks. Tank Pl: 3xM5 lt tanks.

The Airborne Division

Although the airborne division was not one of the 'basic' divisions in Third Army, two airborne divisions (17th and 101st) did come under command in late 1944–early 1945, so a brief examination of their basic organisation will not go amiss. The airborne division had undergone a complete re-organisation in late 1944, its manpower being increased almost to that of the standard infantry division. The complete airborne division now had a strength of 12,979 all ranks, so that it fielded some 1,274 less manpower than the infantry division. At full strength it comprised two Infantry Parachute Regiments and one Infantry Glider Regiment, plus supporting troops which included Div Arty (pack hows), an AA/ATk Bn, a Para Maint Coy, an Engr Bn, a Medical Coy and Special Troops (MP platoon, Recce platoon, Ord Maint Coy, QM Coy, Signal Coy and HQ Coy). Para Regts had three battalions (each of 36 officers, 1 WO and 669 enlisted men), plus a Service Coy and an HQ Coy. The Glider Regt was similarly organised, but had, in addition, an Anti-tank Coy of 9x57mm towed ATk guns and 9 Bazookas. Div Arty totalled one battery of 16x75mm pack hows, plus two batteries each of 12x75mm pack hows (gliderborne) and 10 liaison aircraft. The AA/ATk Bn contained 24 x 57mm ATk guns and 36 x .50 cal HMG. Divisional transport of some 1,000 plus vehicles consisted, of course, of mainly light trucks, all being 2½-ton or under (there were nearly 800 jeeps!) except for one 4-ton wrecker. There was also a large number of 1-ton and ¼-ton trailers (756 total). Like all airborne forces they were really too lightly equipped for sustained action.

A Divisional Headquarters in Action

In his first Letter of Instruction to all Corps, Divisional and Separate Unit Commanders, Patton laid down certain principles which he wished to be strictly adhered to by all commanders. These will be covered in full later. They included such detail as to where corps and divisional Command Posts (CPs) should be located – as one might guess, this was to be as far forward as possible, so that less time was wasted getting to the forward troops. 'Remember,' he told his commanders, 'that your primary mission as a leader is to see with your own eyes and to be seen by the troops when engaged in personal reconnaissance.'

In his book on the US 6th Armored Division, entitled *The Super Sixth*, Professor George F. Hofmann gives an excellent description of how a divisional headquarters (HQ) functioned in action:

'Division HQ Company provided the administrative supply and service personnel and the local security for both Forward and Rear Echelon of Division Headquarters. The Forward Echelon included the Division Commander, Assistant Division Commander, their aides and the liaison officers from subordinate and adjacent headquarters, Chief of Staff, Assistant Chiefs of Staff G-1, G-2, G-3 and G-4[5] Division Surgeon, Signal and

Engineer Officers (the latter also commanded the 25th Engineers and was usually represented by an Assistant Division Engineer). The Division Chemical Officer and the Military Government Officer joined the Forward Echelon when appropriate. G-1, G-4 and the Division Surgeon rotated between Forward and Rear Echelon as the situation demanded. Forward Echelon was located, both on the march, in combat or in bivouac, as far forward as practicable to facilitate communication and personal contact with combat units. The Division Commander or the Assistant Division Commander, their aides and, from time to time officers from the G-2 and G-3 sections, constituting an "advance party", kept in close personal touch with the "main effort" during combat and at the same time, in radio touch with the Division CP where the Chief of Staff, in touch with all units through radio, wire or liaison personnel, kept the Commander informed and issued orders as directed or, if necessary, on his own, in accordance with the plan. The magnificent communication facilities rarely failed to keep all commanders and staff personnel in touch.

'The Headquarters Commandant with the security platoon was charged with moving, locating and protecting the Division CP as directed by the Chief of Staff. On rapid advances, this frequently took the party under fire as they sought a forward position in anticipation, usually proven justified, of continued advance.

'The Rear Echelon was under control of the Division Trains Commander for movement and security. The latter duty often fell to the Band as well as the MP Platoon. In addition to HQ and HQ Company of Division Trains, the following sections of Division HQ, constituting the Rear Echelon, were normally present: The Adjutant General, Inspector General, Division Chaplain, Special Services Officer (including Graves Registration), Postal Officer, Finance Officer, Provost Marshal and when not with the Forward Echelon, the Military Government Officer and Chemical Officer, as well as attached speciality teams and Red Cross Field Directors.

'There was, obviously, constant interchange between Forward and Rear Echelons, particularly between G-1 and G-4 section personnel. The Rear Echelon moved less frequently than the Forward and was billeted in more permanent shelter whenever practical as was fitting to their duties.'

Preparing for Battle

The spring and early summer months of 1944 were hectic ones for everyone and GSP made it his personal business to see that his troops were ready for action, visiting the most important units on more than one occasion. The 'Super Sixth' (6th Armd Div), for example, saw him first on 8 March – for his famous 'off the cuff' talk which lasted for 40 minutes and was followed by his 'sticking his head into tents and messes, meeting unit COs and inspecting the 15th Tank Battalion'. He was back again on 22 April, and again in June when the division was carrying out range firing. During this last period 'A' Coy of the 15th Tk Bn was selected to go to Salisbury Plain to try out their new tank guns and Patton was on hand to watch them. However, it was not his style to sit and watch, so he quickly decided to try out one of the guns himself. 'He was the gunner,' recalled Edgar Foster, 'I was the assistant gunner. We travelled about a mile and he had fired several rounds when the tank stopped half-way down the range.' The driver endeavoured to re-start the engine but had no luck. After a while an Ordnance officer drove up in a jeep, checked the tank and found that the gas tank was empty – the crew had forgotten to fill up. 'Patton really chewed everyone out!'[6] Later, the first Soldier's Medal for Heroism was awarded by General Grow (Commanding General) to a member of 76th Armd Medical Bn for rescuing a tanker from a burning tank.

However, it was not all training; there was time to drink warm, watered beer in the local pubs, provided one could elbow one's way through a wall of khaki to the bar, others managed to visit London to see the sights, a number falling victim to the 'Piccadilly Commandos', who plied their trade around the boarded-up statue of Eros.

Annex 'A' to Chapter 4: Shoulder Patches

Coloured patches had first been used for identification purposes during the American Civil War. The shoulder patches as used in the Second World War had been officially introduced in 1918. Different types were used: some embroidered on felt with coloured threads or silver and gold wire, others were entirely embroidered in coloured silks. Backgrounds were generally khaki to blend with the uniform.

Shoulder Patches of the Initial Corps in Third Army Personnel at Corps HQ wore the corps shoulder patch, whose design was mainly a pictorial reference to its number.

Corps	*Shoulder Patch*
XV	Blue 'X' on white 'V' inside a blue circle with khaki background
VIII	White '8' inside a white octagon on blue background
XX	Two yellow 'X's superimposed on one another on a blue shield with a yellow edge, on top of a similarly shaped red shield
XII	A windmill (blades) in red on a blue shield. It symbolised the city of New York (New Amsterdam)

Nicknames and Shoulder Patches of the Initial Divisions in Third Army

Div	*Nickname*	*Shoulder Patch*
INFANTRY		
5th	Red Diamond	A red diamond
8th	Pathfinder	A yellow arrow passing through a white 8 in a blue shield

Div	*Nickname*	*Shoulder Patch*
Infantry		
28th	Keystone	A red keystone (unit was from the 'Keystone State' of Pennsylvania)
35th	Santa Fe	A dark blue circle with white crosses of the type used to mark the Santa Fe trail
79th	Cross of Lorraine	A Cross of Lorraine on a blue shield
80th	Blue Ridge	A khaki shield edged in white with three grey mountains on a white line in the centre
83rd	Thunderbolt	'OHIO' in yellow within the letter 'O' in the centre of a black triangle-point down
90th	Tough Ombres	A red monogram of the letters 'TO' in a square representing the states from which the unit was recruited (Texas & Oklahoma). The nickname is a corruption of the Spanish for tough men
Armour		
4th	None*	Standard armour triangle divided into three with top yellow, bottom left blue and bottom right red. Division number in black on yellow section. In centre, an armoured vehicle track in black under a red lightning bolt
5th	Victory	ditto
6th	Super Sixth	ditto
7th	Lucky Seventh	ditto

*4th Armored was occasionally called 'Breakthrough', but they considered that 4th Armored was name enough.

Annex 'B' to Chapter 4
Strengths and Principal Weapons of the US Infantry Division, circa 1944.

	Strength
Entire division	14,253
Division HQ	158
Infantry (total)	9,354
Inf Regt (3 per div)	3,118
HQ and HQ Coy	108
Service Coy	114
Anti-tank Coy	165
Cannon Coy	118
Inf Bn (3 per regt)	871
HQ and HQ Coy	126
Heavy Weapons Coy	166
Rifle Coy (3 per bn)	193
Field Artillery (total)	2,160
HQ and HQ Bty Div Arty	114
Lt Arty bn (3)	509
HQ Bty	132
Service Bty	77
Firing Bty (3 per bn)	100
Med Arty Bn	519
HQ Bty	115
Service Bty	77
Firing Bty (3 per bn)	109
Auxiliary Units (total)	2,074
Reccce Troop	155
Engr Bn	647
Med Bn	465
QM Coy	193
Ord Coy	147
Sig Coy	226
MP Platoon	73
Div HQ Coy	110
Band	58

Auxiliary Units (total)	2,074	PRINCIPAL WEAPONS	
Reccce Troop	155	Rifles .30 cal	6,518
Engr Bn	647	Auto rifles .30 cal	243
Med Bn	465	MG .30 cal	157
QM Coy	193	MG .50 cal	236
Ord Coy	147	Mortars 60mm	90
Sig Coy	226	Mortars 81mm	54
MP Platoon	73	Bazookas	557
Div HQ Coy	110	Anti-tank guns 57mm	57
Band	58	Howitzers 105mm	54
Attached Medical	494	Howitzers 155mm	12
Inf Regt (3)	135		
Div Arty	57	VEHICLES, all types (except	
Engr Bn	17	boats and aircraft)	2,012
Special Troops	15	(Source T/O and E 7 and allied tables,	
Attached Chaplains	13	15 July 1943)	

Annex 'C' to Chapter 4
Strengths and Principal Weapons of the US Armoured Division, circa 1944.

Entire Division	*Strengths* 10,937	PRINCIPAL WEAPONS	
Div HQ	164	Rifles .30 cal	2,063
Tank Bns (3) each	729	Carbines .30 cal	5,286
Inf Bns (3) each	1,001	MGs .30 cal	465
CC HQ and HQ Coy (2) each	184	MGs .50 cal	404
Div Trains HQ and HQ Co	103	Mortars 60mm	63
CCR HQ	8	Mortars 81mm	30
Field Arty	1,623	Bazookas	607
Auxiliary Units		Howitzers 57mm	30
Cav Recce Sqn (Mech)	935	Howitzers 75mm	17
Engr Bn	693	Howitzers 105mm	54
Med Bn	417	Medium Tanks	186
Ord Bn	762	Light Tanks	77
Sig Coy	302	Armoured cars	54
MP Platoon	91	Half-track carriers	455
Div HQ Coy	138	Half-tracks (81mm	
Band	58	mortar carriers)	18
Attached			
Medical	261	VEHICLES, all types (except boats	
Chaplains	8	and aircraft)	2,650
		Less Combat Types	1,761
		(Source: T/O 17 of 14 September 1943).	

Notes to Chapter 4

1. Quoted in *The Supreme Commander* by Stephen E. Ambrose.
2. Colonel Allen describes the arrival of Patton and his Africa/Sicily veterans as being like 'a heady shot of bourbon on HQ Third Army. Overnight it began

flourishing like a green bay tree.'

3. From Captain (later Major) E. Ray Taylor, and quoted in *Patton's Third Army at War* by George Forty.
4. Of the 89 divisions in existence at the end of the war, there were 66 infantry, sixteen armoured, five airborne, one mountain and one cavalry.
5. The General Staff Branches mentioned were: G-1 Personnel; G-2 Intelligence; G-3 Operations and G-4 Supply.
6. As quoted in *The Super Sixth* by Professor George F. Hofmann.

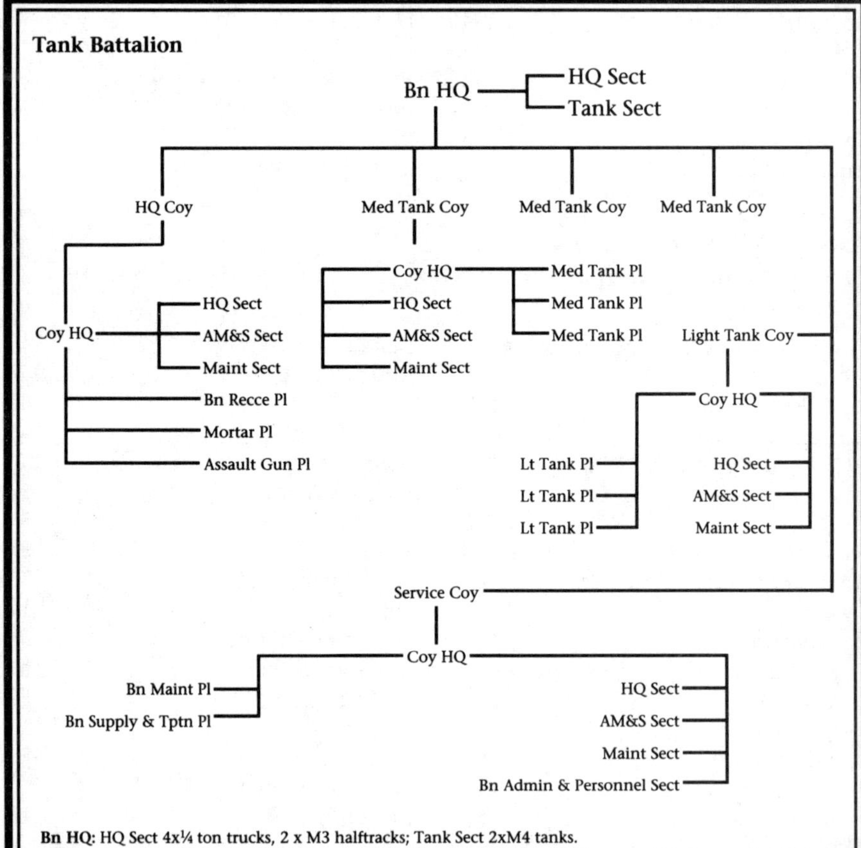

Bn HQ: HQ Sect 4x¼ ton trucks, 2 x M3 halftracks; Tank Sect 2xM4 tanks.
HQ Coy: *Coy HQ:* HQ Sect 1x¼ ton truck, 1xM3 halftrack; AM&S Sect 1x2½ ton truck, 1x1 ton trailer; Maint Sect 1x¼ ton truck, 1xM3 halftrack. *Bn Recce Pl:* 5x¼ ton trucks, 1xM3 halftrack. *Mortar Pl:* 1xM3 halftrack, 3xM21 81mm mortar carriers. *Assault Gun Pl:* 2xM3 halftracks, 3xM4 tanks (105mm hows), 4xM10 ammo carriers.
Med Tank Coy: *Coy HQ:* HQ Sect 1x¼ ton truck, 2xM4 tanks, 1xM4 (105mm how); AM&S Sect 1x2½ ton truck, 1x1 ton trailer; Maint Sect 1x¼ ton truck, 1xM3 halftrack, 1xM32 ARV. Three *Tank Pls* each of 5xM4 med tanks.
Lt Tank Coy: *Coy HQ:* HQ Sect 1x¼ ton truck, 2xM5 lt tanks; AM&S Sect 1x2½ ton truck, 1x1 ton trailer; Maint Sect 1x¼ ton truck, 1xM3 halftrack, 1xlt ARV. Three *Tank Pls* each of 5xM5 lt tanks.
Service Coy: *Coy HQ:* HQ Sect 1x¾ ton truck; AM&S Sect 1x2½ ton truck, 1x1 ton trailer; Maint Sect 1x¼ ton truck, 1x2½ ton truck, 1x1 ton trailer; Bn Admin & Personnel Sect 1x2½ ton truck, 1x1 ton trailer. *Bn Maint Pl:* 1x¼ ton truck, 1x¾ ton truck, 2x2½ ton trucks, 2x1 ton trailers, 2xM32 ARV, 2xheavy wreckers. *Bn Supply & Tptn Pl:* 1x¼ ton truck, 1x¾ ton truck, 29x2½ ton trucks, 15x1 ton trailers, 13xM10 ammo trailers.

Armoured Infantry Battalion

Bn HQ

HQ Coy
Coy HQ — HQ Sect, AM&S Sect, Maint Sect
Bn Recce Pl
Mortar Pl
MG Pl
Assault Gun Pl

Rifle Coy
Rifle Coy
Rifle Coy
Coy HQ — HQ Sect, AM & S Sect, Maint Sect
ATk Pl
Rifle Pl
Rifle Pl
Rifle Pl

Service Coy
Coy HQ — HQ Sect, AM&S Sect, Maint Sect
Bn Supply & Tptn Pl
Bn Maint Pl
Bn Admin & Personnel Sect

BN HQ: 4x¼ ton trucks, 2xM3 halftracks.
HQ Coy: *Coy HQ:* HQ Sect 1x¼ ton truck, 1xM3 halftrack; AM&S Sect 1x2½ ton truck, 1x1 ton trailer; Maint Sect 1x¼ ton truck, 1xM3 halftrack, 1x1 ton trailer. *Bn Recce Pl:* 5x¼ ton trucks, 1xM3 halftrack. *Mortar Pl* 1xM3 halftrack, 3xM21 81mm mortar carriers. *MG Pl:* 3xM3 halftracks. *Assault Gun Pl:* 2xM3 halftracks, 3xM7 105mm hows, 4xM10 ammo trailers.
Rifle Coy: *Coy HQ:* HQ Sect 1x¼ ton truck, 1xM3 halftrack; AM&S Sect 2x2½ ton trucks, 2x1 ton trailers; Maint Sect 1x¼ ton truck, 1xM3 halftrack, 1x1 ton trailer. *ATk Pl:* 1x¼ ton truck, 3xM3 halftracks, 3x57mm guns. Three *Rifle Pls* of five squads – three rifle, one mortar and one LMG: each squad 1xM3 halftrack.
Service Coy: *Coy HQ:* HQ Sect 1x¾ ton comd car; AM&S Sect 1x2½ ton truck, 1x1 ton trailer; Maint Sect 1x¼ ton truck, 1x2½ ton truck, 1x1 ton trailer; Bn Admin & Personnel Sect 1x2½ ton truck, 1x1 ton trailer. *Bn Supply & Tptn Pl:* 1x¼ ton truck, 1x¾ ton truck, 9x2½ ton trucks, 5x1 ton trailers, 4xM10 ammo trailers. *Bn Maint Pl:* 1x¼ ton truck, 1xM3 halftrack, 2x2½ ton trucks, 1x6 ton heavy wrecker, 1xM32 ARV, 2x1 ton trailers.

Armoured Signal Company

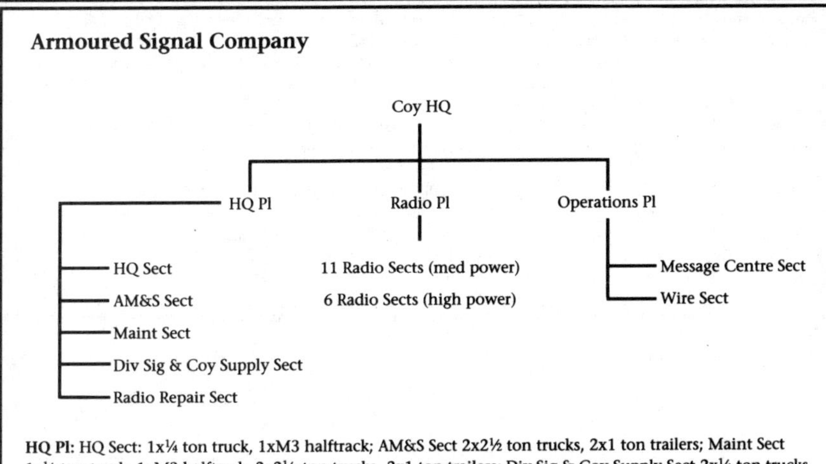

HQ Pl: HQ Sect: 1x¼ ton truck, 1xM3 halftrack; AM&S Sect 2x2½ ton trucks, 2x1 ton trailers; Maint Sect 1x¼ ton truck, 1xM3 halftrack, 2x2½ ton trucks, 2x1 ton trailers; Div Sig & Coy Supply Sect 2x¼ ton trucks, 1x¼ ton trailer, 4x2½ ton trucks, 4x1 ton trailers; Radio Repair Sect 2xM3 halftracks, 2x2½ ton sig repair trucks, 2x2½ ton trucks, 2x1 ton trailers. *Ops Pl:* Message Centre Sect 14x¼ ton trucks, 2xM3 halftracks; Wire Sect 5x¼ ton trucks, 2xM3 halftracks, 3x2½ ton trucks. *Radio Pl:* 11 Radio Sects med power each 1xM3 halftrack; Six Radio Sects high power each 1x2½ ton radio truck, 1xK52 signal trailer.

Cavalry Recce Squadron

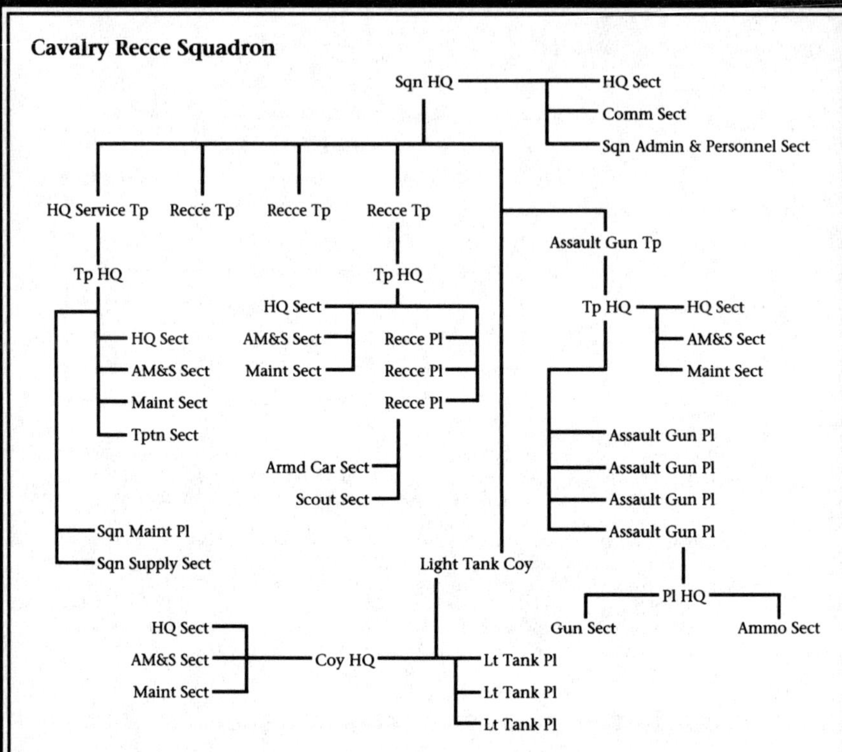

HQ & HQ Service Tp: *Sqn HQ:* HQ Sect 2x¼ ton trucks, 2xM3 halftracks; Comm Sect 4x¼ ton trucks, 3xM8 armd cars, 1xM3 halftrack; Sqn Admin & Personnel Sect 1x¼ ton truck, 1x2½ ton truck, 1x1 ton trailer.
HQ Service Tp: *Tp HQ:* HQ Sect 1x¼ ton truck; AM&S Sect 1x2½ ton truck, 1x1 ton trailer; Maint Sect 1xM3 halftrack, 1x1 ton trailer; Tptn Sect 1x¼ ton truck, 6x2½ ton trucks, 4x1 ton trailers, 2xM10 ammo trailers. *Sqn Maint Pl:* 1x¼ ton truck, 1xM8 armd car, 1xM32 ARV, 1xM3 halftrack, 1x6 ton heavy wrecker, 2x2½ ton trucks, 2x1 ton trailers. *Sqn Supply Sect:* 3x2½ ton trucks, 3x1 ton trailers.
Recce Tps: *Tp HQ:* HQ Sect 3x¼ ton trucks, 2xM8 armd cars; AM&S Sect 3xM3 halftracks, 1x2½ ton truck, 4x1 ton trailers; Maint Sect 1x¼ ton truck, 1xM8 armd car, 1xM3 halftrack, 1x1 ton trailer. Three *Recce Pls* each of: Armd Car Sect 3xM8 armd cars; Scout Sect 6x¼ ton trucks.
Assault Gun Tp: *Tp HQ:* HQ Sect 1x¼ ton truck, 1xM3 halftrack; AM&S Sect 1x2½ ton truck, 1x1 ton trailer; Maint Sect 1x¼ ton truck, 1xM3 halftrack, 1xlt ARV. Four *Assault Gun Pls* of: Pl HQ 1xM3 halftrack; Ammo Sect 1xM3 halftrack, 1xM10 ammo trailer; Gun Sect 2xM8 75mm carriage hows, 2xM10 ammo trailers.
Lt Tank Coy: *Coy HQ:* HQ Sect 1x¼ ton truck, 2xM5 lt tanks; AM&S Sect 1x2½ ton truck, 1x1 ton trailer; Maint Sect 1x¼ ton truck, 1xM3 halftrack, 1xlt ARV. Three *Lt Tank Pls* of: 5xM5 lt tanks.

Armoured Engineer Battalion

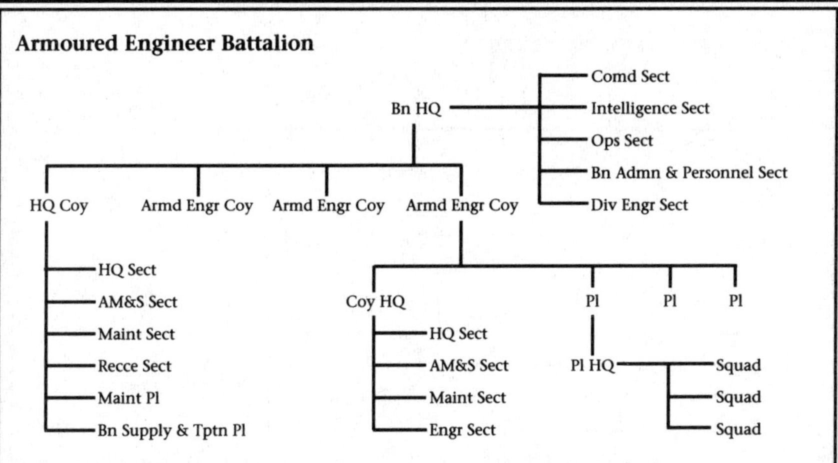

HQ & HQ Coy: *Bn HQ:* Comd Sect 1x¼ ton truck, 3xM3 halftracks; Intelligence Sect 1x¼ ton truck; Ops Sect 1x¾ ton truck; Div Engr Sect 1x¾ ton truck; Bn Admin & Personnel Sect 1x2½ ton truck, 1x1 ton trailer.
HQ Coy: *Coy HQ:* HQ Sect 1x¼ ton truck; AM&S Sect 1x2½ ton truck, 1x1 ton trailer; Maint Sect 1x¼ ton truck, 1x¾ ton truck; Recce Sect 4x½ ton trucks. *Maint Pl:* 1x¼ ton truck, 1x¾ ton truck, 1x6 ton heavy wrecker, 1x motorised shop, 1x welding equipment trailer, 2x2½ ton trucks, 1x1 ton trailer. *Bn Supply & Tptn Pl:* 1x¼ ton truck, 1x truck mounted compressor, 3x3 ton bridge trucks, 4x water equipment trailers, 11x2½ ton trucks, 9x1 ton trailers, 2xM10 ammo trailers.
Armd Engr Coy: *Coy HQ:* HQ Sect 1x¼ ton truck, 1xM3 halftrack; AM&S Sect 1x2½ ton truck, 1x1 ton trailer; Maint Sect 1x¼ ton truck, 1x¾ ton truck; Engr Sect 1x truck mounted compressor, 1x65dbhp tractor (bulldozer), 1x20 ton semi-trailer and tractor, 1x6 ton bridge truck. *1 Pl:* Pl HQ 1x¼ ton truck, 1x2½ ton cargo truck, 1x1 ton trailer, 1x2½ ton utility trailer pulled by squad M3; three Squads each with 1xM3 halftrack. *2 & 3 Pl:* Pl HQ 1x¼ ton truck, 1x2½ ton cargo truck, 1x1 ton trailer, 1x2½ ton utility trailer pulled by squad truck; three Squads each with 1x2½ ton dump truck.

Division Artillery HQ Battery

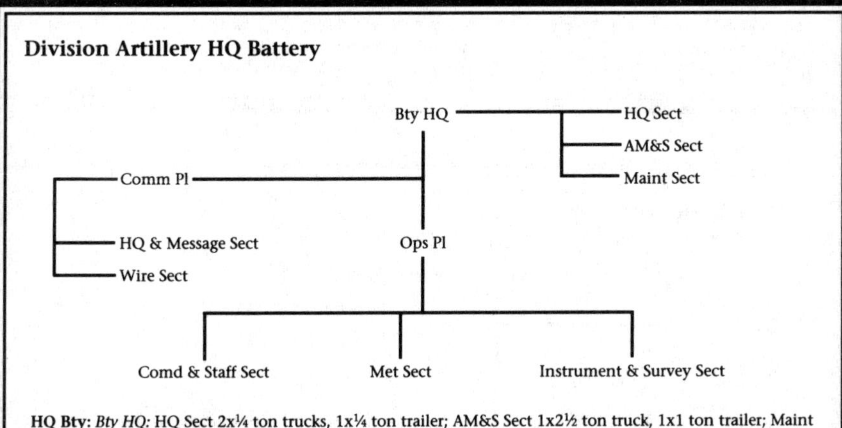

HQ Bty: *Bty HQ:* HQ Sect 2x¼ ton trucks, 1x¼ ton trailer; AM&S Sect 1x2½ ton truck, 1x1 ton trailer; Maint Sect 1x¼ ton truck, 1x¼ ton trailer, 1x¾ ton truck, 1x2½ ton truck, 1x1 ton trailer. *Comm Pl:* Wire Sect 2x¾ ton trucks, 1x2½ ton truck; HQ & Message Sect 3x¼ ton trucks, 1x¾ ton truck. *Operations Pl:* Met Sect 1x2½ ton truck, 1x1 ton trailer; Instrument & Survey Sect 1x¼ ton truck, 1x¾ ton truck; Comd & Staff Sect 3x¾ ton trucks, 1xM8 armd car, 1x2½ ton truck, 1x1 ton trailer, 2x liaison aeroplanes.

Armoured Field Artillery Battalion

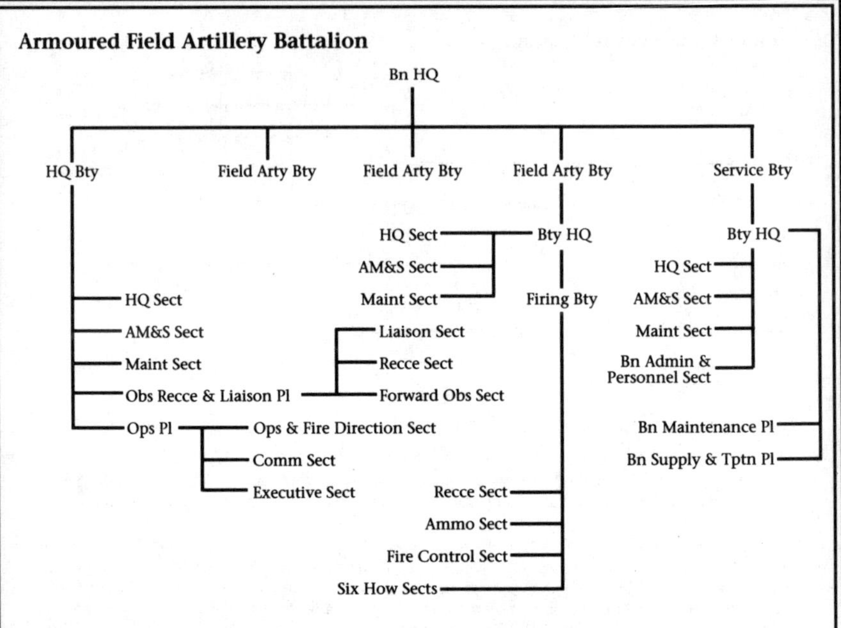

Bn HQ: 4x½ ton trucks, 1xM3 halftrack.
HQ Bty:HQ Sect 1x¼ ton truck. AM&S Sect 1x2½ ton truck, 1x1 ton trailer. Maint Sect 1x¼ ton truck, 1xM3 halftrack, 1x1 ton trailer Obs, Recce & Liaison Pl: Liaison Sect 1xM3 halftrack; Recce Sect 1x¼ ton truck, 1xM3 halftrack; Forward Obs Sect: 3xM4 tanks. Ops Pl: Op & Fire Direction Sect 3xM3 halftracks; Comm Sect 2x¾ ton trucks, 1xM3 halftrack; Exec Sect 1x¼ ton truck, 1x¼ ton trailer, 1x¾ ton truck, 1xM3 halftrack, 2x L5 lt planes.
Field Arty Bty: *Bty HQ:* HQ Sect 1x¼ ton truck, 1xM3 halftrack; AM&S Sect 1x2½ ton truck, 1x1 ton trailer; Maint Sect 1x¼ ton truck, 1xM3 halftrack, 1x1 ton trailer. *Firing Bty:* Recce Sect 1x¼ ton truck, 1xM3 halftrack; Ammo Sect 2xM3 halftracks, 2xM10 ammo trailers; Fire Control Sect 2xM3 halftracks; Six Howitzer Sects each of 1xM7 105mm SP how, 1xM10 ammo trailer.
Service Bty: *Bty HQ:* HQ Sect 1x¾ ton truck; AM&S Sect 1x2½ ton truck, 1x1 ton trailer; Maint Sect 1x¼ ton truck, 1x2½ ton truck, 1x1 ton trailer; Bn Admin & Personnel Sect 1x2½ ton truck, 1x1 ton trailer. *Bn Maint Pl:* 1x¼ ton truck, 2x2½ ton trucks, 2x1 ton trailers, 1x6 ton heavy wrecker, 2xM32 ARV. *Bn Supply & Tptn Pl:* 1x¼ ton truck, 2x¾ ton trucks, 16x2½ ton trucks, 7x1 ton trailers, 9xM10 ammo trailers.

Division Trains HQ Company

Coy HQ
HQ Sect
AM&S Sect
Maint Sect
Recce Pl
Tptn Pl

HQ Coy: *Coy HQ:* HQ Sect 2x¼ ton trucks; AM&S Sect 1x¾ ton truck, 2x2½ trucks, 2x1 ton trailers; Maint Sect 1x¼ ton truck, 1x¾ ton truck, 1x2½ ton truck, 1x1 ton trailer. *Recce Pl:* 4x¼ ton trucks. *Tptn Pl:* 1x5 passenger car, 5x¼ ton trucks, 8x¾ ton trucks, 6x2½ ton trucks, 6x1 ton trailers.

Ordnance Maintenance Battalion

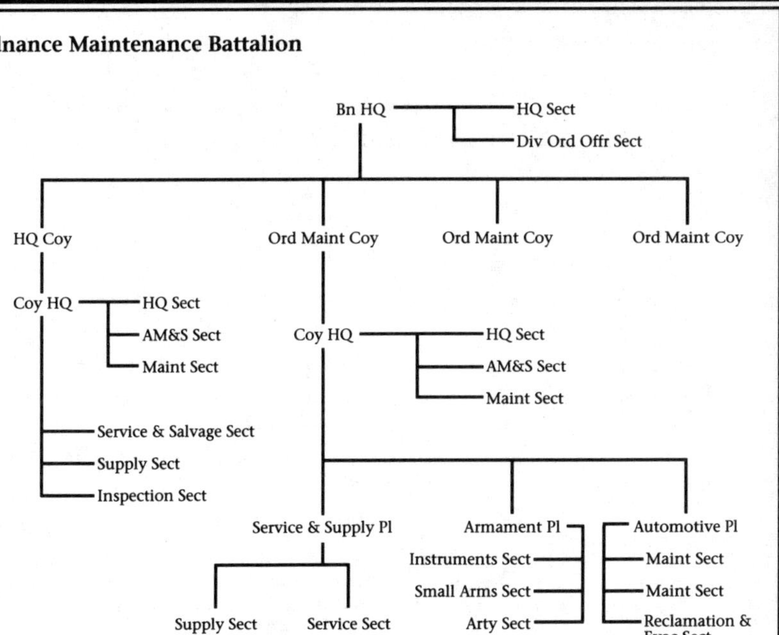

Bn HQ: Div Ord Offr Sect 1x¼ ton truck, 1x¾ ton truck, 1x2½ ton truck, 1x1 ton trailer; HQ Sect 3x¼ ton trucks, 1x¾ ton truck, 1xM3 halftrack, 2x2½ ton trucks, 1x1 ton trailer.
HQ Coy: *Coy HQ:* HQ Sect 1x¾ ton truck; AM&S Sect 1x2½ ton truck, 1x1 ton trailer; Maint Sect 1x¼ ton truck, 1x¾ ton truck. *Service & Salvage Sect:* 2x6 ton heavy wreckers, 2x2½ ton machine shop trucks, 3x2½ ton trucks. *Inspection Sect:* 3x¼ ton trucks, 1x2½ ton truck. *Supply Sect:* 26x2½ ton trucks, 26x1 ton trailers.
Ord Maint Coy: *Coy HQ:* HQ Sect 1x¼ ton truck, 1xM3 halftrack; AM&S Sect 1x2½ ton truck, 1x1 ton trailer; Maint Sect 1x¾ ton truck. *Service & Supply Pl:* Service Sect 1x¾ ton truck, 1x2½ ton truck, 1x2½ ton machine shop truck; Supply Sect 6x2½ ton trucks, 6x1 ton trailers. *Armament Pl:* Arty Sect 1x¼ ton truck, 1x2½ ton arty repair truck, 1x2½ ton truck, 1x1 ton trailer; Small Arms Sect 1x¼ ton truck, 1x2½ ton small arms repair truck; Instrument Sect 1x¼ ton truck, 1x2½ ton instrument repair truck. *Automotive Pl:* Pl HQ 2x¼ ton trucks, 1x¾ ton truck, 4x2½ ton trucks, 4x1 ton trailers, 1x2½ ton decontamination truck, 1x2½ ton electrical repair truck, 1x6 ton heavy wrecker; two Maint Sects each with 1x¾ ton truck, 1x2½ ton truck, 1x1 ton trailer; Reclamation and Evac Sect 2x6 ton heavy wreckers, 1x2½ ton truck, 1x1 ton trailer, 3x transporter tractor trucks, 3x transporter semi-trailers.

MP Platoon

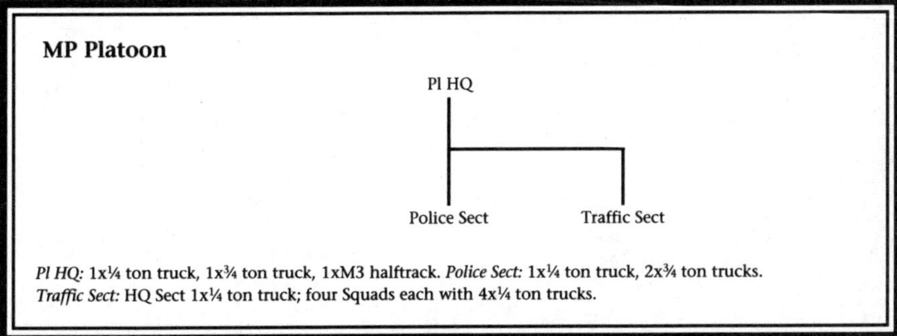

Pl HQ: 1x¼ ton truck, 1x¾ ton truck, 1xM3 halftrack. *Police Sect:* 1x¼ ton truck, 2x¾ ton trucks. *Traffic Sect:* HQ Sect 1x¼ ton truck; four Squads each with 4x¼ ton trucks.

Armoured Medical Battalion

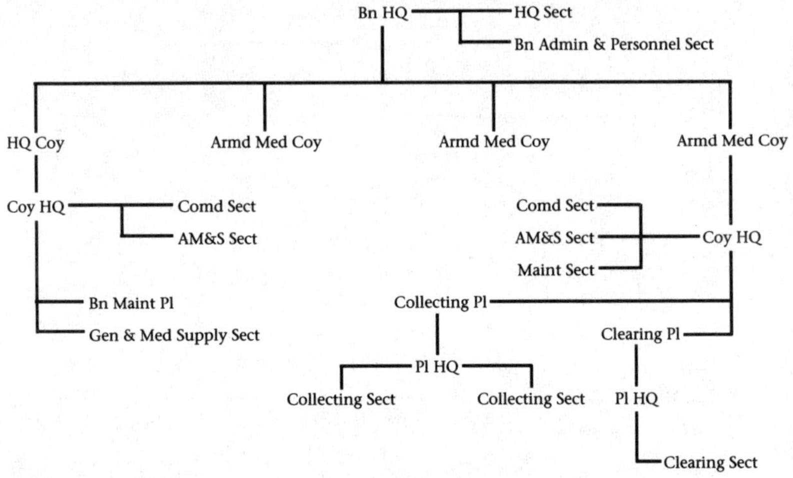

Bn HQ
HQ Sect
Bn Admin & Personnel Sect
HQ Coy
Armd Med Coy
Armd Med Coy
Armd Med Coy
Coy HQ
Comd Sect
AM&S Sect
Comd Sect
AM&S Sect
Coy HQ
Maint Sect
Bn Maint Pl
Collecting Pl
Gen & Med Supply Sect
Clearing Pl
Pl HQ
Collecting Sect
Collecting Sect
Pl HQ
Clearing Sect

Bn HQ: HQ Sect 2x¼ ton trucks, 1x¾ ton truck, 1xM3 halftrack; Bn Admin & Personnel Sect 1x¾ ton truck. **HQ Coy:** *Coy HQ:* Comd Sect 1x¾ ton truck; AM&S Sect 1x2½ ton truck, 1x1 ton trailer. *Bn Maint Pl:* 1x¼ ton truck, 2x2½ ton trucks, 2x1 ton trailers. *Gen & Med Supply Sect:* 1x¼ ton truck, 5x2½ ton trucks, 5x1 ton trailers. **Armd Med Coy:** *Coy HQ:* Comd Sect 1x¼ ton truck, 1xM3 halftrack; AM&S Sect 1x2½ ton truck, 1x1 ton trailer; Maint Sect 1x¾ ton truck. *Collecting Pl:* Pl HQ 1x¼ ton truck, 1x¾ ton truck; 1st Collecting Sect 5x¾ ton ambulances; 2nd Collecting Sect 5x¾ ton ambulances. *Clearing Pl:* Pl HQ 1x¾ ton truck; Clearing Sect 1x¾ ton truck, 2x2½ ton trucks, 2x2½ ton surgical trucks, 2x1 ton trailers, 2x250gal water trailers.

5
Patton, His Immediate Staff and His Third Army Commanders

'I am a genius. I think I am.'

From the very first moment of contact with their new commander, nobody in Third Army had any doubts whatsoever as to who was in charge. Throughout his army career Patton had always had the ability to dominate every unit he commanded. Yet, as Robert Allen explains in his book *Lucky Forward*: '... in dominating he did not domineer. Patton always led his men. He did not rule them.' Well before he took over Third Army GSP had come to the conclusion that he was a man of destiny, that he did have the ability both to lead and to inspire: 'I am a genius,' he wrote in his diary on 3 November 1942, but then added the rider, 'I think I am.' Certainly the enemy had no doubts as to his abilities, but the American public would blow hot and cold towards him throughout his life and only describe him with such phrases as 'the greatest soldier of this terrible war', 'essential to the nation', 'the greatest general America has seen', when he lay dying. There was seldom any doubt in the minds of his soldiers. When a sergeant in the beleaguered garrison of St-Vith heard that units of the Third Army were on their way to rescue them, his comment was: 'That's good news. If Georgie's coming we have got it made.' However, Patton did not inspire such loyalty by being soft on his men. Eisenhower once said of him: 'The more he drives his men the more he will save lives and the men of the Third Army know this to be true.' When criticised for being too tough on his troops he replied: 'Goddammit, I'm not running for Shah of Persia. There are no practice games in life. It's eat or be eaten, kill or be killed. I want my bunch to get in there first, to be the "fustest with the mostest". They won't do it if I ask them kindly. That was the only mistake Robert E. Lee ever made. He gave suggestions instead of orders and it cost him the war.'

Patton's Aides

There was nothing stuffy or pompous about GSP, so he was not really a difficult man to serve, although he demanded unswerving loyalty and constant devotion to duty. He was also always able to maintain a 'distance' between himself and his immediate staff, being formally known as 'The General', although among themselves they would refer to him as 'Georgie'. His immediate personal staff was not large, considering that, for most of the period when he commanded Third Army, he was in charge of more than 300,000 men. He had two permanent aides: Lieutenant Colonel Charles R. Codman and Major Alexander C. Stiller; a third, Captain Francis P. Graves, Jr; plus a 'steel-nerved' personal pilot, Captain William J. Wellman.

Charles Codman, a Bostonian, had been a brave and famous air force pilot during the Great War, having been awarded the Croix de Guerre. Rich and widely travelled, he was an authority on France, especially its food and wines. He was first appointed GSP's aide before the invasion of Sicily in early May 1943 and always remained with him thereafter. He possessed all the right qualities to make him invaluable to Patton – a natural ability as a linguist, being as fluent in French as in English, he had demonstrated his courage and coolness so could be relied upon to remain calm in any crisis, together with (to quote Martin Blumenson) 'all the social graces and perceptive intelligence, that would make Patton increasingly dependent on his loyal and devoted service'. For his part Codman wrote of Patton: 'He brings to the art of command in this day and age the norms and antique virtues of a classic warrior. To him the concepts of duty, patriotism, fame, honor, glory are not mere abstractions, nor the shop-worn ingredients of Memorial Day speeches. They are basic realities – self-evident, controlling.... In the time of Roger the Norman, or in ancient Rome, General Patton would have felt completely at home.' Codman was Patton's constant companion, well able to keep up with him at every level yet always in the background, never trying to outshine his friend, a constant 'rock' on which GSP could lean whenever necessary. Martin Blumenson quotes Codman as saying of GSP: 'I know of no one living who equals the boss in one respect, namely as regards that amazing capacity for instant rightness and lucid anger. It's a rare and invaluable quality.... You can't fake it. You either have it or you haven't.'

Alexander 'Al' C. Stiller could not have been more different from the charming, cultivated Codman. A stocky, hard-bitten Texan, Stiller had been one of Patton's tankmen in the Great War. Blumenson describes him as being 'rough and unlettered'. He would serve Patton faithfully and well, principally as a bodyguard – it is said that he was as good a pistol shot as GSP and went everywhere with him. His love and loyalty are typified in a letter that he wrote to Beatrice Patton in March 1944, which included the words: 'You have more reason to be proud of "your man" than even you know. He is the real "Leader" of this war. And before it is over he will again demonstrate it in no uncertain terms. I am very proud of the privilege to serve with him. I will never let him down. And will do my very all to return him to you. When the job is finished. You can depend on it.' GSP asked Al Stiller to go with the Hammelburg mission to rescue John Waters, Patton's son-in-law, and other prisoners of the Germans from behind enemy lines, and

Stiller agreed. Unfortunately, he was later reported missing in action, possibly wounded and captured. However, he survived this ordeal and was safely back with GSP by early May 1945.

Francis P. Graves, Jr, of the Field Artillery, was the son of GSP's Californian cousin. He is listed in Third Army's After Action Report as General Patton's third aide.

A Personal Physician. Among GSP's small group was a doctor, Colonel Charles B. Odom, an eminent New Orleans surgeon. Patton describes in a letter to Beatrice of 31 January 1945 as him being 'the Dr who lives with us – my personal physician?' Although GSP had an iron constitution and was seldom ill, there were occasions when he needed urgent medical assistance; after all, he was at an age when most men have retired from active soldiering, had been badly wounded in the Great War, suffered untold breaks, etc., during his sporting, riding and hunting career, and was now under the sort of workload that would have laid low most men. So the 'on hand' personal attention which Charles Odom was able to administer, quickly and effectively, was a real life saver. Patton quotes one example, concerning the rapid assistance which Odom gave him in January 1945. It was necessary because GSP had been driving an open jeep for about eight hours in bitterly cold weather in the Ardennes. On his return to 'Lucky Forward', he got into a hot bath, and turned on a sun lamp ('to give a tropical aspect'). But the lamp was too close and after the effects of its rays on top of the bitter cold and snow, GSP woke in the night in great pain and with streaming eyes. Odom put cold boracic compresses on his eyes, and gave him a shot of morphine and a sleeping-powder, which knocked him out for twelve hours. Needless to say, he survived and was none the worse for the experience! Colonel Odom was the most decorated medical officer of the war in the ETO with the Silver Star, Legion of Merit, Bronze Star, Purple Heart (he was wounded in action) and Croix de Guerre with Gold Star.

GSP's Orderly. Next in the Patton ménage was his orderly, Master Sergeant William George Meeks, a veteran Negro cavalryman from GSP's days in Fort Riley and the Desert Training Center. Meeks was responsible for his immaculate appearance, his uniforms and all their many accoutrements being his top priority. He was also, as we have already seen, responsible for the safety of GSP's precious pistols. 'He is about the only man who can find anything,' Patton once wrote to the Adjutant General, Major General James Ulio, when asking him for help in getting Meeks transferred, so that his invaluable orderly could remain with him. 'If you are unable to do this ... I will have nothing to wear'! Knowing the importance which Patton placed upon his own immaculate dress, clearly the quiet, unobtrusive orderly was worth his weight in gold. Meeks served him faithfully in North Africa, Sicily and Europe, going everywhere with him (including on leave) and being promoted every time GSP went up a rank, until by the end of the war he was a Master Sergeant. And he was still there at the end, proudly helping to carry Patton's coffin, shedding a silent tear for the great man he had served so well for eight years.

Personal Driver. Master Sergeant John L. Mims was GSP's personal driver from September 1940 until May 1945, so like George Meeks, he went with Patton everywhere. He saw GSP in all his moods, and marvelled at his ability to change so quickly from rage to calm. One minute he could be raising hell, the next smiling and pleasant. Mims once commented that he thought the major quality which endeared Patton to his men was his ability to admit his mistakes, honestly and sincerely – he was a 'straight shooter' and they admired him for this. 'He never used his stars to cover his errors,' is how Mims put it.

Best Damn Cook in the US Army! The last human member of Patton's immediate staff was his personal cook, Mess Sergeant Thue P. Lee, an American-born Chinese, whom GSP had 'captured' in the North Africa beachhead. 'It was the first night, very dark and the situation was very tense,' recalled Colonel Robert Allen. 'Everyone had his finger on the trigger. The challenge was "George", the reply "Patton". He [GSP] was all over the beachhead, prodding and directing, when suddenly a nearby sentry yelled: "Halt, who's there!" A long silence followed. Again the sentry barked, "Who's there! George!" Again, no reply for a moment. Then, in squeaky, broken English a voice said, "Me no George. Me Sergeant Lee. Best damned cook in the US Army." Before the sentry could reply, Patton shouted, "Sentry, grab that man. If he's the best damned cook in the Army, I want him. Bring him here." That was the way Sgt Thue P. Lee, American-born Chinese, precipitously transferred from an Engineer battalion to Patton's personal entourage, to cook appreciatively for him until he died.'

Willie. I referred to Sergeant Lee as being the last 'human' member of GSP's immediate staff advisedly, because, of course, there was another VIP, in the shape of Willie, a white bull-terrier, whom Patton bought in England on 4 March 1944. The little dog was 15 months old and had previously belonged to an RAF pilot who had been killed over Germany. Patton, always an ardent dog lover, saw him in a London kennel and bought him on the spot. 'My bull pup ... took to me like a duck to water,' GSP wrote excitedly to Beatrice that evening, '... pure white except for a little lemin on his tail which to a cursory glance would seem to indicate that he has not used toilet paper.' Willie had quite a fierce appearance, but was in fact usually a very amiable dog and obviously loved his master, although he is reputed to have given GSP a wide berth whenever the General was off smoking. As soon as Patton started to smoke his cigars again, Willie (and the rest of the staff for that matter), heaved a sigh of relief as things returned to normal.

Personal Accommodation

In England, of course, GSP had lived in some luxury in Peover Hall. Later, in Europe, especially in Germany, whenever possible he would take over a suitable country house conveniently near to Lucky Forward. But like other field commanders he often lived and worked in two truck-trailers. One, a converted Ordnance lorry, with steps up at the rear, was used for sleeping and as living-quarters. This had a built-in bed, a small wash-stand, a bath, a small desk with side drawers, electric light and two telephones – one for talking to his corps commanders, the other, fitted with a scrambler, for calls to Eisenhower and Bradley. The second trailer was set up as an office, with a desk, map boards and telephone. A mobile generator supplied all the necessary current.

Corps Commanders (during the periods between 1 August 1944 and 9 May 1945, when the various Corps were under command)

Commanders and Chiefs of Staff of the six Corps that served under Third Army were:

III Corps	CG:	Maj Gen John Millikin – 31 Oct 1944 to 11 Feb 1945
		Maj Gen James A. Van Fleet – 18 Apr to 9 May 1945
	COS:	Col James H. Phillips
V Corps	CG:	Maj Gen Clarence R Huebner
	COS:	Col S. B. Mason
VIII Corps	CG:	Maj Gen Troy H. Middleton
	COS:	Brig Gen C. H. Searcy
XII Corps	CG:	Maj Gen Gilbert R. Cook – 1 to 17 Aug 1944
		Maj Gen Manton S. Eddy – 17 Aug 1944 to 20 April 1945
		Maj Gen S. LeRoy Irwin – 20 April to 9 May 1945
	COS:	Brig Gen R. J. Canine
XV Corps	CG:	Lt Gen Wade H. Haislip
	COS:	Brig Gen Pearson Menoher
XX Corps	CG:	Lt Gen Walton H. Walker
	COS:	Brig Gen W. A. Collier

Of the Corps, XII and XX served the longest with Third Army, both being assigned for 281 days; VIII Corps served for 160 days, III Corps for 157, XV Corps for 56 and V Corps for just 3 days.

Pen Portraits of the Corps Commanders

Major General John Millikin was born at Danville, Indiana, in 1888. He graduated from West Point into the Cavalry on 15 June 1910. His first unit was the 5th Cavalry and he served in Hawaii until December 1912 when he was ordered to Arizona for border patrol duty around Nogales. He joined the AEF in France early in 1918, serving as Executive Officer of the Army General Staff College at Langres until 1919, when he was appointed Chief of the Military Police Division of the Provost Marshal General's Department. He was awarded the DSM for his services in the war. Returning to the USA in June 1919, he had a series of staff jobs in Washington, Hawaii and Fort Riley, Kansas. After attending both the Command and Staff School and the Army War College, he was appointed Chief of the Department of Tactics and Director of Instruction at the Cavalry School, Fort Riley, Kansas. His first command appointment was in September 1939, as CO 6th Cavalry, then on 20 May 1941 he was assigned to command 2nd Cavalry Division at Fort Riley, Kansas.

There followed periods of command as CG 83rd Inf Div (May-August 1942), 33rd Inf Div (Aug 1942 – October 1943), then he was designated CG III Corps at Fort McPherson, Georgia, and moved with III Corps to the Presidio of Monterey, California. In the autumn of 1944 HQ III Corps moved overseas and on 10 October, together with 95th Inf Div, the HQ was assigned to Third Army. Colonel Robert Allen comments that III Corps' staff was: 'green, but high-powered and willing'. GSP told Millikin to send up all his senior corps staff to do duty with their opposite numbers at Third Army HQ, so that when they became operational they would know what to expect. Patton was initially opposed to having Millikin as CG, because he believed it was wrong to put an officer in charge of a corps who had never commanded a division in battle, while all his division commanders were veterans. This apart, Patton considered him to be an excellent general and soon got over his initial misgivings.

HQ III Corps left Third Army in mid-February 1945 for First Army and troops under their command were later to capture the famous Ludendorff Railway Bridge at Remagen. General Hodges was unimpressed with Millikin's grasp of the situation, comment being made of his 'unaggressive style of management'. In mid April 1945, when General Wogan, CG 13th Armd Div was seriously wounded, General Millikin took his place. He remained commanding 13th Armd Div and returned to the USA with them in July 1945.

General James A. Van Fleet took over III Corps in April 1945, having commanded 90th Infantry Division. Born in 1892 in Coytesville, near New York, he graduated from West Point in 1915 (a classmate of both Eisenhower and Bradley) and was commissioned into the infantry. He commanded the 17th Machine Gun Battalion in the AEF during the Great War and was wounded in the Meuse–Argonne offensive. On D-Day he landed on Utah Beach, commanding 8th Infantry Regiment of 4th Infantry Division and distinguished himself in the capture of Cherbourg (22–7 June 1944), winning several awards and being promoted to Brigadier General. As Asst Comd of 2nd Infantry Division, he took part in the siege of Brest (August–September 1944) and was then made CG 90th Infantry Division in Third Army. In his autobiography Patton wrote of him: 'General Van Fleet, who made a wonderful Division and Corps commander ... was among the first officers to be recommended for temporary promotion.' After the war he was chosen by President

Truman to head the military advisory mission to Greece and Turkey, being responsible for the training, organisation and tactical deployment of the Greek Army against the communist uprising in 1948–9. In 1951 he replaced General Ridgway as CG Eighth Army in Korea and succeeded in halting the communist offensive. An able and tough commander, he clashed with his superiors on a number of occasions in Korea, when he wanted to conduct a more aggressive type of warfare. He retired from the Army in February 1953.

Major General (later General) Clarence R. Huebner commanded V Corps. He was once described by Eisenhower as being 'tops'.[1] Born in Bushton, Kansas, in 1888, he enlisted in the Army in 1910 and served with the 18th Infantry Regiment until 1916, when he was commissioned and served in the AEF during the Great War. CG of 1st Infantry Division ('The Big Red One') in 1943, he brought them to the UK in early 1944 and on D-Day landed with them on Omaha Beach in the first wave of the Normandy landings. His division had a tough battle on 'Bloody Omaha', but eventually succeeded in beating back the Germans. Later, he was appointed CG V Corps and remained in that post until the end of the war. He was awarded the DSC with Oak Leaf Cluster, the DSM with two Oak Leaf Clusters, the Silver Star, the Legion of Merit and the Bronze Star. Among his foreign decorations were the Legion of Honour and the Croix de Guerre from France, the CB from Great Britain and similar awards from Belgium, Russia, Luxembourg and Czechoslovakia. Post-war he was CG US Army Europe in 1947, then acting commander of US Forces in Europe. He retired in 1959 and died in 1972.

Major General Troy H. Middleton. The VIII Corps commander throughout the campaign in Europe. Born near Georgetown, Mississippi, in 1889, he enlisted in 1910 and was commissioned two years later. He took part in the Vera Cruz operation in 1914, and in France commanded 1st Bn, 47th, then 39th Infantry Regiment, gaining distinction in the Meuse–Argonne offensive, so his combat experience was considerable. When he got to Third Army he had already demonstrated his competence as a divisional commander in both Sicily and Italy, commanding the 45th Infantry Division. Several months before the Normandy invasion, he assumed command of VIII Corps, which became operational in France just nine days after the landings, with the mission of protecting the rear of the forces driving on Cherbourg. He led his corps on the breakout at St-Lô and later bore the brunt of the unexpected German assault in the Ardennes. Middleton's calm, efficient response played a major part in the Allied success there and in the subsequent advance across the Rhineland. He was the most methodical of GSP's corps commanders, and probably the best tactician. Patton described him as being 'one of the easiest Corps Commanders to do business with .... and also one of the most efficient'. He retired as a Lieutenant General in 1945 and died in 1976.

Major General Gilbert R. Cook. Initially commanding XII Corps was the hard-fighting and able Gilbert R. Cook, 'a fine soldier and an audacious leader' (Patton's words), whom GSP was very sorry to lose only a few days after the breakout had begun, Cook being hospitalised with bad arteries. Patton visited him in hospital and afterwards wrote in his diary that his circulation was so bad that his legs were turning black. GSP talked to him for a long time and finally had to tell him that in justice to both himself and his men, he could not retain him in command any longer. 'Doc' Cook had taken over the corps from Major General W. H. Simpson in early November 1943, while they were still training in the USA. A Westerner, born in 1889 at Texarkana, Arkansas, he was well over six feet tall, and had a lifelong interest in athletics. He graduated from West Point in 1912. His record in the Great War with a combat infantry unit was outstanding, winning the Silver Star with Oak Leaf Cluster and credit for five engagements. When he assumed command of the corps he had already received the Bronze Star for Pearl Harbor. Cook had spent much of the inter-war years teaching at service schools, and came to XII Corps from 104th Infantry Division, having activated the 'Timberwolves' from scratch to a state of high combat efficiency. 'Doc' Cook was well liked by his men. He was the holder of two Croix de Guerre with gilt star, the Legion of Honour, two Silver Stars with Oak Leaf Clusters and two Distinguished Service Medals. On his return to the USA he served at HQ Army Ground Forces and retired in 1948. He died in September 1963.

Major General Manton S. Eddy. Plump, 'high-tensioned' Manton, or 'Matt' as he was called, took over XII Corps from 'Doc' Cook, having previously commanded 9th Infantry Division. Colonel Frank Veale, who came with him to XXI Corps from 9th Div, analysed his qualities: 'Sparking the General throughout his campaigns was a constant demand, almost a mania, for mobility. In combat particularly he displayed the most conspicuous aversion to allowing either his person or the persons of his troops to remain in any location longer than it took to prepare for the next move. Immobility was his dread. He was at his happiest, most buoyant and confident, when the situation was moving rapidly. When his troops stopped moving he worried, fretted and seemed to preoccupy himself in devising ways of stirring up action. When he himself became immobilised he was miserable. To spend an entire day, even an afternoon, in his headquarters was almost torture for him; he would fidget, try to become absorbed in administrative matters, and then finally give up, call for his jeep and be off down the road.

'His optimism was highly contagious; so were his rare moods of pessimism. When things were moving quickly his infectious good humour bolstered the staff. He seemed to believe that nothing succeeded like success and often sensing opportunities, would exploit the most minor successes with impetuosity and daring. When things slowed up or began going badly he began to lose – never his courage, nor even his confidence – but his impulsiveness. It was during the most critical periods that he became most careful in formulating his decisions. Intuition would defer to judgement, and at these times he would rely most heavily on fact – and on his staff.

'Quick as he was to censure, he was even quicker to praise – and showed the keenest personal pleasure and satisfaction in learning of and rewarding on the spot, individual acts of heroism. Often in the middle of presenting a medal in the field he would become so impressed with the citation being read that he would return the medal to his aide and call for one of the next higher degree (his aide generally carrying a supply for just that purpose).

'Day in day out, his energy, aggressiveness, and personal courage were inspirations to those who came in contact with him. Most remarkable to those who lived with him was his prodigious daily pace; the combination of his long, exhausting hours, his healthy appetite and his light sleeping, would have done in many a younger man in a few weeks.'[2]

A regular army officer since November 1916, Eddy was not a West Pointer, but he had a distinguished record in the Great War and during the inter-war years. He had been designated CG of 9th Infantry Division in June 1942 and had commanded them in the USA, North Africa, Sicily and elsewhere in Europe, with First Army. When he took over XII Corps he had already been awarded the DSC for his part in the capture of Cherbourg, the citation speaking of his repeated acts of heroism between 14 and 26 June 1944. Writing in the *Saturday Evening Post* on 6 July 1946, Thomas R. Henry commented: 'After Cherbourg they called "Matt" Eddy the country's most brilliant division commander.'

Nevertheless, he was not without moments of uncertainty; for example, soon after he had assumed command he became very jittery about his Corps' long open flank and took the matter up with Patton. 'Manton,' said GSP, 'if I had worried about flanks, we'd all still be sitting in the hedgerows in Normandy. You have an open flank, but it's nothing to worry about. First of all, the enemy is on the run. Second, he has nothing south of you mobile enough to make an attack in strength before our Air can spot it. The thing for you to do is advance in depth, one division echeloned behind the other. That will give you striking power and at the same time cover your flank.'[3] General 'Hap' Gay, Patton's Chief of Staff, once summed up his opinion of XII Corps' commander by saying: 'When a decision has been made he always does as he is told, but is always worried about some other corps commanders getting a better deal.'

I think that probably the most accurate description of Eddy was given by Ernie Pyle in his book *Brave Men*: 'General Eddy looked more like a schoolteacher than a soldier. He was a big, tall man but he wore glasses and his eyes had a sort of squint. Being a midwesterner, he talked like one. He claimed Chicago as home, although he had been an Army officer for 28 years. He was wounded in the last war. He was not glib, but he talked well and laughed easily. In spite of being a professional soldier he despised war and, like any ordinary soul, was appalled by the waste and tragedy of it. He wanted to win it and get home just as badly as anybody else.... We liked him because he was absolutely honest with us, because he was sort of old-shoe and easy to talk with and because he was a mighty good general. We had known him in Tunisia and Sicily and then there in France.... General Eddy especially liked to show up in places where his soldiers wouldn't expect to see him. He knew it helped soldiers' spirits to see their commanding general right up at the front where it was hot. So he walked around the front with his long stride, never ducking or appearing concerned at all.'

Undoubtedly, the affection and esteem in which 'Matt' Eddy was held knew no limitations in rank. The GIs who served under him loved him, but also respected his know-how for winning battles with as few casualties as possible. A great general, he was a fitting member of Patton's team. But the strain of years of command finally told, and on 20 April 1945, having read the doctor's report, Patton ordered him back to the USA for medical attention.

Major General S. LeRoy Irwin took over XII Corps in the closing weeks of the war in Europe, after having commanded 5th Infantry Division throughout XII Corps' operations in ETO. 'Red' Irwin's division had performed exceptionally well, being awarded the DSM for effecting the first assault crossing of the Rhine. 'The fighting general', as he was known, commanded XII Corps for the remaining weeks of combat and the period of occupation, until the Corps was deactivated. Irwin was born in March 1893, graduated from West Point in 1915 and entered the 11th Cavalry at Fort Oglethorpe, Georgia, taking part in the punitive expedition to Mexico. After further service with the 11th Cavalry, he transferred in the rank of captain to 80th Field Artillery in June 1917. He next spent a year at Yale University as Assistant Professor of Military Science and Tactics, returning to 1st Field Artillery at Fort Sill, Oklahoma, in July 1920. Once war had been declared his service included Iceland and the ETO, being initially CO and CG 9 Inf Div Arty, then Colonel Field Artillery 5th Inf Div before being appointed as CG. His decorations included the DSM and the Bronze Star with Oak Leaf Cluster (USA), CBE (Great Britain), Legion of Honour and Croix de Guerre with Palm (France), Croix de Guerre (Belgium) and Croix de Guerre (Luxembourg).

Lieutenant General Wade H. Haislip. Commander of XV Corps, Haislip was a West Pointer, who graduated in 1912. He took part in the Vera Cruz expedition and had served in France during the Great War as a staff officer in V Corps. After service between the wars with 16th Inf Regt and at various military schools as an instructor, he was appointed Assistant Chief of Staff G-1 on the War Department General Staff. This important post was followed by divisional command, as CG 85th Inf Div. In February 1943 he was selected to command XV Corps. His corps trained in Northern Ireland as part of Third Army, so both he and his headquarters staff were well known to GSP and his staff. His Corps HQ arrived in France in mid July and fought throughout all the major campaigns. GSP had great confidence in Haislip and was 'very depressed' when his Corps left Third Army on the Moselle. He went on to command Seventh Army in June 1945, and was vice COS of the US Army 1949–51. His decorations included a DSM with three Oak Leaf Clusters, the Legion of Merit and the Bronze Star with Oak Leaf Cluster. His foreign decorations included a French Legion of Honour and a Croix de Guerre with Palm. He retired in 1951, and died in 1971.

Lieutenant General Walton H. Walker. CG of XX Corps, Walton Harris 'Johnnie' Walker, another West Pointer who had also served in France in the Great War, was an infantryman who had turned to armour. Born in 1899, he graduated from West Point in 1912, went to France in April 1918 with the 13th Machine Gun Battalion, 5th Division, saw action in the St-Mihiel and Meuse–Argonne offensives and had reached the rank of temporary lieutenant colonel by 1919. In January 1942 he took command of 3rd Armd Div, being promoted to temporary major general the following month. In September he took over IV Armd Corps and two months later was named as commander of the Desert Training Center on the California–Arizona border. He was still commanding IV Armd Corps when, in October 1943, it was redesignated XX Corps. Ordered to the UK in February 1944, XX Corps landed in France in July 1944 and was a vital element of Third Army thereafter. It captured Reims, crossed the Moselle in November 1944, reduced the fortress of Metz and broke through the Siegfried Line in February 1945, earning the nickname the 'Ghost Corps' because of its speed of advance. In April it liberated Buchenwald. Always the most willing and co-operative of Patton's corps commanders, 'Johnnie' Walker was a tough and pugnacious leader, willing to fight at any time, any place with anything the Army Commander desired to give him! In 1950, at the outbreak of the Korean War, he commanded the army of the Republic of Korea and the other UN forces as they arrived, fighting a stubborn withdrawal action and successfully defending the vital port of Pusan. He continued to fight bravely and with great skill until, on 23 December 1950, he was killed in a jeep accident on the road between Seoul and the front.

Of the many divisions that served in Third Army, those with the longest record of service were: 4th Armd 280 days; 5th Inf 276 days; 80th Inf 274 days; 90th Inf 272 days; 6th Armd 252 days.

A list of all Divisional CGs and Assistant Divisional Commanders is given in Annex 'A' to this chapter. A selection of short biographies is given below.

Armour Commanders

4th Armored Division. Probably the most famous of Patton's thrusting armour commanders was Major General John S. 'Tiger Jack' Wood, CG of 4th Armd, whom Sir Basil Liddell Hart, eminent English historian, once described as being 'the Rommel of the American forces ... one of the most dynamic commanders of armour in WWII and the first in the Allied Armies to demonstrate in Europe the essence of the art of and tempo of handling a mobile force'. His leadership qualities were without parallel; he was not only loved and admired by his troops, but idolised. General Jacob L. Devers simply said: 'They [his men] would follow him to hell today.' 'Wood's division set the pattern for armor operations in Europe,' wrote Brigadier General Albin F. Irzyk in an article about 4th Armd in *Armor* magazine in 1987. 'Operating like cavalry, his division slashed, side-stepped with speed and surprise. It was confident and cocky, and demonstrated a daring, audacious, hard-riding, fast shooting style.' On other occasions, especially during the German counter-attacks on the Nancy bridgehead in September 1944, the division showed that it could fight in defence just as well as it could raid and pursue.

Unfortunately, the very 'hands on' way in which Wood led his division took its toll of the man himself. In the end, Patton had to relieve him of command in early December 1944, GSP writing to Beatrice: 'I got P [meaning Wood – the 'P' was West Point jargon for 'professor', because Wood had often tutored less gifted students while he was there as a cadet] sent home on a 60 day detached service. He is nearly nuts due to nerves and inability to sleep. I hope I can get him a job in the States. He is too hard to handle.' This was a very difficult decision for Patton to make as they were great friends. Wood was replaced by Major General Hugh G. Gaffey, who had of course been GSP's Chief of Staff from April 1944, and was himself replaced as COS by Major General 'Hap' Gay. Later, 4th Armd had a third CG – William Hoge, who, while a combat team commander in 9th Armd Div, had captured the Remagen Bridge. He was later to be responsible for the Hammelburg mission. Nat Frankel, in his informal history of 4th Armd goes into some detail about the rights and wrongs of Wood's being replaced, but, while agreeing that both Gaffey and Hoge were good competent commanders, ends his remarks by saying that '... when history remembers the 4th Armored Division, it remembers John Wood'. He was awarded the DSC, DSM, Silver Star, Bronze Star with Oak Leaf, Air Medal with Oak Leaf, plus the French Legion of Honour and Croix de Guerre with Palm. 'Tiger Jack' retired from the Army in 1946 and worked with a government organisation for refugees in Austria until 1951. He died in 1966.

5th Armored Division. Major General Lunsford E. Oliver was born in Nemaha, Nebraska, in 1889. He graduated from West Point in 1913 into the Corps of Engineers. After serving in Texas and various other parts of the USA, he was sent to France in 1919, and spent a short time with 2nd Engineers in Germany. From 1920 to 1922 he was in charge of construction of the Key Bridge across the Potomac River. After various District Engineer jobs in such diverse localities as Mississippi and Alaska, he was assigned to 1st Armd Div and commanded CCB in Tunisia, being promoted to major general (temp) in November 1942. His Combat Command were the first US troops to confront the Germans on the ground. He was ordered back to the USA to command 20th Armd Div in January 1943, but before it was activated his assignment was changed to CG 5th Armd Div. The division spearheaded XV Corps' advance through Vitre and le Mans to Argentan and was heavily involved in the Falaise pocket. They passed through Paris and advanced rapidly to the Belgian border as part of V Corps. They were also the first Western Allied Powers to enter Germany, took part in all the subsequent operations of Third Army and finished on the Elbe which they had reached on 12 April 1945. After a period of occupation duties Major General Oliver was posted to command 4th Armd Div and was then Assistant COS Army Ground Forces from September 1945 to August 1946 when he joined the Atomic Energy Commission. His decorations included DSM (for the Oran landings), Oak Leaf Cluster to DSM (for 5th Armd Div operations), Silver Star (for 5th Armd Div's advance across France), Legion of Merit (for 5th Armd's advance to the Elbe), Oak Leaf Cluster to Legion of Merit (for his part in the development of the treadway bridge in 1941), Bronze Star (by Patton for the rapid advance which created the Falaise pocket), Oak Leaf Cluster to Bronze Star (for work in the marshalling areas in the UK prior to the invasion), and a second for the advance from the Roer to the Rhine. He received foreign decorations from Ecuador, France, Luxembourg and the Netherlands.

6th Armored Division. Another excellent armour commander was Major General Robert W. Grow, CG of 6th Armd Div. Bob Grow had been S3 (equates to adjutant in the British Army) to Colonel Van Voorhis, the very first commander of the Mechanised Force of 1930, so, although like Patton he had begun soldiering in the cavalry, he was steeped in armour traditions and teachings. Less flamboyant and theatrical than his Army Commander, he was described by Patton as being: 'one of the best armored force commanders the war produced'. Grow had started his military career as a private in the Minnesota National Guard in 1914, while attending the University of Minnesota. He graduated in 1916 and transferred from the National Guard to the Regular Cavalry, being commissioned in November 1916. He was appointed commander of CCB, 8th Armd Div in April 1942, then in May 1942 took over as CG of 6th Armd. He would continue to command the 'Super Sixth' throughout the rest of the war. In his farewell address on 14 June 1945 Grow said: 'You have made history, history that will be recorded and read as long as men cherish gallantry and glory in the record of success in combat. For your story is the story of men who never failed. The

Super Sixth has earned its name.' His division's successes were due in no small way to Bob Grow's leadership.

7th Armored Division. Major General Lindsay M. Sylvester was born in Portsmouth, Virginia in 1889. He was commissioned into the infantry in 1911. Like Patton he served in the Mexican Punitive expedition and with the AEF, taking part in the Aisne, Champagne–Marne, St Mihiel and Argonne offensives, first with 30th then with 7th Inf Divs, being wounded in October 1918. His first command of tanks was in 1931–5 with 66th Inf (light tanks), and he was then chief of the tank section at the Infantry School, Fort Benning, 1937–8, and later commanded 67th Inf (medium tanks), then 69th Armd Regt and 1st Tank Group at Fort Knox, 1940–1. He was awarded the DSC, Silver Star Citation, Purple Heart and French Legion of Honour. He died in 1963.

In November 1944 Major General Sylvester relinquished command to Major General Robert W. Hasbrouck who had been commanding the division's CCB. Hasbrouck was born in Kingston, New York, in 1896. In August 1917 he graduated from West Point as a Second Lieutenant in the Coast Artillery Corps. He served in the USA, Poland (Polish Relief Commission) and Germany, later becoming an instructor at the MT Corps School there. In 1920 he transferred to Field Artillery. In 1941 he was appointed to command 22nd Armd Fld Arty Bn of 4th Armd Div, later becoming Exec Officer of 4th Armd's artillery, then COS 1st Armd Div in Mar 1942 and going overseas with them. He returned to the USA as a combat commander in 8th Armd Div, and in August 1943 was appointed Deputy COS 1st Army Group in ETO (later designated 12th Army Group). His next assignment was as commander of CCB 7th Armd Div in September 1944, and he was given command of the division on 1st November. The division was rushed from US Ninth Army's sector to St Vith in the Ardennes to protect this vital road centre, and received special praise from both Eisenhower and Montgomery for holding out against six German divisions until being ordered to withdraw on 23 December, having been credited with splitting the German offensive. The division also won fame when it spearheaded III Corps' breakout from the Remagen Bridge over the Rhine, and again in the liquidation of the Ruhr pocket. 7th Armd Div was then attached to British Second Army and finished the European war on the shores of the Baltic. General Hasbrouck went on to become Deputy COS Army Ground Forces in September 1945, then, in December, acting COS AGF until August 1946. His decorations included the DSM, Silver Star, Legion of Merit, Bronze Star, French Legion of Honour and Croix de Guerre with Palm, and the Polish War Cross.

8th Armored Division. Major General John M. Devine was born in Providence, Rhode Island, in 1895. He graduated from West Point in 1917. An artilleryman, he taught at West Point and Yale from 1932 to 1940, before joining the Armored Force in July 1940. He went overseas

Right: A young George Patton, aged 12, with a small friend, on a fishing trip at Lake Vineyard, California, 1897. (Patton Museum)

Right: Cadet Adjutant George Patton, photographed during his final year at West Point (1908-9) - he was there six years before either Eisenhower or Bradley. He graduated only 46th out of 103, but excelled at sports. (Patton Museum)

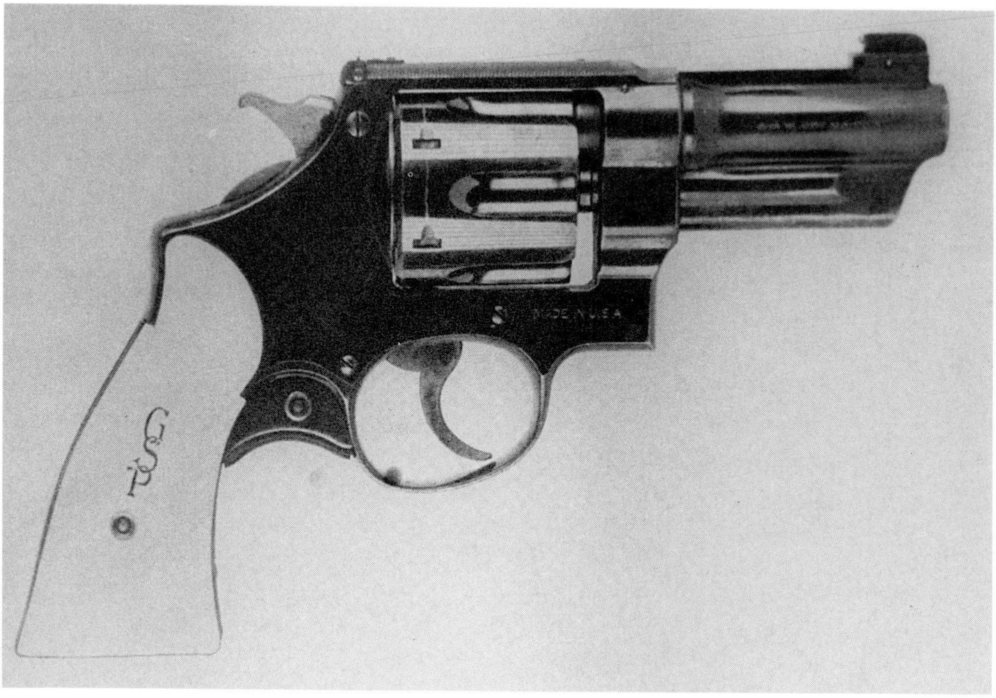

Opposite page: Lieutenant George Patton, photographed in Mexico, in 1916, with Pershing's expedition against Pancho Villa, during which he shot Julio Cardenas, Villa's bodyguard and at least one other man. He had already started to wear one of his famous pistols. (Patton Museum)

Two of Patton's favourite pistols. **Above:** An ivory handled .357in Smith & Wesson. **Below:** A Colt 44/45 single action. (Mike Province)

Left: GSP with his first child, Beatrice Ayer Patton (late Mrs J. K. Waters), *circa* 1915-16. (Patton Museum)

Above: A column of American light tanks (French-built FT17s) leaving a village during operations in 1918. (Patton Museum)

Right: Col George S Patton, Jr, photographed in France, in 1919, before returning to the Cavalry. He is already highly decorated, having been awarded both the Distinguished Service Cross and the Distinguished Service Medal. (Patton Museum)

Black Sea Bass
Wt. 280# Time 15 min
Capt.
C. Wickman
Our Catch at Catalina Isl. Cal.

Left: 'Gone fishin!' GSP with friends after what was clearly a highly successful fishing trip, *circa* 1919. (Patton Museum)

Lower left: A delightful family portrait of GSP with his wife Beatrice, elder daughter Beatrice, younger daughter Ruth Ellen and son George, at Fort Meyer, Virginia, 1929. (Patton Museum)

Right: Col Patton and members of his staff at Fort Meyer, 1940, where he commanded both the post and 3rd Cavalry. This was almost at the end of his 'between the wars' career with the cavalry and he would soon be returning to tanks. (Patton Museum)

Right: Close-up of a line of M1 combat cars, the commanders all manning their .30in Browning machine guns on AA mounts, while the .50in and .30in MGs in the turret can also be seen. The little 8.77 ton tank also had a third .30in MG in the hull. (US Army)

Above left: A hot and dusty GSP, now CG 2nd Armd Div, during the Louisiana manoeuvres of 1941. Patton wears the tanker's grey-green coveralls, while his tank helmet lies on the ground. Note also the radio earphones, leather pouches, binocular case and 'Hell on Wheels' armour badge on his pocket. (Patton Museum)

Left: A reflective Patton sits at ease during the Louisiana manoeuvres, 8 September 1941. (US Army)

Above: Some of the 'Trojan chariots', which made up the US Armored Force of the 1940s. The front row are all M2 and M2A1 17-18 ton medium tanks, whilst behind them are a mixture of twin-turreted light tanks and M1 and M2 combat cars. (US Army)

Below: Maj Gen Patton, now immaculate in cavalry jodphurs and riding boots, gets ready to speak after the Louisiana manoeuvres, 25 October 1941. (Patton Museum)

Left: GSP, immaculate as ever, despite the heat and dust, at the Desert Training Center, Indio, California, June 1942. (Patton Museum)

Below: Operation TORCH. Victorious American troops, headed by 'Old Glory', march off to Maison Blanche aerodrome, which was captured early on the morning of 8 November 1942. (US Army)

Right: Behind the scenes in North Africa, Patton was making sure that the fighting troops got everything they needed, like these brand new M4 medium Sherman tanks being prepared in a camp at Oran, which have just arrived from the USA. (US Army)

Right: GIs inspecting knocked-out German tanks, after their successful counter-attack battles which lessened the shock of their initial defeat at Kasserine Pass in Tunisia. (US Army)

Above: Gen Patton, accompanied by Gen Geoffrey Keyes, on the beach at Gela, Sicily, 11 July 1943, about to 'walk into town'. (Patton Museum)

Left: GSP discusses operations with Gen Harold Alexander, senior British general and Eisenhower's deputy in North Africa and Sicily. Patton considered Alex to be 'very quiet and good looking'. (Patton Museum)

Right: Patton visits the wounded. GSP talks to Pte Frank A. Read of 7th Infantry, 3rd Division, whilst he and other casualties wait for air evacuation to North Africa from Sicily, 25 July 1945. The 'slapping incident' was quite out of character; although he hated cowards and malingerers, he was far more likely to shed a few tears over those in hospital rather than to strike them. (Patton Museum)

Below: Gen Patton giving one of his 'off the cuff' addresses to his troops. GSP spent a great deal of time in England, visiting units of Third Army to talk to them – and the troops loved his salty pep talks! (Patton Museum)

Above: GSP talking at the opening of the 'Welcome Club' in Knutsford, on 25 April 1944, when his unscripted remarks were deliberately misquoted by the American press. (Author's collection)

Below: Gen Patton receiving the Order of the Bath in London in March 1944, from Field Marshal Alan Brooke who is reputed to have said: 'Don't wince Patton, I shan't kiss you!' (Patton Museum)

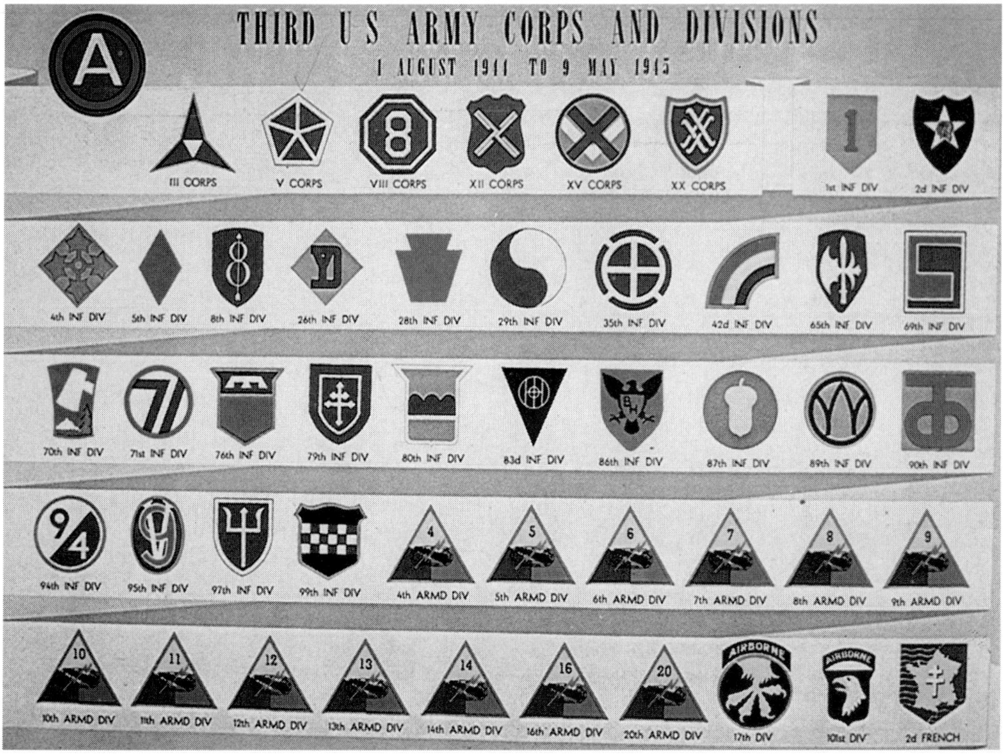

Above: Third US Army Corps and Divisional Insignia. (Taken from the US Third Army After Action Report)

Below: Patton had to go much farther afield than just England to visiting his troops whilst they were on training. Here he visits the men of 10th Inf Regt, 5th Inf Div near Kilkeel, County Down, Northern Ireland, 30 March 1944. (US Army)

Left: Col Charles R. Codman; charming, cultivated and brave, he was an ideal aide and companion, whom GSP came to depend upon more and more. (Mike Province)

Below: Sitting with GSP at a Red Cross Show in Sicily are two more essential members of his staff: Capt (later Maj) Al Stiller (far left) who was his bodyguard and Brig 'Hap' Gay, one of his two Chiefs of Staff. (Mike Province)

Right: Master Sergeant William George Meeks, Patton's orderly from 1942 onwards. He served GSP faithfully and was responsible for his immaculate turnout. (Patton Museum)

Below: Sgt John L Mims was GSP's driver from 1940 onwards. Here he drives Patton's jeep in N. Ireland, 1 April 1944, during another inspection tour. He wears the division insignia of 2nd Inf Div. (Patton Museum)

Top left: Willie, GSP's little white bull terrier, seen here at his 'birthday party' at Peover Hall, with Patton cutting Pvt Willie Alexander's birthday cake. (Note his 'dawg tags'!) (Patton Museum)

Corps Commanders

Left: Maj Gen Troy H. Middleton, CG VIII Corps, confers with two of his division commanders, Gen Simpson and Gen Stroh. (Tank Museum)

Above: Maj Gen James A. Van Fleet, CG III Corps. (Tank Museum)

Above right: Maj Gen Clarence R. Huebner, CG V Corps. (Tank Museum)

Right: Maj Gen Gilbert R. Cook, CG XII Corps. (Tank Museum)

Opposite page, top left: Maj Gen Manton S. Eddy, CG XII Corps. (Tank Museum)

Opposite page, top right: Maj Gen S. LeRoy Irwin, CG XII Corps. (Tank Museum)

Opposite page, lower left: Maj Gen Wade H. Haislip, CG XV Corps. (Tank Museum)

Opposite page, lower right: Maj Gen Walton H. Walker, CG XX Corps. (Tank Museum)

Above: Brig Gen Otto P. Weyland, CG 19th Tactical Air Command USAAF, seen here with GSP and Lt Gen Omar N. Bradley, 12th Army Group Commander. (Willie sleeps in his master's armchair!) (Patton Museum)

Gen Patton and the Staff of HQ Third Army, Luxembourg, January 1945.
Back row, left to right: Col Cheever, JA; Col Van Buskirk, SPEC SERV; unknown; Col Busch, QM; unknown; Col Clayton, PM; unknown; Col O'Nall, CHAP; unknown; Col Hammond, SIG OFF.
Centre row, left to right: Brig Gen Conklin, ENGINEER; Col Cummings, DEP A/S ADM; Col Park, INSP GEN; Col

Wallington, CHEM OFF; Col Chamberlain, A A OFF; Col Niyon, ORD; unknown. **Front row, left to right:** Col Mathews, G-1; Col Koch, G-2; Brig Gen, Gay, C/S; Gen Patton; Col Harkins, Dep C/S OPS; Brig Gen Maddox, G-3; Brig Gen Mullere, G-4; Col Campanole,G-5. (Patton Museum)

Above: Gen Patton busy planning with his other Chief of Staff, Maj Gen Hugh Gaffey, Seine River area, France, 26 August 1944. Also present is Maj Halfers, Special Intelligence Officer. (US Army)

Below: On the way to the ETO. Heavily laden GIs boarding ship at New York bound for 'Fortress UK'. This photograph gives a good indication of the amount of kit that one soldier carried – note, all personal weapons of this party seem to have been loaded separately. (National Archives)

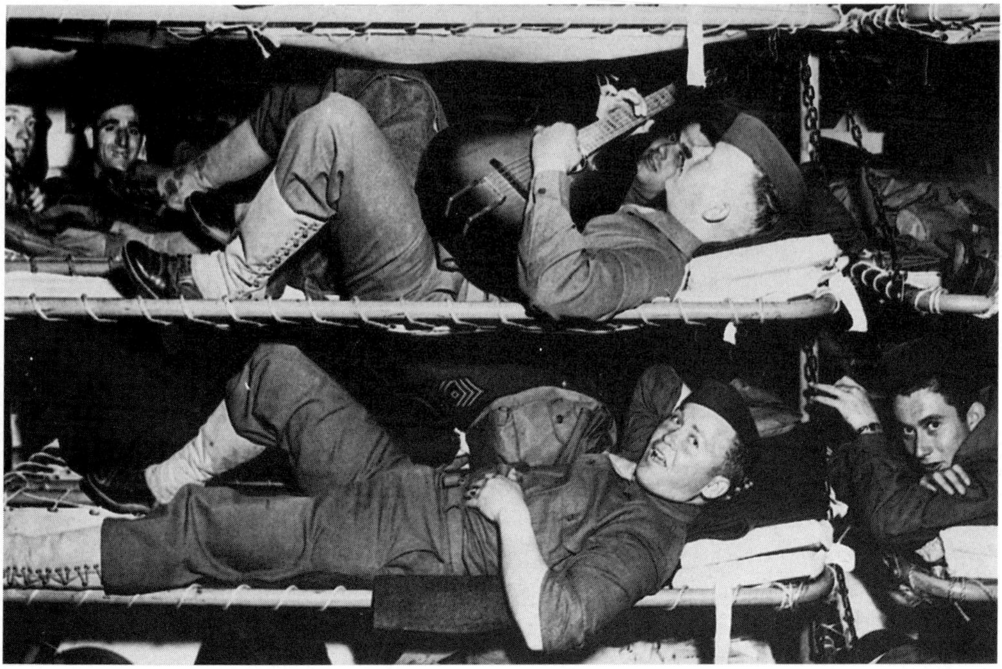

Above: There was little comfort on board, with the rows of 'standee' bunks occupied on a double shift system. (National Archives)

Below: These Third Army infantrymen of 83rd Inf Div, were in St Malo, 17 August 1944. They show what the GI carried in summertime combat. Note waterbottles and entrenching tools clipped to the belt and the mixture of rifles and carbines carried. The GI half obscured by the wall has the squad Browning .30in machine gun, with its belt of ammunition draped over his shoulder. (US Army)

Above: When the weather got colder it was necessary to wear more clothing – some of these GIs of 11 Inf Regt, 5 Inf Div, wear the longer thigh length 1943 jacket, but not all. Note the heavier, water-cooled version of the .30in Browning MG on an AA mount on the jeep. (Real War Photos)

Below: Sgt Bob Grady's tank crew (Co B, 37th Tk Bn, 4th Armd Div) provide a good example of standard tankers dress, note especially the highly prized windcheaters. Webbing was worn so that crewmen could be more easily rescued from a 'brewing-up' tank. (Col James Leach)

Above: The differences between standard infantry and airborne forces dress can be seen here in this squad from 101st Airborne Division – note the high laced airborne jump boots, capacious pockets in the zippered jacket and trousers, carbine in its waterproof case and helmet with moulded chin-cup strap. (Real War Photos)

Below: Basic living was in a two man 'pup' tent – each man carrying a half shelter plus guy line, wooden pins and folding pole. It was not always easy to keep weapons and clothing dry, especially during the spring thaw. (US Army)

Above: The .30in M1 rifle was the US infantryman's basic weapon of WW2, although some still carried the old 1903 bolt action WW1 rifle. This photo also shows some attempts at winter camouflage, by using whitewash or making ad hoc white oversuits locally. (US Army)

Below: The M1 self-loading carbine was the other standard basic weapon for enlisted men not equipped with rifles – over six million were produced. These men in the French bocage play a deadly game of 'hide and seek' with the enemy. (The disassembled machine gun in the foreground is an incomplete German MG 42.) (US Army)

Above: Standard heavy support machine gun was the .50in Browning, which was produced in greater quantity than any other MG as it was used by all three Services. (Real War Photos)

Right: A feared weapon was the manpack flamethrower M2-2 which had a range of some 25 to 40 yards. Although used by combat troops they were held and maintained by the CWS. (Tank Museum)

Top: The anti-tank rocket launcher M1 and M9 was popularly known as the Bazooka. It was highly effective against tanks at short ranges. Nearly half a million were manufactured during WW2. (US Army)

Above: This 57mm anti-tank gun M1 is in action near Brest, 14 September 1944. It replaced the smaller 37mm and was also used mounted on the M3 half track (then known as the GMC T48). (US Army).

Below: The 105mm howitzer M2A1 was the backbone of the American field artillery and over 8,500 were produced. The carriage M2A2 had pneumatic tyres and split trail and was very reliable and sturdy. (US Army)

Bottom: The M3 halftrack was used for a wide variety of jobs, but its basic role was as a troop and weapons carrier. Note this halftrack mounts a .50in Browning, plus two .30in BMGs to provide covering fire for the infantry squad. This halftrack belonged to 5th Armd Div and was passing a blazing barn some 12 miles from the Elbe River. (US Army)

Left: Gen Patton rides in his M20 armoured utility car, the turretless version of the M8 Greyhound. Some 4,000 of these versatile scout cars were built and used for a variety of tasks. Riding with him is Averell Harriman, Ambassador to Russia, during a visit to Third Army in November 1944. (US Army)

Below: The only armoured car to be used in any great numbers by the US Army was the M8 Greyhound, seen here in front of a burning farmhouse. Its turret contained a 37mm gun and .30in coaxially mounted machine gun, whilst on top was a .50in AA MG. (Tank Museum)

with 90th Div Arty and became CG 8th Armd Div in Oct 1944. He retired in 1952 and became Commandant of Cadets at Virginia Polytechnic from 1952 to 1960. His decorations included the Bronze Star, Silver Star, Legion of Merit, DSM, French Legion of Honour and Croix de Guerre, Dutch Order of Orange-Nassau (Knight Commander with Swords), War Cross and Order of White Lion from Czechoslovakia.

9th Armored Division. Major General John W. Leonard was born in Toledo, Ohio, in 1890. In June 1915 he graduated from West Point into the infantry. He served with the punitive expedition into Mexico in 1916, and then went to France in April 1918 with 6th Inf Div, where he was awarded the DSC, Purple Heart and two French awards for bravery. He became CO 6th Inf Regt in December 1918, and took part in the French and British Victory Parades in Paris and London. His regiment the returned to the USA as General Pershing's bodyguard. He became CO 18th Tank Bn in July 1921, and after various appointments (including service in Brazil surveying their defences) was assigned first to 4th Armd, then to 9th Armd Div in July 1942 when it was activated, assuming command of CCB. In September 1942 he became CG vice Major General Keyes. The division became famous in the Battle of the Bulge, where CCR assisted 101st Ab Div to hold Bastogne. After a period of rest and re-organisation, 9th Armd was in action again in March 1945, and was responsible for the capture of the Ludendorff railway bridge at Remagen on the 7th. The division continued the victorious advance, ending up near Karlsbad in Czechoslovakia. General Leonard was later assigned to command 20th Armd Div for the invasion of Japan, and was still commanding when the division was de-activated in April 1946. He next commanded 2nd Armd Div and the Armored School at Fort Knox. His decorations included the DSC, DSM, Legion of Merit, Silver Star, Bronze Star, Purple Heart, Army Commendation Ribbon with Oak Leaf Cluster, French Legion of Honour and Croix de Guerre (Great War), and the same for the Second World War.

10th Armored Division. Major General William H. H. Morris Jr. was born in Ocean Grove, New Jersey, in 1890. He graduated from West Point in 1911. In early 1942, as a brigadier general, he took command of 6th Armd Div on its formation at Fort Knox, remaining with the 'Super Sixth' until May 1943 when he was appointed CG II Armd Corps. In September 1943 he moved to XVIII Corps then, in July 1944, took command of 10th Armd Div. He remained in command of 'Armored Tiger' until May 1945 when he became CG VI Corps. He was commanding 10th Armd during the capture of Metz, the Battle of the Bulge, capture of Trier, the breakthrough to the Rhine, capture of Heidelberg and Ulm, and crossing the Alps to Garmisch. He was awarded the DSC, DSM, Purple Heart, Silver Star, Legion of Merit, Bronze Star, French Legion of Honour and Croix de Guerre, Belgian Croix de Guerre, Brazilian Order of Military Merit, plus medals from Panama and Ecuador.

11th Armored Division. Brigadier General Charles S. Kilburn had been nicknamed 'Rattlesnake Pete' early in his career in the cavalry, and was an outstanding horseman and polo player. He was born in Silver City, New Mexico, in 1895. He graduated from West Point in 1917. After serving in Mexico in the campaign against Pancho Villa, he went overseas with the AEF to France. He took command of 11th Armored (the Thunderbolt Division) early in 1943 and was commanding them during the Battle of the Bulge when they trapped thousands of German troops near Bastogne in January 1945. Later the division made a 15-mile advance across the River Nabev to a town fourteen miles west of Kaiserslautern, sealing a 300-square mile pocket containing an estimated 2,000 enemy soldiers. In March 1945 he relinquished command to Major General Holmes E. Dager who commanded it for the remainder of the war. He died in 1978.

Major General Dager was born in Astbury Park, New Jersey, in 1893. He was appointed as an infantry second lieutenant in the NJ National Guard in 1912, and was commissioned into the Regular Army in 1917. In France, he took part in the Meuse–Argonne offensive with 51st Inf Regt. After service in the USA and Puerto Rico, he was assigned in January 1942 to 2nd Armd Div, then to 8th and finally, in August 1942, he became a combat commander in 4th Armd Div. He led troops of this division in the capture of Coutances, Avranches and Lorient, and continued with them until he was assigned to 11th Armd Div. The 11th was the first division in Third Army to meet Russian troops (7th Paratroop Guard Division, at Amstetten in Austria), and on VE-Day was the easternmost ground force of the entire US Army in Europe. In September 1945 Dager was in command of 5th Armd Div in occupied Germany before returning to the USA in November. His decorations included Silver Star with Oak Leaf Cluster, Bronze Star with two Oak Leaf Clusters, Legion of Merit, DSM and DSC. Foreign decorations were French Legion of Honour (Knight) and Croix de Guerre with Palm, Luxembourg Croix de Guerre, Soviet 'Defence of the Fatherland' (1st Degree).

12th Armored Division. Major General Roderick R. Allen was born in Marshall, Texas, in 1894. He was commissioned into the 16th Cavalry in 1916. He served as a Captain in 3rd Cavalry with the AEF, and became Comd CCA 4th Armd Div in April 1942. In October 1943 he took over command of 20th Armd Div, a post he held until September 1944 when he became CG 12th Armd, remaining in command of the 'Armored Hellcats' until the end of the war. Post-war he served in Japan and Korea (CG XVI Corps 1951–2). His decorations included the DSM, Silver Star, Legion of Merit, Bronze Star, French Legion of Honour and Croix de Guerre with Palm, Order of White Lion of Victory and War Cross (Czechoslovakia). He died in March 1970.

13th Armored Division. Major General John B. Wogan was born in New Orleans in 1890. He was commissioned into the Coast

Artillery in 1915, served on the Mexican border and then with the AEF Coast Arty Corps in 1917, taking part in the St-Mihiel and Meuse–Argonne offensives. Transferring to field artillery in 1920, he became Commander CCB 2nd Armd Div in 1942. He commanded 13th Armd Div from July 1942 until 15 April 1945 when he was severely wounded in the Ruhr battle and had to retire. Decorations: DSM, Silver Star, Legion of Merit, Purple Heart, French Legion of Honour and Croix de Guerre with Palm. He died in 1968. He was replaced by Major General John Millikin (see page 88).

14th Armored Division. Major General Albert C. Smith was born in Warrenton, Virginia, in 1894. He graduated from West Point in April 1917 and was commissioned into the cavalry. In October he went to France with 7th Cavalry, took part in the Meuse–Argonne offensive and later was aide to General McGlachin at VII Army Corps HQ. After various postings between the wars, he was appointed Plans and Training Officer of the Armored Force Replacement Center at Fort Knox in November 1940. He performed the same role with 4th Armd Div in April 1941, and then became CCA of that division. He assumed command of 14th Armd Div in July 1944, took them to Europe and remained their commander throughout the entire combat service of the division, and later during occupation duties until they were deactivated in September 1945. He served in Japan and the USA until he retired in 1955. Decorations: DSM, Silver Star, Bronze Star, French Legion of Honour and Croix de Guerre with Palm. He died in 1974.

16th Armored Division. Brigadier General (later Major General) John L. Pierce was born in Dallas, Texas, in 1895. He was commissioned into the infantry from Texas Agricultural & Mechanical College in 1917. He served in France and Belgium with the AEF, and enrolled at The QM School in 1930. His first armour appointment was as S-4 Supply Officer of 67th Armd Regt in January 1941. He was then assigned as Div Transportation Officer 2nd Armd Div. From April 1941 to April 1942 he was ACOS G-4 3rd Armd Div, then ACOS G-4 II Armd Corps, being designated COS II Armd Corps in November 1942. He was next assigned as a combat commander, first with 9th Armd Div in June 1943, then with 16th Armd Div in March 1944. He assumed command of the division in Aug 1944 and remained with them until the end, including the occupation of Czechoslovakia.

20th Armored Division. Major General Orlando Ward was born in Macon in 1891. He graduated from West Point in 1914 and was commissioned into the US Cavalry. After serving in Mexico with the Punitive Expedition in 1917, he transferred to the field artillery and served in France with 10th Fd Arty. He became CG 1st Armd Div at Fort Knox in 1941 and the following year was appointed to command the Tank Destroyer Center at Camp Hood, Texas. In 1943 he took over the Field Artillery School until October 1944, when he became CG 20th Armd

Div and stayed with them until the end of the war. One of his post-war appointments was as head of the Historical Division of the Army from 1949 to 1953. Decorations: DSC, Legion of Merit with Oak Leaf Cluster, Purple Heart, DSM and Bronze Star. He died in 1972.

Infantry Commanders

1st Infantry Division. Major General Clift Andrus took over 'The Big Red One' on 11 December 1944 from Major General Clarence R. Heubner (who went to command V Corps) and continued in command for the remainder of the war. Andrus was born at Fort Leavenworth in 1890. He was commissioned into the 2nd Field Artillery in 1912 and remained with the artillery throughout his service, being the 'Divarty' commander of 1st Div prior to taking command. There was a saying: 'The US Army consists of the 1st Division and ten million replacements!' Undoubtedly they fought well throughout the war, one senior German officer remarking: 'Where the 1st Division was, there we would have trouble.' That 'trouble' would undoubtedly have been of Andrus's making. His decorations included the DSC, DSM, Silver Star with Oak Leaf Cluster, Legion of Merit with Oak Leaf Cluster, Soldier's Medal, and Bronze Star with Oak Leaf Cluster. He died in 1968.

2nd Infantry Division. Major General Walter M. Robertson was born in Nelson County, Virginia, in 1888. He graduated from West Point in 1912. He served in Hawaii and with the AEF, was CO 9th Inf Regt from November 1940 to December 1941 when he was appointed Asst Div Commander of 2d Inf Div. He became CG in May 1942 and commanded the division throughout the war; he was CG XV Corps (occupation forces in Austria) and Deputy Comd Seventh Army in 1947. Decorations: DSC, DSM, Legion of Merit, Silver Star, Bronze Star, CB (British), Legion of Honour and Croix de Guerre with Palm (French), Military Cross and Order of White Lion (Czech), Order of Wars of Fatherland (USSR). He died in 1954.

4th Infantry Division. Major General Raymond O. Barton was born in Grenada, Colorado, in 1889. He graduated from West Point in 1912 and was commissioned into the infantry. He went to France with the AEF, where he commanded the Motor Overhaul Park. After various postings during the inter-war years he was appointed COS 4th Inf Div in July 1940, and later joined 85th Inf Div. In June 1942 he assumed command of 4th Motorised Div (which subsequently became 4th Inf Div), took them to Europe in 1944 and remained with them until March 1945. He then became CG Infantry Training in the USA. He retired in 1946. He was awarded the DSM for his assault on Utah Beach on D-Day. He died in 1963.

His successor in March 1945 was Major General Harold W. Blakeley, who had been the division's artillery commander since August 1943. Blakeley was born in Malden, Massachusetts, in 1893. In 1917 he was commissioned into the Field Artillery from the reserve. In 1919 he served as a special courier between HQ Paris District and officials in Holland and Austria. After various inter-war postings he was assigned to 1st Armd Div in October 1941, then became Div Arty Officer, 5th Armd Div in January 1942. The following June he was named as commander CCA of 5th Armd Div and held that post until joining 4th Infantry Division.

5th Infantry Division. Major General S. LeRoy Irwin was CG until he was appointed to replace Major General Manton Eddy as XII Corps commander on 20 April 1945. He handed over to Major General A. E. Brown for the remainder of the war. Major General Albert E. Brown was born in Charleston, South Carolina, in 1889. He graduated from West Point in 1912 and was commissioned into the infantry. He went to France with the AEF and took part in various offensives, returning to the US in February 1919. After various inter-war appointments (including being a member of the Infantry Board 1935–8), he was designated CG of 7th Mech Div (redesignated 7th Inf Div) in May 1942, then, following an overseas assignment, became CG Infantry Replacement Training Center at Camp Wheeler in June 1943. Going overseas, he commanded troops during operations on Kiska and Attu Islands in the Aleutians, before being posted to the ETO in December 1944 for duty with 35th Inf Div. He assumed command of the ETO Ground Force Reinforcement Command in February 1945, then was nominated as CG 5th Inf Div in April vice Major General Irwin when he became XII Corps commander. He returned to the USA with the division in August 1945.

8th Infantry Division. Major General Donald A. Stroh was born in Harrisburg, Pennsylvania, in 1892. He was commissioned into the cavalry in 1912. He held various intelligence posts between the wars and was appointed CO 339th Inf Regt on its activation in February 1942, subsequently becoming CG 9th Inf Div five months later. He took part in Operation 'Torch' and fought in Tunisia and Sicily. In July 1944 he was assigned to command 8th Inf Div and remained their CG almost until the end of the war, being transferred to command 106th Inf Div in February 1945. Decorations: DSM, Legion of Merit with Oak Leaf Cluster, Bronze Star, French Legion of Honour and Croix de Guerre with Palm. He died in 1953.

26th Infantry Division. Major General Willard S. Paul was born in Worcester, Massachusetts, in 1894. He enlisted in the Field Artillery in 1916 and was commissioned the following year. His period in command of 26th Inf Div was followed by a G-1 appointment at SHAEF and he was promoted to lieutenant general in 1948. He died in 1966.

28th Infantry Division. Major General Norman D. Cota was born in Celsea, Massachusetts, in 1893. He graduated from West Point in 1917 and was commissioned into the infantry. He was appointed COS 1st Inf Div in 1942 and landed with them in North Africa in October. In February 1943 he was assigned to British Combined Operations

HQ in London and helped to evolve amphibious landing techniques that were used on D-Day. In October 1943 he became Asst Comd 29th Inf Div, landing with a forward HQ detachment of the 29th on Omaha Beach, where his work won recognition from both the US and British authorities, leading to his being awarded the DSC (US) and the DSO (UK). In August 1944 he was given command of 28th Infantry Division and led them for the remainder of the war in Europe, returning to USA with them in August 1945, to prepare for combat against Japan. He retired because of physical disability in June 1946, but returned to active duty the following month. His decorations, in addition to the DSC and DSO, included: the DSM, Legion of Merit, Silver Star with Oak Leaf Cluster, Bronze Star with Oak Leaf Cluster, Purple Heart, plus the French Legion of Honour.

29th Infantry Division. Major General Charles H. Gerhardt was born in Lebanon, Tennessee, in 1895. He graduated from West Point in 1917 and was commissioned into the cavalry. He went to France with the AEF and took part in the St Mihiel and Meuse–Argonne offensives. After tours in the USA and the Philippines, he served with 1st Cav Div in July 1941 and, in May 1942, was assigned as CG 29th Inf Div upon its activation and commanded them throughout the war. His decorations included the Silver Star (for gallantry during the capture of Isigny in three days of bloody fighting), DSM, Bronze Star, Legion of Merit and foreign awards from France, Belgium, Holland and the USSR.

35th Infantry Division. Major General Paul W. Baade was born at Fort Wayne, Indiana, in 1889. He graduated from West Point in 1911 and was commissioned into the infantry. Before the Great War he served in Manila, and then was with 81st Inf Div in the AEF, returning to the USA with his regiment in June 1919. After various inter-war appointments, he became CG Puerto Rican General Depot and Mobile Force from July 1942 until July 1943 when he was appointed Asst Div Comd 35th Inf Div in Southern California. In January 1943 he became CG and landed with his division in Normandy on 6 July 1944, entering the battle of Normandy two days later as part of XIX Corps in First Army. He continued to command the 35th until April 1945. His division was the closest American or British unit to Berlin. His decorations included the DSM, Silver Star with Oak Leaf Cluster, Legion of Merit, Bronze Star with two Oak Leaf Clusters and the Purple Heart. He also had decorations from France and Holland. He died in 1959.

42nd Infantry Division. Major General Harry J. Collins was born in Chicago in 1895. He was commissioned into the infantry reserve from the University of Chicago in 1917 and received his regular commission the same year. After service in the USA and Hawaii he became Intelligence Officer of 11th Inf Div in 1940, then IO of IV Corps in November 1941. The following April he activated 354th Inf Regt, and four months later was appointed Asst Commander 99th Inf Div. In April

1943 he became CG of 43rd (Rainbow) Inf Div which, in December 1944, played a major role in stopping the German Ardennes offensive. After reforming they relieved 45th Div on the Moder River, then attacked through the Harz mountains and the West Wall, crossed the Rhine and reached Munich. By D-Day they had occupied eastern Tyrol and then Land Salzburg, eventually being responsible for the entire US zone in Austria, with Major General Collins as military governor. Post-war his appointments included MA in Moscow. Decorations: DSM, Silver Star, Bronze Star, Army Commendation Ribbon; foreign decorations included the French Legion of Honour (Knight) and Croix de Guerre with Palm, and the Order of the Crown of Italy.

65th Infantry Division. Major General Stanley E. Reinhart was born in Polk, Ohio, in 1893. He graduated from West Point in 1916 and was commissioned in the Field Artillery. He served with the AEF in France, seeing action with 17th FA, and in 1918 became COS VI Army Corps Arty. In 1919 he was a member of the AEF Historical Section in France. After service in the USA and Hawaii, he was appointed CG 65th Infantry Division, took them to ETO and was in command until March 1945. In July 1945, he took command of 26th Inf Div in ETO and in the autumn returned to the USA for hospitalisation. His decorations included the DSM (awarded in 1918), Legion of Merit (for action in Oahu in July 1943) and Oak Leaf Cluster to DSM in 1945 for his meritorious service as CG 65th Infantry Division.

69th Infantry Division. Major General Emil F. Rheinhardt was born in Bay City, Michigan, in 1888. He graduated from West Point in 1910. He was appointed CG of 69th Division in April 1942 and commanded them throughout the war. It was his division that made the first contact with the Soviet army on the River Elbe. He retired in 1946 and died in 1969.

70th Infantry Division. Major General Allison J. Barnett was born in Kentucky in 1892. He served in the Kentucky National Guard from 1907 to 1913, being discharged as a sergeant. On the outbreak of war he re-enlisted, was commissioned as a captain in the 3rd Kentucky Infantry in 1917, then, in 1920, received a Regular Army commission as a first lieutenant in the infantry. After various inter-war postings, including some with the Air Corps, he became a Regt Comd in the 95th Inf Div in May 1942 and later that year was ordered to Numea in the South Pacific. In August 1944 he was appointed CG of 70th Inf Div in the USA, took them to ETO in December 1944 and commanded them for the remainder of the war. After 70th Div he commanded 94th Inf Div, and then served as Asst COS First Army.

71st Infantry Division. Maj Gen Willard G. Wyman was born in Augusta, Maine, in 1898. He graduating from West Point in 1918 into the Cavalry. He would eventually reach the rank of full general, his first senior appointment being as Assistant CG 1st Inf Div 1943–4 before being appointed to command 71st Inf Div 1944–5. He was then G-2 AGF 1945–6; thereafter his appointments included CG IX Corps, CG Sixth Army, CG US Continental Army Command (1956–8). Decorations: DSC, Silver Star, Bronze Star with Oak Leaf Cluster, Legion of Honour and Croix de Guerre (France), Russian Order of Great War 1st Class, DSM with 1st Oak Leaf Cluster. He died in 1969.

76th Infantry Division. Major General William R. Schmidt was born in Verdigre, Nebraska, in 1889. He graduated from West Point in 1913. He emerged from the Great War as a major, so he brought a wealth of experience to 76th Inf Div whose command he assumed in December 1942. The division was composed of men from all over the USA. They began their combat record in the Ardennes and fought through Luxembourg, the Siegfried Line, Trier, the Moselle, the Rhine and onwards, making a 'mad dash' across central Germany from the Fulda to the Mulde in order to link up with the Russians. In total, they covered more than 400 miles in 110 days of continuous combat. General Schmidt was awarded the Legion of Merit and the Silver Star while with the division; his other awards included: DSM, Bronze Star, Legion of Honour and Croix de Guerre with Palm (France), Order of Orange-Nassau with Swords (Holland), War Cross (Czechoslovakia), Croix de Guerre (Belgium). After the war his senior commands included 3rd Inf Div and 101st Ab Div. He died in 1966.

79th Infantry Division. Major General Ira T. Wyche was born in Ocracoke, North Carolina, in 1887. He graduated from West Point in 1911 and was commissioned into the infantry. He went to France with the AEF after serving in Texas and Alaska and transferring to the Field Artillery. On his return after various postings he was appointed to command 4th Fld Arty in 1938, then 7th Fld Arty Bde in 1941. In May 1942 he became CG 79th Inf Div and commanded them throughout all their battle operations in Europe. The division fought under First, Third, Seventh and Ninth Armies, covering 2,300 miles in the process. It took part in the capture of Cherbourg, was first across the Seine, bore the brunt of the German offensive in the Ardennes and was one of the first divisions across the Rhine. In May 1945 General Wyche became Corps Commander III Corps. His decorations included: DSM, Silver Star, Bronze Star with two Oak Leaf Clusters, French Legion of Honour and Croix de Guerre with Palm.

80th Infantry Division. Major General Horace L. McBride was born in Madison, Nebraska, in 1894. He graduated from West Point into the Field Artillery in 1916. He went to France with the AEF, commanded 347th Fld Arty Bn of 91st Inf Div and participated in the Meuse–Argonne offensive. He commanded 2nd Fld Arty Bn in the Panama Canal Zone in 1940–1, and in May 1942 was assigned as Arty Comd 80th Inf Div, becoming CG in July 1944 and taking them overseas for duty in the ETO. His division was one of the longest-serving with Third Army (274 days) and took part in all the campaigns, assisting in closing the Falaise pocket, establishing the first American bridgehead across the Moselle, breaching the Maginot Line and driving deep into the southern flank of the German armies in the Bulge to make contact with the 101st Ab Div in Bastogne. They penetrated the Siegfried Line, made an assault crossing of the Rhine and finished the war in contact with the Russians on the Enns River in Austria. The division took the surrender of the Sixth German Army. General McBride became CG XX Corps in October 45 and later commanded the First Service Command in Boston in 1947. His decorations included: DSM, Legion of Merit, Silver Star with Oak Leaf Cluster, Bronze Star Medal, with foreign awards from Poland (Cross of the Brave), France (Legion of Honour and Croix de Guerre with Palm and Star), Luxembourg (Croix de Guerre) and USSR (Order of Alexander Nevsky and Order of War of the Fatherland).

83rd Infantry Division. Major General Robert C. Macon was born in Washington DC, in 1890. He was commissioned into the infantry in 1916. After various inter-war postings in the USA, he commanded 80th Armd Regt in 4th Armd Div, then joined 3rd Inf Div as CO 7th Inf Regt, commanding them during the landings in North Africa. Returning to the USA in April 1943, he became Asst Div Comd 83rd Inf Div, then CG in January 44. He remained in command until the division was deactivated in April 1946, when he was appointed as MA Moscow.

86th Infantry Division. Major General Harris M. Melasky was born in Austin, Texas, in 1893. He graduated from West Point in 1917 and was commissioned into the infantry. In October 1918 he served with the Army Staff School, Langres, France, and was later sent to Siberia, commanding troops at Razdolnoe. Service in the Philippines and then Tientsin, China, followed. In 1941 he commanded 550th Ab Inf Bn in the Panama Canal Zone. Assigned to 77th Inf Div in July 1942, he was then appointed to command 86th Inf Div in January 1945 and took them to ETO in March 1945. He commanded the division for the remainder of the war.

87th Infantry Division. Major General Frank L. Culin Jr. was born in Seattle in 1892. He was commissioned into the infantry in 1916. Decorations: Silver Star (1918), with Oak Leaf Cluster (1943), second Oak Leaf Cluster (1945), Bronze Star, Air Medal, DSM, Legion of Honour and Croix de Guerre with Palm (France), Croix de Guerre with Palm (Belgium). He retired in 1946, and died in 1967.

89th Infantry Division. Major General Thomas D. Finley was born in Annapolis, Maryland, in 1895. He graduated from West Point in 1916 and was commissioned in the Corps of Engineers. He went to France with 7th Engineers in 1918 and later commanded a battalion of the 7th in Luxembourg. He was with the MA in Paris during 1927 and enrolled in the French Tank School. After a variety of appointments, he was designated Asst Div Comd, 89th Inf Div in May 1942. He became CG the following year and took the division to ETO and commanded them for the remainder of the war.

90th Infantry Division. Major General Raymond S. McLain was born in Washington County, Kentucky, in 1890. He enlisted as a private in the National Guard in 1912. He was commissioned, served on the Mexican Border and during the Great War. In 1940 he was a brigadier general in the Oklahoma National Guard, then CG of 45th Inf Div Arty in Sicily and Italy. He was transferred to the UK in April 1944 as CG 30th Inf Div Arty and on 9 June was appointed CG 90th Inf Div, then in July 1944 was promoted to lieutenant general and selected to command XIX Corps for the remainder of the war. His decorations included the DSC with Oak Leaf Cluster, DSM with Oak Leaf Cluster, Silver Star, Bronze Star with Oak Leaf Cluster, Legion of Honour and Croix de Guerre with Palm (France), Order of Orange-Nassau (Holland), Order of Leopold and Croix de Guerre (Belgium). He retired in 1952 and died two years later.

He was replaced in 90th Inf Div by General J. A. Van Fleet (see entry above under III Corps) and when Van Fleet was promoted to command III Corps, Patton recommended Brigadier General Herbert L. Earnest to succeed him as CG of 90th Infantry Division. Earnest was a tank-destroyer expert, a Third Army veteran and an outstanding combat commander. But General Eisenhower personally overruled the choice and ordered that one of his friends, Major General Lowell Rook, who was later to be made head of UNRRA, should take over, in order for him to gain some operational experience before getting a SHAEF desk job. Rook held the post for about a month, with Earnest as his assistant divisional commander. Then Earnest took over as CG, did a brilliant job and was promoted to major general. His decorations included: DSM, Legion of Merit, Silver Star, Bronze Star with two Oak Leaf Clusters, DSO (Britain), Legion of Honour and Croix de Guerre with Palm (France), Czech War Cross. He died in 1970 aged 75.

94th Infantry Division. Major General Harry J. Malony was born at Lakemont, New York, in 1889. He graduated from West Point into the infantry in 1912. He served in the Panama Canal Zone and with the AEF in France during the Great War. He was appointed CG 94th Inf Div in 1942, and led them throughout the war. Post-war, he was Chief of the History Division, War Department. He retired in 1949 and became a Deputy Director UN for the Kashmir plebiscite. Decorations: DSM with Oak Leaf Cluster, Silver Star, Bronze Star, Legion of Honour, Croix de Guerre and Ordre d'Etoile Noire (France). He died in 1971.

95th Infantry Division. Major General Harry L. Twaddle was born in Clarksfield, Ohio, in 1888. He graduated from Syracuse University and was commissioned into the infantry in April 1912. He served in the USA, Alaska and the Philippines and at numerous posts in the USA, until he was assigned to command 1st Bn, 38th Inf Div, (the demonstration battalion at the Fld Arty School) in 1933. After various other postings, he was designated CG 95th Inf Div in March 1942 and activated the division in Texas. They went to the UK in August 1944, arrived in France the following month and assisted in operating the 'Red Ball Route' until October when the division went to the Metz area. They subsequently took part in the XX Corps offensive through the Maginot Line and on to the Siegfried Line in the Saar Valley. Joining VIII Corps, they moved to Bastogne, then further north to Maastricht. Later they conducted defensive operations as part of VIII Corps, British Second Army. Following the crossing of the Roer and then the Rhine, they arrived in the vicinity of Münster. In April 1945 they took part in a southern offensive across the Leippe toward the Ruhr, capturing Hamm, Soest and Dortmund. They finished the war near Lüdinghausen. General Twaddle brought his division home in June 1945, deactivating them in October. He had the unique distinction of being the only US divisional commander to activate, train, move overseas, fight, return to the USA and deactivate his division during the Second World War.

97th Infantry Division. Brigadier General Milton B. Halsey was born in Huntsville, Alabama, in 1894. He graduated from West Point in 1917 and was commissioned into the infantry. In 1919 he served in the AEF with 50th Inf Div at Mayen. In December 1941 he was assigned as COS 29th Inf Div, then moved to 44th Inf Div as Asst Div Comd. In January 1944 he was made CG 97th Inf Div and continued to command them for a period of 20 months, including their service in ETO and their re-deployment to Japan. First engaged in the Rhineland, the division later participated in the elimination of the Ruhr pocket. On VE-Day, as part of Third Army, they had reached Pilsen in Czechoslovakia. In their 43 days of front-line service the Trident Division had taken 2,000 square miles of territory and more than 47,000 POWs. Brigadier General Walsey's decorations included the Order of the White Lion and the Military Cross (Czechoslovakia), Legion of Honour and Croix de Guerre with Palm (France).

99th Infantry Division. Major General Walter E. Lauer was born in Brooklyn in 1893. He was commissioned into the US Army Reserve in 1917 and thence to the Regular Army the same year. After serving as COS 3rd Inf Div in Tunisia in 1943, he was appointed CG 99th Inf Div in 1943 and commanded them throughout the war. Retiring as a major general in 1946, he joined UNRRA, being in charge of all surplus property in Europe. Decorations: DSM, Silver Star with Oak Leaf Cluster, Legion of Merit, Bronze Star with two Oak Leaf Clusters, Purple Heart, Royal Crown and Croix de Guerre with Palm (Belgium), Legion of Honour and Croix de Guerre with Palm (France), Order of Red Banner (USSR), War Cross (Order of White Lion) (Czechoslovakia). He died in 1966.

Airborne Commanders

Commanding 101st Airborne Division was MAJOR GENERAL MAXWELL DAVENPORT TAYLOR, one of the most brilliant airborne commanders of the war. He was born in 1901. He graduated from West Point in 1922 and was commissioned into the engineers, but later transferred to artillery. By 1942, he was a brigadier general and COS 82nd Airborne, then its artillery commander on operations in Sicily and Italy. He took over the 101st for the Normandy invasion and continued to command them throughout the rest of the war. Post-war he held various senior appointments, such as CG US Forces in Berlin 1949–51, commander Eighth Army in Korea in 1953, commander US Forces in the Far East 1954–5 and, finally, Chief of Staff of the US Army 1955–9. Retiring in 1959, he was recalled as Chairman of the Joint Chiefs of Staff 1962–4 and then became Ambassador to South Vietnam.

Although Major General Maxwell Taylor was the CG of the 101st, it was his deputy commander, BRIGADIER GENERAL ANTHONY G. MCAULIFFE, who was in temporary command when the division carried out its heroic defence of Bastogne (called by some the 'Gettysburg of WWII'). His now famous laconic response to the German ultimatum to surrender: 'Nuts!', earned him the immediate award of the Distinguished Service Cross pinned on him personally by Patton on 28 December for the 101st's epic struggle, which had materially helped to halt German progress in the Ardennes. His first message to Patton once the siege was lifted read: 'Losses light. Morale high. Awaiting orders to continue the counter-offensive.'

MAJOR GENERAL WILLIAM M. MILEY, commander of 17th Airborne Division, was born in Fort Mason, California, in 1897. He graduated from West Point in 1918 and was commissioned into the infantry. His airborne career started in October 1940 when he assumed command of 501st Para Bn at Fort Benning. Later he activated and commanded 503rd Para Regt at Fort Bragg. After a period as Asst Div Comd 82nd Ab Div, he was appointed CG 17th Ab Div in April 1943, and took them to the UK in August 1944. When the Germans broke through in the Ardennes, the division was flown to France, and went into battle on 4 January 1945. After 30 days of bitter fighting they moved forward towards the Siegfried Line. Withdrawn in February, they were flown into Germany on 24 March, landing by parachute and glider to capture the city of Münster. They then attacked southwards, taking Essen, Mülheim and Duisburg. After VE-Day they performed occupational duties until the area was taken over by the British. The division was deactivated in September 1945. General Miley went on to a series of senior appointments, including CG US Army in Alaska. He retired in 1955. His decorations included the DSM, Silver Star with Oak Leaf Cluster, Bronze Star with Oak Leaf Cluster; his foreign decorations included the British DSO.

Foreign Commanders

Mention must also be made of the one foreign division that served with Third Army, namely the French 2nd Armoured Division. Its commander was MAJOR GENERAL JACQUES LECLERC. His name was in fact a '*nom de guerre*' which he had adopted in order to protect his family against German retaliation in occupied France. After the war, the French government allowed him the legal use of the name and he became the Vicomte Philippe François Marie Leclerc de Hautecloque. The division had its origins in French Equatorial Africa, when, in August 1940, the *Régiment de Tirailleurs Sénégalais du Tchad* had joined General de Gaulle's Free French forces. In December 1940 Colonel Leclerc took over command in Tchad and carried out a series of highly successful raids on enemy outposts in Libya. He then took his force on a long march to join the British Eighth Army in North Africa, being reinforced on the way by Free French units from Syria and Dakar, also by loyal Frenchmen from all over the world. After the victory in North Africa they sailed for England, where they were known as the French 2nd Armoured Division.

They arrived on French soil on 1 August 1944 as part of XV Corps, whose CG, Wade Haislip, was himself a graduate of the Ecole Supérieure de Guerre and consequently well able to get the best out of Leclerc's division. Any casualties they received during their advance on Paris were swiftly made up by eager volunteers from among the local population, as the liberation continued. Like his troops, Leclerc was a tough, widely experienced commander, to whom Patton gave the honour of liberating Paris. 'Leclerc of the 2nd French Armored Division came in, very much excited,' wrote GSP in his diary on 15 August. 'He said, among other things, that if he was not allowed to advance on Paris he would resign. I told him in my best French that he was a baby, and I would not have division commanders tell me where they would fight and that anyway I had left him in the most dangerous place. We parted friends.' Leclerc clearly held Patton in great esteem, and, during the Battle of the Bulge asked to be reassigned to Third Army from Seventh Army.

Up and Coming Officers

In addition to those who held senior command, there were a number of officers in Third Army, who were still too young and junior really to 'hit the heights'. However, their gallant actions got them noticed and earmarked them for future greatness. Two such men were Bruce C. Clarke, who made his name commanding the heroic stand at St-Vith, and Creighton W. Abrams, whose 37th Tank Battalion was one of the most outstanding units in Third Army.

Clarke of St-Vith. Brigadier General (later General) Bruce C. Clarke joined the US Army in 1918 at the age of seventeen, served in the ranks and was commissioned into the Corps of Engineers in 1925. In

1940 he was appointed CO of 24th Engineer Battalion, which was part of the Armored Force[4] and became the acting engineer office for the Force. Later, he was Chief of Staff 4th Armd Div and went overseas in December 1943 as the CO of CCA 4th Armd Div. In August 1944, after some of the heaviest fighting, he was awarded both the DSC and the Silver Star. In November 1944 he was CG of CCB 7th Armd Div, and found himself thrust into a much wider command, covering a hodgepodge of units in one of the key sectors in the Ardennes, around the small town of St-Vith. Here he was able to hold up the enemy thrusts by using mobile 'hit and retire' tactics. 'As the commander of CCB,' he later wrote, 'I analyzed the situation and decided that the probable objective of the German attack was not just St-Vith or a bridgehead over the Salm River, but rather a decisive objective far to my rear, probably toward the English Channel. I could well afford to be forced back slowly, surrendering a few kilometers of terrain at a time to the German forces while preventing the destruction of my command and giving other units to my rear the time to prepare a defense and a counter-attack. Therefore by retiring a kilometer or so a day, I was winning, and the Germans, by being prevented from advancing many kilometers a day, were losing, thus proving my concept that an armored force can be effectively employed in a defense and delay situation as in the offensive.'

General Hasso von Manteuffel, the able and tough commander of 5th Panzer Army, later described Clarke's actions as being 'one of the best models of this method of fighting'. By his clever tactics Clarke had undoubtedly prevented a link-up between 5th and 6th Panzer Armies and completely upset the timetable of the German Ardennes offensive. He went on after the war to command both 1st and 4th Armd Divs, I and VII Corps during the Korean War, US Seventh Army and later, NATO's Central Army Group during the Berlin crisis. General Bruce Clarke wrote later of Patton: 'Patton was a unique commander, and a unique person and had a unique influence over the officers and men under him and, I am sure, over his enemies in battle as well.... He changed the US Army's concept of the role of tanks in WWI, from an accompanying and supporting weapon of foot infantry, to that of the principal component of a balanced, combined arms division made up of tanks, armored cavalry, armored infantry, armored field artillery and armored engineers, supported by tactical air and adequate logistics units.'[5]

CO 37th Tank Battalion. Also serving with Clarke in 4th Armored Division was Lieutenant Colonel (later General) Creighton W. Abrams, commanding 37th Tank Battalion. A brilliant armour commander, Patton once said: 'I'm supposed to be the best tank commander in the Army, but I have one peer – Abe Abrams.' He won distinction when his tank battalion led 4th Armd Div into Bastogne, to relieve the beleaguered 101st Airborne Division. He was born in Springfield, Massachusetts, in 1914. He graduated in 1936 into the cavalry, transferring to armour in 1940. Post-war he held many senior appointments including CG 3rd Armd Div 1960–2, CG V Corps in Germany in 1963 and Deputy Commander US Military Assistance Command Vietnam (MACV) 1967–8, where he directed the Tet offensive in March–April 1968. In the summer of 1968 he took over from General Westmoreland as Commander of MACV and was responsible for the 'Vietnamisation' of the war and the disengagement of US forces. His last appointment was as Chief of Staff of the US Army, a post he held from 1972 to 1974, when he died of cancer. His name has now been commemorated in the latest American main battle tank, the M1 Abrams.

Annex 'A' to Chapter 5
Division Commanders and Assistant Division Commanders who served with Third (US) Army between 1 August 44 and 9 May 1945

Division	*Commander*	*Asst Divisional Commander*
1st Inf	Maj Gen (MG) Clift Andrus	Brig Gen (BG) G. A. Taylor
2nd Inf	MG W. M. Robertson	BG J. A. Van Fleet
		BG J. H. Stokes, Jr
4th Inf	MG R. O. Barton	BG J. S. Rodwell
	MG H. W. Blakely	
5th Inf	MG S. LeRoy Irwin	BG A. D. Warnock
	MG A. E. Brown	
8th Inf	MG D. A. Stroh	BG C. D. W. Canham
26th Inf	MG W. S. Paul	BG H. N. Hartness
28th Inf	MG N. D. Cota	BG G. A. Davis
29th Inf	MG C. H. Gerdhart	BG L. H. Watson
35th Inf	MG P. W. Baade	BG E. B. Seebree
		BG B. B. Miltonberger
42nd Inf	MG H. J. Collins	BG H. Linden
65th Inf	MG S. E. Reinhart	BG J. E. Copeland
69th Inf	MG E. F. Rheinhardt	BG L. H. Gibbons
70th Inf	MG A. J. Barnett	BG T. W. Herren
71st Inf	MG W. G. Wyman	BG O. S. Rolfe
76th Inf	MG W. R. Schmidt	BG F. A. Woolfley
79th Inf	MG I. T. Wyche	BG F. U. Greer
		BG J. S. Winn, Jr
80th Inf	MG H. L. McBride	BG O. Summers
		BG G. W. Smythe
83rd Inf	MG R. C. Macon	BG C. B. Ferenbaugh
86th Inf	MG H. M. Melasky	BG G. V. W. Pope
87th Inf	MG F. L. Culin, Jr	BG J. L. McKee
89th Inf	MG T. D. Finley	BG J. N. Robinson
90th Inf	MG R. S. McLain	BG W. G. Weaver
	MG J. A. Van Fleet	BG J. M. Tully
	MG H. L. Earnest	

Division	*Commander*	*Asst Divisional Commander*
94th Inf	MG H. J. Malony	BG H. B. Cheadle
95th Inf	MG H. L. Twaddle	BG Don C. Faith
97th Inf	BG M. B. Halsey	BG F. H. Partridge
99th Inf	MG W. E. Lauer	BG H. T. Mayberry
4th Armd	MG J. S. Wood	BG W. L. Roberts
	MG H. J. Gaffey	
	MG W. H. Hoge	
5th Armd	MG L. E. Oliver	
6th Armd	MG R. W. Grow	BG G. W. Reed, Jr
7th Armd	MG L M Silvester	
	MG R W Hasbrouck	
8th Armd	MG J. M. Devine	
9th Armd	MG J. W. Leonard	
10th Armd	MG W. H. H. Morris, Jr	
11th Armd	BG C. S. Kilburn	
	MG H. E. Dager	
12th Armd	MG R. R. Allen	
13th Armd	MG J. B. Wogan	
	MG John Millikin	
14th Armd	MG A. C. Smith	
16th Armd	BG J. L. Pierce	
20th Armd	MG Orlando Ward	
17th Ab	MG W. M. Miley	BG J. L. Whitelaw
101st Ab	MG M. D. Taylor	BG G. J. Higgins
		BG A. G.McAuliffe
French 2nd Armd	MG F. M. Leclerc	

Notes to Chapter 5

1. As quoted in *Breakout and Pursuit* by Martin Blumenson.
2. *XII Corps, Spearhead of Patton's Third Army* by Lieutenant Colonel George Dyer, 1947.
3. *Lucky Forward* by Colonel Robert S. Allen.
4. On 25 May 1940, a recommendation was made after a meeting in the basement of a high school in Alexandria, Louisiana, between General Adna R, Chaffee, Colonel (later General) Alvan C. Gillem, Colonel (later General) George S. Patton, Jr and General Frank Andrews (a member of the War Department General Staff). The 'Alexandria Recommendation', as it was called, was to authorise the creation of an Armored Force which came into being on 10 July 1940.
5. See Foreword to *Patton's Third Army at War.*

6
Patton's Staff

'Lucky Forward'

It was standard practice for headquarters to be allocated code-names, not merely to disguise them, but also to make it easier and quicker to communicate with them. The Supreme Headquarters Allied Expeditionary Force (SHAEF) was called 'Liberty', 12th Army Group was 'Eagle' and US First Army was 'Master'. General Patton was a great believer in luck, saying that it was 'the instantaneous realisation of a problem by the inner mind before the outer mind could get into gear'. His own choice of code-word for Third Army was 'Lucky'. He felt that it would epitomise the victorious career and ebullient character of this, his newest and largest command. And certainly history proved him to be perfectly correct on both scores!

GSP's Battle Command Post was therefore known as Lucky Forward, again most appropriate, because 'Forward!' was the only direction in which Patton would be going! Lucky Forward moved a total of nineteen times between 1 August 1944 and 8 May 1945, when Third Army was operational, travelling 1,225 miles in the process. Full details of these moves are given in Annex 'A' to this chapter.

THE FORWARD ECHELON consisted of:

The Commanding General
Chief of Staff
Secretary of the General Staff
G-1, G-2 and G-3
Engineers, Field Artillery, AA Artillery, Signals and Co-operating Air
Sub-sections of the Provost Marshal, Special Troops and an HQ Commandant
Liaison representatives from G-4, Ordnance, Medical, QM and G-5 sections.

When necessary, an even smaller Advance Tactical Headquarters could be split off, which contained the following:

The Commanding General
Forward Echelon Chief of Staff
A small operations section of G-2, G-3, Engineers, Field Artillery and Signals, plus,when required, a liaison group from G-4.

The Rear Echelon, comprising the rest of the Army HQ, was left under command of G-4.

Whenever possible these three elements would be co-located and certainly Rear Echelon was never to be more than three hours' drive from the Forward Echelon. GSP always insisted that ample wire communications must exist between Forward and Rear. He also laid down a number of other rules for headquarters, covering such basic requirements as having a standard plan for the layout of all headquarters no matter their size. In this way, he correctly reasoned, anyone arriving at a strange headquarters would be able to find their way about without difficulty. Sleeping arrangements for senior officers was another area of concern; one could not always rely upon taking over suitable buildings. So every senior officer at CG and COS level should have his own truck or trailer – this was in fact standard practice in most armies. Buildings rather than tents should be used wherever possible for offices, dining-rooms and kitchens.

GSP also considered it essential that, at the Forward Echelon headquarters, there should be sufficient separate office trailers for the CG and his COS, the heads of G Branches, the Secretary of the General Staff and all the clerks and stenographers, so that paper work could continue no matter the weather. He insisted that it was essential for the telephone in any staff office or trailer to be placed near the principal map, so that the officer could refer to the map while talking on the telephone – a simple point but one often forgotten; he comments wryly that in its 23rd CP Lucky Forward still had the main map and telephone on opposite sides of the room!

He felt that it was essential for the Commanding General to answer his own telephone, reasoning that no one would call the Commander unless it was very important and then they should speak to him immediately. By night it should be answered by an aide who should be able to buzz the CG/COS as necessary. He stressed that a means of recording, either by stenographer or machine, should always be on duty so that written transcripts of important conversations were taken (showing date, time, place and the two speakers) and were then available to stop mistakes and 'acrimonious discussion' afterwards.

He was very insistent that everyone in a headquarters got sufficient exercise, sleep and meals. He rightly appreciated that there were normally two peak loads in every 24-hour period during which the maximum number of staff was needed to be on duty. At other times the maximum number of officers and enlisted men should be off duty, but performing one of the three essentials – eating, sleeping or taking exercise. Too many officers made themselves useless by being too conscientious at the start of a campaign, thinking they were indispensable.

He considered that a secretary was vital for the General Staff, with a competent Deputy COS, to ensure that the subsections and sections of the General and Special Staffs did not get too independent and issue contradictory orders. The Deputy COS was the vital 'bottleneck' through which such orders must go, so that he could vet them before they were issued.

He deemed it essential at all headquarters of divisional level or above, that the Forward Echelon of each staff conduct a staff meeting or briefing session daily, and that this meeting should be held as soon as the HQ had obtained the necessary information for the day. Patton reckoned that this time varied depending upon level of command as follows: Division – one hour after dawn; Corps – two hours after dawn; Army – three hours after dawn.

He was insistent that Staff Officers did not live in 'ivory towers' completely detached from the sharp-end soldiers and their battles. To this end he laid down that one officer from each staff section at Corps and Army headquarters should go to the front daily and visit his opposite number in the next lower echelon. In addition to collecting information for his own branch, he was also to collect general information. Anything of vital importance had to be passed to the COS immediately on his return. If it were not vital, he was to raise it at the next staff conference. Not only staff officers, but the CG or the COS must visit part of the front daily after the briefing.

The CG or the COS of the Tactical Air Command, which was operating with an Army, should be present at all staff conferences and planning meetings. Without this personal contact it was impossible to maintain maximum co-operation with the vital air arm. The A-3 must work with the G-3 and the A-2 with the G-2.

Finally GSP put his finger on the need to get rid of 'bad apples', or as he described them, 'officers of inharmonious disposition'. He considered that, irrespective of their ability, they had to be removed. 'A staff cannot function properly unless it is a united family.'

Principal Staff Officers in HQ Third Army

CHIEF OF STAFF: Major General Hugh J. Gaffey* April–December 1944; Major General Hobart R. Gay* December 1944 until end of war (he was also Deputy COS initially under Gaffey)

DEPUTY COS: Colonel Paul D. Harkins*

SECRETARY GENERAL STAFF:	Lieutenant Colonel G. R. Pfann
G-1 (Personnel):	Colonel Frederick S. Matthews
G-2 (Intelligence):	Colonel Oscar W. Koch
G-2 Air:	Colonel H. M. Forde
G-3 (Operations/Training):	Brigadier General Halley G. Maddox
G-4 (Logistics):	Brigadier General Walter J. Muller*
G-5 (Civil Affairs):	Colonel Nicholas W. Campanole; Colonel R. L. Dalfres

ADJUTANT GENERAL:	Colonel Robert E Cummings*
ANTI-AIRCRAFT:	Colonel Frederick R. Chamberlain, Jr; Colonel T. F. Gallagher
ARTILLERY:	Brigadier General Edward T. Williams
CHAPLAIN:	Colonel James H. O'Neill
CHEMICAL WARFARE SECTION:	Colonel Edward C. Wallington
ENGINEERS:	Brigadier General John F. Conklin
FINANCE:	Colonel Charles B. Milliken
HQ COMMANDANT:	Colonel Rufus C. Bratton
INSPECTOR GENERAL:	Colonel Clarence C. Park
JUDGE ADVOCATE GENERAL:	Colonel Charles E. Cheever
MEDICAL SECTION:	Brigadier General Thomas D. Hurley; Colonel T. J. Hartford
ORDNANCE SECTION:	Colonel Thomas H. Nixon*
PROVOST MARSHAL:	Colonel John C. MacDonald; Colonel P. C. Clayton
PUBLIC RELATIONS OFFICER:	Colonel K. A. Hunter; Lieutenant Colonel J. T. Quirk
QUARTERMASTER:	Colonel Everett Busch
SIGNALS:	Colonel Elton F. Hammond*
SPECIAL SERVICES OFFICER:	Lieutenant Colonel Kenneth E. Van Buskirk
TANK DESTROYER:	Brigadier General H. L. Earnest; Colonel L. C. Berry
XIX TACTICAL AIR COMMAND:	
COMMANDER:	Brigadier General O. P. Weyland
COS:	Colonel R. Q. Browne

*All on GSP's Western Task Force HQ for Operation 'Torch' in similar positions as with Third Army. (Source: Appendix 'F' to Patton's *War As I Knew It.*)

While the above is an accurate summary of the staff during the entire operational period, Third Army's After Action Report lists GSP's staff as at 1200 hrs 1 August 1944 as being:

COS:	Major General H. J. Gaffey
DCOS:	Brigadier General H. R. Gay
DCOS (Opns):	Colonel P. D. Harkins
ACOS G-1:	Colonel F. S. Matthews
ACOS G-2:	Colonel O. W. Koch
ACOS G-3:	Colonel H. G. Maddox
ACOS G-4:	Colonel W. J. Muller
ACOS G-5:	Colonel N. W. Campanole
ACOS G-6:	Colonel C. C. Blakeney
AG:	Colonel R. E. Cummings

AAA:	Colonel F. R. Chamberlain
Arty:	Colonel E. T. Williams
BUILD-UP CONTROL ORGANISATION:	Colonel R. F. Perry
CHAPLAIN:	Colonel J. H. O'Neill
CHEMICAL WARFARE:	Colonel E. C. Wallington
ENGINEERS:	Colonel J. F. Conklin
FINANCE:	Colonel C. B. Milliken
HQ COMDT:	Colonel R. S. Bratton
INSPECTOR GENERAL:	Colonel C. C. Park
JUDGE ADVOCATE::	Colonel C. C. E. Cheever
PROVOST MARSHAL:	Colonel J. C. Macdonald
QM:	Colonel E. Busch
SIGNALS:	Colonel E. F. Hammond
SPECIAL SERVICES:	Colonel K. E. Van Buskirk

The Chief of Staff

The most important member of the Staff, he was the Commanding General's right-hand man and in dire emergency might have to take over command until a replacement could be found. Patton was fortunate to have two high-calibre officers as his COS, namely, Major General Hugh J. Gaffey and Brigadier General (later Major General) Hobart R. Gay. Both Hugh Gaffey and 'Hap' Gay had served with GSP before he took over Third Army, Gaffey having been with him at the Desert Training Center, then as Deputy Commander of 2nd Armored Division in North Africa and subsequently as CG of 2nd Armored in Sicily; Gay had been Patton's COS throughout both operations. Nicknamed 'Hap' – short for 'Happy' – Gay epitomised his nickname. He was utterly devoted and completely loyal to Patton. A splendid companion, who loved to hunt and shoot, he was in some people's opinion just too 'dumb loyal' for his own good or GSP's for that matter. Patton had made Gay his Chief of Staff when he took over Third Army, having brought him with him expressly for that purpose. Gay initially served in the appointment from 28 January 1944 until 1 April 1944.

Unfortunately, General Eisenhower was unhappy about the arrangement, and told GSP that, while he would not order him directly to replace Gay, he felt that Gay did not have the necessary presence to represent him at other headquarters or to take over should Patton be killed. Others felt the same way, but it was Ike's objection which most affected GSP and put him in a very difficult situation. 'I owe him [Eisenhower] a great deal,' he wrote in his diary. 'On the other hand, I have paid my way ever since. I am very reluctant to supersede Gay, but it looks to me and to Hughes [General Everett Hughes was Eisenhower's personal representative], and others with whom I have talked, that if I don't, I will be superseded myself, so I will have to make the change.' He decided to make a clean breast of the whole affair and to tell Gay the exact truth, namely that Eisenhower had ordered him to replace his chosen COS. 'Gay was fine,' GSP noted in his diary on 6 March 1944, 'could not have been better. I told him the exact truth, that Ike had ordered me to do it.'

Patton now had to chose between two men to fill the post of COS vacated by Gay. They were Hugh Gaffey and Troy Middleton. Of the two, he preferred Gaffey, as he knew him better, having served with him at the Desert Training Center and in Tunisia. A third possibility was General Geoffrey Keyes, who had been his deputy on Operation 'Torch' and again on Operation 'Husky'. 'If something should happen to make Keyes available, I would take him like a shot,' wrote GSP in his diary, after dining with Eisenhower and discussing the problem. In the end the choice was Gaffey who, although he had no wish to give up command of 2nd Armored Division, cheerfully accepted GSP's request. He said (as GSP records in his diary) that he: 'owed me so much, he would do it, if I can get Bradley to turn him loose'. Gaffey was undoubtedly a staff officer of genius and, like Patton, a tank expert, so he was ideally suited to the post. So it was that HQ Third Army began operations with Major General Hugh Gaffey as its Chief of Staff, and with Brigadier General Hobart Gay as his deputy[1] – GSP had the best of both worlds and must have been secretly delighted with the outcome of this seemingly impossible situation.

At the end of 1944, GSP would have to use Gaffey to replace Major General 'Tiger Jack' Wood as CG of 4th Armored Division, when he was too exhausted to continue in command. General Gay automatically took over and remained as Chief of Staff for the rest of the war. The Chief of Staff's job was an onerous one, but there was never any doubt in anyone's mind as to who was actually in charge. As Colonel Robert Allen puts it in his book *Lucky Forward*: 'The Chief of Staff, Section Chiefs and other senior officers were important. But not all-important. Under Patton, only one man ruled the roost – Patton.'

Chiefs of Staff: Biographies

Hobart R. Gay was born on 16 May in Rockport, Illinois. Graduating from Knox College, Galesburg, Illinois, in 1917 with a Bachelor of Science degree, he was commissioned into the US Cavalry Reserve on 15 August 1917. Two months later, on 26 October, he was commissioned into the Regular Army as a second lieutenant. He joined the 12th Cavalry at Hachita, New Mexico, and five months later was transferred to the 7th Cavalry at Fort Bliss, Texas. In September 1923 he enrolled in the Cavalry School at Fort Riley, Kansas, and, following his graduation in June 1924, remained there for the special advanced equitation course, after which he served at the Cavalry School as an instructor for four years until June 1929. His next posting was to the

Reno Quartermaster Depot and Remount Purchasing and Breeding HQ, Fort Reno, Oklahoma in July 1929. Two years later, in August 1931, he became Acting Officer in Charge of Remount Purchasing and Breeding HQ. In July 1934 he became CO of the Reno QM Depot and of the Purchasing and Breeding HQ.

In 1936, he was appointed Post Quartermaster at Fort Clayton, Panama Canal Zone, where he stayed for two years, returning home in August 1938 to enter the Quartermaster School at Philadelphia, Pa, and graduated the following June. He was then appointed Post QM at Fort Myer, Virginia. He enrolled in the Army Industrial College, Washington DC, in August 1940 and on completing the course was appointed Assistant to the CO, Washington QM Depot. Between February 1941 and February 1942, he was Divisional QM and later CO, 14th QM Bn, 2nd Armd Div and QM Officer, I Armd Corps, Fort Benning, Georgia. In March 1942 he moved with I Armd Corps to the Desert Training Center, Camp Young, California and was serving in that capacity when he became Chief of Staff, HQ I Armd Corps and later Western Task Force, Camp Young, and Camp AP Hill, Virginia.

In November 1942 he took part in Operation 'Torch' , landing at Fedala on 8 November, as Chief of Staff, I Armd Corps. It was here that he was awarded the Silver Star for his outstanding gallantry in going through hostile lines in an attempt to get the commander of the Vichy French troops to cease hostilities. His citation reads: 'The trip involved passages through a zone occupied by hostile troops and penetration of the hostile area as far as the Admiralty in Casablanca, at the time it was being heavily bombed from the air. Colonel Gay was fired on by hostile infantry, but continued boldly forward with utter disregard for his own safety. Colonel Gay's complete calm, boldness and courage made possible the successful completion of the trip and cannot but have greatly impressed hostile troops with the courage of Americans under fire.'

After North Africa he became COS Seventh Army and took part in the amphibious landings in Sicily, then went with GSP as COS Third Army. He remained with Third Army until the end. Post-war, he was COS Fifteenth Army for four months, then CG for one month. For the next twelve months, from February 1946, he held a series of command appointments, the longest being as CG 2nd Constabulary Brigade and Munich Military Community. He retired from the Army on 18 February 1947.

General Gay's US decorations were: DSC, DSM, Legion of Merit with Oak Leaf Cluster, Silver Star with Oak Leaf Cluster, Bronze Star with Oak Leaf Cluster, Air Medal and Army Commendation Ribbon. His foreign decorations were: DSO (Great Britain), Knight of the Legion of Honour, Officer of the Legion of Honour, Croix de Guerre with Palm (France), Fourragère (66th *Régiment d'artillerie d'Afrique*), Ouissam

Alaouite (Morocco), Order of the 4th Army (Fatherland, Class I) (Russia), Order of the White Lion Class II (Czechoslovakia), Commander of the Order of Adolphe of Nassau with Crown, Croix de Guerre with Palm (Luxembourg), Ordre de la Couronne (Commandant avec Palm), Croix de Guerre 1940 with Palm (Belgium).

Hugh Joseph Gaffey was born in Hartford, Connecticut, on 18 November 1895. He attended the University of Pennsylvania and was commissioned in the Field Artillery reserve on 15 August 1917. Promoted to first lieutenant on 19 October 1918, he was commissioned in that rank in the Field Artillery of the Regular Army on 1 July 1920. His first assignment after attending officers' training school in 1917 was to 312th Field Artillery at Camp Meade, Maryland, and in August 1918 he went to France with the 312th. In May 1919 he joined the 12th Field Artillery in Germany, returning to the USA with that regiment to Camp Travis, Texas. In February 1922 he transferred to 15th Fld Arty and then entered the Field Artillery School at Fort Sill, Oklahoma. On graduation he was assigned to 1st Fld Arty at Fort Sill. In July 1926 he became a Professor of Military Science and Tactics at Cornell University, New York, returning to 1st FA in September 1930. He transferred next to 18th FA in January 1935 at Fort Sill, and that August entered the Command and General Staff School at Fort Leavenworth, Kansas. Graduating in June 1936, he was assigned to 68th FA (Mechanised) at Fort Knox, Kentucky, which was the beginning of his service with armour. In March 1937, he became the Assistant Plans and Training Officer of 7th Cavalry Brigade there. In October 1938, they moved to Fort Riley, Kansas, with Gaffey now Intelligence Officer. He remained with the brigade when it was mechanised in November 1938, and in July 1939 returned to Fort Knox as Acting Plans and Training Officer of the 7th Cav Bde (Mech). In January 1940 he joined 19th Fld Arty at Fort Knox.

July 1940 saw him become Assistant to the Plans and Training Officer, G-3, of I Armored Corps at Fort Knox, and in April 1941 he became the Corps Plans and Training Officer. In January 1942 they moved to Fort Benning, Georgia, and that July he was assigned to 2nd Armd Div. In November 1942 he was assigned to duty overseas and in April 1944 designated COS Third Army in the ETO. In December 1944 he was named CG 4th Armd Div.

In June 1943 he was awarded the DSM, the citation reading: 'For exceptionally meritorious service in a position of great responsibility. From March 7 to April 10, 1943, General Gaffey performed the function of COS, II Corps. During this period the active operations of the Corps included the battle of El Guettar and adjacent combats. His courage, energy, foresight, force and technical ability were largely responsible for the outstanding success achieved during these operations.'
(Source of biographical details: US Army Military History Institute).

Composition and Duties of Third Army HQ Staff

As we have seen, below the COS were a number of General Staff Sections (G-1 to G-5 inclusive), plus a larger number of special staff sections, covering such specialised subjects as the fighting arms (artillery, tank destroyers, engineers, etc.), the supporting arms (Ordnance, Quartermaster, etc.) and 'A' matters (discipline, spiritual welfare, entertainment, etc.).

G-1 SECTION (PERSONNEL):

ASSISTANT COS G-1 (Personnel)
EXECUTIVE OFFICER

G-1 Sub-Sections:

ADMINISTRATION: Administrative checking; duty rosters; files and reference material; routing of correspondence.
MISCELLANEOUS: Awards and decorations; graves registration; law and order; mail; morale; Post Exchange (equivalent to British NAAFI services); Red Cross; rewards and punishment; uniform.
PERSONNEL: Appointments; assignments and re-assignments; discharge; leaves; passes; personnel reinforcements; re-classification; rotation.
REPORTS: Daily casualty summaries; statistical information; strength of units; weekly G-1 reports.

As can be seen from this list, the G-1 Section was concerned with all matters to do with the personnel of the command, which included both civilians and prisoners of war. As the section chief, Colonel Frederick S. Matthews, wrote in his 'After Action Report': 'Battles are won by men. The experience of Third US Army has been that sufficient personnel, properly assigned, is the most important factor in the success of any military undertaking. Arms, machines, equipment and supplies supplement and support the soldier; they cannot replace him. The best laid plans are only words on paper or lines on maps until executed by resolute men with determination to fight and the indomitable will to win. It is men who win battles, men who occupy ground, men who are the first concern of all commanders. With this thought paramount the G-1 section has devoted its principal effort to furnishing sufficient qualified personnel when and where needed.'[2]

G-2 SECTION (INTELLIGENCE)

ASSISTANT COS G-2
SPECIAL LIAISON UNIT (direct liaison with higher echelons of command)
EXECUTIVE OFFICER

Main G-2 Sub-Sections:

SITUATION: Collection, production and dissemination of combat intelligence; G-2 situation and work maps; journal and work sheets; intelligence summaries and bulletins and information bulletins; periodic reports; G-2 estimates; target area analyses; liaison visits; research; G-2 briefings; organisation and supervision of War Room; maps.

ADMINISTRATION: G-2 message centre; mimeograph reproduction; general files; transportation; dissemination; personnel and supplies; preparation of monthly 'after action report' required by AR 345105.

AUXILIARY AGENCIES: Supervision, co-ordination and administration of attached auxiliary agencies; allocation through Field Interrogation Detachment of intelligence specialist teams to corps and division headquarters; organisation through Field Interrogation Detachments of the Interrogation of POW teams at Army POW cages; location and control of Military Intelligence Interpreter teams; guidance and supervision of OSS/SI activities; supervision of Psychological Warfare Branch activities; evaluation and dissemination of intelligence reports received from intelligence specialist teams.

SECURITY: Counter-espionage; counter-sabotage; counter-subversion; counter-intelligence directives; military security; intelligence funds; document security; counter-intelligence information; passwords and replies; censorship; security missions; counter-intelligence reference files; counter-intelligence control line; personality files; Allied security liaison.

G-2 AIR: Map and model policies (in conjunction with engineers); collection of enemy information from graphic presentation (including air targets); co-ordination of requests and presentation to Air Force; tactical and photo reconnaissance; night photos; gridded obliques; artillery adjustments; vectographs; photo mosaics; dissemination of air reconnaissance information; co-ordination of Photo Interpretation teams at corps and divisions; liaison between air and ground headquarters.

Minor G-2 Sub-Sections:

(i) under Situation

ORDER OF BATTLE TEAM: Enemy organisation, strength, location, disposition, equipment and tactics.

WAR ROOM: Mapped and graphic information displayed for army commander and staff.[3]

NAVY LIAISON: Maintenance of liaison between army and navy units.

(ii) under Auxiliary Agencies

PSYCHOLOGICAL WARFARE BRANCH: Employment of propaganda by leaflets, loudspeakers and radio to attack enemy morale.

ENEMY DOCUMENTS SECTION: Seizure, examination, analysis and disposal of captured enemy documents.

OFFICE OF STRATEGIC STUDIES/SECRET INTELLIGENCE: Collection of enemy information through OSS services.

FIELD INTERROGATION DETACHMENT: Co-ordination and supervision of IPW and MII teams under subordinate commanders; organisation and super-

vision of interrogation of army POW cages.
INTERROGATION OF POW TEAMS (IPW): Collection and preparation of information from captured enemy personnel.
MILITARY INTELLIGENCE INTERPRETER TEAMS (MII): Collection of intelligence information by interrogation of refugees and civilians of country in which army is operating.
EVASION AND ESCAPE UNITS: Identification and interrogation of Allied evaders and escapers and instruction of troops on escape methods.
(iii) under Security
COUNTER-INTELLIGENCE CORPS: Headquarters security; counter-intelligence; known and suspected enemy agents; security of army installations.
OFFICE OF STRATEGIC SERVICES/SPECIAL COUNTER-INTELLIGENCE: Counter-intelligence liaison – higher headquarters.
(iv) under G-2 AIR
PHOTO CENTRE (at airfield or reconnaissance group): Photo interpretation; reports; photo file and library; preparation of defence traces for production of collated maps; distribution of photos, daily reports and defence traces.
ATTACHED PHOTO INTERPRETATION TEAMS
AIR RECCE COORD OFFICERS: Duty with Tac Air Command. Presentation of requests received from G-2 Air to Air Force for action; assistance in briefing of TAC staff on enemy situation; co-operation with TAC target section; dissemination of recce results to army units.
GROUND LIAISON OFFICERS: Duty recce group and squadrons. Briefing and interrogation of pilots for army missions; dissemination of results of recce to ARCO; liaison between ground and Air Force re current ground situation.

Colonel Oscar W. Koch, G-2 section head, writes in *Third Army's After Action Report* that the main task of his section was to ensure a smooth working military intelligence organisation for the accurate and rapid collection, production and distribution of effective Combat Intelligence and Counter-Intelligence. In *Lucky Forward,* Colonel Robert Allen describes Koch as being 'brilliant, quiet-spoken and hard-working'. Koch was commissioned in the Regular Cavalry from the Wisconsin National Guard for overseas service in the Great War. He translated a number of important foreign military volumes and wrote a notable study on the Army's first armoured-car manoeuvres. Patton brought him to 2nd Armored Division soon after the illustrious 'Hell on Wheels' was organised, and took him to Africa as Chief of Staff of one of the Task Forces. Later he made him his G-2. Allen again: 'Koch is the greatest G-2 in the US Army. His record is without equal in every phase of intelligence.... Koch was the spark plug of HQ Third Army. Because of his exceptional abilities, unfailing effectiveness and the wide range of G-2 activities, he was constantly being tossed the ball. Patton and the COS were always assigning him tasks outside his sectional duties.' Another military historian of the period (Major General H. Essame) described the scholarly, self-effacing incredibly industrious Koch, as being, 'in the field of intelligence, the most penetrating brain in the American Army'.[4] Perhaps the most important opinion of his capabilities was GSP's, who merely said: 'Oscar Koch is the best damned intelligence officer in any United States Army Command!'

G-3 SECTION (OPERATIONS AND TRAINING)

ASSISTANT COS G-3
EXECUTIVE OFFICER

G-3 Sub-Sections:

OPERATIONS: Outline plans, directives and orders; G-3 periodic reports; situation reports; situation maps; signal communications; co-ordination; operational diary; War Room maintenance (in conjunction with G-2).
AIR: Air-Ground planning, training and liaison; supervision of AF liaison squadron; Tac Photo Recce (in conjunction with G-2); situation map records of air activities; ground targets – recommendations and priorities.
TROOP MOVEMENTS: Unit assignments and attachments; troop lists/Order of Battle; unit re-organisation and activation; locations of units; unit movement orders and co-ordination of unit movements.
ADMINISTRATION: Message recording and distribution; journal maintenance; personnel rosters; typing and filing; offices and field security; office supplies; section movement and organic transport; field/office section arrangement.
TRAINING, HISTORICAL AND MISCELLANEOUS: Training directives and programmes; procurement and co-ordination; army schools organisation; training facilities; special training; historical/operational records; equipment studies; dissemination of War Department information; supervision of orientation activities; army educational programme – planning, administration and supervision.
LIAISON AND ACCOMMODATION: Liaison with Corps and adjacent higher echelons; co-ordination and dissemination of current information; situation maps; covered accommodation; unit arrival accommodation.
PASSIVE AIR DEFENCE: Advice to units on planning, operations and training; Civil Affairs co-ordination; inspection of accommodation; establishment of a control centre (when necessary).
SPECIAL FORCES DETACHMENT: Co-ordination and control of Resistance forces; HQ liaison.

Also linked to G-3 was the Army Information Service whose job it was to liaise with front line units in order to furnish latest tactical information to Army HQ in the most expeditious manner.

Colonel Halley G. Maddox, a wiry and imperturbable West Pointer, was, according to Colonel Allen, 'a high powered and smoothly functioning G-3. He always took everything in his stride, coolly and efficiently.'

G-4 SECTION (SUPPLY)

ASSISTANT COS G-4
LIAISON (daily contact with corps and divisions; check of army supply points; reception of new units; contacts with higher echelons)
EXECUTIVE OFFICER (Supervision and co-ordination of work of sub-sections; execution of policies of Section chief)

G-4 Sub-Sections:

ADMINISTRATION: Personnel; publications; records and reports; internal security; distribution of orders; correspondence control; Section supply; reproduction.
SUPPLY AND STATISTICS: Supply levels; procurement and distribution; allocations; unit equipping; equipment maintenance; salvage; captured material; supply to attached Allied units; supply summaries and periodic reports.
FISCAL: Procurement policies and procedures: general supplies, services and facilities; real estate and billets; allocation of civilian labour between services; sub-allotment of funds; exploitation of local resources; appointment of purchasing and contracting personnel.
OPERATIONS: Movement of service units; G-4 situation map; compilation of administrative orders; co-ordination of lines of communication; plans Army's rear boundaries; accommodation for units in Army services.
TRANSPORTATION: Highway movements; traffic control; operation of transport units; rail movements; railhead regulation.

Writing in *Third Army's After Action Report*, Brigadier General Walter J. 'Maud' Muller said that from the planning phase in the UK and throughout the operations in Europe his section had been 'confronted with all of the complex problems supply, transportation and evacuation of a modern army. Standard procedures were often followed but scrapped or altered without hesitation if proven inadequate. Many situations were entirely new and procedures were developed to meet them. As operations through France progressed with increasing speed and supply lines turned both east and west, then north and south, and lengthened by the hour, the problems of supplying the Army assumed unprecedented proportions. All available means of transportation – motor, rail, air and water – were all utilised. Ammunition and gasoline were strictly rationed. Captured supplies were exploited to the fullest. A rail line was reconstructed and operated by the Army. In the formulation of plans and policies, consideration was given to the overall picture, but our primary objective, always was to provide the frontline soldier with the essential materials for combat.'

'Maud Muller was the gettingest G-4 in the ETO,' comments Colonel Allen in *Lucky Forward*. 'If it was to be got, he got it – and often when it wasn't. Stocky, driving and razor-tongued, Muller operated on a fixed policy of keeping several steps ahead of Patton on supplies. It was a very sound rule. It saved Muller a lot of headaches and kept Third Army happy and potent.

'Patton never asked Muller how and where he got his supplies and equipment and the latter never bothered Patton with needless details. In Third Army this was considered a very sound arrangement and everyone was immensely proud of Muller's unfailing effectiveness.' In essence, he was the bane of SHAEF and higher headquarters, yet the firm friend of the fighting troops, some going so far as to call him the ablest Quartermaster since Moses!

G-5 SECTION (CIVIL AFFAIRS)

ASSISTANT COS G-5
EXECUTIVE OFFICER

G-5 Sub-Sections:

PERSONNEL AND ADMINISTRATION: Internal arrangement of administration and supply; selection and requisition of personnel; maintenance of records; co-ordination with Plans and Operations Section for securing, reinforcing and replacing personnel.

INTELLIGENCE: Collection of information in uncovered areas; dissemination of information to higher and lower units; compilation of information for direction of policy; control of Top Secret documents and enforcement of security; publicity and history; public works and utilities; communications.

PLANS AND OPERATIONS: Movement and employment of Civil Affairs troops; training preparations and inspections; refugees and Displaced Persons; Civil Affairs operational map and location list.

RELIEF AND SUPPLY: Relief supplies; economics (labour, agriculture and local resources); transportation; relief agencies.

GOVERNMENT AFFAIRS: Political activities; legal affairs; public health and sanitation; fiscal affairs; public safety; arts and monuments.

The G-5 Section was sometimes not referred to as a G section but just called 'Civil Affairs'. G-5 section had only been established in the US Army since the early 1940s, when it was realised that a special section would be needed to control the civilian population in the country where the Army was fighting. Colonel Roy L. Dalferes, the second incumbent of the post of Assistant COS G-5, wrote in Third Army's After Action Report: 'The mission of this Section was to further military objectives and this was achieved by a thorough control of the civil population and an employment of civilian resources in the common aim of destroying the enemy. Success in accomplishing this mission is the result of complete co-operation of all sections of the Army, its corps and divisions, the whole-hearted assistance of the peoples of the liberated countries and the strict enforcement of regulations prescribed for Military Government in Germany.'

SPECIAL STAFF SECTIONS AND DUTIES

ADJUTANT GENERAL SECTION

Adjutant General
Executive Officer

Sub-Sections:

Miscellaneous Division: ***Cables Section*** – processing of all incoming teletype and radio messages, dispatch of all outgoing electrically transmitted messages. ***Mail and Records Section*** – all permanent records, receipts, routes and preparing of all correspondence for dispatch. ***Publications Section*** – reproduction and assembly of all directives, orders, circulars, bulletins and memoranda; maintenance of stock of current directives, requisitions for publications and blank forms, WD and theatre directives, issue of WD and AGO forms. ***Distribution Section*** – dispatch of all correspondence and publications; maintenance of inter-office messenger service; determination of distribution.

Executive Division: ***Casualty Section*** – battle casualty reports, individual battle and non-battle casualty histories, casualty statistics; reports of burial, reports of stragglers, missing or missing in action personnel; identity of unknown soldiers; hospital admissions and dispositions; reports, letters of inquiry concerning casualties, letters of condolence. ***Machine Records Unit***[5] – officers and enlisted men's status file, strength reports, AWOL reports, battle casualty cards and reports, patients' location cards, non-battle casualty cards, personnel survey reports, weekly station list. ***Postal Section*** – supervision of postal service, mail handling procedures, methods and facilities; inspections and investigations; location of general assignment APOs, location recommendations of postal regulation section; assignment of non-divisional units to APOs; transportation arrangements for mail, assistance with civilian postal service. ***Top Secret Section*** – all incoming or outgoing top secret documents; receipt file and top secret journal, cardex file showing location of top secret documents; downgrading of documents; periodic inventory of top secret documents.

Personnel Division: ***Classification Section*** – classification and assignment procedures; personnel replacement (reinforcement) requisitions, replacement statistics; inventory of specialists; balance of units surpluses and shortages; scarce categories of skill, administration of tests, interview and preparation of qualification cards. ***Officers' Section*** – transfers, appointments and promotions, for permission to marry, rotation, efficiency reports; appointments, promotions and terminations of warrant officers; details, assignments and resignations of officers, identification cards; re-classification of officers; rosters. ***Enlisted Men's Section*** – transfers, discharges, applications for permission to marry; pay and allowances; leave and passes; rotation, allotments, naturalisation, changes of name, birth dates. ***Morning Report Section*** – maintenance of morning report for Third Army HQ.

Colonel R. E. Cummings wrote in his portion of *Third Army's After Action Report* that the main activities had concerned his Casualty Sub-section, the Machine Records Unit and the Army Postal Service, while all the rest had functioned throughout the operation 'both in method and tempo, in a manner most similar to the routine functioning of these activities in non-operational situations'.

ANTI-AIRCRAFT ARTILLERY SECTION

AA Officer
Executive Officer

Sub-Sections:

AA1: Administration; correspondence; requests for personnel; requisitions; citations; files.
AA2: Unit report analysis; weekly intelligence reports; daily sitreps; communications; radar; claims (damaged/destroyed); aircraft recognition.
AA3: Operations directives; missions; defence priority lists; situation maps; attachments; journal; unit locations; Order of Battle; history.
AA4: Supply; ammunition; matériel; transportation.
Training: Attached instruction teams.

Charged with the defence of ground installations, the AA officer, Colonel F. R. Chamberlain, Jr, explains that his units were mainly defending lines of communications, supply points and vital areas in both the Army and Corps areas. It is of considerable interest that the Third Army AA shot down a staggering total of 1,648 enemy aircraft (1,084 destroyed and 564 probably destroyed) during their period of operations.

ARTILLERY SECTION

Artillery Officer
Executive Officer

Sub-Sections:

Sub-Section 2: Collection, evaluation and dissemination of artillery intelligence; co-ordination of supply of maps and aerial photography to included gridded obliques; co-ordination of counter-battery procedure and activities.

SUB-SECTION 3: Training; operations; troop movements; Arty/R; communications; liaison.
SUB-SECTION 1 – 4: Ammunition; supply; maintenance; personnel.
SUB-SECTION ARTILLERY–AIR: Training; operations; supply and maintenance; personnel.
SUB-SECTION CHIEF CLERK: Clerical; message centre; drafting.

Brigadier General Edward T. 'Molly' Williams wrote in the *After Action Report*: 'Third US Army and the artillery thereof, has operated over many kinds of terrain under strikingly diversified climatic conditions.... There have been swift pursuits of fleeing enemy, repeated assaults of river lines great and small, assaults of defensive positions ranging from hasty field fortifications to the fortress city of Metz and the redoubts of the Siegfried Line. There have been resolute unyielding defenses against counterattacks ranging from a handful of infantry with a tank or two to that of an Army Group including a Panzer Army. Against all these conditions the infantry and tankmen of Third Army have built a record of magnificent success. To this record the artillerymen with the Army have contributed unceasingly and materially. They have consistently received the one real reward of the artilleryman, the appreciation of the supported troops expressed in the words "well done".'

CHAPLAIN SECTION

CHAPLAIN: Adviser to CG on matters pertaining to chaplains, their activities and religious work in Third Army. Technical supervision and inspection of chaplains and their work as religious leaders in subordinate units within the limits prescribed by the CG. To ensure a maximum of spiritual guidance and instruction for military personnel in the Third Army. Transfer and relief of chaplains in co-operation with G-1.
EXECUTIVE ASSISTANT: Assists the Chaplain Third Army. Supervision of plans and training, and PR sections. Supervision and direction of the work of chaplains when the Army Chaplain is absent. Provides religious services for military personnel as required. Liaison with clergy, churches and welfare.
ADMINISTRATIVE ASSISTANT: Assists the Chaplain and Executive Assistant. Supervises personnel, funds, equipment and supplies. Publishes church bulletins and programmes for special observance days for all groups as required. Arranges itinerary of inspection trips to include schedule overlay and advance notification letters.
TEN SUB-SECTIONS: Plans and training; public relations; graves registration; inspections; conferences; correspondence; religious and pastoral (personal); personnel; funds; equipment and supplies.

It was Colonel James H. O'Neill whom Patton ordered to produce a 'prayer for fine weather' in mid-December 1944, so that Third Army could get on with killing the enemy. Colonel Paul Harkins, then Deputy COS, recalled the incident: 'On or about 14 December 1944, Gen Patton called Chaplain O'Neill and myself into his office in Third

Headquarters at Nancy. The conversation went something like this:

GEN PATTON: 'Chaplain, I want you to publish a prayer for good weather. I'm tired of these soldiers having to fight mud and floods as well as Germans. See if we can't get God to work on our side.'

CHAPLAIN O'NEILL: 'Sir, it's going to take a pretty thick rug for that kind of praying.'

GEN PATTON: 'I don't care if it takes a flying carpet. I want the praying done.'

CHAPLAIN O'NEILL: 'Yes sir. May I say, General, that it usually isn't a customary thing among men of my profession to pray for clear weather to kill fellow men.'

GEN PATTON: 'Chaplain, are you teaching me theology or are you the Chaplain of the Third Army? I want a prayer.'

CHAPLAIN O'NEILL: 'Yes sir.'

'Outside the chaplain said: "Whew, that's a tough one! What do you think he wants?" It was perfectly clear to me. The General wanted a prayer – he wanted one right now – and he wanted it published to the Command.

'The Army Engineer was called in, and we finally decided that our field topographical company could print the prayer on a small-sized card, making enough copies for distribution to the army. It being near Christmas, we also decided to ask Gen Patton to include a Christmas greeting to the troops on the same card with the prayer. The General agreed, wrote a short greeting, and the card was made up, published and distributed to the troops on the 22nd of December.

'Whether it was the help of the Divine guidance asked for in the prayer or just the normal course of human events, we never knew; at any rate on the 23rd, the day after the prayer was issued, the weather cleared and remained perfect for about six days. Enough to allow the Allies to break the backbone of the Von Rundstedt offensive and turn a temporary setback into a crushing defeat for the enemy.'

Patton was delighted, remarking to Harkins that 'O'Neill sure did some potent praying' and ordering him to fetch the Chaplain so that he could pin a medal on him. The weather was still clear when O'Neill arrived the next day. Patton came from behind his desk, with his hand outstretched. 'Chaplain,' he smiled, 'you're the most popular man in this Headquarters. You sure stand in good with the Lord and soldiers.' With that, GSP pinned a Bronze Star on Chaplain O'Neill, while his Army got back to the business of killing Germans, with clear weather for battle! (The card is illustrated in the picture section.)

CHEMICAL WARFARE SERVICE SECTION

CHEMICAL OFFICER: Adviser to the CG and staff on Chemical Warfare. Planning and supervision of chemical operations; supervision of protective training; supply of CW protective material and ammunition.

Three Sub-Sections:

INTELLIGENCE AND TECHNICAL SUB-SECTION: Combat and technical intelligence; intelligence maps and reports; study of transmission of information on CW developments.

OPERATIONS AND TRAINING SUB-SECTION: Planning, supervision and co-ordination of chemical operations; operations maps and reports; chemical defence orders and training schools.

ADMINISTRATION AND SUPPLY SUB-SECTION: ***Executive*** – Administration – office supervision, mail, records, statistics and publications. Supply – protective items and CWS ammunition supply, maintenance and salvage of CWS material, requisitions and reports.

Colonel E. C. Wallington, the Chemical Officer, explained in the After Action Report how Chemical Mortar battalions had participated in all major operations, employing both HE and smoke in support of forward elements, commenting that the use of chemical smoke generator companies during river crossings had reached a new high during the campaign.

ENGINEER SECTION

ARMY ENGINEER
EXECUTIVE OFFICER

Sub-Sections:

ADMINISTRATION: Operated the Section message centre; maintained the correspondence files; consolidated daily logs of the several sub-sections and incorporated them into the Section log; co-ordinated through G-1 all administrative personnel actions affecting engineering troops with the army, including allotment of school quotas; co-ordinated through HQ Commandant all details concerning local defence, movement, office supply and operation of the office establishment of the Engineer Section. Co-ordinated through HQ Commandant all matters of military discipline affecting the Engineer Section; co-ordinated through Adjutant General the distribution of Engineer technical publications; supervised the use of transportation allotted to the Engineer Section; performed all functions of an administrative nature necessary to the comfort and orderly conduct of the Section.

INTELLIGENCE: Collected, evaluated and disseminated Engineer intelligence pursuant to the policies established by the Army Engineer or prescribed by higher authority; arranged through G-2 for the collection of Engineer intelligence from Army intelligence agencies; maintained a reference library of technical, geographical and geological data pertinent to present or prospective operations; maintained maps to show current status of engineer intelligence situation; supervised and controlled operations of Engineer Technical Intelligence Teams assigned to Army Headquarters; designed, in conjunction with other sub-section chiefs, Engineer intelligence reporting devices and procedures to ensure complete coverage, by recce agencies, of data essential to Engineer operations and initiated their promulgation to units concerned.

OPERATIONS AND TRAINING: Outlined training objectives and prescribed standards of technical proficiency to be attained by all Engineer troop units with the Army; prepared plans for the disposition of Army Engineer Troops, co-ordinated with G-3 if such plans affected tactical displacement, and with G-4 if they affected troop movements; prescribed the nature and scope and supervised the training undertaken by Army Engineer troop units; co-ordinated through the Administrative Officer the distribution of training publications; conducted training inspections and tested Engineer troop units with the army; kept the Engineer informed of current Engineer troop dispositions by maintaining the Engineer Troop dispositions map; drafted the Engineer paragraphs and Engineer annexes to Field Orders.

SUPPLY: Computed Class II Engineer requirements for the Army; assembled, evaluated and consolidated all Engineer supply requirements, initiated the procurement and follow up to ensure their delivery in the desired quantities, at the proper places and on time; co-ordinated through G-4 preparation of the Engineer supply plan and drafted Engineer paragraphs and annexes to Administrative Orders; took all necessary actions to effect the Engineer Supply Plan; maintained stock records of Engineer items of supply and kept Engineer informed of current status of Engineer supply; prepared the Engineer Equipment Maintenance Plan for the Army and co-ordinated through Engineer Operations Officer the disposition of Engineer Maintenance Companies with the Army.

TECHNICAL: Prepared estimates of construction requirements of the Army; translated them into phased bills of materials and labour requirements, then transmitted to Supply Officer and Operations Officer, respectively, for procurement; drew plans and specifications for specific construction projects as directed by Army Engineer; developed plans for the construction, repair, maintenance and operation of utilities necessary for the functioning of the Army; prescribed standards of construction, maintenance and operational tasks charged to agencies, other than Engineer Troop units, operating under the direct control of the Army Engineer; inspected for technical efficiency the execution of Engineer operational tasks by Engineer Troop Units with the Army; collected detailed engineering data and prepared engineering plans pertaining to: fortifications, minefields and barriers, demolitions, assault of fortified zones, camouflage, floating bridges and water supply; reconnoitred available road net and recommended action necessary fully to exploit its capacity with the minimum attendant maintenance; maintained schedules, progress charts and operations maps to reflect current status of all construction, maintenance and utility operations under supervision of the sub-section; acted as consulting agency for

Army on technical engineering; discharged all functions pertaining to the acquisition and disposal of Real Estate delegated to the Engineer by Higher Authority.

TOPOGRAPHIC: Planned and supervised procurement, production, storage and distribution of maps, map substitutes, photographs, charts and models for the Army; co-ordinated the survey activities of the Corps Topographic Companies and the Army Topographic Battalion to the end that the survey requirements of the Army as a whole were best satisfied; worked in close liaison with the Army Artillery Officer in formulating survey plans so that full utilisation would be made of the combined survey means available to the Army; prepared, subject to G-2 approval, the Army Map Plan as an appendix to Field or Administrative Orders; supplied the reproduction needs of Army HQ; maintained records affecting accuracy of maps and survey control in current use and took immediate action to disseminate corrections to affected unit headquarters.

The Army Engineer was initially Colonel David H. Tulley, ex-West Point wrestling champion, whom Colonel Robert Allen remembers as being a 'human dynamo' in action and whose invariable response to any demand was 'Can do!' He was supported by Lieutenant Colonel Daniel Kennedy – one of the greatest map experts in the USA – and Lieutenant Colonel Robert J. Foley, a bridge-building wizard. Later, Tulley handed over to Brigadier John F. Conklin, who wrote in the After Action Report that the largest single engineering work done was bridging – which covered both floating and fixed bridges. Other major tasks undertaken included: breaching enemy obstacles, locating and removing mines, assault river crossings, road maintenance and construction, construction of PoW enclosures, rehabilitation of damaged billets and hospitals, water supply, camouflage, fire-fighting, mapping and many other engineering tasks.

FINANCE SECTION

FINANCE OFFICER
ADMINISTRATIVE FISCAL OFFICER
DISBURSING OFFICER AND DEPUTY DISBURSING OFFICER
CHIEF CLERK

Sub-Sections:

ADMINISTRATIVE AND FISCAL: fiscal and report; filing, distribution, stenographic.

DISBURSING: commercial accounts; pay and allowances; accounting and cashier.

The Branch had the mission of disbursing and accounting for all of Third Army's funds. It paid the salaries and any amounts due for Army purchases.

HEADQUARTERS COMMANDANT SECTION

HEADQUARTERS COMMANDANT
CO SPECIAL TROOPS
EXECUTIVE OFFICER

Sub-Sections:

HQ COMMANDANT'S OFFICE: Planning and training; mess functioning (officers and enlisted men); supply; billeting (selection of exact sites for Army HQ for both forward and rear echelons, allocation of office, garage and storage space); purchasing and contracting (requisition of covered accommodation and furniture for all troops and attached troops; quartering of all officers, enlisted men and visitors); utilities (water, electricity); automotive and transportation.

HQ SPECIAL TROOPS: Adjutant (maintenance of records for HQ personnel, discipline including summary and special courts-martial); Special Service operations; Post Exchange (including PX, barbers' shops, tailoring and dry cleaning); Surgeon (operation of aid stations); HQ Company (furnishing personnel for messes, supply room, motor pool, APO 403, orderlies, police, fatigues, firemen for boilers and furnaces); Band (employment of 61st AGF Band).

It was this section that was responsible for the smooth running of Third Army's HQ unit. It was a difficult and onerous task for which little source material was initially available to assist the Commandant to visualise the requirements and arrange for their fulfilment.

INSPECTOR GENERAL SECTION

INSPECTOR GENERAL: Responsible for all work of the section and all action papers processed by them. Reviewed all reports of investigations and inspection reports. Conducted investigations and inspections. responsible for replacing inspectors general of subordinate units.

EXECUTIVE OFFICER: Assisted the Army Inspector General. Conducts investigations and inspections. Supervised Section administration.

Three Sub-Sections:

INVESTIGATIONS SUB-SECTION: Completed investigations and prepared thorough and complete reports.

INSPECTION SUB-SECTION: Inspected all types of Army unit and any or all phases of their activities as ordered and prepared reports showing deficiencies and irregularities noted.

ADMINISTRATIVE SUB-SECTION: Executed all reports issued by the Army Inspector General and Sub-sections; maintained complete indexed Army regulations, War Department and ETO circulars, filing of records and reports and administration of the section.

Colonel C. C. Park, the Inspector General, says in the After Action Report that the main task of the Inspector General was to promote the efficient administration of the command.

JUDGE ADVOCATE SECTION

JUDGE ADVOCATE

EXECUTIVE BRANCH: Administration; personnel; processing claims; maintenance of legal library.
WAR CRIMINALS BRANCH: Investigation of charges; preparation of reports; trials by Military Commissions; liaison with all Sections concerned.
LEGAL ASSISTANCE BRANCH: Advising military personnel on all civil and military matters; preparation of wills, powers of attorney and other legal papers.
MILITARY JUSTICE BRANCH: Processing charges and actions under AW 104; trials by general court-martial; review of records of trials; general supervision of military justice within Army.
MILITARY AFFAIRS BRANCH: Legal advice to Commanding General and Staff.

MEDICAL SECTION

SURGEON MEDICAL CORPS
EXECUTIVE OFFICER
LIAISON MEDICAL OFFICER (attached – for liaison with 12th Army Group on all medical matters)

Sub-Sections:

ADMINISTRATION AND PERSONNEL: Medical Section Message Centre. Maintenance of Section files, classified documents and all outgoing correspondence; co-ordination with G-1 and other staff Sections regarding transfers, temporary duty, and all other matters relating to Medical Department personnel, including promotion of officers; advice to subordinate medical units relative to personnel and administrative matters; responsible for personnel and administration within the Medical Section.
PREVENTIVE MEDICINE: Prevention and control of disease and injury through:

1. Investigation and recommendations regarding all epidemiological problems.
2. Recommendations on portability of all water supplies for Army, including that contaminated by chemical and other agents.
3. Recommendations of all technical matters pertaining to sewage and waste disposal within Army.
4. Evaluation and dissemination of information relating to Medical Intelligence.
5. Correlation of civilian and army Venereal Disease problems and recommendations and institution of corrective measures.

Special investigations for Surgeon and advice on all public health matters in occupied territory; technical supervision of Army Medical Laboratory; processing and supervision of all monthly sanitary reports, VD reports, and medical statistical reports from subordinate units; maintenance of weekly medical statistical charts and consolidation of same monthly and yearly.

OPERATIONS AND TRAINING: Operational planning for the medical service; evacuation within Army Zone, including air evacuation and co-ordination of evacuation from Army to Com Zone installations; hospitalisation within Army; training of medical units and other units of the Army on medical matters; inspection of medical units in the Army Zone, including detachments, with regard to personnel, their technical knowledge, station set-up, care of patients, sanitation and medical service rendered and received; initiation of reinforcement and/or replacement of medical services where needed, including Corps and Divisions; maintenance of operations map and admin records in connection with hospitalisation, evacuation, location of medical units and other operational matters.

SUPPLY AND FINANCE: Responsible for all matters relative to policies concerning medical supply and finance within the Army. Constant liaison with combat troops, Regulating Stations, Com Zone Depots and Civil Affairs agencies, in order to determine status and serviceability of medical supplies available. Technical supervision of two Army Medical Depot Companies. Purchasing and Contracting Officer (Medical) for purchase of medical supplies from local sources. Inspection of captured enemy medical equipment and supplies to determine the advisability of reissue. Edited requisitions for controlled items of medical supplies and requests for equipment in excess of Tables of Equipment.

CONSULTANT: All matters relative to technical training. Qualifications, capabilities and performance of personnel assigned or attached to surgical, medical, neuropsychiatric and nursing services to ensure that all technique involved was in accordance with modern accepted principles of practice. Inspection and supervision of nursing service and recommendations for policies involving standardisation and improvement of nursing service within Army, as well as all matters pertaining to general welfare and distribution of nurses (female) within Army. Co-ordination with Army Medical Supply Officer relative to requirements for surgical supplies, drugs and biological products for use within Army. Maintained close liaison with G-5 Section and promulgation of measures for treatment of civilians with contagious diseases. Co-ordinated evacuation, care and treatment of chemical warfare casualties within Army.

DENTAL: All matters relative to technical training, qualifications, capabilities, performance and distribution of personnel assigned or attached to Army Dental Service. Inspection and supervision of dental service in order to assure:

1. That all dental technique involved was in accordance with modern accepted principles and practice.
2. Proper use and disposition of all dental teams.
3. Compliance with correct dental administration procedures and submission of required dental records.

Preparation of consolidated monthly dental records. Maintenance of information relative to status of dental care of all units.
VETERINARY: Inspection of food at, and sanitary supervision of, all Class I rail truck-heads and other ration breakdown points within entire Army. Sanitary inspection, instruction and supervision of all units' messes of Army and Corps units (and Divisions) including cleanliness of personnel and utensils, reception and storage of rations, preparation and serving of food and proper kitchen waste disposal. Instruction and supervision of all units in the preparation of dehydrated food and special Army rations.

The major effort of the Medical Section was to save lives, conserve military strength and ensure the earliest possible return to duty of all casualties. This required prompt provision of medical attention and surgery in forward areas, coincident with speedy and efficient evacuation to Army hospitals, where more adequate facilities were available. This led to one of the lowest mortality rates achieved by the Medical Service of any Army in military history.

ORDNANCE SECTION

ARMY ORDNANCE OFFICER
ASSISTANT ORDNANCE OFFICER

Sub-Sections:

ADMINISTRATION: Received, dispatched, circulated and filed all correspondence and official documents from, to and within the Ordnance Section. Maintained personnel records, including promotions, transfers, awards and decorations.
OPERATIONS: Prepared daily Ordnance Station List. Maintained Ordnance operational map and Army troop lists. Prepared abstracts for Administrative Orders. Prepared daily report of captured, destroyed and lost material.
SUPPLY: Supervised and co-ordinated procurement and distribution of all Ordnance Class II and IV supplies to troops of the Army. Contracted for procurement of standardised equipment.
MAINTENANCE: Administrative supervision of activities in Ordnance maintenance units. Developed new Ordnance ideas. Contracted for and aided in local manufacture of new Ordnance equipment.
AMMUNITION: Responsible for all administrative functions of Class V* supply in the field. Procurement of allocations and proper distribution of ammunition to using units.
69TH ORDNANCE GROUP: Combat Troop Support. Major Equipment Reclamation. Replacement Parts/Assembly. Supplies. Supervision of subordinate battalions.
70TH ORDNANCE GROUP: Major Equipment Supply. Major Equipment Replacement. Major Equipment Maintenance, Reclamation and Evacuation. Supervision of subordinate battalions.

82ND ORDNANCE GROUP: Ammunition supply. Supervision of subordinate battalions.
(*The Ordnance section was responsible for obtaining and distributing weapons and ammunition, which were coded as Class V Supply. It was also involved in improving older weapons and developing new ones.)

PROVOST MARSHAL SECTION

PROVOST MARSHAL (PM): adviser to CG and Staff on all matters pertaining to Military Police (MP) and PM activities
EXECUTIVE OFFICER: supervisor of PM Office

Sub-Sections:

ADMINISTRATION: Correspondence and reports. Maintenance of files and records. Running message centre. Policies and statistics.
INVESTIGATION: Investigated reported crime. Apprehended offenders. Prepared crime reports. Liaised with G-4, Transportation, G-3, Engineers and Ordnance Sections. Completed investigation reports and submitted to higher and lower headquarters.
TRAFFIC: Traffic control in Army area. Established traffic policies. Liaised with other Sections (*see* Investigation). Reconnoitred road nets. Controlled convoy movements. Liaised with civil agencies.
MAINTENANCE OF LAW AND ORDER
LAW ENFORCEMENT: Apprehended and controlled AWOL and stragglers. Liaised with other Sections (*see* Investigation). Disciplinary Reports. Supervised and maintained Army General Prisoner Stockade. Supervised and operated Army Summary Courts. Liaised with civilian agencies.
PRISONERS OF WAR (PoW): PoW control. Controlled and ran internment camps; controlled ex-Allied PoW in camps overrun by Army.
DEFENCE: ***Lines of Communication*** – supervised, controlled and guarded vital installations in the Army Area (highway bridges, railroad bridges, signal centres, etc.). ***Signal Communications*** – operated MP traffic and Lines of Communications road net. ***Command Pos***t – prepared and maintained current plans for the internal security and defence of the CP, maintained emergency striking force to repel enemy attack.

PUBLIC RELATIONS SECTION*

PUBLIC RELATIONS OFFICER
CORRESPONDENTS: copy and pictures for newspapers, radio networks and wire services

Sub Sections:

CAMP COMMANDANT: Housekeeping, movement, supply, etc. of Press Camp. Administration – maintenance of records, supply and procurement. Service Group – transportation, mess and housekeeping of Press Camp.

PRESS: News dissemination from Army channels, assistance to Press correspondents. Copy Room – copy control to censors and transmission agencies.
PHOTO: Pictorial coverage within Army, and assistance to photographers.
RADIO: Radio material production within Army, and assistance to radio correspondents.
INFORMATION: Operation of Press Camp War Room.
PRESS CENSORS: Responsible for security censorship of all copy originating at Army level.
COMMUNICATIONS PLATOON: 399 Radio Operator and Teleprinter to other headquarters, Paris and London.
RADIO MACKAY: Continuous wave and phone transmission of copy direct to USA.
(*This Section was sometimes known as the G-6 Section.)

QUARTERMASTER SECTION
QUARTERMASTER
EXECUTIVE OFFICER
The QM Section was responsible for the provision of all the basic supplies needed to fight a war (except Class V [ammunition] which was an Ordnance responsibility). These were:
CLASS I: All items such as rations and free Post Exchange items that were used up at a regular rate.
CLASS II: Items issued to units or individuals such as clothing, Post Exchange sales items and Red Cross supplies.
CLASS III: Items such as all POL products and solid fuel.
CLASS IV: Miscellaneous items not covered elsewhere.

Sub-Sections:
ADMINISTRATION: Purchasing and Contracting activities. Personnel and administrative matters for the QM Section.
GRAVES REGISTRATION: Evacuation from divisional collecting points. Identification and burial of all Allied and enemy dead. Operation of all cemeteries and other Army Graves Registration activities.
FIELD SERVICE: Supervision of all QM troop units through Group and Battalion commanders. Operation and assignment of QM labour units. Operation of laundries, fumigation and bath units. Salvage and equipment repair. Collection and disposal of captured enemy supplies.
OPERATIONS: Regulation of movement of supplies to Army QM supply installations.

SIGNAL SECTION
SIGNAL OFFICER
EXECUTIVE OFFICER
HEADQUARTERS

Supervision and co-ordination of all activities of the Signal Section staff, Army Signal troops, Signal Section staffs and troops of subordinate echelons.

Sub-Sections:

ADMINISTRATION AND PERSONNEL: Maintained signal files. Procured and assigned reinforcements (including Signal Corps Officers). Reproduced and distributed signal documents. Supervised rear echelon communications.

COMMUNICATIONS: Planning, direction and supervision of the tactical employment of Signal Operation and Signal Construction Battalions of the Army Signal Service. Signal Systems Information including the preparation and continuous revision of Line Route Map, Circuit Diagram, Radio Net Diagram and VHF Radio Relay Diagram. Studied traffic handling in all Army units so as to advise on changes and improvements. Prepared frequency and call sign allocations, row register index, air warning broadcast, air/ground visual code, identification panel code, pyrotechnic code and telephone code-names. Prepared signal circulars.

PLANS AND OPERATIONS: Co-ordinated activities of operational signal units and of Army Signal sub-sections with policies and directives laid down by the Signal Officer, Third Army and higher headquarters. Maintained tactical situation map, location of operational units and station troop lists. Supervised section and unit histories. Investigated and inspected billeting areas. Organised reception of visitors.

PHOTOGRAPHIC: Co-ordinated photo assignment activities of Photo Assignment Officer and CO of Signal Photo Company. Controlled and approved all orders for photo prints needed for tactical and historical purposes. Responsible for transmittal of War Department film to Army Pictorial Laboratories.

SIGNAL INTELLIGENCE SERVICE: Liaison with G-2 staff section. Supervision of all operational activities of Army and corps radio intelligence companies. Radio counter-measures. Signal counter-intelligence. Solution of special codes and ciphers. Examination and reproduction of captured signal intelligence and communications documents and dissemination. Interrogation of special PoWs and dissemination of material obtained. Maintenance of cryptographic, transmission and physical security in the Army. Preparation and distribution of codes and ciphers. Supervision of Army SIAM Company, Army Signal Pigeon Company and the Army Weather Detachment. Supervision of all Army messenger and message centre activities. Supervision of wire, radio and messenger facilities for signal intelligence purposes.

ENEMY EQUIPMENT INTELLIGENCE: Collection, evaluation and disposition of captured enemy signal equipment. Technical reports.

SUPPLY: Procurement, storage and issue of signal equipment and maintenance of records. Supervision of Army Signal Depot and Army Signal

Repair. Procurement of non-standard items from captured enemy equipment. Collection, reclamation and salvage of equipment and reports on all losses of signal equipment.

As the Signal Officer, Colonel Elton F. Hammond, comments in the After Action Report: 'The initial signal plans called for a greater number of Signal Corps Troops than were ever available during operations on the Continent. There never was a period when additional signal personnel could not have been used to great advantage. This disadvantage was overcome, however, by the ingenuity, loyalty and persistence of the Signals Corps soldier who remains imbued with our traditional slogan: "Get the message through".' Colonel Robert Allen describes 'Demon' Hammond as being responsible for the installation and maintenance of Third Army's wide, constantly shifting and complex communications network. 'The chunky, insatiably curious West Pointer was constantly being called on to perform miracles. He never failed. Sometimes he groaned in despair, but he always produced.' Allen goes on to explain how after a number of difficult weeks in the most awful weather and terrain, 'Demon' had completed an elaborate wire system in preparation for the expected offensive through the Palatinate. Overnight the plan had to be jettisoned and he had to set up an entirely new network to cope with Third Army's turning north to halt the German assault in the Ardennes (in a matter of hours and under even worse conditions). 'He and his heroic Signal battalions did it without a hitch.' Colonel Allen also makes special mention of Major Charles Flint's radio-interception agency (Special Intelligence Service), 'young, trigger-smart expert, it worked closely with G-2 on a dual mission: maintaining a vigilant security check on friendly communications and intercepting enemy messages. The unit performed outstandingly in both fields. Its reports plugged up an unwitting leak from a Mechanised Cavalry source, capable of revealing important troop-movement information to the enemy. And at a critical period in the Battle of Bastogne, the unit broke a coded German message that enabled heavy losses to be inflicted on the redoubtable 5 Para Division.'

SPECIAL SERVICES SECTION

Chief of Section
Executive Officer

Sub-Sections:

Third Special Service Company: Handled all entertainment for Army troops, including soldier stage shows, movies and orchestras. Supplemented same work done by Special Service Companies attached to Corps when necessary.

Supply and Distribution: Requisitioned, collected and distributed to Corps Special Service sections all athletic and recreational supplies; handled

issues of all supplies to Army troops directly from this HQ.
AMERICAN RED CROSS: Supervised and co-ordinated all American Red Cross functions within the command, including Field Service, Home Service, Hospital Service, Club Service and Clubmobiles.
ARMY EXCHANGE OFFICER: Supervised the setting-up of exchanges within subordinate Army units and other units in the Army area; advised units on policies and operations; made local purchases to supplement regular supplies.
CINEMA: Received and distributed all films to Corps libraries; ran film library for Army troops; repaired and serviced cinema projectors and radios, co-ordinated with 3283rd Signal Service Detachment.
ATHLETIC AND RECREATIONAL: Planned and presented special athletic events; supervised programmes at Red Cross Clubs and similar installations.

The Section was thus responsible for entertaining the troops, providing a little bit of home away from home in the broadest possible way.

TANK DESTROYER

CG 1ST TANK DESTROYER BRIGADE
Commanded all groups and battalions under Army control. Chief of TD Section.
EXECUTIVE OFFICER

Sub-Sections:

S-1 AND S-4: Maintained records of equipment and personnel and assisted units in their equipment and personnel matters.
S-2: Technical information collection, collation and distribution. Ditto for German armour.
S-3: Maintained records of unit location, equipment reports, training and personnel; collected and disseminated combat experiences; plans and orders for tactical operations.
ADDITIONAL STAFF: HQ Commandant, Liaison Officer, Communications Officer and Aide (for CG).

(The source of the information contained in this explanation and breakdown of Staff Sections of HQ Third Army is Vol. II of Third Army's After Action Report)

XIX TACTICAL AIR COMMAND

The Headquarters of XIX Tactical Air Command was always established conveniently near to HQ Third Army, both headquarters working closely together at all times. HQ XIX TAC worked closely with both the Air sub-sections of the G-2 and G3 Sections of HQ Third Army.

The mission of XIX TAC was simply to provide air support for Third Army and it was the G-3 section which provided the connecting link between the two headquarters. Examples of the type of support given during the month of August 1944 were:

a. Attacking ground targets in direct support of armour and infantry columns.
b. Air cover for columns and assaults.
c. Armed reconnaissance.
d. Area patrols, for both ground and air targets (especially air).
e. Railroad reconnaissance and attacks on rail targets.
f. Pre-planned point target attacks (dive-bombing).

During August and September 1944, they rendered devastating damage to the enemy. The pace of activity continued high, but tailed off as the months passed and fewer targets existed once ground forces reached Germany and the enemy was on the verge of defeat. Most casualties during this latter period were from enemy AA, as there were few air-to-air engagements. XIX TAC consistently provided all that Third Army asked for, and its commander was highly thought of by GSP and all ranks of his Army. Patton once wrote to General George C. Marshall, US Army Chief of Staff: 'The co-operation between the Third Army and the XIX Tactical Air Command ... has been the finest example of the ground and air working together that I have ever seen.' He had the highest regard for Brigadier General Otto P. Weyland (nicknamed 'Opie') who always loyally supported Third Army. For example, Weyland took part in a high-powered conference at SHAEF at which a Group plan to allocate most of the air bomber force to First and Ninth Armies was discussed. Despite the fact that Weyland was the only one-star general present he protested vigorously: 'Third Army,' he told Eisenhower, 'has fought for months with very little bomber support. Under this plan it would continue to get only what First and Ninth Armies can't use. That is not only unfair, but unsound tactically.' For a few moments the silence was so thick that it could have been cut with a knife. Then Eisenhower spoke: 'Weyland is absolutely right. The plan needs revision to insure that our Air power is used in a manner to obtain maximum results.'[6] This completely changed the meeting and in a few minutes Group's plan was 'junked' and Third Army was guaranteed full-scale bomber support.

Annex 'A' to Chapter 6
Locations of Lucky Forward between 5 July 44 and 3 May 1945

Date	*Location*	*Miles travelled*
5-7 Jul 1944	Néhou, France	
1 Aug	Lebignard, France	25
2-3 Aug	Beauchamps, France	36
8 Aug	Poilley, France	32
12 Aug	St-Ouen, France	35

Date	*Location*	*Miles travelled*
14-15 Aug	La Bazoge, France	67
20 Aug	Brou, France	73
25 Aug	Courcy-aux-Loges, France	68
30 Aug	La Chaume, France	80
4 Sept	Marson, France	99
15 Sept	Braquis, France	68
22-8 Sept	Etain, France	5
11 Oct	Nancy, France	60
28 Dec	Luxembourg City	90
27-8 Mar	Idar-Oberstein, Germany	80
3 April	Frankfurt, Germany	85
11 April	Hersfeld, Germany	85
22 April	Erlangen, Germany	150
2-3 May	Regensburg, Germany 87	
TOTAL	19 Locations	1,225

Source: Patton's Third Army After Action Report

Notes to Chapter 6

1. The Headquarters staff list also shows Colonel Paul D. Harkins as Deputy Chief of Staff (Operations). He was another 'Patton Man' from the Sicily operation.
2. Taken from Third Army's After Action Report, Vol. II.
3. The major feature of the War Room was a 1/250,000 scale Situation Map of the entire Western Front, showing the position of every Allied and German division. This map was flanked by two others covering the Eastern Front and Third Army's zone. The latter was a 1/100,000 scale map and showed the disposition of units down to battalions. The maps were mounted on boards which could be dismantled (they were made at HQ Third Army). When the CP moved, the maps were taken down and rolled up in blankets, the sections of the boards unscrewed and all packed on a truck. The black and red symbols used on the maps were cut from cardboard and stuck with scotch tape on to the acetate (which was always in short supply) covering the maps.
4. See *Patton the Commander* by H. Essame.
5. The Machine Records Unit used electrical accounting machines (EAMs) which were the forerunners of today's computers.
6. Quoted in *Lucky Forward.*

7
Georgie's Boys

Regular, National Guardsman, Organised Reserve or Draftee, the US Third Army, like all the rest of the units large or small in the American Army, was made up of professional soldiers, part-time soldiers and conscripted civilians. The first group, of which Patton was a prime example, needs no further explanation, except perhaps to point out that, on 1 July 1939, the total strength of the active Army of the United States of America was just 174,000 men, most of whom were scattered across country in more than 130 posts, camps and stations. About 25 per cent were overseas. They were woefully short of modern equipment, motor transport, tanks (less than 400 in service) and other AFVs. The second group can be divided into two parts, the first being the National Guard, some 200,000 in all. Until 1933, each state had its own Guard, then the National Guard of the United States came into being. They were very like the British Territorial Army, attending 'drill evenings' some 48 times a year, plus two weeks' field duty (annual camp). Their equipment and weapons were not only in short supply, but also even more antiquated than those of the Regulars. The remainder of this second group were the Organised Reserves. They existed in mobilisation blueprints only, but did contain a pool of more than 100,000 trained officers, mainly graduates of the Reserve Officers' Training Corps. They would prove an invaluable asset when expansion began. The remaining group, and by far the largest in size, was the vast horde of drafted civilians. Together these elements would form one of the finest and best-equipped armies the world has ever seen.

MOBILISATION AND TRAINING
'A Prodigy of Organisation'

The average GI[1] who made up the vast proportion of units in Third Army, was a product of an amazing training machine which turned the woefully inadequate American Army of 1939, in which most units were still organised, trained and equipped to fight the Great War, into the mightiest Army in the world, numbering more than 8,300,000 men, armed and equipped with superb weapons, vehicles and clothing, and having all the necessary strategic mobility and logistic capability to enable it to fight anywhere in the world. The US Army, which absorbed more than three-quarters of the total manpower in the American Forces, was only exceeded in size by the Russian Army, but was infinitely better equipped, especially with regard to transport and at the basic soldier level. No wonder Winston Churchill described what America had achieved as being 'a prodigy of organisation, an achievement which soldiers of every other country will always study with admiration and envy'.

The Selective Service Act

When the Second World War began in 1939, the American nation continued its isolationist policies, fervently hoping that the 'European War' would not involve them. During 1940, however, while the Germans were overrunning Europe, the gravity of the world situation at last appeared to galvanise the people of the United States into action. The threat which Adolf Hitler's Nazi regime posed to the world suddenly became a reality to them and there was a public outcry that something should be done to strengthen the woefully inadequate armed forces before it was too late. Large sums of money were authorised by Congress, and the Selective Service Act was signed by President Roosevelt on 16 September 1940. This Act allowed the size of the Army to be raised to 1,400,000, of which half a million would be Regulars, 270,000 National Guardsmen and the remaining 630,000 Selectees chosen from a country-wide draft. A month later, in schools and other public buildings all over America, men between the ages of 21 and 35 started to register. From early October 1940 to July 1941, a staggering seventeen million were registered, but initially, only 900,000 of these were permitted by the Act to be inducted into the Army. A few weeks before Japan's 'Day of Infamy', on 7 December 1941, when they struck without warning at Pearl Harbor, Congress renewed the Selective Service Act – by a majority of just one vote in the House of Representatives!

By the summer of 1941, the Army had almost reached its agreed ceiling of 1,400,000. The ground forces within the United States now consisted of four Armies, containing a total of nine corps and made up of 29 divisions, together with various overseas garrisons. One of these four armies was Third Army, located in the south-east, with its headquarters alternating between Fort Sam Houston, Texas, and Atlanta, Georgia.

As already explained, at that time Third Army was part of the training machine and did not become a combat army until 31 December 1943, when it was ordered to prepare for movement overseas. In December 1941, however, there was still much to be done. Only seventeen of the 34 divisions in the USA had received sufficient training to fit them for combat, and there was a critical shortage of all types of weapons and equipment. GHQ in Washington had originally estimated that some 200 divisions of all types would be needed, and set themselves an immediate target of raising 72 divisions by the end of 1942, at the rate of three or four each month beginning in March. Existing units would provide the cadre, or training nucleus, for each new unit which would be brought up to full strength by voluntary recruitment or the draft. Before assignment, these new recruits had to be put through a basic training course at replacement training centres. Officers for the new units would initially be drawn mainly from the Officers' Reserve Corps, to supplement the officers already in each cadre. In this way armies would be brought up to full strength and would then be responsible for the preparation of their own tactical units for combat.

Time was of the essence; the War Department's schedule allowed only 44 weeks for a division to be formed, staffed, equipped and trained to combat readiness. This period was broken down as follows:

17 weeks	establish initial organisation and complete basic training
13 weeks	unit training up to regimental level
14 weeks	combined tactical training, including one division-level exercise.

The strain was probably greatest on the small number of experienced officers and enlisted men who formed the basic unit cadres. They had to be drawn from an existing division, put through special training at the service schools, while the selected divisional commander and his staff attended the Command and General Staff School, to prepare them for the onerous tasks which lay ahead. Most of the remaining officers would come directly from officer candidate schools, and the enlisted men from replacement training centres. Despite all the problems, mobilisation proceeded at a cracking pace, and by the end of 1942 virtually all the initial ground combat units had been mobilised. Thereafter, their striking power was improved only by re-organisations and economies from within the 89 divisions now in existence – just under half GHQ's original estimate.

Training

The average Second World War GI had to learn many more complex and technical skills than had his father in 1918. Even an infantryman had to be able to use any of a dozen or so different weapons. He also needed to know about camouflage and concealment, mines and booby traps, patrolling and map reading, tank and aircraft recognition, how to deal with PoWs, how to use captured enemy equipment, first aid and field hygiene, how to live in the field for long periods under the most trying conditions and in all weathers. The list of individual skills was endless and most of them were skills that were not taught in civilian life. Their forefathers, the pioneers, the backwoodsmen or the mountain men, would have found most of these skills second nature, but the civilised, urban-dwelling young American of the 1940s had to learn them all from scratch. And above all, he had to learn how to become a member of a team, be it in a rifle squad, a tank, or a gun crew. He had to learn to obey orders without question, yet retain the spark of individuality that would place him above the automaton. He also needed to become physically fit, mentally alert, to build up stamina and a high morale, that would endure no matter how difficult and dangerous the going became. In other words, he had to become a match for any professional or volunteer soldier and learn his trade, quickly and well.

Basic training. In early 1940 the only military training establishments in the USA were the General and Special Service Schools, small organisations able to train only limited numbers of key individuals. The much larger task of basic training for all newly joined recruits was left to units. Obviously this was unacceptable given the enormous influx of 'citizen soldiers' produced by the draft. So, in 1940, the War Department adopted an entirely new plan, with special training organisations – known as Replacement Training Centers (RTC) – being established all over America. Their role was to provide a steady stream of trained men to tactical units, thus relieving units from their training burdens during mobilisation and combat. Twelve such RTCs ere established in March 1941: four for Infantry, three for Coast Artillery, three for Field Artillery, and one each for Armor and Cavalry. By the end of 1941 they had trained more than 200,000 men. Once war was declared the RTCs had two basic requirements: to supply 'filler replacements' to occupy initial vacancies in units being activated; to provide 'loss replacements' for units already in training or combat. Additional RTCs were later set up to cover such new arms as Anti-Aircraft Artillery and Tank Destroyers.

The 'filler replacements' were fed through to large Replacement Depots, located fairly well to the rear of the operational area in whichever theatre of war the army was operating. Each depot had several replacement battalions attached to it. Troops of all classifications – infantrymen, artillerymen, tankmen, radio operators, technicians of all descriptions – were fed from the RTCs to the depots and thence into the Replacement Battalions. When a front-line unit needed replacements, perhaps because of casualties, it put in a requisition direct to its Corps Replacement Battalion for the needed number of men of certain specified categories. It was thus possible to keep units at full strength or nearly so, at all times. In this way a division could remain in continuous combat for months on end.

The RTCs trained the newly inducted men in basic military subjects and in the elementary specialist techniques of their particular arm of service. The former covered such subjects as military discipline, personal hygiene, first aid, guard duties and the care and handling of personal weapons. Initially courses lasted 12–13 weeks, but soon after Pearl Harbor many RTC programmes were cut to eight weeks. This was found to be too short, however, and by the end of 1943, with a few specialist exceptions, all courses had been fixed at seventeen weeks.

Service schools. These establishments trained individual officers, officer candidates and enlisted men in the special skills required by their arm of service. From July 1940 to August 1945, more than half a million men completed courses designed to fit them for such diverse jobs as infantry battalion commander or AA control technician. Eight of these schools operated under control of the Army Ground Forces (AGF); four of them had been established in peacetime (Cavalry, Coast Artillery, Field Artillery and Infantry), and there were four new ones (Armored, AA Artillery, Tank Destroyer and Parachute). The Parachute School was more than just an arms school as it had to train all paratroop replacements, so was in effect both an RTC and a school.

Officer training. Officer candidates were selected for commissions and trained in an element of each service school, known as Officer Candidate School (OCS). Their aim was to convert enlisted men of the particular arm to combat officers, to meet the mobilisation requirements which could not be filled by Regular, Reserve or National Guard officers. Courses lasted from twelve to seventeen weeks, the candidate being trained in the basic duties of an officer of that particular arm. It also decided whether or not he was fit to be recommended for a commission. By the end of 1943, when mobilisation was nearly completed, about 19,000 National Guard officers were in federal service, some 180,000 officers had been drawn from the Reserve Officer Training Corps, and almost 100,000 civilians had received direct commissions – just under half were doctors, dentists and chaplains, the rest were technical or administrative posts. Despite continual agitation to raise the length of the OCS course to six months, this never happened and no substantial changes were ever made. The official history comments: 'While the AGF officer candidate schools fulfilled an indispensable mission becoming the main source of junior officers, it was the combination of school and unit training that produced the successful junior officer for the ground combat arms in WWII.'

Personal reactions to induction. In the XII Corps history, *Spearhead of Patton's Third Army*, there is a good example of a new recruit's early days at his RTC: 'When I first went into the army I was very unhappy,' wrote Ralph Ingersoll. 'The process by which I ceased to be unhappy was the process of absorption into that vast community which is the Army of the United States. To each man this process is personal, intimate and individual.... I can put it best by going back to my thoughts and emotions in the first month or two of training. I was then so physically tired that I could only get through a day by using every five or ten minute breathing spell to lie flat on my back and luxuriate in my aches and pains.... Then there was the food, generally of good quality, but often badly cooked and at best monotonous and unfamiliar to many of the new soldiers. And the almost universally unfamiliar discomforts of life in the open. And in the summer, dust. And in spring and fall, something else: one divisional commander described his regimental areas as "disconnected islands in a sea of mud". And the inadequacies of green officers, little more experienced than the recruits they were required to lead. And shortages of everything, individuals had no musette bags, no shoulder packs, no fur caps, gloves, mufflers or shoulder insignia ... officers had no bedding rolls. There were no field ranges.... Training aids and facilities were not available.'[2] Clearly these shortages did not last once the 'Battle for Production' had been 'fought and won' all over the USA, but at the start things were very difficult.

Another recruit, Curtis W. Tarr, joined the army on 9 April 1943. He was destined to serve as a field artilleryman in the 11th Armored (Thunderbolt) Division of Third Army. He was 6 feet 5 inches tall and had hoped to join the Navy as he had always yelled for them when he listened to Army–Navy football games. 'Sorry, you might get caught in a hatch somewhere and we'd lose the whole war!' the Navy recruiter had told him. 'But the Army took me, and with no propaganda either. They accepted every man who passed the physical examination. I stood before the flag where an officer administered the oath that seemed about as impressive as saying "Ah" for the doctor a few minutes before. Thus I became Private Curtis Tarr.... Immediately an Army lieutenant gave me orders to take seven other men the next day to the Presidio at Monterey.... I gathered my men and we headed for the Southern Pacific depot not far away. There we received a special "Army" meal in part of the dining room separated by a rope. Although the government was charged the going rate I noted some quality control problems in what we were served.... The next morning an Army truck took us back to the railroad station where we boarded a troop train for Monterey.... The Army would not be entirely foreign to me. I had learned close order drill in the Boy Scouts and I knew something about how to care for myself in the open. I had marched with the ROTC at Reno High School several years earlier.'

On arrival at the Presidio, they had a meal and were then assigned to their barrack room, drawing the necessary bedding and being taught by a 'crusty' sergeant how to make a bed 'Army style'. 'Not being a highly literate man, he went over the details again and again, confusing some of the men as he helped others. And he required everyone to make his bed well enough to pass inspection before he would allow any of us to retire. Finally we did so at two in the morning! But the sergeant's lesson made quite an impression on me: each day since then I have made my bed in that prescribed manner.' Reveille was at five a.m., so it was a very short night for the new recruits, who then found that they had 'many things to be cleaned, policed, shined or repaired before breakfast in order to satisfy the privates first class who sternly supervised our efforts'. After breakfast, they attended the test centre for a series of aptitude tests – the Army General Classification Test (AGCT). This was followed by marching to the clothing warehouse to get their uniforms, their civilian clothes first being removed and packed away for shipment home. 'Next we stood naked awaiting the government issue of necessities. By that time most of us had gotten used to standing naked and waiting, two essentials of soldierly patience.

'As we drew our military clothes, I heard many boys complain about the fit. "Don't worry, it will shrink", often was the reply. Strangely, in most cases, the quartermaster sergeant was right.... My shoes though, were unusual. Since they were 13Bs, the Army considered them "non-tariff" size. The sergeant warned me to take good care of them because it would be difficult to order others like them, but they were so large that I had no chance of losing them. More than once they made me a conspicuous sight on a pass in town: some of my friends called them landing craft. That army clothing warehouse was the last building I have ever entered where I could find an entire wardrobe of clothes to fit me.... Finally, at the end of the second day in the Army we got haircuts. We looked innocent with no insignia on our uniforms, little hair on our heads, and meagre expectations of what the future might hold.' After a week of waiting at the Presidio, doing odd jobs, Private Tarr was posted to Camp Roberts, for basic training in field artillery.

Tactical training. Third Army was responsible for a massive area of the continental United States, with hundreds of units varying from corps to small detachments, located in scores of camps, posts, manoeuvre areas and other military installations, which stretched from Mississippi to Arizona and from Arkansas to the Mexican border. Troop strength was generally more then 750,000. The best-known training centre was the Louisiana manoeuvre area, which Colonel Robert Allen describes as being 'a 40 x 90 mile sparsely settled, chigger and tick infested bayou and pitch pine section between the Sabine and Red rivers, the region is rugged and historic. For more than a decade after the Louisiana Purchase, it was law-of-the-gun "no man's land".... Major terrain features are Pearson Ridge and Burr Ferry. More sham battles and river crossings were fought at these two points than in all the campaigns of World War II.

'Pearson Ridge is a stump-knobbed sector that was once part of the vast virgin pitch-pine forests that covered this portion of Louisiana. Hundreds of thousands of troops sweated, froze, and choked in dust on Pearson's sandy trails and denuded slopes.... Burr Ferry, 15 miles west of Leesville, was the site of a Confederate camp for Union PoW. Now it is noted for a handsome concrete bridge connecting Louisiana and Texas, and as the scene of countless river-crossing exercises. Most of the crack divisions learned their art of war there. They learned it the hard way because the Sabine is as treacherous as a Nazi Gauleiter. It can be an inoffensive rivulet one day and a raging, ruthless killer the next. It was a rare manoeuvre that did not take a toll of a number of drownings.... The manoeuvre area was Third Army's finishing school. Units came there after completing their D problems at home stations.'[3]

The field manoeuvre period lasted for some two months and pitted division against division, with all elements taking part, including AAA, TD and Air. Units lived and operated under battle conditions, irrespective of the weather. 'In Louisiana,' comments Colonel Allen, 'when it's hot, it's torrid, and when it's cold, it's freezingly bitter!'

Testing took place at all levels of training, and for the Louisiana manoeuvres, HQ Third Army maintained a large special staff in a field camp near Leesville, known as Director Headquarters, HQ Third Army. The commander of this staff was the Commanding General Third Army, and at least once during every exercise period, Lieutenant General Lesley J. McNair, CG Army Ground Forces, would fly in from Washington for an inspection tour.

At this time Third Army was under the command of the dynamic Lieutenant General Walter Kreuger who was, to quote Colonel Allen, 'without a peer as a troop trainer'. His debriefs were always 'stellar, and sometimes hotly dramatic, instructional events. He didn't hesitate to tell off Corps and Division commanders in blunt terms.' He had shot to prominence during the Louisiana war games of 1941, when his Third Army had chased Lieutenant General Ben Lear's Second Army right out of Arkansas! His Chief of Staff at the time was the then unknown and newly promoted Brigadier General Dwight D. Eisenhower, and his 'principal sledge-hammer' in the rout of Second Army had been the 'Hell on Wheels' 2nd Armored Division, commanded by Major General George S. Patton, Jr, who had: 'whiplashed around Lear's flank and turned his rear, forcing him to abandon strong positions and retreat'.[4]

After this spectacular performance Kreuger, although well over sixty, carried on training troops with characteristic energy and zeal. When an exercise was taking place in the manoeuvre area, he would leave the Exercise CP well before dawn and 'gnaw his way up' a zone of advance until far into the night, constantly stressing the importance of individual and low-level training – 'the little details that make the difference between dead men and live veterans.... But he never jumped an enlisted man. He always summoned the responsible officer and worked him over.' His exercise debriefs were held in a large cinema at Camp Polk and attended by all officers and selected NCOs, Allen said: 'There was nothing like them in any other United States Army.'

Overseas training. Third Army did not stop training when it moved overseas, indeed, the training intensified. One novel feature of the move was that units left practically all their quartermaster and ordnance equipment behind and drew new equipment on arrival in the UK.

This was done to speed the build-up, only the troops with their personal gear and some light, scarce articles being embarked in the ships for overseas.[5] This allowed heavy equipment, guns, trucks, etc., to be shipped and stored in the UK months in advance, while the troops were still training in the USA. 'When they arrived overseas the units were issued fine new equipment of every description, all of the latest design, ready for the rigors of what proved to be a long and strenuous campaign.'[6]

The Move Overseas

For most of the Third Army, apart from its commander and his small number of hand-picked senior staff members, who came from the Mediterranean Theatre, the UK was the initial arrival point in Europe. The procedure for getting the US troops from their camps and training locations in the USA was perfected during the early war years, so that when the majority of Third Army came to be moved, together with thousands of other GIs, WACs, nurses and all the rest, the system was well and truly in place. Obviously, it was from the east coast ports that the main UK-bound convoys departed: Hampton Roads, Virginia, Boston and even Charleston serving as outports for New York, which in mid-1943 had been assigned responsibility for the European and Mediterranean theatres.

As New York had been declared one of the major departure ports for the ETO, the first leg of the troops' journey was usually by train to 'The Big Apple', as it is now nicknamed, from anywhere in the vast continental United States. Private Curtis Tarr moved from Camp Cooke in California to New York in a train of 'troop sleepers'. He recalls: 'The troop sleeper had a boxcar chassis and frame, but it contained double metal bunks, the lower of which could be converted into a crude sofa during the day. A porter in each car kept it orderly and helped us with the bunks. At one end the car had washing and toilet facilities. The large windows let the sun roast us, but we could see fully the sights along the route. The car had no amenities but it did furnish basic essentials, and I preferred these accommodations to sleeping with another unfortunate in a regular Pullman lower berth.'

The train moved southward to join the Santa Fe railway system in the California desert, then turned eastwards. They proceeded at a leisurely pace, with frequent stops for exercise. Apparently it was so routed as to avoid most large cities, so it took ten days to reach Camp Kilmer, New Jersey, the transit post for troops destined for shipment overseas. During his stay here, Curtis had two passes into New York City. He had hoped to see some major-league baseball but 'somehow that thrill escaped us. Instead we visited the conventional soldiers' haunts in Manhattan: the Pepsi-Cola Service Center, the Empire State Building, Rockefeller Building.' He tried queuing for 'Oklahoma' which was playing to capacity audiences, but discovered that there no seats available for three months! He comments wryly: 'We had much to learn about metropolitan ways.'

In Camp Kilmer everyone had to pass the 'Overseas Physical' and so all lined up ready: '... by then we had no reservations about standing naked at attention, even if we had to assemble in drill formation! ... Finally a whistle blew and we marched smartly through in our appropriate lines. Soon I saw that the doctors in this outfit gave rapid physical examinations. While one man looked at our medical records, presumably for the proper "shots", others inspected our mouths, noses, eyes, teeth, feet, buttocks. The "short arm" inspection for VD took the longest time. Almost before we realised it, the overseas physicals were completed – and we all passed.'

Embarkation. A few days later, they boarded another train for their 'last train ride in the States', taking with them their personal clothing and equipment. Curtis had a major problem – his 13Bs taking up at least a third of his total usable space! 'Of course I had the shoes filled with small objects. But still I had my sleeping bag, blankets, clothes, raincoat, mess kit, toilet kit, personal items and books. What a relief when we closed the bags and tied them together. But they were so unwieldy to carry that it was difficult to walk in a straight line.

'Despite all our training, we had never before tried the shoulder harness which we used when we boarded the ship. The man who designed that harness disliked soldiers. The object was to permit a man to put a musette bag on his back, a gas mask and carbine over his arms, a pistol belt around his waist and wear his overcoat and steel helmet over his helmet liner. The harness hooked to the straps of the musette bag so that the snap rested on the top of a man's shoulder, cutting in at a most sensitive spot.

'Quickly we tired with all of our heavy clothing heating us to fever temperatures. Loaded so heavily, we had to help each other boost barrack bags up on our shoulders. But of course each time we stopped we repeated the process. Once aboard the train we could hardly sit with so much paraphernalia strapped to us. An officer in our car warned us not to take anything off, because our ride would be short.... When the train stopped, the more rugged test began ... the walk to the ship, quite a distance, considering the weight of the duffel. The bags could be slung over one shoulder, but with a carbine slipping down one arm and a gas mask falling off the other, the choice of shoulder presented difficulties. But no matter where you put them, you found quickly that another position, any position, would be preferable.'

One can well imagine how they struggled, even before they reached the slippery gang-plank, so they were very relieved when they were met by Red Cross ladies at the wharf, with hot coffee and doughnuts, 'Forever after I have admired the Red Cross. They knew just where to be in order to help us that night.'

Curtis Tarr, with 4,999 other men, sailed in an old Cunard vessel, SS *Samaria*. Many thousands of American troops of course sailed in the *Queen Mary* (SS490 as she was known in wartime) and her sister ship *Queen Elizabeth*, each of which could carry 15,000 troops at a time. The usual hammocks were replaced by 'standee bunks' up to eight tiers high, which were erected everywhere. But these could only accommodate 8,000 sleeping at one time, so a two-shift system was instituted, two men being allocated to each bunk! Because of the overcrowding, safety was a constant priority, boat and raft drill being practised daily and everyone had to carry his lifebelt at all times. Anyone caught without one had to remove his shoes and surrender them to the military police, only getting them back when he reported to the shoe store with his lifebelt. 'The finest incident I saw on any of my trips,' reported one distinguished official who crossed the Atlantic many times during the war, 'was the sight of an American admiral stopped by a GI sentry and ordered to remove his shoes because he had no lifebelt. I can see the great man now, padding obediently away in his socks over the wet decks and returning meekly with the belt.'[7]

Another GI who made the journey 'over there' was Frank J. Paskvan, who served with the engineers in Third Army. He recalls: '... all of us slowly went up the gangplank and inside the ship. Down, down, down we went, until I thought we would come out at the bottom. By this time my pack was so heavy that I had lost all interest and only wanted to sleep in my stateroom. Someone asked the Captain when we would be allowed to go to our staterooms. He said, "Staterooms, this is your stateroom" and he left in a hurry! To make something out of nothing, one of the sailors gave us some hammocks, and I hung one up, almost fell out a couple of times, but found out if I held my breath I didn't fall out and was soon asleep. Morning was breaking when I noticed the lamp above me was swaying slowly. I told my buddy that the ship was moving. He looked at the lamp and said "Naw, no way is this ship moving." I told him to listen and you could hear the motors of the ship. When he heard them he immediately got sea sick, so did several others. It took ten days to cross the Atlantic and my buddy was sick for the whole ten days. I thought he was going to die.'[8]

Liverpool was the main reception port for Third Army, and as Curtis Tarr recalls: '... no one argued when we received orders to disembark, glad to be away from our congested, foul quarters'. Final training would then have to take place, the English weather in all its many guises would have to be borne stoically, as would warm beer, absence from loved ones and all the rest. All too soon they would be in action, most for the very first time. Before looking at Third Army's combat record, let us look in some detail at the dress, equipment, personal weapons and rations of the average GI.

UNIFORMS

Non-Combat Dress

This consisted of an open-necked tunic with four straight-flapped pockets, a pair of straight trousers, brown leather boots or shoes, plus a peaked cap or the 'envelope-type' overseas cap. All clothing was olive drab in colour, but varied considerably in tone. Ties and shirts varied from olive to light tan. Officers wore a similar service dress, but with a dark worsted band around each cuff, which was the mark of an officer of any rank. Later in the war, many officers wore the 'Ike' jacket, which resembled a British battledress top – but had numerous variations in colour, style and cut. The American uniform was far superior to its British equivalent in material, design and cut, which was undoubtedly the cause of much admiration from the girls and much envy and resentment from British Tommies!

Badges of Rank. These were worn on all types of uniform, including shirts and, sometimes, on helmets.

Cap and Collar Badges. All ranks wore the coat of arms of the USA as a cap badge in the peaked cap. The officers' version was 3 inches by 2 inches; enlisted men wore a smaller version which was attached to a disc about 1.6 inches in diameter. Both were made of brass or gilded brass. Collar badges, also of brass, were worn by all ranks and, as with the cap badges, enlisted men wore slightly smaller badges, again attached to brass discs. The collar badges denoted the arm of service (armour, artillery, infantry, etc.).

Officers wore collar badges in pairs (except on shirts in summer uniform when badges of rank took the place of the left-hand collar badge), with the US national insignia above the branch badge. Enlisted men wore them singly, with the 'US' on the right and the branch badge on the left.

Breast Badges. A wide variety of breast badges was worn in addition to medal ribbons. These included for example, Combat Infantryman, Paratrooper and General Staff identification badge.

Shoulder Patches. Divisional, Corps and Army shoulder patches were worn as appropriate, the Third Army shoulder patch being worn by all HQ personnel and any Army troops. Corps HQ personnel and Corps troops wore their own corps patch; the vast majority of troops wore their own divisional patch.

Combat Dress

M1 Helmet. The average GI wore the M1 steel helmet (see later for tank crews and airborne troops). It was manufactured in three parts: an outer steel shell, usually painted olive drab, sometimes worn with a scrim net for taking camouflage material and fitted with an adjustable webbing chin strap (often worn shortened and looped over the rear of the helmet). Divisional insignia may well have been painted on the front of the helmet. This steel outer fitted snugly over the top of a fibre liner, exactly the same shape, but slightly smaller in size. It had a cradle of straps inside it and a thin leather chin strap which was usually slipped over the front rim. This inner was sometimes worn on its own. The third component was the notorious 'beanie', an olive-coloured knitted cap, designed to be worn under the helmet, but often worn on its own, as it formed a comfortable, warm, but casual item of head-dress – akin to the British cap comforter. The 'beanie' was anathema to GSP – so pity the poor unsuspecting GI he caught wearing one! The outer was not only used for protection, it also formed a washing bowl, cooking pot, emergency entrenching tool – its uses were legion!

M1943 HBT Fatigues. Introduced in 1943, the Herringbone Twill two-piece fatigues comprised a thigh-length jacket, and trousers of similar material. The 1943 jacket replaced the M1941 model which was only hip length and only windproof, the new jacket being also waterproof and tear resistant. In addition it had zip fasteners, good-sized pockets and could accept both a built-in liner and hood for winter. Unfortunately most of the uniforms worn for the Normandy invasion were heavily impregnated with an anti-vesicant chemical (to protect against mustard gas), which made them clammy, heavy and foul smelling! Under the fatigues the GI would wear an olive drab flannel, open-necked shirt and, when cold, a sweater(s) and even a white undershirt. Underwear was issued in wide variety of styles, including short underpants, longjohns, etc., all made of wool/cotton and available in both green and white. Socks were made of wool and cotton. A simple peaked, cloth field cap was also issued.

Footwear. The trousers were normally tucked into calf-length leggings made of canvas. Later these were replaced by a new boot which had a built-in gaiter and fastened with two small straps and buckles. Finally, in 1945, an even taller boot was produced, which resembled the high-laced paratrooper's boot.

Miscellaneous. Other general items of uniform included long greatcoats, raincoats, high-necked pullovers, scarves, Balaclava helmets, herringbone twill suits (for mechanics), rubber storm boots, metal-fastened rubber galoshes (to wear over combat boots), olive wool or brown leather gloves. Improvised white snow camouflage hooded jackets and over trousers (some 'acquired' from the British) were later worn in the Ardennes and elsewhere.

Specialised Clothing

Tank Crews. In addition to their normal uniform tankmen were issued with four special items:

a. A tight-fitting fabric 'helmet' resembling a Great War pilot's head gear, with housings for earphones. It was universally hated!
b. A composition crash helmet with a padded and ventilated top. It was liked by crews and worn in preference to the steel helmet.

c. One-piece olive drab herringbone twill overalls.
d. Finally, the most sought-after item of clothing in the entire US Army, a zippered windcheater, with knitted cuffs and waistband. It had no shoulder-straps, so officers had to pin their rank badge on the jacket.

AIRBORNE TROOPS. They undoubtedly were treated right royally as far as their personal uniform was concerned, with the following special items:

a. M1C helmet. This was a conversion of the normal helmet, with extra harness inside the liner and a moulded chin strap, so that it would act as a crash helmet.
b. Jump jacket. With four distinctive large patch pockets, with flaps, the beige cotton-poplin jacket had a full-length covered, heavy duty metal zip and a light canvas belt with a buckle. Three pleats in the back gave full freedom of movement.
c. Jump trousers. Made of similar material, with two large pockets on the thighs, running down to the knees.
d. Jump boots. Made of brown leather, with twelve pairs of eyelets, these high leg boots were much sought after by other troops.

BADGES OF RANK IN COMBAT. As a general rule, rank and unit insignia were kept to a minimum on combat dress. Sometimes badges of rank were painted on the front or back of steel helmets, but this 'dead give-away' was discouraged. Medical personnel invariably wore red crosses on white discs, and MPs broad white bands with the letters 'MP' on the front of the helmet. The only unit insignia worn universally were divisional shoulder patches. The obvious exception to these rules was of course the Commanding General! Patton wore all his badges of rank, as flamboyantly as possible, not out of vanity, I hasten to add, but because he rightly realised what a morale booster they helped to make him! No one was ever in any doubt that the bestarred man who was helping unscramble the traffic jam, or 'tearing a strip' off some miscreant, or visiting the wounded in a forward aid post, or generally encouraging his men to greater heights of endeavour, could only be 'Georgie'!

'DOG TAGS'. Every soldier, irrespective of rank, was supposed to wear his identification tags (known universally as 'dog tags') at all times, waking or sleeping. These were two identical rectangular metal tags worn around the neck, on a string or metal chain. They bore the wearer's name and number, and the name and address of his next of kin, although this latter information was discontinued from about 1943. In the event of his being killed, one tag would be left on the body and one taken for casualty identification purposes.

PERSONAL EQUIPMENT

Webbing

All enlisted men and a fair number of officers, wore the basic webbing, which consisted of one of two patterns of broad web belt, both of which fastened with a buckle in the front. The cartridge or magazine belt had five thin webbing pouches on each side of the buckle, each holding a clip of Magazine rifle or Garand ammunition. Also attached to eyelets on the belt was a M1924 first-aid pouch, and a canteen and cup in a 1910 M1 canvas cover, but of course the wearer could choose to add or substitute other items. The second type of belt was designed for those soldiers who did not usually carry a rifle, such as tank crewmen, machine-gunners and officers. It was basically a pistol belt for the large Colt .45 pistol and two spare magazines. There was plenty of room also for a canteen and a first-aid pouch, plus whatever else the wearer chose to fix on to the row of metal eyelets top and bottom of the belt. Webbing shoulder braces could be attached. These crossed in the centre of the back via stitched loops for greater stability, then came down vertically over the shoulders to the top of the chest, then divided into two narrower sections and were finally fixed by snap-hooks on to the top of the belt. The long bayonet for the M1903 or M1903A1 Magazine rifle fitted into the side of the backpack (see below), but the shorter M1 bayonet was carried, in its scabbard, hooked on to the belt. Another useful item which could be hooked on to the belt was a pair of M-1938 wire-cutters in a webbing pouch.

When the M1928 backpack was worn, it was attached to the top row of eyelets on the belt. It had a back pocket for the mess-tin, and one of its closure straps held the handle of the entrenching tool. The pack contained a raincoat (5-button, rubberised), underwear and socks, towel, toiletries (provided by the PX), a sewing kit ('Housewife' in British parlance), knife, fork and spoon and personal items – writing materials, books, cigarettes, etc.

Also stowed in the haversack or worn about the person were items of special equipment:

a. Water-purifying tablets, heat tablets, emergency rations.

b. Anti-gas equipment. detector armband (changed colour in presence of vesicant gases), M4 gas mask or the lighter M5 gas mask, anti-dim cloth, cellophane anti-gas cape, woollen protective hood, eye-shields and protective ointment. (Most of these items were carried in the gas mask bag.)

Carried on unit transport – it was hoped – would be the rest of the GI's personal kit, although those with their own transport – jeep, tank or SP gun – would keep their kit close by. Every soldier quickly learnt to look after his own kit above all else. Such items were:

a. One shelter half, with its guy line, wooden pins and folding pole. So two men could make up a two-man bivouac.
b. Two blankets.
c. Spare clothing, stowed in the soldier's duffel bag which bore his name and serial number.

PERSONAL WEAPONS

All officers and soldiers, with the obvious exception of medical personnel and chaplains, carried a personal weapon – pistol, submachine-gun, carbine or rifle. (NB. All other small arms are dealt with in subsequent chapters.)

AUTOMATIC PISTOL, .45 CAL M1911 AND M1911A: The 2½lb (1.1kg) automatic pistol was a recoil-operated, self-loading hand weapon. The magazine held seven rounds and two spare magazines were carried in a webbing pouch which normally accompanied the pistol in its russet leather holster. The pistol was very powerful, but was not easy to fire accurately. Two other handguns issued to US forces were the .45 cal Smith & Wesson revolver and the .45 cal Colt revolver, both being M1917 models. Most officers carried handguns, although infantry officers usually preferred to be more heavily armed.

SUBMACHINE-GUN, .45 CAL M1 AND M1A1: The .45 cal Thompson M1 weighed about 10½lb (4.74kg) and was usually fitted with a 50-round drum magazine, which made it very heavy and very wasteful on ammunition (cyclic rate of fire was 700rpm). It was followed by a lighter, simpler version, the M1A1, which would accept either a 20- or 30-round straight box magazine. It had no pistol grip.

SUBMACHINE-GUN, .45 CAL M3: Lighter than the Thompson at 8½lb, and resembling the British Sten gun, it had a straight, vertically loaded 30-round magazine, a cyclic rate of fire of 350–450rpm and a maximum range of 100 yards. Although an experienced shot could squeeze off single rounds, the M3 was designed to fire only on automatic. It was cheap and cheerful and could be adapted to accept 9mm Parabellum ammunition. It was issued from December 1942.

MAGAZINE RIFLE, .30 CAL, M1903 AND M1903A1: Although this rifle dated from the Great War, it was still preferred by many soldiers to the Garand rifle or to the carbine. It weighed 9lb (4.1kg) and could be fitted with the 1905 long-pattern bayonet. Its magazine held five rounds. The sniper's version was fitted with the Weaver telescope sight.

RIFLE, .30 CAL M1 GARAND: The 9½lb M1 .30 cal (7.62mm) semi-automatic gas operated rifle, was the US infantryman's basic weapon. It had gone into mass production in 1939. It had a maximum range of 3,000 yards but an effective range of only about 500 yards. Its magazine held eight rounds. Its cyclic rate of fire was 20 rounds per minute, so a trained solider could fire eight aimed rounds in about 20 seconds. By 1945, more than 5½ million Garands (named after its designer) had been produced.

CARBINE, .30 CAL M1 AND M1A1: For those who did not carry a rifle, the Winchester self-loading carbine was introduced. Much lighter, only 5.2lb, it had a magazine capacity of either 15 or 30 rounds. More than six million were produced. It had a high rate of fire (30rpm) but was not as accurate as the rifle. A later version, the M2 carbine, was fully auto-

Above: The M5A1 light tank was widely used and was known as the Stuart by the British. It mounted a 37mm gun and weighed 15 tons. Towards the end of the war it was replaced by the M24 Chaffee. This M5A1 is passing one of the German juggernauts – a massive Jagdtiger, which weighed 70 tons and was armed with a 128mm gun. (Tank Museum)

Right: Most widely used and prolific tank of the war was the M4 medium Sherman. Nearly 50,000 were built, representing over 50% of the total US tank production and far more than either the total tank production of Great Britain or Germany. Its main armament was a 75mm gun. (US Army)

Opposite page, top: Blockbuster 3rd was the command tank of Co B, 37th Tank Battalion, 4th Armd Div and is seen here in Luxembourg in 1945. It was the upgunned version of Sherman which mounted an improved 76mm gun. (Col James Leach)

Above: Standard equipment for the artillery battalions of American armored divisions was the M7 HMC, which mounted a 105mm howitzer on the M3 medium tank chassis. Known as the Priest by the British Army. (US Army)

Left: The Tank Destroyer Command lived up to its motto: 'Seek, Strike and Destroy'. First of the specially built TDs was the M10 Wolverine, which was based upon the M3 medium tank and mounted a 3inch gun in an open-topped turret. The British upgunned it with their 17pdr, when it was known as the M10 Achilles. (Real War Photos)

Above: An M1 155mm howitzer in action. Some 4,000 of these very accurate weapons were produced. The M1A1 was made of stronger steel. (US Army)

Below: Gen Patton once said that it was the 2½ton lorry that had won the war. Certainly the 'Deuce and a half', or 'Jimmy' (GMC) as it was affectionately called, was the backbone of the Quartermaster Corps resupply system. Over 800,000 of these robust 6x6 vehicles were produced and could tackle most terrain, such as the thick mud of a Belgian winter. (Tank Museum)

Above: Combat engineers built a vast number of bridges across rivers and canal all over Europe. Here men of 5th Inf Div hold a pontoon raft close to the river bank, whilst a 'Deuce and a half' is loaded. (Real War Photos)

Below: The 'Red Ball Express' resupply system kept the trucks rolling across Europe. Especially useful were the truck and trailer, the prime mover being able to detach its load and pick up a new one with the minimum of delay. (Tank Museum)

Above: The medical services made full use of the ubiquitous jeep to get casualties out of tricky situations. Here a jeep fords the Moselle River, carrying stretcher cases back to the Aid Post. (US Army)

Left: Gen Patton always took a close interest in the work of his soldiers and realised how important were the fitters and repair technicians, such as this Ordnance Corps Technician Third Grade who is working on a vehicle. (US Army)

Right: GSP talks with an Ordnance Corps Technician Fifth Grade, who is responsible for giving a pile of battle-damaged rifles some 'tender loving care'. (US Army)

Right: One of the most important parts of a soldier's daily life was receiving letters from home. Here men of an Army Post Office sort letters into unit sacks. (US Army)

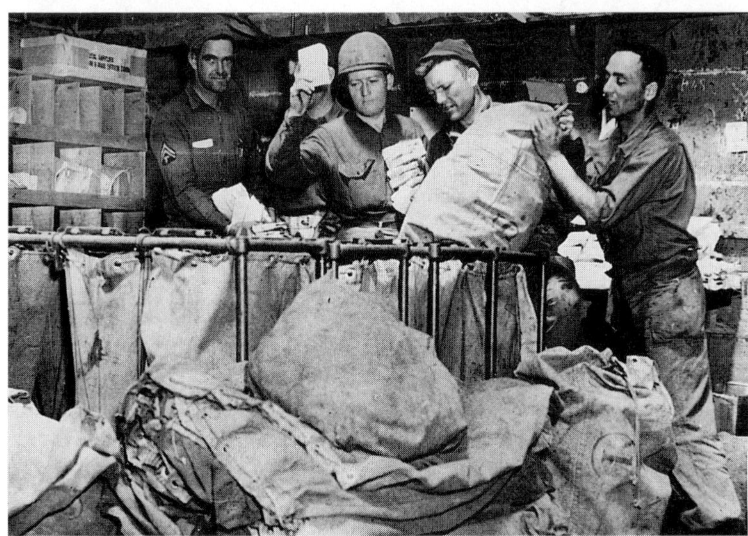

Right: The end result of the postal chain. A contented tank crew read their mail sitting beside their M5 light tank. (US Army)

Opposite page, top left: 4th Armd - Maj Gen 'Tiger Jack' Wood. (Tank Museum)

Opposite page, top right: 6th Armd - Maj Gen Robert W. Grow. (Patton Museum)

Opposite page, lower left: 11th Armd - Maj Gen Charles S. 'Rattlesnake Pete' Kilburn. (Tank Museum)

Opposite page, lower right: 76th Inf - Maj Gen William R. Schmidt. (Tank Museum)

Above: 80th Inf - Maj Gen Horace L. McBride. (Tank Museum)

Above right: 101st Ab - Maj Gen Maxwell D. Taylor. (Tank Museum)

Right: 101st Ab - Brig Gen Anthony G. McAuliffe who was commanding the division in Bastogne. (Real War Photos)

Above left: Fr 2nd Armd – Maj Gen Jacques LeClerc. (Author's collection).

Above: Col (later Gen) Bruce C. Clarke, hero of St. Vith. (Patton Museum)

Left: Lt Col (later Gen) Creighton Abrams, CO of 37th Tank Battalion. (Patton Museum)

Above: On the roll! A Sherman of 2nd Platoon B Company (see sign B-11 on rear) of one of the tank battalions of 4th Armd Div, leaving Periers on its way to the front lines at Coutances for the Third Army breakout on 21 July 1944. (US Army)

Below: Welcome to the Liberators! Men of XX Corps receive a rapturous welcome in the narrow, crowded streets of Angers. The welcoming banner is still being put up as they enter town! (US Army)

Opposite page, top: The infantry were always 'at the sharp end' and the fighting was at very close quarters in the thick bocage hedgerows of of Normandy. Here newly captured prisoners are quickly de-briefed before being taken to the rear. (US Army)

Above: Patton tactfully allowed the 2nd French Armoured Division to 'liberate' Paris, 25 August 1944. Here they are greeted by the citizens, some of whom still seem to be giving a Nazi salute – just in case! (Real War Photos)

Left: An excellent photograph showing men of the 11th Infantry Regiment, 5 Inf Div advancing, not in immediate action. In addition to providing good examples of GI clothing one can also spot in the general background, jeeps, halftracks and, on the extreme right, an HMC M8 105mm SP howitzer. (Real War Photos)

Above: Was it Napoleon who said that an army 'marches on its stomach'? Here GIs line up in a Chow Line for hot food – a welcome change from 'K' rations. Note also the good close up of an immaculate M1 rifle. (US Army)

Below: Searching the skies for signs of enemy aircraft. A Third Army GMC M15A1 (a multiple gun mount of a 37mm cannon and twin .50in HMGs based on a halftrack) keeps watch near Bastogne. (US Army)

Above: German prisoners march out of Fort Jeanne d'Arc at Metz after its capture by III Corps on 13 December 1944, ending the long-drawn out siege of Metz. (US Army)

Below: Two gaunt members of the heroic garrison of Bastogne exchange a few words after their relief by 4th Armored Division. (US Army)

PRAYER

ALMIGHTY and most merciful Father, we humbly beseech Thee, of Thy great goodness, to restrain these immoderate rains with which we have had to contend. Grant us fair weather for Battle. Graciously hearken to us as soldiers who call upon Thee that armed with Thy power, we may advance from victory to victory, and crush the oppression and wickedness of our enemies, and establish Thy justice among men and nations. Amen.

Above: Winter conditions made the fighting and movement exceptionally difficult. Here a tank column passes a line of infantry in a shell-marked village street. Sometimes whitewash was used to camouflage AFVs, but this snow appears real! (US Army)

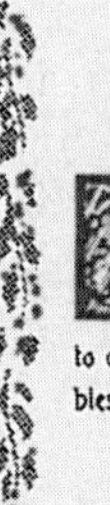

HEADQUARTERS
THIRD UNITED STATES ARMY

TO each officer and soldier in the Third United States Army, I wish a Merry Christmas. I have full confidence in your courage, devotion to duty, and skill in battle. We march in our might to complete victory. May God's blessing rest upon each of you on this Christmas Day.

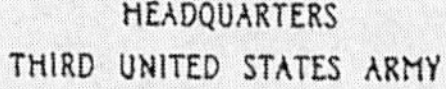

G. S. PATTON, JR.,
Lieutenant General,
Commanding, Third United States Army.

Left: GSP issued this Christmas Card in December 1944 – as will be seen it includes his 'prayer for fine weather' (see page 130). (via Mike Province)

Right: Gen Patton presenting BG Anthony C. McAuliffe with the DSC, 29 December 1944. McAuliffe commanded the 101st Ab Div garrison at Bastogne and his laconic reply of 'Nuts!' to the German ultimatum to surrender is now part of airborne history. (US Army)

Below: Men of 76th Infantry Division advance down a street in Echternach, 7 February 1945. The instinctive crouch helps to make them think they were a less conspicuous target; however, an infantryman's life was always fraught with danger. (US Army)

Above: Men of 90th Infantry Division pass through some of the 'dragon's teeth' of the Siegfried Line near Heckuscheid, Germany, in February 1945. (US Army)

Below: The combat engineers were always busy at every water obstacle. Here they construct a pontoon bridge across the Moselle River, whilst other GIs wait to cross. (US Army)

Above: Men of 354 Inf Regt, 89 Inf Div, VIII Corps, crossing the Rhine at St Goar on 26 March 1945. This was one of Third Army's seven crossings and was some days after the initial 1st Army crossing at Remagen (7 March) and XII Corps, first crossing at Oppenheim (22 March). (US Army)

Right: Raising 'Old Glory' at the Lorelei. Third Army troops raise the Stars and Stripes on top of the Lorelei Rock, overlooking the Rhine, 28 March 1945. (US Army)

Left: Burning buildings greet Shermans of 11th Armd Div in Kronach, near Bayreuth, in April 1945. By now there was little heavy opposition, just relief that the war was ending. (US Army)

Below: Here GIs dodge sniper fire as they clear Oberdoria, Germany, 4 April 1945, with tank support. (US Army)

JOHNNIE
THE GHOSTS OF
PATTON'S ARMY

Opposite page, top: Members of the 2nd Cavalry Group of Third Army gather around a fire to read about their exploits in 'Stars & Stripes'. (US Army)

Opposite page, bottom: Some of the unspeakable horrors uncovered as the advance continued were the concentration camps, like this one at Ohrdruf, Germany, where hundreds of Polish prisoners had been murdered by the SS just hours before the arrival of 4th Armd and 89th Inf Divs. 8 April 1945. (US Army)

Below: The 'Master Race' is vanquished. Tanks of 6th Armd Div roll on past vast columns of German prisoners. This group is walking down the centre island of the autobahn near Giesen. (US Army)

U.S.

Left: Four star General George S Patton, Jr, wearing his 'war face'. (US Army)

Above: Patton salutes his soldiers. The officers and enlisted men of HQ Third Army march past their Commanding General, in Germany in 1945. (Patton Museum)

Below: Patton addresses HQ Third Army after a parade in Germany in 1945. (Patton Museum)

Right: Gen Patton accompanying US Secretary of War, Henry L. Stimson, on an inspection of 2nd Armored Division, in Berlin. 20 July 1945. (Patton Museum)

Opposite page, top: Gen Patton and Lt Gen Nikonov Dimitrievitch Zahwataeff, CG 4th Soviet Guards Army, salute a guard of honour near Linz, Austria on 12 May 1945. GSP had a deep suspicion of all communists and saw them as a far greater menace than even the Germans. (Patton Museum)

Above: Patton with his grandchildren, taken in June 1945 at the Walter Reed Hospital, Washington, where his daughter, Ruth Ellen worked as a volunteer. L to R: George Patton Waters (4), Michael Walker Totten (3), Beatrice Willoughby Totten (2) and John K Waters, Jr. (7). (Patton Museum)

Left: Gen Patton stands by as Beatrice talks with Gen Henry 'Hap' Arnold, Chief of the USAAF. Although this photo is not dated, GSP wears four stars and Third Army insignia, so it was probably taken during his first post-war visit to the USA in June 1945. (Patton Museum)

Above: GSP receiving one of the many decorations presented to him by Allied countries during his various tours in October – November 1945. (Patton Museum)

Opposite page, top: Gen George S. Patton, Jr, addresses his beloved Third Army troops for the last time, as he hands over to a very sombre-looking Gen Lucian K. Truscott, formerly CG Fifth (US) Army, at Bad Tolz, Germany, 7 October 1945. (Patton Museum)

Opposite page, bottom: Snuggled up against his late master's belongings a disconsolate Willie waits to be shipped home. (Patton Museum)

MP
LT. GEN. 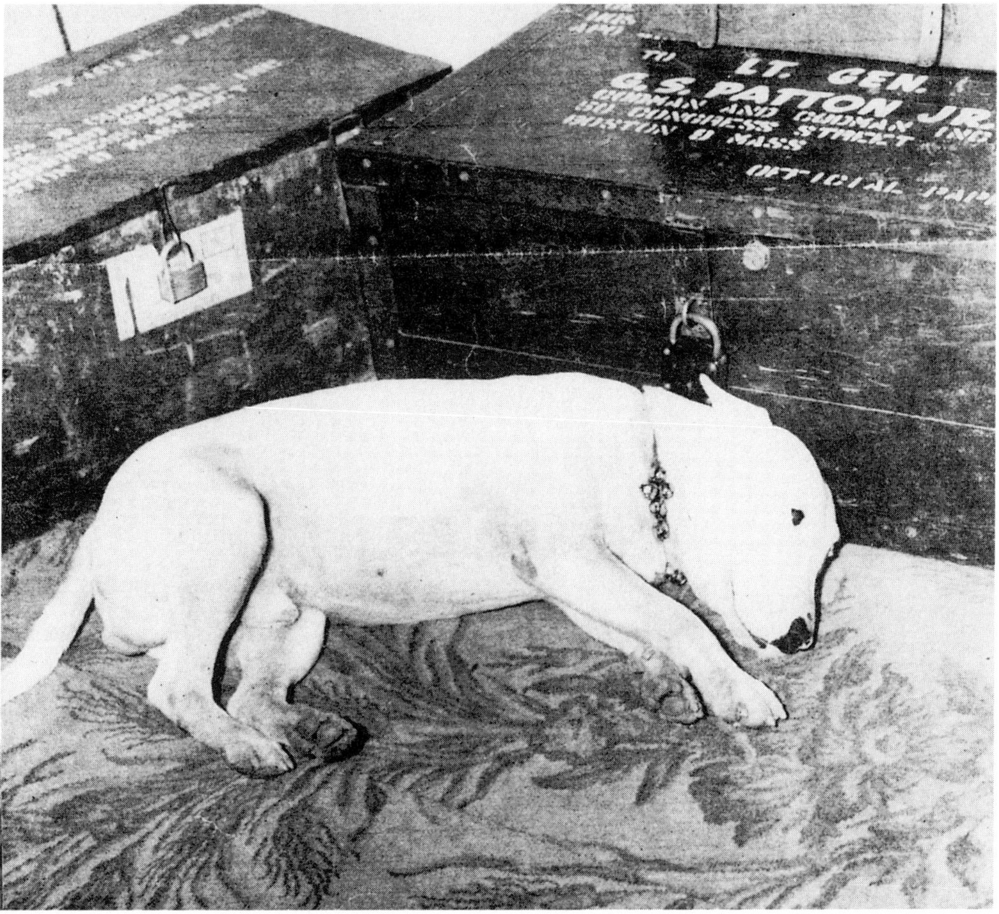
G.S. PATTON JR.

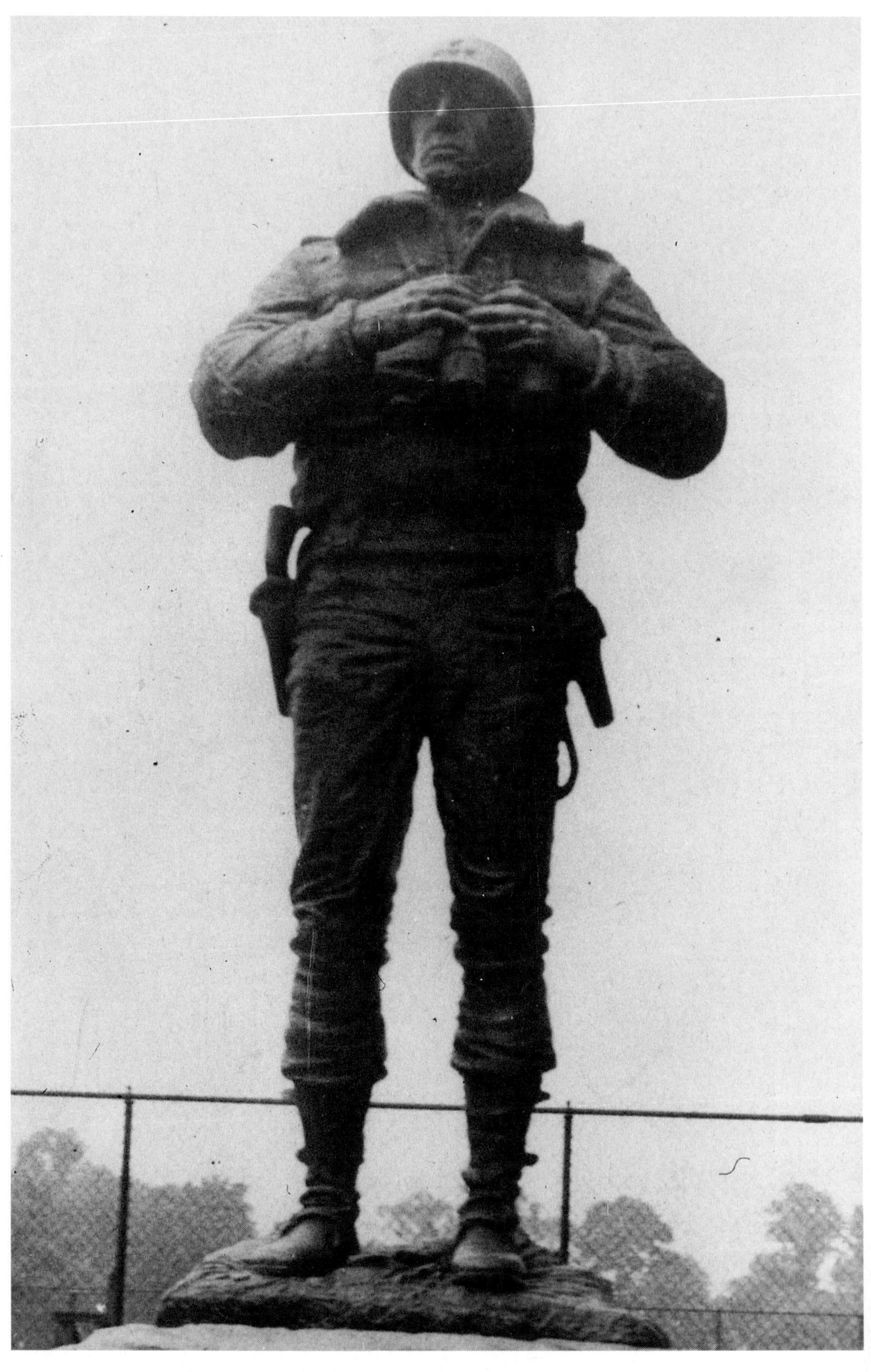

Above: Gen Patton's statue at West Point Military Acadamy. It's a copy of the original statue at Ettelbruck, Luxembourg. (US Army)

matic. Curtis Tarr, who, as an artilleryman, was armed with a carbine as his personal weapon, recalled in his autobiography that he 'acquired' a rifle as well, because, as he rightly decided, it would be more accurate and have a greater range in a fire fight. 'I found one easily; M1 rifles were available, everywhere, abandoned by the killed and wounded. I cleaned it, learned how to care for it and to fire it. I thought it would be better protection in case enemy troops stormed our command post. But my interlude with the M1 ended a few days later, when a man from Ordnance took it away from me, saying that I was authorised only a carbine!'

GRENADES: There were two main types of hand-grenade: the M2A1 fragmentation grenade which was pineapple-shaped and had its outer surface segmented (cf: British Mills 36 grenade). It weighed 1.31lb (0.6kg) and had a 4-second fuse. The second type was the M3A fragmentation grenade which was cylindrical, weighed 0.84lb (0.38kg) and had a 4½-second fuse.

AIRBORNE FORCES' PERSONAL WEAPONS: Every paratrooper carried a .45 cal pistol and an M1 rifle. Officers were supposed to carry only a pistol, but many sensibly also preferred a rifle or Thompson submachine-gun. Each man jumped with his personal weapons, but machine-guns, mortars, reserve ammunition, radios, medical equipment, etc., were packed in bundles or 'para-packs' which were dropped from six bomb racks under the belly of the Dakota, or pushed out of the door by the jumpmaster.

RATIONS

There were five different types of field ration scales in the US Army, known by the letters 'A', 'B', 'C', 'D' and 'K'.

FIELD RATION 'A': This was almost the same as the garrison ration and the diet of soldiers in the USA, containing as it did some 70 per cent fresh food.

FIELD RATION 'B': Similar to 'A' but with non-perishable items substituted for fresh, e.g., canned meats, fruits and vegetables, dehydrated eggs and potatoes. As more refrigerated space became available in cargo ships, more fresh foodstuffs were shipped overseas. 'B' Ration was sometimes called 'Ten in One', one pack containing sufficient food for ten men for one day. Two hot and one cold meal could be served from this pack.

FIELD RATION 'C': Under development just before the war, this ration was designed to replace the reserve ration of the Great War. It consisted of small cans of meat and vegetables (ten different ones – meat & beans; meat & vegetable stew; meat & spaghetti; ham, eggs and potatoes; meat & noodles; meat & rice; frankfurters & beans; pork & beans; ham & lima beans; chicken & vegetables). Jam, biscuits (crackers), powdered drinks, sugar, cereals, etc., were also included.

FIELD RATION 'D': This comprised a highly concentrated chocolate bar, containing cocoa, oat flour and skim milk powder, weighing just four ounces, but containing 600 calories. It was designed for emergency use only, replacing the Iron Ration of the Great War.

FIELD RATION 'K': Originally developed for paratroops, it was soon very familiar to all front-line troops. One individual meal was packed in a waterproofed cardboard box, just 6 inches long. The boxes were marked with the type of meal they contained: BREAKFAST, DINNER or SUPPER. Breakfast contained a fruit bar, Nescafé powdered coffee, sugar, crackers and a small tin of ham and eggs. Dinner and Supper contained a can of cheese or potted meat, crackers, orange or lemon powder, sugar, chocolate or other sweets and chewing-gum.

Both the 'C' and 'K' Rations could be eaten hot or cold. Each man usually carried one or two meals in his pack or pockets, while all vehicles normally had more 'C' or 'K' Rations on board. Many GIs carried paraffin pocket heaters, heat tablets, matches and candles. Outposts would be issued with small gasoline stoves, while units had larger gasoline ranges. Most commanders liked to send up hot meals whenever possible in containers (called 'Marmite' cans) which kept food hot; platoons and squads rotating back to a suitable location to eat. For much of the time, however, front-line troops had to depend on 'B', 'C' or 'K' rations, supplementing them with hot drinks whenever they could make a fire on which to 'brew up'. Curtis Tarr recalled that his battery kitchen served two hot meals a day and that they supplemented these with 'K' and 'C' rations as well as food from home.

LIVING CONDITIONS

These varied depending on location, time of year and, in particular, how near the 'sharp end' one happened to be. Those with vehicles, AFV crews and the like, probably had a better built-in capability to provide themselves with warm, dry accommodation, and a ready supply of gasoline meant that making a fire was never difficult. But, as every soldier knows, only a fool is uncomfortable, and so even the infantryman on his two feet was able to find warmth and shelter, except in the most desperate situations. 'Cover from view' was not always 'cover from fire', so a wet foxhole was sometimes far more sensible than a dry shelter above ground level. Private Tarr soon discovered many things essential to existence in open-air conditions, none being more important than the open-air bathing technique: 'You began with a pot of water on the small Coleman gasoline stove: how I loved that stove for heating rations as well as water for shaving and bathing! You filled your helmet with the heated water, propped it up so that it would not roll over and empty and there you had a satisfactory basin for washing. You needed a warm place to stand, and one perfect spot was the hood of the half-track while the engine ran to charge the battery for the radio; the engine heated the hood and made a warm pad for your feet. Then you took off your clothes, despite temperatures below freezing, and bravely in this exposed position applied soap and water to your body beginning with your face and ending with your hair. What luxury clean clothes were after such a bath.

'But then you had the dirty clothes to launder. Some fellows used gasoline on their woollens, others used soap and water. I never developed a satisfactory method until I learned that the older women in the village needed soap for their own use and that dirty clothes plus extra soap produced clean and pressed clothes. How they did it, I could not determine. But they did it well.'

MORALE

Good morale starts at the top with the man in charge who must motivate everyone else by his leadership and example. Third Army could have had no better example of this adage than Patton, who was one of the finest motivators of men in the American Army. His own example for bravery was legendary, and the example he set on dress, deportment and discipline was faultless. He demanded the same high standards from his men – as II Corps swiftly discovered when GSP took charge of them in Tunisia. This was the same standard he expected from Third Army personnel at all times; pity the poor GI caught dirty, unshaven or without his necktie and helmet, when there was every reason why he should have been clean, smart and properly dressed. Patton obviously made allowances for troops in action, but they were still always required to maintain a proper level of self-respect. Anyone entering the Third Army area was always impressed by the fact that every man was clean-shaven, had polished boots and wore his helmet and necktie. Third Army's Provost Department must have had their work cut out maintaining their Commanding General's high standards. There is supposed to be a fully documented case of MPs arresting three members of a bomber crew shot down over the Third Army area, for 'failing to wear helmets, liners and neckties'![9]

Third Army men were always proud to proclaim that they were in Third Army. When the US Secretary of War, Robert Patterson, was visiting wounded in base hospitals in the UK, he found it was always possible to spot a Third Army man. When asking a patient what unit he was in, men from other Armies invariably named their regiment or division, very few knowing what Army they were in, or the name of their Commanding General. 'But a Third Army man always replied: "I was with the Third Army". And he not only knew who commanded it, but usually had a personal anecdote about Patton.'[10]

Patton had very definite views on morale: 'Wars may be fought with weapons,' he once wrote, 'but they are won by men. It is the spirit of the men who follow and the man who leads that gains the victory.' He was also conscious of the fact that loyalty was a two-way business: 'There has been a great deal of talk about loyalty from the bottom to the top. Loyalty from the top to the bottom is much more important and much less prevalent. It is this loyalty from top to bottom which binds juniors to their seniors with the strength of steel.' Furthermore he was adamant that commanders should lead their men: 'Each, in his appropriate sphere, will lead in person. Any commander who fails to obtain his objective and who is not dead or severely wounded, has not done his duty.'

Cocky Bastards. The 'Patton Spirit' undoubtedly pervaded Third Army. Colonel Robert Allen says that Third Army men were proud of themselves and their ever-victorious battle prowess and made no bones about it. Therefore the HQ Staff were most surprised when Eisenhower, during a visit in late March 1945, told them that they were too modest, that they didn't boast enough about their achievements, saying: 'Don't be modest about yourselves. You've done great things and we need that kind of publicity right now...' The staff were surprised and the visiting liaison officers dumbfounded. 'Finally, one groaned, "Keerist! He must be nuts. Telling you guys not to be modest. Doesn't he know what the hell is going on in his Theater? You are already the most blowharding bastards over here. From now on, you'll be completely unbearable." "You and the goddamned krauts said it," gleefully whooped a brash young captain. "Cocky bastards, that's us!"'

Notes to Chapter 7

1. 'GI' was coined from the term 'Government Issue' and replaced the term 'Doughboy' which had been used to describe the US soldiers of the AEF.
2. Quoted in the XII Corps History as coming from the introduction to *The Battle Is the Payoff* by Ralph Ingersoll.
3. Quoted from *Lucky Forward*. 'D' stands for division and represents the period of divisional training, when all the major components operated together for the very first time.
4. Ibid.
5. This had not of course applied to troops going to North Africa for Operation 'Torch'. They were 'combat loaded' because they went into action immediately on landing.
6. *Patton and His Third Army* by Brigadier General Brenton G. Wallace.
7. Quoted in *XII Corps, Spearhead of Patton's Third Army*.
8. Quoted in *Patton's Third Army at War*.
9. Quoted in *Lucky Forward*.
10. Quoted in *Patton the Commander* by H. Essame.

8
The Combat Arms, Weapons, Vehicles, Equipment and Tactics

Combat Arms and the Technical Services

When the US Army was re-organised in 1942, the Technical Services were grouped under Army Service Forces(ASF), but they did include many elements of the Army Ground Forces which were also included in the Troop Basis and thus considered as combat arms. There was a strong body of opinion that some of them, such as the Corps of Engineers and Corps of Signals, should be considered as 'Arms' not 'Services' (cf: the British Army). As some of their vehicles and equipment were also common to all arms and services, the division of this and the next chapter is purely arbitrary. I have therefore chosen for reasons of balance to cover Engineers and Signals here, but I will leave the remaining five Services (Chemical Warfare, Quartermaster, Ordnance, Medical and Transportation) to the next chapter, when I shall also cover the 'specialists', such as Provost, Chaplains and Special Services including the PX.

The All Arms Team. The tactics employed by Third Army were those of the all arms team, in other words the use of a fully mobile, mixed force of armour and infantry, with the support of artillery, engineers, signals and elements of all the other arms and services which, together with air support, produced a balanced force under one commander. Whenever possible the individual commanders were linked on one radio communication net, so that they could all talk to one another, all hear what was going on and, most importantly, enable the commander of the force to impose his will and personality on the battle. This was especially important in the fluid, armoured warfare which rapidly became the hallmark of Third Army's battle plan and the reason for their continued success. Their two major characteristics can best be described as the ability to 'move and shoot', while constant momentum became their trademark. But this was not all. As we shall see later, Third Army's fast-driving, fast-shooting armoured divisions also proved that they could stand and fight on the defensive when the need arose. Patton had used tanks in the Great War, he fully understood their capabilities, he had fully embraced and understood the tactics of mobile warfare which the Germans had exemplified so well in their *Blitzkrieg*, so he above all other Allied commanders appreciated the need for speed and for the use of aggressive thrusts in the most unlikely places.

'Violent and rapid attack with the marching fire is the surest means of success in the use of armor,' wrote Patton in his last 'Notes of

Combat', issued after the war in early November 1945. In order to achieve such speed of reaction and offensive action his troops needed to be properly equipped, so a short examination of their basic weaponry will not come amiss.

INFANTRY WEAPONS

The heavier infantry weapons – machine-guns, mortars, some types of chemical weapons such as flame-throwers, anti-tank guns and rockets – were not exclusively used by the infantry although they clearly were the major users. The inclusion of anti-tank weapons shows that infantry divisions were expected to do their own anti-tank fighting rather than always depend upon armoured divisions, or on permanently attached tank destroyer units, which were better employed if kept as a pool by Corps or Army. The range of weapons also assisted in deciding where they would be located within the infantry division. So mortars, both 60mm and 81mm, were kept concentrated in separate sub-units, the former in the weapons platoon of the rifle company, the latter in the battalion heavy weapons company. The same applied to machine-guns, Browning LMGs and HMGs being similarly placed. The 57mm anti-tank gun was found in both the HQ company of the infantry battalion and the anti-tank company of the infantry regiment.

Machine-Guns

BROWNING AUTOMATIC RIFLE (BAR) MODEL 1919A2 .30IN (7.62MM).

The twelve-man rifle squad had three main elements: a two-man scout section (Able), a four-man fire section (Baker) which included the squad's automatic rifle, and a five-man manoeuvre and assault section (Charlie). The Browning automatic rifle thus provided the primary infantry squad support weapon. First developed in 1917, the Model A2 (the Great War variant) had a butt monopod fitted in addition to the bipod and shoulder-strap and flash-hider of the 1918A1 model (the original Model 1918 had been hand-held). The A2 had two rates of automatic fire instead of selective fire, but this feature was sometimes removed. Basic details:
Length: 47.8in (121.4cm)
Weight: 19.4lb (8.73kg)
Rate of fire: 3–500rpm or 5–600rpm
Type of feed: 20-round box magazine.

US MACHINE-GUN MODEL M1917A1 .30IN (7.62MM)

This was the US Army's standard support machine-gun during the Second World War. Water-cooled, it resembled the British Vickers in many respects. In the ground support role it was fired from a tripod mounting, but there was also an AA mounting. More than 53,000 of the A1 Model were manufactured.

Length: 38.64in (98cm)
Weight: 85.75lb (38.5kg) less water
Rate of fire: 450–600rpm
Type of feed: 250-round fabric a metal link belt.

US MACHINE-GUN MODEL M1919 .30IN (7.62MM)
The major difference between this MG and the M1917 model was that it had an air-cooled barrel. It was one of the most widely used machine-guns of the war, it being fitted in AFVs as well as serving in the ground role. The M1919A4 was the initial infantry version, next was the A5 for AFVs and, finally, the A6 as an infantry squad weapon, with bipod, butt and carrying handle added.
Length: 41in (104cm)
Weight: 31lb (13.95kg)
Rate of fire: 450–500rpm
Type of feed: 250-round fabric or metal-link belt.

US MACHINE-GUN MODEL M2 .50IN (12.7MM)
First produced in 1921, it was basically a larger version of the .30in M1917, with similar mechanism, firing a .50in round (based on the German 13mm anti-tank rifle round). Like the .30cal it had many uses both on the ground (AFVs and AAA as well as infantry) and in the air (nearly 1½ million of the aircraft version alone were manufactured), being produced in greater quantity than any other US machine-gun of the war.
Length: 65.1in (165.4cm)
Weight: 84lb (37.8kg)
Rate of fire: 450–575rpm
Type of feed: 110-round metal-link belt.

Mortars
60MM MORTAR M2.
This was the standard light infantry mortar, which fired mainly HE rounds (normally the M49A2), but could also fire the M83 illuminating round.
Barrel Length: 28.6in (72.6cm)
Range: 100–1,985 yards (91-1,816m)
Weight in action: 42lb (19.07kg)
Bomb weight: 3lb (1.36kg).

81MM MORTAR M1.
Capable of firing a wide range of projectiles, using a range of six charge increments. It could be carried into action by two men, but was also transported in a special mule pack or the M6A1 handcart. In addition, there was a variety of mobile mounts fixed in the M2 and M3 half-tracks.
Barrel Length: 49.5in (125.7cm)
Range: 100–3,290 yards (91–3,010m)

Weight in action: 136lb (61.7kg)
Bomb weight: HE 6.87lb (3.12kg) and 10.62lb (4.82kg); Chemical 10.75lb (4.88kg).
NB. The larger, 4.2in mortar was a Chemical Warfare Service (CWS) weapon and is covered in the next chapter.

Flame-Throwers

PORTABLE FLAME-THROWER M2-2.
Three versions of man-portable flame-thrower were produced during the war, the M1, M1A1 and M2-2. This final version appeared in March 1944. All were very similar in appearance, comprising two fuel tanks and a pressure tank (carried on the back). The weapon was more widely used in the Pacific campaigns but saw some service in the ETO.
Range: 25–40 yards (22.9–36.5m) (M1 had a shorter range)
Weight in action: 62–72lb (30.9–32.7kg)
Duration of fire: 8–9sec (M1 8–10sec).
Although these weapons were used by combat troops, they were held and maintained by the CWS – see next chapter.

Anti-Tank Weapons

ANTI-TANK RIFLE GRENADE M9A1.
This was the standard US rifle grenade, which could penetrate up to 4in of homogeneous armour. The nose-impact grenade weighed 1.31lb (0.59kg) and was fired from the M7 launcher (M1 rifle) or M8 (M1 carbine).

ROCKET LAUNCHER M1 AND M9 'BAZOOKA'.
One of the most original weapons produced during the war – the Germans copied it in their *Raketenpanzerbusche 43* series – which comprised a metal tube from which a small hollow-charge rocket could be fired. It needed a two-man team, one to fire the weapon, one to do the loading, the battle range being usually some 150 yards. The M6A1 and M6A3 HE rockets were carried three to a canvas bag (two bags carried by the loader). Smoke and incendiary rounds were also available. It had a dangerous back blast area, but was highly lethal to most types of AFV at close range. The M9 could be broken down into two halves. Nearly half a million Bazookas were manufactured during the war.
Length: M1 4.5ft (135cm), M9 5ft 1in (155cm)
Max range: 700 yards (640m)
Weight of rocket: 3.4lb (1.53kg)
Armour penetration: 4.7in (11.75cm) at 90°.

ANTI-TANK GUN M1 57MM.
Replacing the older 37mm anti-tank gun and based upon the already proven British 6pdr, it was in general use in ETO before D-Day, twelve

57mm in the anti-tank company and three in the anti-tank platoon of each HQ company, making a total of 57 in an infantry division. Its armour-piercing shell could penetrate 2.7in (6.75cm) of armour at 20° at a range of 1,000 yards (914m). It was normally towed, but was also mounted on the M3 half-track as the T48 Gun Motor Carriage.
Length: 9ft 9in (297cm)
Traverse: 90°
Elevation: -5° to +15°
Travelling weight: 2,700lb (1,225kg)
Muzzle velocity: 2,700fps (900m/s)
Shell weight: 6.28lb (2.83kg)
Maximum range: 10,260 yards (9,380m).

Artillery

105mm Howitzer M3. Also within the Infantry Regiment was the Cannon Coy, armed with six of the short-barrelled version of the 105mm M2 towed field howitzer on the M3A1 carriage, which could be turned through 180° to lower the piece on to the firing pedestal, thus giving added stability when firing. It had a split trail and pneumatic tyres. It weighed 2,495lb complete, had a shell weight (M1 HE) of 33lb and a maximum range of 7,250 yards. A total of 2,580 were built during the war.

The task of the infantry has always been to close with the enemy, so as to capture and hold ground. It is they who have to meet the enemy, face to face, more often than the troops of any other arm. Despite the increased individual firepower of the average rifleman, it is interesting to note that post-war studies of the infantry in the Second World War have shown that only between 15 and 30 per cent of riflemen actually fired a shot at the enemy during any particular battle, nor do these figures mean that those riflemen fired continually throughout the battle, but rather indicated the percentage of those who tried to shoot at the enemy at least once.[1] Nevertheless, infantry battles were invariably difficult, exhausting, bloody encounters, as these two short extracts from the history of 76th Infantry Division's actions in February 1945, while they were operating in the Siegfried Line area, show: 'At 1550 the pallid, death signal of a green flare appeared in the sky; the artillerymen understood. They ceased firing, their concluding shell a screaming echo of the whisper in their hearts, "Good luck, doughboys, give'em hell!" Immediately two .50 caliber machine-guns north of Ernzhof opened up with crossfire on the pillbox. From the adjacent woods it also received the whooshing rockets of bazookas. Up the ridge in a staggered wedge formation came the assaulting infantrymen. An anti-personnel mine exploded, the wire tripped accidentally by Lt Henderson. He and Pfc Jack W. Wardle were slightly injured, but the lieutenant continued to lead the assault. The pillbox was completely buttoned up; fire from machine-guns, bazookas, automatic and M-1 rifles completely prevented the enemy from firing. The assault group was now 25 yards from the fort. The machine-gunners lifted their fire and the demolition carrier, Pfc Leslie M. Roderick, rushing forward, placed one of the satchel charges against the door of the large front embrasure. Part of the door was blown away. A second charge was placed but failed to explode, so Sgt Pusco dashed up and tossed two grenades through the hole made by the initial explosion. By this time however, the Germans, deserting the firing compartment, had fled via the rear exit to the quarters compartment. Members of the assault team worked their way into position and grenaded the new defense point. The Germans had enough. Out of the pillbox came a complete manning crew of 15 men led by a staff sergeant, who was made to deactivate the minefield surrounding the fortification. The entire assault operation lasted one hour and fifteen minutes with only two of our men wounded in the action. 40 pillboxes to a square mile and this is the saga of only one. Simple, wasn't it?'

Later, having taken out 110 pillboxes, the weary troops were relieved. 'Now the company, led by 1st Lt Richard Bluhm, came stumbling and slipping down the slimy side of the mountain they and the other companies had won in pain and darkness six days ago. All that could be seen in those dirty whiskered faces, in the sag of wet shoulders, in the shuffle of mudcaked feet, was the weariness of men who had lived with continuous danger, little food and less sleep for nearly a week – complete utter fatigue. "It took us three hours just to climb that mudbank, slipping back a step every time we took one forward," said Lt Bluhm, "but we reached our objective on that flat hilltop and we hung on." Elsewhere in that weary conglomeration of tired humanity a GI was speaking: "Did you hear about Lt Mears? He led assault squads against three emplacements which were defended against hell and high water, but he took the fortifications and fifteen of the enemy. Then two days later he led his platoon from Company K through machine-gun fire that came so fast it was like solid steel. He assaulted a pillbox singlehanded, armed only with a jammed carbine and a hand-grenade and forced the surrender of its nine kraut defenders. Gosh, what a guy."'

ARMOURED FIGHTING VEHICLES

There were AFVs of various types – light tanks, medium tanks, tank destroyers, armoured cars, scout cars and a variety of specialised armoured vehicles (e.g., tracked recovery vehicles) – to be found in tank battalions, tank destroyer battalions and cavalry reconnaissance squadrons, either within armoured divisions or attached to infantry divisions. In addition, of course, there were the ubiquitous, more lightly armoured half-tracks which were used for a wide variety of roles.

Light Tanks

M5 AND M5A1.

By the time that Third Army reached the ETO, all the little M3s and M3A1s – the 'Honey' as the British drivers in the Western Desert had nicknamed this excellent little tank – had been replaced in US operational service (except in the Pacific theatre) by the later M5 model and its successor, the M5A1. The M5 had first seen combat with units of the 2nd Armored Division, during Operation 'Torch' in the Casablanca area of the North Africa coast. With a four-man crew and dual driving controls, both the M5 and M5A1 were powered by two 8-cylinder, 90 degree V-type liquid cooled engines, located in the rear of the hull. The flywheel end of each engine was connected to a hydromatic transmission. The propeller shaft from each powerplant went forward through the fighting compartment to a transfer unit located at the right of the driver's seat. The transmission, plus the two-speed transfer unit, provided six forward and one reverse gears. The tanks were wired for radio installation and for an intraphone system within the tank. The basic hull armour plate was a completely welded structure, except for portions of the front, top and rear which were removable for servicing. Armour on the front was 1⅛-inch thick (apart from the nose casting which was 1½-inch). Two drivers' hatches were located in the fighting compartment roof and two more in the turret roof. Access to the engine was via hinged double doors at the rear of the hull. On the M5A1 there was also an escape hatch in the hull floor behind the assistant driver.

Specifications	***M5***	***M5A1***
Combat weight:	33,138lb	33,484lb
(with rubber tracks; steel tracks added 1,200lb to the M5A1)		
Width:	7ft 4.5in	7ft 4.5in
Height:	7ft 6.5in	7ft 6.5in
Length:	14ft 6.75in	14ft 6.75in
Engine horsepower at 3,400rpm:	110	110
Armament: One 37mm gun and one .30 cal MG M1919A5 fixed, in combination gun mount M23, in the turret; one .30 cal MG M1919A4 flexible in ball mount in bow; one .30 cal MG M1919A4 flexible AA on turret roof. 123 rounds of 37mm ammo carried (39 HE, 65 AP and 19 canister).		
Armour:	12mm to 67mm	12mm to 67mm
Radio:	SCR 508 (SCR 506 in command vehicles)	
Fuel capacity:	89gal	86gal
Max speed (roads):	40mph	40mph
Road radius:	180 miles	172miles
Vertical obstacle:	2ft	2ft
Fording depth:	3ft	2.5ft
Trench crossing:	5ft 5in	5ft 5in

Variants. Among the variants which saw service were:
M5 Command tank – basic M5 with turret removed and a box-like superstructure fitted, with a .50cal HMG in a flexible mount.
M5 Dozer – basic M5 less turret and fitted with a front-mounted bulldozer blade.
T8 Recce vehicle – basic M5 less turret, and with a .50cal HMG on a ring mount fitted plus extra storage racks for land-mines.
Howitzer Motor Carriage M8 – see below
Other fittings included an E7-7 flame gun in place of the 37mm; a loud-hailer and PA equipment for psy-warfare; Culin hedgerow cutter for dealing with *bocages* (hedgerows).

M24 CHAFFEE.
Entering US Army service during the winter of 1944, during the Battle of the Bulge, the four-man M24[2] used the assistant driver as loader in the turret for the 75mm gun when the tank was in action. When man-power allowed, the tank could take a five-man crew. The layout was normal – driving compartment in front, fighting compartment in the centre and engine compartment at the rear. Dual controls were provided and the tank was powered by two 8-cylinder 90 degree V-type liquid cooled Cadillac engines, through two hydromatic transmissions, a transfer unit with mechanically selected speed ranges – two forward and one reverse – a controlled differential for steering and braking (located in the front of the hull), two final drives and connecting propeller shafts. Tracks were steel, 16 inches wide. The hull was completely welded (except for servicing entrances), the turret was 5 feet in diameter and mounted on a continuous ball-bearing mounting, with 360° traverse, by means of hydraulic or hand wheel.
Specifications:
Combat weight: 40,500lb
Length: 18ft
Width: 9ft 4in
Height: 7ft 3in
Armament: one 75mm M6 gun, with 48 rounds stowed, plus two .30 cal MG (one coax and one in hull) and one .50 cal AA MG
Armour: 9mm to 25mm
Max speed (road): 35mph
Road radius: 100 miles
Fording depth: 3ft 4in
Vertical obstacle: 3ft 4in
Trench crossing: 8ft.
Although no light tank can seriously be expected to win the tank v. tank battle against a heavier opponent, the Chaffee undoubtedly held its own against all but the heaviest German tanks. It was simple, reliable and rugged, with satisfactory hitting power for a tank of its size and weight.

Medium Tanks – The M4 Sherman Series

As with the M3 lights, the M3 mediums had mainly been phased out of front-line service in the US Army, except in secondary roles (e.g., as tracked recovery vehicles) by the time that Third Army reached the ETO. They had been replaced by the 'tank that won the war', namely the M4 medium, named the 'Sherman' after the famous Civil War general. During the war a staggering total of 49,234 Sherman gun tanks of all types were built: the USSR's T34 was the *only* tank to have been built in similar quantity and it represented more than the total *combined* tank output of Britain and Germany during the whole of the war! By the time production ceased in 1944, no fewer than six basic models of the gun tank had been produced (M4 to M4A6 – the M4A5 being the US designation for the Canadian Ram I), together with seven other gun models including the 105mm Close Support version and the various upgunned 76mm versions. Not all Models of the M4 served in Third Army, but certainly most did, and a myriad of adaptations were to be seen, including tank destroyers, tank recovery vehicles, mine clearers, rocket carriers, etc.

The basic M4 was a five-man tank, armed with a 75mm gun – later upgunned to 76mm – powered by a variety of engines (M4 and M4A1: Continental R-975 radial, 420hp; M4A2: Twin GM diesels, 375hp; M4A3: Ford GAA V-8, 500hp; M4A4: Chrysler Multibank, 370hp; M4A6: Caterpillar radial diesel, 450hp). Various models had cast/rolled armour plate, yet others the earlier three-piece bolted nose. Sherman's protection was not good and it quickly earned the nickname 'The Ronson Lighter' for obvious reasons, so reworking with appliqué armour to the hull sides, front and turret sides took place. But the main improvements were to the main gun, when it was decided to fit the 76mm gun,[3] and to mobility by the fitting of the HVSS (horizontal volute spring suspension) to replace the normal vertical volute spring suspension.

Example Specifications	*M4*	*M4A2(76)W*4*
Combat weight	66,900lb	70,000lb
Length	19ft 4in	19ft 10.5in
Width	8ft 7in	8ft 9in
Height	9ft	9ft 9in
Armament	75mm Gun M3	76mm Gun M1A1
	plus two .30 cal MG (one coax and one in bow), one .50 cal AA MG and one 2in mortar M3 (smoke) fixed in turret	
Armour	12-75mm	12-100mm
Engine	Continental R975C1 9-cylinder radial	GM 6046 twin 12-cylinder inline
Max speed (roads)	24mph	30mph
Road radius	120 miles	100 miles
Vertical obstacle	2ft	2ft
Fording depth	3ft 4in	3ft 4in
Trench crossing	7ft 6in	7ft 6in

Variants. The 105mm Close Support howitzer M4 was fitted to 1,641 M4s and 3,039 M4A3s, to give a close support weapon, normally held in Company HQ, while only 254 of the M4A3E2 assault tank, nicknamed 'Jumbo' were built. This AFV had much thicker armour (175mm on the gun shield alone) which put its weight up to 84,000lb. Like its predecessor, the Sherman was adapted as the Tank Recovery Vehicle M32, the gun and turret being replaced by a fixed turret, with a 60,000lb winch, plus a pivoting A-frame jib. The M1 dozer blade could also be fitted to the front of the tank. Probably the most recognisable of the 'funnies' were Calliope (fitted with the T34 rocket-launcher which held 60 x 4.5in rockets) and Aunt Jemima (the mine exploder T1E3(M1)).

Heavy Tanks

Mention must be made of the T26E3 PERSHING, whose 90mm M3 gun was undoubtedly the most powerful tank gun in US Army service. However, only a small number of Pershings entered service before the war ended, a handful in 3rd Armd Div and just nine to 9th Armd Div, which served with Third Army for a short time in December 1944 and May 1945. The Pershings were used to good effect by 9th Armd Div during the historic seizure of the Ludendorff railway bridge at Remagen in early March 1945, but at that time they were not part of Third Army.

In April 1945, Third Army received 90 Pershings, 40 of which were released to 11th Armd Div, the remainder being held in the main army combat vehicle pool. At the same time ten modified tank transporters were also issued. None of these tanks saw action. The 92,355lb Pershing's armour was more than 100mm thick on its gunshield, and it was without doubt the best all-round fighting tank produced by the USA during the war, but it arrived too late to have any effect upon Third Army's campaign.

Tank Destroyers

Three types of TD were to be found in service with TD Battalions in Third Army. These were the M10 WOLVERINE, the M18 HELLCAT, and the M36. All had five-man crews - commander, driver and three-gun crew. The M10 was based upon the Sherman chassis, power train and running gear, but with a very different armour profile (thick in front, thinner elsewhere, open top) which reduced its weight considerably and gave it excellent battlefield mobility, which was, after firepower, the major prerequisite of the tank destroyer. The M18 was designed from scratch as a TD, some 2,500 being built of this, very fast, agile, but lightly armoured AFV. The last of the trio, the M36, was probably the best, its 90mm gun and slightly thicker armour more than making up for its slower speed. Initially M10A1 hulls were used to mount the redesigned turret, but later Sherman M4A3 and M10 hulls were also used, for the M36A1 and M36A2 respectively. A total of 2,324 M36s of all three models were produced.

Specification	*M10*	*M18*	*M36*
Combat weight	66,000lb	40,000lb	62,000lb
Length	22ft 5in	21ft 10in	24ft 6in
Width	10ft	9ft 9in	10ft
Height	9ft 6in	8ft 5in	10ft 9in
Armament	3in gun plus .30 AA MG	76mm gun plus .50 AA HMG	90mm gun
Armour	12-37mm	7-12mm	12-50mm
Engine	Twin GMC diesels	Continental R975	Ford GAA
Max speed	30mph	50-55mph	26-30mph
Road radius	200 miles	150 miles	150 miles
Vertical wall	2ft	3ft	2ft
Fording depth	3ft	4ft	3ft
Trench crossing	7ft 6in	6ft 2in	7ft 6in

Although armour did often operate on its own, it was far more likely that a force of all arms would deal with a task, such as the day in November 1944, when 80th Infantry and 6th Armored Divisions were co-operating to seize the river crossing and road and rail junction of Han-sur-Nied. The Combat Record of 6th Armd Div reads: 'CCA (Hines): At 0700 a ten-minute artillery preparation was placed on the town of Béchy. At 0710 CT9[5] continued its advance and by 0900 it was fighting for entry into this town. The road leading into town was blocked by a minefield which damaged two tanks. Dug-in enemy riflemen resisted strongly in a brief but bitter fight and the Combat Team continued its advance. On the eastern side of Béchy CT9 again met resistance but overcame it and continued toward the Nied River under heavy artillery fire.

'The bridge at Han-sur-Nied was intact. Light and medium tanks and tank destroyers of the advance guard covered the bridge with fire and knocked out several enemy vehicles and guns which were trying to retreat across it. A hasty assault against the bridge was organised by the advance guard in conjunction with a battalion from the 80th Inf Div. A platoon of Co B, 68th Tk Bn moved down the hill, followed by infantry and a detachment of four men of Co B, 25th Armd Engr Bn. They were covered by fire of the tank destroyers and the remainder of the company of medium and light tanks. The medium tank platoon succeeded in crossing the bridge although one tank was knocked out and the platoon leader was killed. The engineers, working under heavy fire of all types, succeeded in cutting the wires to the prepared demolition charges, on and under the bridge. 80th Inf Div troops together with a few of the 9th Armd Inf Bn and a platoon of tanks from 68th Tk Bn succeeded in holding the bridgehead the remainder of the day though under continuous fire. For this heroic action, Co B 68th Tk Bn and its attachments later received a Presidential Citation.'[6]

Armoured Cars and Scout Cars

Although the USA built a variety of armoured cars and scout cars only three saw operational service in US armoured units, numerous others being built specifically for the British Army (e.g., Staghound). These were one armoured car and two scout/utility cars.

M8 Greyhound

This four-man AFV was the main armoured car of the US Army, 8,523 having been built by the Ford Motor Company by the end of the war. Very fast and very quiet, its chassis was also used for the M20 utility car.

Specifications:
Combat weight: 17,400lb
Length: 16ft 5in
Width: 8ft 4in
Height: 7ft 4.5in
Armament: 37mm M6 gun, plus one .30 cal MG (coax) and one .50 cal HMG AA
Armour: 3-20mm
Engine: Hercules JXD petrol 110hp
Max speed on roads: 56mph
Road radius: 350 miles.

M20 Utility Car

The turret and 37mm gun of the Greyhound was removed and replaced by a superstructure, including a .50 cal HMG on a ring mount. Also built by Ford, 3,791 were produced; they were used as a command vehicle and personnel carrier.

M3A1 White Scout Car

Widely used by many branches of the US Army, its original role was as a scout vehicle for the armoured cavalry. With a crew of two, it could also carry a further six men in the rear compartment, upon which a .50 cal HMG and a .30 cal MG were mounted by means of a 'skate' rail.

Specifications:
Combat weight: 12,400lb
Length: 18ft 5.5in
Width: 6ft 8in
Height: 6ft 6.5in
Armament: one .50 cal HMG and one .30 cal MG
Armour: 7mm
Engine: Hercules JXD petrol, 87hp
Max speed on roads: 50mph
Road radius: 250 miles.

Patton's Household Cavalry. General Patton always needed to know what was happening in the whole of the Third Army battle area so that he could take advantage of enemy setbacks, move his armour quickly and effectively, etc. He therefore made considerable use of his 6th Cavalry Group, under Colonel Edward M. Fickett. He renamed it officially as the Army Information Service (unofficially it was known as 'Patton's Household Cavalry'!) and transformed it into a communications unit. A varying number of reconnaissance platoons (each usually with two officers, 28 men, six armoured cars and six jeeps) sent back a steady stream of information to their headquarters, who would then teletype it direct to the Third Army advance command post. It thus happened that although both corps and divisions monitored the messages, the army staff were better informed on a particular situation than the corps directing the operation!

HALF-TRACKS

The highly successful M series half-tracks M2 and M3, were built by Autocar, Diamond T, International and White. Their front end was similar to the White scout car, but they were powered by more powerful engines – 147hp 6.3-litre White AX in the Autocar, Diamond T and White versions, and a 143hp IHC in the International. All had four-speed gearboxes, with two-speed transfer boxes and drive to the front axle as well as the tracked bogie. A wide series of variants were built: M2 Armored Personnel Carrier (10 seats); M3 APC (13 seats); M4 81mm mortar carrier; M5 APC (13 seats); M13 and M14 multiple AA gun carriers (2 x .50cal HMG); ditto A1 version with one 37mm AA gun as well as the 2 x .50cal HMG; T12 75mm Gun Motor Carriage; T30 75mm Howitzer Motor Carriage.

Specifications of M3 half-track:
Combat weight: 20,000lb
Length: 20ft 2.5in
Width: 7ft 3.5in
Height: 7ft 5in
Armament: one .50 cal HMG, one .30 cal MG
Armour:6.35–12.75mm
Engine: White 160 AX
Max speed on roads: 45mph
Road radius: 215 miles.

FIELD ARTILLERY

'Artillery won the war.' All divisions had their complement of either towed or self-propelled, light/pack and medium field artillery, while additional medium and heavy artillery was available to back this up from Corps and Army sources. 'I don't have to tell you who won the war, you know our artillery did.' So said Patton – quite an admission for one so strongly biased towards armour as GSP! The field artillery's task was to give close and continuous fire support to forward combat troops. It also gave support in depth with counter-battery fire, and fire on enemy reserves, restricting movement in rear areas or disruption of command arrangements. It had to be able to deliver this fire quickly and accurately, whenever and wherever it was needed, no matter the visibility, terrain or weather. The fire had to be quick, accurate, of the right type and calibre, with or without ranging (known as 'adjustment' in US parlance). Fire was well controlled via the 'Fire Direction Center' (FDC) and the wide use of Forward Observation Officers (FOO) and spotter planes – such as the Piper Cub.

Towed Field Artillery

105mm Howitzer M2A1

Within the infantry division field artillery were three light artillery battalions each armed with twelve x 105mm field howitzers M2A1, which had replaced the 75mm M1897A4 as the standard field artillery piece. Sturdy and robust, it became the backbone of US field artillery during the war. Mounted on the M2A2 carriage, which had a split trail and pneumatic tyres, a total of 8,536 were produced. Total weight was 4,260lb, shell weight was 33lb and its maximum range was 12,500 yards.

155m Howitzer M1 and M1A1

The fourth field artillery battalion in the infantry division was a medium battalion armed with 12 x 155mm M1 or M1A1 on the Carriage M1. First issued in 1942, 4,035 had been produced by the end of the war. Weighing 11,926lb, the shell weight was 95lb and the maximum range 16,000 yards. It was a very successful and popular weapon, with a conventional split trail Carriage M1. The later version, the M1A1, was constructed from higher grade steel.

There were two other medium field pieces in service with the Third Army in Europe: the 4.5in Gun M1 and the 155mm Gun M1917 and M1918M1. The former was designed in 1940 so that British and US forces could interchange ammunition, but this proved unpopular because the British ammunition was less powerful. The M1 fired a 55lb shell to a range of 21,125 yards. The 155mm Gun originated as the French 155mm GPF gun and was improved over the years. Despite its age it was widely used; it fired a 94.71lb shell to a range of 20,100 yards.

Heavy Towed Artillery

8in Howitzer M1

Entering service in 1942, the M1 used the same carriage and breech mechanism as the 155mm Gun M1, just over 1,000 being built during the war. It weighed 32,005lb, had a shell weight of 200lb and a maximum range of 18,510 yards.

240MM HOWITZER M1

In April 1940, work began on this howitzer, which came into service in 1943. The barrel was carried on a semi-trailer, while the split-trail carriage hooked on to a tractor, so that the two trail wheels formed a four-wheel trolley. It proved difficult to semi-trail cross country, so the idea was changed and the barrel was carried on a six-wheel wagon and the carriage on another. It needed a 20-ton mobile crane to assemble the two pieces. Its weight was 64,700lb and it fired a 360lb shell to a maximum range of 14.3 miles.

8IN GUN M1

Designed as a 'partner' for the 240mm howitzer, it entered service in 1942 and was also very heavy (69,300lb), normally being towed by a converted M3 medium tank. It could also be transported in pieces, the gun in a transport wagon, the huge split trail in another special wagon. Like the howitzer, it needed a mobile 20-ton crane for assembly. It fired a shell weighing just over 240lb to a maximum range of 20.2 miles.

Self-Propelled Artillery

During the war the USA produced more different types of SP artillery guns than any other nation, with the possible exception of Germany. Early models included the GMC M3 which was a 75mm howitzer mounted on a half-track. A number of 75mm howitzers were also fitted to the M5 light tank chassis and formed the basis of an assault platoon and/or combat team. The SP was known as the Howitzer Motor Carriage (HMC) M8; some 1,778 were built between September 1942 and January 1944 and used by many divisions, especially armoured. The standard 105mm howitzer was mounted on the M3 medium tank chassis, known as the HMC M7 ('Priest' in British parlance). It was followed by the Gun Motor Carriage (GMC) M12, which mounted the 155mm M1918 gun on the M3 chassis and proved highly successful. A cargo-carrying variant, the M30, was used to carry ammunition for the GMC M12. Sent to Europe in June 1944, they were used for heavy bombardment. Further SPs included the GMC M40, but this only arrived in ETO towards the end of the war. In all cases, the gun was mounted on a pedestal at the rear of the chassis with plenty of space all round it. Some armour protection was provided to the sides, and at the rear was fitted a 'spade' (bulldozer blade) which could be dug in to help counter the shock of firing.

PIPER 'GRASSHOPPER' AIRCRAFT

The main light liaison and artillery observation aircraft was the Piper L-4, based on the civil J-3 Cub Trainer. It had tandem cockpits, usually with dual controls, a swivelling seat for the observer and a rear table, and in some versions, a two-way radio. The standard engine was the 65hp Continental.

Wingspan: 35ft 2in
Length: 22ft 3in
Gross Weight: 1,220lb
Max speed: 87mph.

A German view. 'Allied artillery merits the highest praise,' read a German Intelligence bulletin. 'It is adaptable and is skilled at concentrated precision fire delivered by large formations. Observation by spotting aircraft and forward observers is incessant and complete. Fire is never halted on account of imperfect observation, but is carried on from the map. German mortar positions, despite frequent moves and careful camouflage are quickly located and engaged, apparently by use of sound-ranging apparatus.... "Shock shells" used at the end of the preliminary bombardment enable the infantry to penetrate German forward defensive positions just as the last rounds are being fired.... The artillery of some armies may be noted for massing fires, and that of others for precision firing. It remains a unique ability of American artillery to deliver massed fires with the greatest precision in space and time.'[7]

Anti-Aircraft Artillery (AAA)

The USA produced a wide variety of AAA, ranging from multiple heavy machine-guns, to combination mounts of AA gun and machine-gun, and on up to 120mm guns, although 90mm was the largest to be found in Third Army. They also manufactured thousands of 'American Bofors', having quickly appreciated the excellence of the Swedish gun, the most successful of all light AA weapons. The lighter AAA weapons were mainly either trailer-borne or mounted on half-tracks, while many AFVs and larger trucks had light and heavy machine-guns specifically mounted for AA protection. Both the .30 cal and .50 cal machine-guns have already been covered, so we will deal here with only the three types of AAA guns: 37mm, 40mm and 90mm, except to note that the quad .50 cal AA MG had the phenomenally high rate of fire of 2,300rpm!

37mm AA Gun M1A2

Development began in 1921, but shortage of money delayed production until 1938. Some 7,000 were eventually produced. The cyclic rate of fire of the 1.34lb shell was 120rpm, to a maximum ceiling of 18,600 feet.

40mm M1 'American Bofors'

With an effective ceiling of 11,000 feet and a rate of fire of 120rpm, the highly effective Bofors soon outclassed the 37mm. It was of course Swedish in origin, the US Army managing to obtain a gun from Britain and then negotiate successfully with Bofors. The carriage was not well suited to American manufacturing methods, so a new one was designed by the Firestone Tire Co., with a welded frame, tubular axles and electric brakes.

90MM M1 AND M1A1

Developed in 1938, it quickly became the standard AA gun of the field army. It had an effective ceiling of 33,800 feet, a rate of fire of 15rpm and a shell weight of 23.4lb.

Battle record. Third Army AAA shot down more than 1,600 enemy aircraft during operations. It was at 1425 hrs on 1 August 44, just 2 hours and 25 minutes after Third Army became operational that AAA scored its first kill – 445th AAA AW Bn attached to 8th Inf Div opened fire on a flight of 15–20 Me 109s and knocked one down. The 390th AAA AW Bn had the distinction of knocking down the last – three Fw 190s were engaged at 2030 hrs on 8 May, just one hour and 31 minutes before hostilities ended. They had flown over the service elements of 26th Inf Div. One smoked as the tracer fire caught it, then burst into flames and crashed.

ENGINEER EQUIPMENT

The Corps of Engineers used a variety of specialised equipment to assist them in their vast range of tasks, which included for example:

A. CONSTRUCTION MACHINERY. For route clearance, obstacle clearance, road building and similar tasks: augers, air-compressors, cranes and shovels (tractor-operated, crawler-mounted and rubber-tyred), crushing and screening plant, bituminous material distributors and other road-making kit, road graders and rollers, concrete mixers, rooters, saws, scrapers (motorised, towed and semi-trailers), crawler tractors, trailers (8–20-ton), electric welders, etc.

B. BRIDGES. All types including: box girder H-10 and H-20, 25-ton steel pontoon, M-2 treadway (including floats), M-3 pneumatic float and fixed steel Bailey type. To give an idea of the number of bridges built by the engineers of Third Army, the figures for September 1944 alone were: 52 treadway, six heavy pontoon, two infantry support, 170 timber trestle and 67 Bailey (fixed).

C. MINE CLEARING DEVICES. These ranged from prodding with a bayonet, to the hand-held SCR 625 mine detector (weighed 7½lb and could detect metal to about a foot depth), non-metallic mine detectors, right up to tank-borne mine exploders such as the T1E3(M1) nicknamed 'Aunt Jemima'. In addition, of course, the engineers had to lay and map minefields as well as clear them, also lay and clear booby-traps.

D. BOATS. Assault M2, rubber recce pneumatic, canvas, storm (plywood), 18ft, gasoline, utility and outboard motor-boats (22hp and 50–55hp).

E. MAPPING EQUIPMENT. Alidades, cameras, compasses, levels, stereoscopes.

F. WATER SUPPLY. Mobile water point equipment, for water points and water distribution points.
G. MISCELLANEOUS. Camouflage, fire defence, engineer supply.

Engineers at work. 'We were in support of the 35th Division, and were assigned the mission of crossing them by boats, supporting them and later building a bridge.' That is how a member of 'C' Bn, 133rd Engr Regt, began his report on his unit's operations at Méréville-sur-Moselle, about 10 kilometres due south of Nancy. He continued: 'In the assault crossing two engineers were assigned to each boat, which takes 6 to 8 infantrymen, fully equipped, depending whether they are armed with rifles or machine-guns. The infantry and engineers carry the boat, made of light wood, having a hand rail around it and square ends, down to the water. Our engineer sits in the bow and strokes the boat, while the others sit in the stern; all of them paddle. There are no seats and everyone kneels. You feel pretty naked out in one of those boats.... I was in the bow and we had about 300 feet of water to cross. We used 14 boats in our sector for one company of infantry. We worked a shuttle service and made approximately four crossings each. Our mission was to get enough troops across to establish a bridgehead, so that a footbridge could be built.... Our first load went over without casualties, but in the second three men were hit by machine-gun fire and we had a lot of near hits from a mortar. The boats brought the three men back and kept on ferrying. One man died. Two assault boats were hit by direct fire and all the men killed. There were approximately 130 men in the company we ferried.

'When we had got them across that ended the first phase and we started building an infantry footbridge. It's built of narrow pontoons about 6ft long and 1½ft wide, which we carried down in sections and clamped treadways onto two pontoons, which made a section.... Our first bridge was hit by shellfire and had to be cleared and new sections put in place. The bulk of the men had crossed before daylight. By this time enemy artillery fire had been silenced sufficiently so that we had an opportunity to build a vehicle bridge. We put in a floating treadway, which is made of huge rubber pontoons.... We built this bridge downstream from the footbridge as it was away from enemy fire and had a good approach on the near shore. We used about 26 pontoons, which we covered with treadway plate made of wood and steel which fits over the top of the pontoons.... That was the end of our assignment. One of our engineers was killed and 17 wounded ... We thought we had completed our job and could rest, but the infantry moved so fast that we had to go to Rosières-aux-Salines (on the R Meurthe) and put in a Bailey bridge across the canal.... That took the rest of the day and that night we got a good night's sleep.'

SIGNALS

Shortages in 1939. In line with the rest of the army, the Signal Corps was short of both men and equipment when war threatened – in 1939, for example, its total strength was under 4,000, although by the time America had entered the war there were more than 50,000 officers and enlisted men, albeit spread across the globe. An enormous expansion was necessary, together with the mass production of radio and radar equipment. The Signal Corps developed, supplied, installed and maintained its specialised equipment, and the radio sets of the US ground forces were soon the envy of all the Allies and never bettered by any nation. Under the 1942–3 re-organisation, the Signals Corps, like the Engineers, was assigned to the ASF, but there were many valid objections to this, especially when one considers that signal communications was (and still is) one of the major functions of command.

Within Third Army there were three times as many signal troops in non-divisional units as with divisions. One of the reasons for this was that much of the signal equipment in combat units was manned by members of that particular arm. Signal units included an operations battalion which furnished communications at Third Army CPs; construction battalions making telephone cable and wire installations down to corps level and back to army rear HQ; signal intelligence companies; a pigeon company and a signal photographic company. To give some idea of the enormity of their task, the figures for Third Army Signallers were: 16,000 miles of telephone cables laid, 4,000 miles of French/German wire rehabilitated and 36,000 miles of underground cable. Their Message Center alone handled a total of seven and a quarter million code groups, while forward and rear echelon switchboard operators handled an average of 14,000 calls daily.

Radios

In Third Army a wide range of radio sets were in service in all types of unit: man-portable and vehicle sets were in three ranges:

A. SHORT RANGE – up to 25 miles, but more usually five miles or less on RT sets. Sets included: Portable, the SCR 536 'hand-talkie' (the smallest Signal Corps set), the SCR 300 'walkie-talkie', SCR 284, both portable and vehicle-borne (rather heavy – 250lb), SCR 694 the successor to the SCR 284, SCR 509 an 80-crystal push-button FM radio, and the AN/PRC3 portable microwave transceiver for the field artillery. Vehicle-mounted, AN/VRC3, an FM set on same frequency band as the SCR 300, so that tank crews could talk to infantry using the 'walkie-talkie', SCR 508 and SCR 510 80-crystal push-button radios.

B. MEDIUM RANGE – 25 to 100 miles. Sets included: Portable, SCR 177 vehicle-carried but operated on the ground. Vehicle-mounted, SCR 245 mobile set with 4-crystal controlled frequencies, SCR 506 standard medium range vehicle set. There were also numerous transportable

radio relay equipments, both terminal and relay sets.
C. LONG RANGE – 100 miles and over. Sets included: Portable, AN/PRC1 and 5, suitcase continuous wave sets for Military Intelligence Service. Mobile sets (either operated in trucks or at rest and powered by trailer-borne generators), SCR 597 and SCR 299, excellent long-range sets, the latter becoming standard for the entire US Army, giving a 100-mile range on voice and many hundreds of miles on Morse.

Wire Communications
There were two main types of wire to be laid:
A. ASSAULT WIRE – very light, twisted pair, which could be quickly laid over the ground. Two types: W130 (30lb/mile) and WD-1/TT (48lb/mile) with a talking range of 5 and 14 miles respectively.
B. FIELD WIRE – heavier and stronger for use in long lines on the ground or on poles. Two types: W-110-B (130lb/mile) and the heavier W-143, with a talking range of 12–20 miles and 27 miles respectively.

Linemen for the Army. A major task for Signal Company GIs was putting in and maintaining telephone lines, a difficult and dangerous task as this extract from the history of the 76th Infantry Division shows: 'The 76th Signal Company had to work fast. Their mission was to get a telephone line across the River Sauer – pronto. On the opposite bank the doughboys who had fought their way into German soil waited for the line that was to connect them with their CP. S/Sgt Thomas Barker, wire chief and his team tried every trick in the book. One of the men crawled across the pontoon bridge, the telephone wire tied to his leg. He got across but a few minutes later an 88 landed nearby and severed the wire. A couple of men swam the wire across, but on reaching the opposite bank found mines and barbed wire blocking their path. They shot the wire across the river with a bazooka. The Jerries blew that line out too. Headquarters kept calling for communication; the infantrymen across the river waited. The signal team again crawled the precious wire across the bridge, this time working under a smokescreen. As they proceeded they hung heavy iron weights at intervals on the wire, swinging out to sink in the 15 foot river. Ten minutes later a floating mine exploded immediately above it but the line at the bottom of the river stayed in.'

Notes to Chapter 8

1. *Men against Fire: The Problem of Combat Command in Future War* by S. L. A. Marshall, as quoted in *Eisenhower's Lieutenants* by Russell F. Weigley.
2. Called the Chaffee after General Adna Chaffee, 'Father of the Armored Force'.
3. 'Our morale went up when we began to receive the Shermans with the long barrel 76mm,' one US tank officer told me. 'The gun had more firepower and greater velocity.' However, it still did not match up to the British 17pdr gun,

which was fitted to a proportion of Shermans in British service (approx one per tank troop) in the highly successful Sherman Firefly.

4. 'W' = wet stowage, the ammunition being stored in water-protected racks below the turret instead of in the sponsons, to reduce the fire risk.
5. CT = Combat Team.
6. Quoted in *XII Corps, Spearhead of Patton's Third Army*.
7. Ibid.

9
The Services, Specialist Weapons, Vehicles and Equipment

Chemical Warfare Service (CWS)

Protection and neutralisation. First and foremost, the task of the Chemical Warfare Service was to protect the troops against enemy gas attacks. Fortunately this threat never materialised in any theatre of war. Initially, in 1940, the entire strength of the CWS had only been 93 officers and 1,035 enlisted men, but by 1943 this had risen to 8,103 officers and 61,688 enlisted men. The CWS were therefore employed in an offensive capacity, but not of course using gas. Instead their weapons were of two main types:

a. Smoke generators
b. Chemical mortars.

Smoke Generators

Two types of mechanical smoke generator were used, the M1 and the M2. The M1 was the heavier, weighing some 3,000lb; the M2 was much lighter and more compact, but it was noisy, so could not be used to support a surprise attack. Neither could be moved once they were in use, so some protective cover was always needed. Where this was impossible the chemical mortar proved more practicable for producing a smoke-screen. The mechanical generators did not actually produce smoke, but rather a form of artificial fog, through the mixing of steam and oil vapour. There was also the 35lb M4 'floating' smoke pot which could be used both on the ground or in water.

A total of four Chemical Smoke Generator companies were normally attached/assigned to Third Army during operations in the ETO, and it was normal practice for single companies to be attached to a corps for a particular operation. Corps often attached these companies to divisions, putting them under command of a specific engineer or AAA unit because one of their main tasks was to cover bridges and bridge sites. Many inventive mounts for generators were developed – for example, to enable them to be used in both an assault boat and a storm boat during river crossing operations.

Chemical Mortars

Third Army's battle experience proved that every infantry division[1] needed its own attached Chemical Mortar Battalion, but in practice this never came about. In August 1944, when Third Army became operational, only one chemical mortar battalion was attached and at peak times there were never more than seven to support as many as eighteen divisions. Nevertheless, full use was made of these mortars, not only for smoke, but also for HE.

4.2in Chemical Mortar

Intended primarily for firing white phosphorus smoke or gas rounds, it could also fire a large (32lb) HE round which was developed for the mortar in 1943. It differed from the infantry mortars in having a rifled barrel. Because of its range and to increase its effectiveness, artillery FOOs and spotter planes were often used to direct the fire of the mortar companies.
Barrel length: 40.1in (101.87cm)
Range: 600–4,400 yards (549–4,026m)
Weight in action: 330lb (149.8kg)
Bomb weight: Chemical M2 – 25½lb (11.58kg), M4 – 32lb (14.5kg).

Other Tasks

The Chemical Decontamination Company, which was assigned to Third Army, fortunately was never required to perform its primary mission. But it was extremely useful for other roles such as fire-fighting, hauling water, washing vehicles and providing bathing facilities, so CWS personnel were in constant demand.

Chemical Depot and Chemical Maintenance Companies were also assigned, the former dealing with the issue of chemical supplies, the latter for repairing chemical weapons. It was Third Army policy to keep all portable flame-throwing weapons, for example, filled and ready for issue at CWS depots, then to issue them to units for a particular operation. The flame-throwers would be returned to the depot when empty. The primary task of the maintenance companies proved to be the maintenance of the 4.2in mortars. 'One off' jobs which CWS were asked to perform included a request to assist camouflage engineer units to produce white snow suits (30 a day) and coloured eye shields (200,000 pairs), for issue to troops in the severe winter weather of January 1945, in order to guard against snow blindness. More mundane tasks included the repair of gas masks, which clearly had to be kept in working order in case the enemy should use gas weapons – 8,000 gas masks were repaired in January 1945 alone.

Quartermaster Corps (QMC)

A determination to succeed. In his first Letter of Instruction to all corps, division and separate unit commanders, dated 6 March 1944, General Patton had this to say about supply: 'The onus of supply rests equally on the giver and the taker. Forward units must anticipate needs and ask for supplies in time. They must stand ready to use all their means to help move supplies. The supply services must get the things asked for to the right place at the right time. They must do more; by reconnaissance they will anticipate demands and start the supplies up before they are called for. The DESPERATE DETERMINATION to succeed is just as vital to supply as it is to the firing line.'

QMC responsibility. Their responsibility was the supply of everything the soldier needed to enable him to fight the war, other than weapons and ammunition which were of course the responsibility of Ordnance. The infantry and airborne division were the lowest level at which QMC units were provided in Third Army. In armoured divisions all had lost their integral QMC battalions, retaining only their divisional staff.[2]

QMC Companies

Within the infantry division the strength of the QMC company was 186 all ranks, and they manned three truck platoons and a service platoon. Truck platoons (one officer and 28 enlisted men) operated sixteen 2½-ton trucks, which drew Class I (rations and free PX) and Class III (POL and solid fuel) daily from army truck-heads and distributed them to vehicles from the combat units at divisional distribution points. The service platoon (one officer and 48 men) manned the distribution point and transferred the supplies. In addition, whenever possible, men from the service platoon went with the trucks to the army truck-heads to help load supplies, because this saved time and time was the most important commodity of all. Trucks that were going back to collect Class I supplies would invariably take back POWs and/or salvage, but this put an extra strain on drivers. Relief drivers could sometimes be found, though with difficulty and certainly not from within the service platoon which had a myriad of other tasks to perform such as collecting salvage, sorting laundry, operating showers, assisting graves registration units (also part of QMC responsibility) – there were never enough 'hands' to go round.

The Red Ball Express. During periods of continuous combat, when the supply lines lengthened and thousands of other combat troops were attached to divisions, the organic QMC company just could not cope alone and whenever possible corps loaned extra troops from its service company to assist. In the ETO every armoured division had two QMC truck companies attached when in combat, one for ammunition and one for all other supplies including POL. However, as the armoured division used so much more POL – twice as much as the standard infantry division – the QMC companies were always fully stretched. One dramatic expedient, tried by the Communications Zone[3] was the Red Ball Express, which took supplies including POL all the way to the combat units. The long-distance 'through-highway system' was inaugurated in late August 1944, designed as an emergency expedient to support the Seine crossings, by getting 82,000 tons of supplies to the Chartres–Dreux area. It was still in operation in November, operating east of the Seine as well. On 25 August, Red Ball convoys began to use two parallel one-way round-trip routes from which all other traffic was excluded and before long more than 100 truck companies were involved. The US Army History 'Breakout and Pursuit' volume quotes as an example the situation on 29 August, when 132 truck companies – 6,000 vehicles – moved more than 12,000 tons of stores. Operating day and night and without blackout precautions, Red Ball had delivered 135,000 tons of supplies to army service areas by mid-September. Unfortunately, the increasingly long round trips decreased the amount of fuel that could be brought forward because the trucks bringing it themselves consumed more and more fuel. In the end the breakout and pursuit across Europe had to be halted, not by enemy action, but simply because they had moved too fast for the supplies to keep pace. Patton appreciated this, even when he was cursing for being held back. 'If you hear we have been halted,' he wrote to Field Marshal Sir John Dill, head of the British Joint Staff Mission in America, on 31 August 1944, 'it will be for reasons other than enemy activity, for so far we have beaten him wherever we have met him and shall continue to do so whenever permitted. The strain on our vehicles and our supplies has, of course, been heavy, but the supply officer of this Army has done an amazing job, and we can continue to go at any time that we are wanted.'

In addition, of course, there was a tremendous strain on both vehicles and personnel, with no time for proper maintenance, rapid deterioration of vehicles and roads, abuse of vehicles from overloading and speeding, plus a large number of accidents through driver fatigue. Nevertheless, the Red Ball Express played a significant part in the gamble to cross the Seine and exploit the existing tactical advantage, but clearly the wherewithal was not available to sustain it indefinitely.

Vehicles Used

Just as with AFVs, the tremendous contribution that the American vehicle industry made to the Allied war effort cannot be overstated, as they provided thousands of trucks for Allied armies as well as their own – more than 400,000 for the USSR alone. This was all the more remarkable because, up to the 1930s, the US Army had been just as short of modern wheeled vehicles as it had been of tanks. It was not until 1939 that a proper standardised programme was laid down, which led to the building of the most well-known American trucks of the war, such as the ¾-ton 4x4 Dodge and the 2½-ton 6x6 GMC. Five main types were standardised: ½-ton (later uprated to ¾-ton), 1½-ton, 2½-ton, 4-ton and 7½-ton. To these would later be added the ¼-ton Jeep. Military purchases rose dramatically and many automobile companies began producing military vehicles to meet the ever-increasing demand. For example, Bantam, Willys and Ford built Jeeps; Chevrolet, Ford, IHD and GMC all produced 1½-ton 4x4s; 2½-ton 6x6s were built by GMC, White, Mack, Corbitt, Brockway, Kenworth and Ward La France. The

7½-ton 6x6s were built by Mack, Reo, Federal and Biederman, while they and other companies also built prime movers for artillery pieces, wreckers and tractors, dumpers and gasoline carriers, refrigerated trailers and all the rest. Some idea of the vast quantity built is given by the following production figures: one million light trucks, half a million 1½-tonners, more than 800,000 2½-ton trucks, more than 150,000 trucks in excess of 2½-tons!

Despite the pressing need for vehicles of all types, the War Department and Joint Chiefs of Staff imposed severe limitations on the use of diesel engines for trucks, because of the fuel's high flash point, so the bulk of diesel fuel went to the US Navy and only two basic truck types were fitted with diesel engines, most of which were supplied to the British.

Staff Cars

Four basic types were used during the war: 5- and 7-seater passenger sedans and ditto passenger station-wagons. All were modified civilian models, having such wartime fittings as blackout lighting. The 5-seaters were made by Chevrolet, Ford and Plymouth, the larger cars included Buicks, Oldsmobiles, Packards and Cadillacs.[4]

Ambulances. See Medical section for details.

Jeeps

In June 1940, the QMC put up a specification for a 4x4 load-carrier, with a capacity of 500lb, a weight of not more than 1,300lb and an engine of at least 40bhp. Interested parties had to produce prototypes within 75 days. The weight limit was purely arbitrary, '... probably a carryover from earlier years when even a 1½-ton 4x4 was considered "too heavy" if it couldn't be manhandled out of a mudhole'.[5] The specification was sent out to many US firms, but only American-Bantam produced a prototype within the deadline and it was well overweight. Nevertheless, they did get a contract and produced some 2,642 Bantam Jeeps by the end of 1941, but they were both under-powered and insufficiently robust. Once Bantam had done the 'leg-work', however, both Willys and Ford expressed interest, the upshot being that by July 1941, they had been given the contract to build Jeeps, based on the Willys design, while Bantam was relegated to building trailers. During the war, 634,569 Jeeps were built, 350,349 by Willys and 281,578 by Ford, the balance being the initial Bantams. It would remain unchanged in service all over the world long after the war ended.

Specifications for both Ford GPW and Willys MB Jeeps:

Weight:	2,440lb
Length:	11ft
Width:	5ft 2in

Height: 5ft 9.75in
Engine: 54hp Willys model 442 L-head 4-cylinder
Range: 500 miles
Max permitted speed: 65mph
Payload: 800lb
Towed load: 1,000lb.

DODGE ¾-TON 4X4 TRUCK

Also widely used by all arms was the Dodge weapons carrier, which had been originally designed to meet the infantry's need to carry the heavier company weapons, but later became used more widely as a versatile cargo and general-purpose truck. Some were fitted with a front-mounted winch.

Specifications:
Weight: 7,350lb
Length: 14ft 8½in
Width: 6ft 11in
Height: 6ft 10in
Engine: 76hp Dodge T 214 petrol, 6-cylinder
Range: 240 miles
Max speed: 54mph
Payload: 1,500lb
Towed load: 1,000lb
Winch pull: 5,000lb.

DODGE 1½-TON 6X6 TRUCK

Because there was such a large demand for 2½-ton trucks, the 1½-tonner was designed as a substitute because available manufacturing facilities couldn't cope with the 2½-ton requirement. It used many of the components of the ¾-tonner, which were already in volume production. It merely had an extra bogie axle and a slightly longer body and chassis, so as to be able to take more cargo. Sometimes a winch was fitted to the front, and a ring-mount for a .50 cal HMG was fitted to the top of the cab.

Specifications:
Weight: 10,525lb
Length: 18ft 8½in
Width: 6ft 11in
Height: 7ft 1in
Engine: 76hp Dodge T 214 petrol, 6-cylinder
Range: 240 miles
Max speed: 50mph
Payload: 3,300lb
Towed load: 3,500lb
Winch pull: 7,500lb.

GMC 2½-TON 6X6 TRUCK

The ubiquitous 'Deuce and a half', also known affectionately as 'Jimmy' (GMC – hence Jimmy) was by far the most important 6x6 truck in the US Army. It was considered at the time (1939) to be the largest truck that could be mass produced. As well as the cargo version of Jimmy, there was a vast range of variations based upon the same chassis. GMC used a special code for each model, the first one, built in 1939, being the ACKWX-353, which stood for:

A	1939
C	conventional cab
K	front wheel drive
W	tandem rear drive
X	non-standard wheelbase (different from any civilian model)
353	164in wheelbase (the alternative 145in wheelbase was coded 352)[6]

This code was followed throughout the war, except that the X suffix was dropped for all versions except the forward control models. Approximate production figures were: GMC 562,750; Studebaker 197,000+; International 37,088; Reo 22,204.[7] They were used for a wide variety of purposes, including: dump truck, petrol tanker (660 or 750 gallons), water tanker (700 gallons), field operating theatre, dental surgery and first-aid post, Clubmobile and Cinemobile, mobile CP, mobile workshops, breakdown equipment and many more, including as the basis for the amphibious DUKW.

Specifications for the CCKW 353 with winch:

Weight:	11,227lb
Length:	22ft 6in
Width:	7ft 4in
Height:	7ft 9in
Engine:	91.5hp type 270 GMC petrol, 6-cylinder in line
Range:	300 miles
Max speed:	45mph
Payload:	9,200lb.

HEAVY TRUCKS

Most trucks for loads of 5 tons and over were 6x6s and there was a wide range of load carriers, wreckers, etc., one of the best being the 6-ton 6x6 Ward La France, which had a GarWood main crane with a 6-ton capacity, and could be used to tow vehicles up to 16,000 pounds with support braces. There were also 8x8s and 10x10s although the majority of those in the latter category were 6x6 tractors with powered semi-trailers.

Always overstretched. Undoubtedly all QMC companies were overstretched throughout the war and there were constant calls for increases, one of the most vociferous coming from the QM of Third

Army, who advocated the expansion of the divisional company into a battalion of two truck companies and a service company. The proposal also included specialised personnel to deal with the hundred and one tasks such as: rations breakdown, POL distribution, provision of baths and laundry, salvage and repair services. Despite the fact that his proposals were supported by a score of battle-experienced divisional QMs, they were rejected by the War Department on the grounds of 'personnel limitations'. Quartermaster units in Third Army area included bakeries, fuel supply, graves registration, laundry, refrigeration, sterilisation, salvage, fumigation and baths, and war dogs.

76th Infantry Division's history gives a graphic indication of the amount of work involved. In the three-month period during which the division was assigned to Third Army (19 January 1945 to 22 April 1945) its QM company, under the command of Captain R. S. Conlisk, was involved: 'Bringing the food and supplies to the division was the twenty-four-hour-a-day job of the 76th Quartermaster Company. The company's "life-line" fleet of 48 two and one half ton trucks travelled more than 368,337 miles over Europe from the division's Sauer River crossing until it established its last bridgehead over the Mulde. During combat QM issued 1,741,672 ration units, 167,405 PX units, 480,990 gallons of gasoline and 13,669 gallons of lubricants. Along with this came 315,714 articles of clothing and equipment and the reissue of 6,732 items of salvage. QM trucks transported thousands of PWs, DPs and liberated Allied PWs. At one time near the end of the war the division was feeding 35,000 German prisoners.'

Third Army's record of travelling is without parallel, their trucks alone transported more than two million tons of stores a staggering 141 million miles during the 281 days of campaigning.

Ordnance

Unit fitters. This is as good a place as any to look at unit fitters, who were especially important in the more mechanised units, for example, in the armoured division, where there were many heavy tracked armoured fighting vehicles to look after. Fitters in such units travelled in Tank Recovery Vehicles (TRV), based on the M3 or M4 medium tank chassis.

Tank Recovery Vehicle T2 M31

This was based on the M3 medium chassis, which had the guns removed (usually a wooden barrel would be inserted in both the 75mm and 37mm gun mantlets), and was fitted with a rear-mounted boom and winch which had a 60,000lb pull.

Tank Recovery Vehicle M32

This was a modified M4 Sherman, the turret and gun being replaced by a fixed turret fitted with an external 81mm mortar (to fire smoke), a

60,000lb winch (in the fighting compartment) and a pivoting 18-foot 'A' frame jib on the hull. Extra towing eyes, tow bars, blocks, etc., were added, giving the M32 an all up weight of 60,000lb (compared with 70,000 to 72,800lb for a gun tank).

To help keep the tanks, tank destroyers, self-propelled guns, half-tracks, trucks and all the other vehicles in Third Army rolling, there had to be a special unit in each division to back up the unit fitters. In the armoured division this was the Ordnance Maintenance Battalion (762 all ranks) and in the infantry division the Ordnance Light Maintenance Company (147 all ranks). Airborne divisions had even smaller companies (just 108 all ranks). But all three types of unit contained the same three elements: supply, armament and automotive. Taking the largest, that is to say the armoured division's Ord Maint Bn, as an example, it was organised as follows:

HQ COMPANY – comprising Inspection, Supply, Service and Salvage Sections.

THREE ORD MAINT COYS – each having a Service and Supply platoon, Armament platoon (contained instruments, small arms and artillery sections). Automotive platoon (two main sections and a reclamation and evacuation section).

While armoured regimental fitters would travel in Tank Recovery Vehicles (TRV), the Ordnance Maintenance Companies held mainly wheeled vehicles, their breakdown being:

Ordnance Maintenance Company

COMPANY HQ
- HQ Section: one Jeep, one M3 half-track
- AM&S Section: one 2½-ton truck with one 1-ton trailer
- Maintenance Section: one ¾-ton truck

SERVICE AND SUPPLY PLATOON
- Service Section: one ¾-ton truck, one 2½-ton truck; one 2½-ton machine shop truck
- Supply Section: six 2½-ton trucks, six 1-ton trailers.

ARMAMENT PLATOON
- Instrument Section: one Jeep, one 2½-ton instrument repair truck
- Small Arms Section: one Jeep, one 2½-ton small arms repair truck
- Artillery Section: one Jeep, one 2½-ton arty repair truck

AUTOMOTIVE PLATOON
- Platoon HQ: two Jeeps, one ¾-ton truck, four 2½-ton trucks, four 1-ton trailers, one 2½-ton decontamination truck, one 2½-ton electrical repair truck, one 6-ton heavy wrecker
- Two Maintenance Sections, each one ¾-ton truck, one 2½-ton truck, one 1-ton trailer
- Reclamation and Evacuation Section: two 6-ton heavy wreckers, one

2½-ton truck, one 1-ton trailer, three transporter tractor trucks; three transporter semi-trailers.

Battlefield recovery of disabled equipment was a unit responsibility, as were basic repairs and maintenance. Units carried out third echelon maintenance to the very limit of their tools and the skill of their fitters. This undoubtedly suited units, because the last thing they wanted was to lose control of their own vehicles. The Ordnance unit was structured with this in mind, so that it could cope with 60 per cent of third-line repairs during quiet periods and 30 per cent during combat.

In addition to normal repair and maintenance tasks, Ordnance had to take on 'one-off', extremely important tasks, such as the up-armouring of all Sherman tanks to bring them in line with the armour on the M4A3E2. This occurred in January 1945, in the vicinity of the 'Battle of the Bulge' area. After a completed model had been submitted to, and approved by, GSP, instructions were given to proceed with the modification. Army Ordnance personnel were assigned the task of removing armour plate from wrecked tanks at collecting points and on the battlefield. Contracts were then made with three local factories as it was rightly considered that the 85 man-hours needed per AFV would seriously hamper normal maintenance. The actual modification involved welding 22 inches of armour plate on to the front hulls of all M4A3s and M4A3E8s. Third Army obtained extra supplies of welding rod, oxygen and acetylene, so that a schedule of ten tanks per day could be achieved. The tanks of three armoured divisions took just three weeks to modify.[8] Not long afterwards all Shermans with 75mm guns had their main armament barrels replaced by 76mm barrels (either from knocked-out 76mm gun tanks, or new barrels through normal supply channels), thus achieving the long-awaited upgunning of their medium tanks.

Medical

Two types of medics. Basically there were two kinds of medical personnel within the operational area. Those who were attached to units as a permanent part of their establishment provided the immediate first-aid and casualty evacuation back to battalion or regimental aid stations. They were supported by the medical battalion (only a strong company in the airborne division). In the infantry division their total strength was about 1,000, less than half of whom were actually serving in the medical battalion. Medical battalion personnel also assisted the unit medics to collect casualties and bring them to the unit aid stations. They were responsible for the evacuation of wounded down the chain to clearing stations, then on to army level evacuation hospitals.

During the period in which Third Army was operational, their medics moved a grand total of 269,187 patients by army ambulances from division level clearing stations to army level hospitals. Of this number, 233,763 were US Army personnel, the remainder being Allies, US Navy, POWs and civilians. Of this total, 164,810 were evacuated from the Third Army area by air, road, ship and rail.

Medical evacuation within the combat zone was by hand-carried stretcher (known as a litter in US Army parlance), or by litter-carrying vehicles, i.e., ambulances.

Ambulances. There were two basic types of ambulance: 'tactical', for off-road work, which were used to take casualties from the front line to field hospitals; and 'metropolitan', fitted with only 4x2 drive and thus unsuitable off decent metalled roads. The former category was provided by the ubiquitous Jeep, of which there were both two- and three-stretcher versions, plus the ¾-ton Dodge for longer journeys. A total of 26,000 Dodge WC54 were built. They could take either four casualties lying on stretchers or seven sitting. White scout cars were also used as ambulances, but they were not entirely satisfactory as they had no back opening, so the stretchers had to be lifted over the vehicle's high sides. The 'metropolitan' category was filled with a variety of 'civilian type' ambulances, based on lengthened passenger car vehicles or vans, but all lacked 4-wheel drive.

Types of hospital. Behind the Combat Zone, within the Army area were evacuation, convalescent and portable surgical hospitals (25 beds only). Behind them in the Communications Zone (Com Z) were field, convalescent, station and general hospitals. The evacuation hospitals were the 'neck of the funnel', through which all casualties (except those evacuated by air) would pass on their way to hospitals in the Com Z. They were located usually about 15–30 miles behind the battle front, on good roads, ideally with airfields, railways and/or waterways close by. Patients who were short term usually stayed at convalescent hospitals in the army area. Field hospitals were mobile hospitals, capable of giving the same level of service as station hospitals, but in the field and only for limited periods. Station hospitals were static units which served a limited assigned area only and did not usually deal with battle casualties from the combat zone. General hospitals were also fixed units with a bed capacity of 1,000, 1,500 or 2,000 and equipped to give complete treatment for all cases in the theatre.

General evacuation plan. The chief surgeon in the theatre of operations was responsible for the general plan for the evacuation and treatment of the sick and wounded. The system was based on the premise that it was the responsibility of rearward units to take casualties off forward units. In addition there was a laid down period that patients should be kept in a theatre for treatment, before they were evacuated to the USA. In ETO this was 180 days – later reduced to 120 days. It is a measure of the success achieved by Third Army medical staff that of the 313,686 total direct admissions to medical establishments, 43.5 per cent were returned to duty without evacuation outside the Army area, while the mortality rate was only 1.4 per cent.

Air evacuation. In a few cases evacuation was possible from the front line, in a light liaison (Piper Cub) aircraft, but there were no helicopters,[9] so air evacuation normally did not start until further along the chain; within the Army area evacuation would be by road, rail or water. Air evacuation to the USA was the responsibility of Air Transport Command, but the Communications Zone had the responsibility of getting patients to airfields and looking after them until they were on board their aircraft.

Under the Red Cross. A typical account of the heroic work of the medics is given in the XII Corps history by Captain John Bourne, a medical officer with a small task force that had been ordered to blow the bridges over the Loire River: 'Suddenly we heard firing up ahead and the convoy stopped. I was pretty sure that someone had been hurt, so I set up my aid station in the back of the truck. This was the first time I was in action. I heard someone calling "Medics", so I took two litter bearers and went up towards the front end of the column. We had heard a great deal of talk about the fact that the Germans were not respecting the Geneva Convention concerning the neutrality of medical personnel. So my litter bearers were not to anxious to go up.

'We had some difficulty in getting the first man who had been seriously wounded in the neck. We brought him back and gave him plasma. It was the first time I had used it in combat. However, he was so seriously wounded that he died. Then a sergeant crawled back and told me that two men were wounded in the lead truck right in front of the road block. I got a jeep and driver, and a helper, and started up. I put a Red Cross flag on the jeep and we drove slowly up the road. I held my hand up for some reason, I really don't know why, but the GIs who were lying in the ditch took it for a signal to stop firing, so they did. The Krauts ceased firing also. Then suddenly overhead a shell exploded. After that there was complete quiet. I was pretty scared. We got up to the injured men, who were right up at the front of the column which had stopped by the roadblock and started to load them. We were unable to handle them without more help, so I got some of the uninjured engineers out of the ditches to help us. They didn't like it, and you can't blame them as they had no armbands. I kept telling them, "They (the Krauts) won't hurt you." We got the casualties loaded, turned the jeep around and drove down the road as fast as we could, and a couple of minutes later the battle started again.'

Military Police

Motorcycles. The US Army's Military Police were among the major users of motorcycles such as the world-famous and extremely reliable Harley Davidson Model WLA, of which more than 60,000 were built. Chain driven by a 23hp V-2 cylinder engine, it weighed 512lb, and could carry a 200lb payload. Another model, the 45XA, was shaft-driven, weighed slightly more (525lb) and had a 300lb payload capacity; 1,000 of them were purchased by the US Army in 1942. Other important models included the Indian Model 74, the Cushman 15M7 and the Crosley. There were also lighter motorcycles for airborne operations, such as the Indian Model 148, which weighed only 250lb, yet could carry a 225lb payload. It was known as the 'Motorcycle Extra Light M1'.

MPs on traffic duty. 'There were six of us MPs,' recalled Sergeant James H. Coyle, of the 76th Infantry Division MP Platoon, in the division's history, *We Ripened Fast*, 'and there were three traffic posts to handle that night. The 385th was sending a battalion to relieve one of the 417th's. There were some real hot corners. The shells dropped steadily from 1000 to 0600 the following morning. Our job was to keep the troops moving past the hotspots on the double. A couple of us were down at the bridge. If anything makes the night unforgettable it was having to stand there and wave those guys into the Siegfried Line.' Pfc Ebel H. Sietsema, a member of the MP squad, had just put up a direction light on the wall opposite his post on 'Suicide Corner' in Echternach, only to watch the wall disintegrate before his eyes a few seconds later under a direct hit. 'Back in Chicago all we had to look out for was drunken drivers,' he said, as he went looking for another wall.

Chaplains

At the end of the campaign, there were 225 chaplains assigned in the seventeen divisions then under Third Army Command, plus a further 120 with other supporting units.

'Taken quickly from civilian life and plunged deep into the maelstrom of battle, chaplains of the Third Army have clearly demonstrated unflagging devotion both to God and to country.' So wrote Third Army's Chaplain, Colonel James H. O'Neill, in the After Action Report. He continued: 'Death, wounds and decorations for some testify to the self-sacrifice of all. It has been well worth the cost. For in the person of each soldier, the chaplain has met something of his Lord, and in trying to give he has received far more than he had to offer.'

Although services were held wherever space allowed, both outdoors and indoors, most of the time chaplains needed some form of tented accommodation, in which to keep their vestments and altar equipment, while one of their most useful items of equipment was a folding organ, although it did suffer in the bad weather. As a result it was recommended that metal pegs be substituted for wooden ones as organ stops, and the use of plastic instead of fabric-covered wood would prevent warping.

Special Services

While the USO brought many shows to the front lines, with famous movie stars such as Marlene Dietrich and Bing Crosby providing the entertainment, probably the most appreciated of all the voluntary organisations were the American Red Cross Clubmobiles, whose brave girls served front-line troops with hundreds of thousands of doughnuts and cups of coffee, cigarettes, sweets, gum and books. For example, in Nancy, the group attached to HQ Third Army opened a 'Clubmobile Annex' at the Rex Theatre and served more than 10,000 doughnuts and 5,000 cups of coffee daily.

The Clubmobiles mainly used the ubiquitous 'Jimmy' as their vehicle, the special body being fitted on to the CCKW 353 chassis. A total of 183 Clubmobiles were operating in the ETO, all staffed by American Red Cross volunteers. In non-operational areas there were also travelling libraries, known as 'Bookmobiles'.

The Special Services also provided movie-projectors and movies for the troops, together with sports equipment. Out of action and in rest areas, there would be *ad hoc* sports facilities established such as softball and touch football. In the USA and UK such facilities were far more lavish and well organised, but the men at the 'sharp end' were probably more appreciative of the efforts made for them by the Special Services Section.

Post Exchange

The 'Post Exchange' – the 'PX' – was the US equivalent of the British NAAFI (Navy, Army and Air Force Institutes), which provided the soldier with what could be described as 'life's little luxuries', but which were at moments of stress probably considered more as necessities. For example, cigars and cigarettes, pipe and chewing tobacco, did not have the stigma they do today, the harmful effects of smoking being not widely known. The PX provided huge quantities of tobacco, some of it free with the rations. The PX system had been in existence since the days of post traders, but unit canteens for enlisted men were not properly organised until the Post Exchange came into being in 1905.

Notes to Chapter 9

1. Third Army never attached chemical mortars to their armoured divisions, rightly considering that these units had neither the mobility nor the protection needed to be able to operate in areas where armoured forces were involved.
2. Outside Third Army, 2nd and 3rd Armored Divisions had retained their QMC Bns, as had cavalry divisions.
3. The Communications Zone (COMZ) in the ETO was the area behind Army rear boundaries, divided into sections (e.g., Seine Section, Channel Base Section [Br area], Brittany Base Section, and Normandy Base Section, with the Advance Section directly behind Army boundaries).
4. GSP was riding in a 1939-model Cadillac limousine when he suffered his fatal accident (see later).
5. *US Military Wheeled Vehicles*, by Fred W. Crismon.

6. Source of this information: *WW2 Military Vehicles, Transport and Halftracks*, by G. N. Georgano.
7. Ibid.
8. Not long afterwards, a modified tank in 6th Armd Div was struck by a 75mm shell from a Panther tank. The only damage was the complete separation of the middle section of armour from the hull. The Sherman stayed in action and was able to knock out the enemy tank.
9. Heliborne medevac did not become widely used until the Korean War.

Part III

The Battle History of Third Army

10
Chronology: Third Army's Battle Record, 1 August 1944 to 8 May 1945

Moving to France

Prior to their first operational day (1 August 1944), Third Army had first to cross to France, and ready themselves for operations. In Chapter 4 we left HQ still at Breamore Hall, near Fordingbridge, GSP having announced to his staff on the evening of 3 July, that they would 'go to war' the following day. In fact they had first to get themselves over the Channel, the UK planning phase officially coming to an end on 5 July, when Lucky Forward's Echelon sailed from Southampton, crossing the water in some fourteen hours. They made the passage in Liberty ships and Landing Ship Tanks (LST). The transports anchored offshore and loads were transferred to small craft and amphibious trucks which then unloaded on Utah Beach, the vehicles driving ashore through the shallows. The LST were beached at high tide, left high and dry when the tide ebbed and debarkation was then able to be carried out across dry land. On reaching shore all the vehicles were moved about eight miles inland to a transit area, where they were de-waterproofed and then driven in convoy some 28 miles to the Headquarters Bivouac Area at Néhou (see map in Chapter 4). This is how Colonel Brenton Wallace described his crossing: 'Late in the afternoon of 4 July the headquarters started to motor down to the port of Southampton in the embarkation area, to board the ships for the passage across the Channel. As we neared the port, our column moved slower and slower, and finally came to a halt in the centre of the city. Despite the light, we realised it was almost midnight and decided that we would probably be stuck there for the rest of the night. So we tried to make the best of it. We all had our own motor equipment, of course, for we had been made independently mobile for the campaign. I personally had my own jeep and trailer and my sergeant driver. All of my equipment, including my CP tent, bedding roll and personal belongings, as well as those belonging to my driver, were in the trailer, covered with a tarpaulin. Earlier in the evening we had become pretty hungry, so opened some K rations and ate them for the first time. They were supposed to be full of vitamins, but to us they tasted terrible. Later on in France we changed our minds and thought they were excellent. Some time after midnight, we located an army kitchen and got some hot coffee. Some of us tried to sleep on the benches in a park, opposite which we were stopped, but I never realised how hard park benches really were. It got pretty cool toward morning and I finally crawled in under the tarpaulin on top of the baggage in the trailer and got a little sleep.

'The following morning we drove our vehicles aboard an LST, which is larger than an LCT. Both have fronts which drop down as the vessel hits the beach, and the vehicles are run off the ship to the beach over the ramp. The LST had two decks, the upper one reached by a large elevator which carries vehicles from deck to deck. The LST was equipped with triple-tier bunks and blankets for the enlisted men and junior officers. The senior officers had bunks in staterooms. The meals going across the Channel were hot and were really excellent. The whole trip was surprisingly comfortable. It took practically all day for our ships to be loaded and our convoy formed and we did not sail until the night of 5 July. When we came on deck the next morning, it was a beautiful clear day and the Channel was quite a sight. In front of us and behind us, as far as the eye could see, were LSTs, Liberty and Victory ships in double column plowing across the Channel. Each ship carried a silver barrage balloon, extending on a cable from its stern. It was really a bridge of ships. On either side of the double column, destroyers flitted here and there and off in the distance could occasionally be seen the low outline of a cruiser or a battleship.

'As we neared the French coast we began to hear the rumble of guns, demolition charges along the coast, with once in a while the explosion of a mine. As we approached Utah Beach we saw a great deal of wreckage, smashed craft and vehicles, and many underwater obstacles, although many of these things had been removed. Our LST beached shortly after noon on 6 July and we drove ashore over the ramp formed by our dropped bow. The beach traffic was fairly well organised although dozens of ships were lined up on both sides of us discharging their loads onto the sand. We drove over a sort of highway marked by the vehicles along the beach and then up a ramp built through an opening in the sea wall onto the land above. Beach strongpoints and enemy gun emplacements which had been captured or smashed were of course visible everywhere. We began to see minefields placed there by the Heinies, marked with a skull and crossbones and the words *Achtung-Minen*. They told us that the white signs marked dummy minefields and the yellow ones the real thing. As we went inland we saw the barbed wire entanglements and the French grey stone houses which had been wrecked by naval and artillery shells and also small fields of crosses where the dead had been buried. When we came to Ste-Mère-Eglise and other towns we found that many civilians still lived there and they welcomed us warmly with smiles and hand waving and an occasional *Vive l'Amérique*! As we got farther inland they even offered us Calvados to drink and threw apples to us. One of the amusing things, however, was to see the little children, six or seven years old, try to give us Churchill's famous victory sign made with the first two fingers of the hand. These little youngsters, having been taught the Nazi salute by the Heinies, and of course knowing no better, would first give us a stiff Nazi salute and then immediately open two fingers making the V-sign at the same time.'

Patton Arrives

General Patton and his Chief of Staff, Hugh Gaffey, left England at 1025 hrs on 6 July to join his headquarters in France. They flew in a flight of three C-47s, each carrying a jeep and escorted by four P-47 fighters. Flying down the west coast of the Cotentin Peninsula, they landed at an airstrip near Omaha Beach. Although he was still meant to be 'a secret', news of his arrival spread like wildfire and a mass of Army and Navy personnel rushed to see him. Perhaps they were disappointed to discover that he was not wearing a gold helmet or his "Green Hornet' uniform, and was carrying only one pistol. But they must have enjoyed the impromptu speech he made, standing in his jeep: 'I'm proud to be here to fight beside you,' he said. 'Now let's cut the guts out of those Krauts and get the hell on to Berlin. And when we get to Berlin, I am going to personally shoot that paper-hanging son of bitch just as I would a snake.' The troops cheered!

Breakout from the Bridgehead

Having established a secure bridgehead on the Normandy coast and built up their troops within it, it was now time to move on to the next phase of operations, namely the breakout from the confines of the Cotentin peninsula, to gain control of Brittany and swing wide to the east. On the left flank, the British and Canadian Armies would mount continuous attacks, with the aim of masking the main effort, which would be made by US First Army on the right. They would pivot on their left flank and swing south on the right, thus securing the whole of the Cotentin peninsula. On reaching the base of the peninsula, VIII Corps would turn west into Brittany, making for Rennes and St-Malo. Third Army would follow on the extreme right of VIII Corps, ready to take command of the breakout when ordered. First Army's operation was known as Operation 'Cobra' and H-Hour was set for 1300 hrs on 24 July, but then postponed for 24 hours because of bad flying weather. Heavy artillery barrages and saturation bombing preceded the attack.

Third Army Goes Operational

On 28 July General Omar Bradley, who was commanding the Twelfth Army Group, issued verbal orders to General Patton to assume operational control of all troops in the VIII Corps zone and to continue the breakout. Third Army would go operational at 1200 hrs on Tuesday, 1 August, with four Corps under command: VIII Corps (Middleton), XV Corps (Haislip), XX Corps (Walker) and XII Corps (Cook). At the same

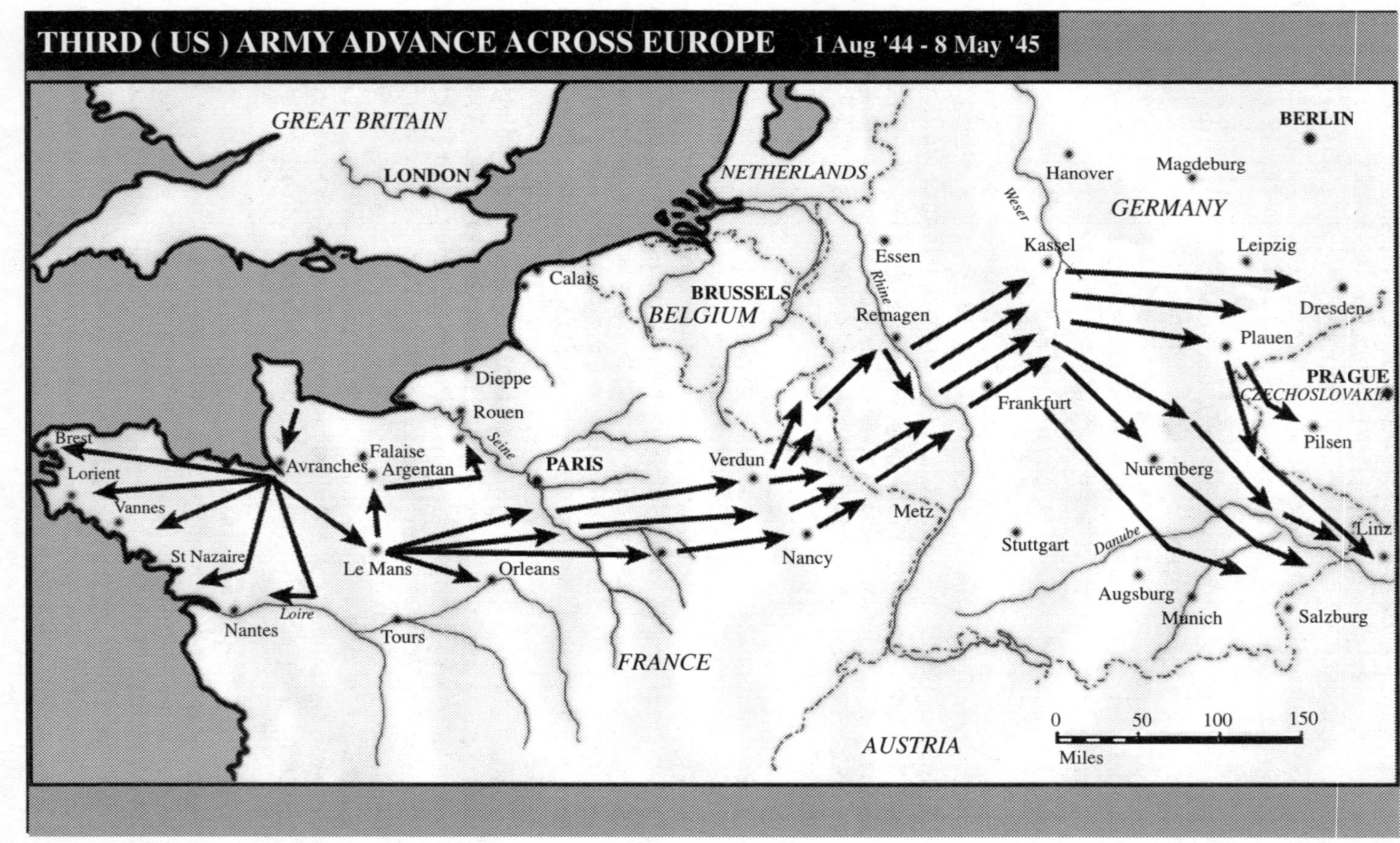
THIRD (US) ARMY ADVANCE ACROSS EUROPE 1 Aug '44 - 8 May '45
GREAT BRITAIN
LONDON
NETHERLANDS
BRUSSELS
BELGIUM
BERLIN
Hanover
Magdeburg
GERMANY
Weser
Kassel
Leipzig
Essen
Rhine
Remagen
Dresden
Plauen
PRAGUE
CZECHOSLOVAKIA
Pilsen
Frankfurt
Nuremberg
Linz
Stuttgart
Danube
Augsburg
Munich
Salzburg
Calais
Dieppe
Rouen
Seine
Brest
Lorient
Vannes
St Nazaire
Avranches
Falaise
Argentan
PARIS
Verdun
Metz
Nancy
Le Mans
Orleans
Nantes
Loire
Tours
FRANCE
AUSTRIA
0
50
100
150
Miles

time, XIX TAC became operational under General Weyland. August operations would be developed in five phases:

a. The conquest of Brittany
b. The encirclement of German Seventh Army in the Argentan–Falaise–Mortain area
c. The advance to the River Seine, including enveloping enemy forces from Mantes Gassicourt to Elbeuf
d. Forcing the enemy to evacuate south-western France
e. Routing the enemy across the Rivers Marne, Aisne and Meuse.

Week 1 (1–6 August 1944)
Uncertain of what to expect, the Germans were unable to present a cohesive front line, although they did establish a number of defensive perimeters with well-emplaced artillery. Third Army spearheads burst out of Avranches and made considerable progress to the south (Rennes captured on 3 August), to the south-east (Mayenne captured on 5 August) and to the west, where Task Force 'A' (based on 1st TD Bde, with 2nd and 15th Cav Gps, 6th TD Gp, 705th TD Bn, 159th Engr Combat Bn and 509th Engr Light Pontoon Coy) made for Brest, capturing Vannes on the 5th, with VIII Corps following up. From Lebignard, Lucky Forward moved to Beauchamps, eleven miles north of Avranches on 2 August. For security reasons, Third Army's name was still not being used.[1] XIX TAC kept the enemy away from the advancing spearheads, attacking enemy positions, guns and AFVs. Patton appreciated that he must keep advancing, never giving the enemy time to stop to organise a proper defence, so, after taking Mayenne (XV Corps), they went swiftly on, crossing the Mayenne river, with Le Mans as their objective in the east. On the other flank, Brest, some 210 miles to the west, was still VIII Corps' main target. By the end of 6 August, Third Army had liberated some 3½ million people in 119 towns and villages. Bread was in short supply all over the area, but the coming harvest should soon solve that problem. During the night of 6 August, Lucky's HQ at Beauchamps was bombed but there were no casualties.

Week 2 (7–13 August)
On 7 August, the only remaining aggressive enemy resistance was against VIII Corps in the St-Malo area, where mines, booby-traps, anti-tank obstacles and guns were all being deployed. St-Malo had been heavily fortified and the harbour locks mined. XV Corps was now only twelve miles from Le Mans (7 August), the enemy offering only token resistance. XII Corps continued with its mission, which was to move newly arriving units from the beaches to their assembly areas. XIX TAC now had nine full fighter-bomber groups operational and continued to attack in all areas, but the Luftwaffe was becoming more aggressive. Thirty-three

enemy aircraft were shot down on the 7th and seven more on the 9th. By 10 August Angers had been captured and the town of St-Malo cleared (less the Citadel). The ration situation was becoming critical, all forward units outrunning their supplies and having to use emergency reserves. On 12 August, GSP ordered XII Corps into action, its objective being to concentrate forces south-east of Le Mans, so as to protect the Army's southern flank. By the 13th, the enemy were withdrawing through the Falaise–Argentan Gap, with XIX TAC destroying many targets – a force of 37 P-47s attacked a concentration of 800–1,000 enemy vehicles on 13 August, claiming 400–500 transports destroyed. The Citadel at St-Malo was now under heavy artillery bombardment. Lucky Forward had reached Poilley (eight miles north-west of Fougères) on 8 August, and St-Ouen-des-Toits (seven miles north-west of Laval) on the 12th.

Week 3 (14–20 August)

Lucky Forward moved to La Bazoge (ten miles north of Le Mans) on 14 August. In the west, the enemy was withdrawing towards Dinard, while in the east they were desperately trying to withdraw to the Argentan–Falaise gap. Twelfth Army Group ordered Patton to hold the southern portion of the gap with XVth Corps and 80th Division, together with VII Corps (First Army), while simultaneously making a rapid movement east, to harass and confuse the enemy. The objective of XX Corps was changed from Dreux to Chartres. On 15 August SHAEF at last announced to the world news agencies that Third Army, under GSP, was now operating in France. By now, the area south of the Seine from Paris to Orleans was already under Third Army control. Dreux was captured by XV Corps on the 16th, and XII Corps took Orleans, despite the fact that there were some 125,000 combat effective enemy troops with 300 tanks in Third Army's area. Patton ordered XII Corps to hold Orleans with a small force, maintain an armoured combat command at La Loupe, move the bulk of the corps south of Janville and press on with recce to the east. By the 18th Third Army had secured bridgeheads over the Eure at Dreux and Chartres, and were closing up to the Seine. By the end of the week, the Argentan–Falaise gap had been finally closed, trapping some 10,000 Germans, while the Brittany peninsula was under Third Army control almost everywhere although some isolated pockets of enemy still held out in certain ports. On 19 August Major General Manton Eddy took over as CG XII Corps from General Cook who retired because of ill health. On 20 August XX Corps launched an attack east of the Seine, having established bridgeheads there, and Lucky Forward was moving to Brou, 22 miles south-west of Chartres.

Week 4 (21–27 August)

On 21 August 4th Armd Div captured Sens, while 35th Inf Div reached Boynes, six miles south-east of Pithiviers, against sporadic enemy resistance. At Champenard, XV Corps had rather more trouble, meeting strong resistance. The Luftwaffe switched from night to day operations and repeatedly attacked the Seine crossing area; 60 aircraft were shot down by AAA, and XIX TAC bagged another 20 aircraft on 22 August. Diesel fuel was supplied to the French farmers so that they could complete their harvest, but HQ ComZ was told that the scheduled Third Army tonnage of all types of supplies had not been delivered and that the situation was becoming critical. With only three corps (XV Corps had been released to First Army on the 24th), one of which was occupied in Brittany, Third Army had captured Fontainebleau and Montargis on 23 August, while its armoured spearheads continued to race eastwards. The Red Ball Express (see Chapter 9) was established by ComZ to meet the severe shortages of fuel supplies. On 24 August Patton ordered XX and XII Corps to push on eastwards and capture bridgeheads from Reims to Vitry-le-François. In the XII Corps area, 4th Armd captured Troyes after some hard street fighting. On 25 August, French 2nd Armd Div, detached to First Army, entered Paris and obtained the surrender of the German garrison that afternoon, and Lucky Forward moved to Courcy-aux-Loges, eight miles south of Pithiviers that same day. Twelfth Army Group now ordered Third Army to cross the line of the Seine–Yonne Rivers to the line Troyes–Châlons-sur-Marne–Reims, protect the right flank eastwards from Orleans and be ready to advance rapidly to seize crossings of the Rhine into Germany, from Mannheim to Koblenz. On 26 August, HQ XV Corps returned to Third Army.

Week 5 (28 August – 3 September)

Rapid progress was made on the 28th, liberating Châlons-sur-Marne, Montmirail and Epernay. But the fuel situation had become critical, mainly because all available fuel was now going to the British, so as to support Montgomery's airborne assault on Arnhem. Patton issued orders that Third Army would continue their advance no matter what happened – one tank would drain the fuel from the rest of their platoon and when that tank ran out of gas, the crew were to get out and walk! Under no circumstances were the soldiers of Third Army to stop their advance. On 30 August, however, 12th Army Group informed Third Army that there would be no further petrol supplies until 3 September. Lucky Forward moved to La Chaume, thirteen miles north-east of Sens. CCA 7th Armd Div captured Verdun, while CCB moved to Eix on 31 August, and 4th Armd reached the vicinity of St-Mihiel. September began with the fuel shortage still acute, but on the plus side the Brittany peninsula was finally subdued by XIII Corps. XIX TAC flew 492 sorties that day, destroying or damaging 39 aircraft, 33 locomotives, 130 AFVs and 817 motor transport vehicles (MT). On 2 September the enemy was cleared from north of the Loire to Orleans, XIX TAC flew another 164 successful sorties, while 7th Armd Div secured its bridgehead across the

Meuse and continued to recce eastwards. German casualties that week were 264,300 infantry and 120,000 panzer troops, leaving him an estimated 106,700 infantry and 78,000 panzer troops on the Third Army front. On 3 September, XII Corps consolidated its positions east of the Meuse, XV Corps concentrated in the vicinity of Nangis, XX Corps secured the Verdun bridgehead and pushed patrols further east towards Germany, while VIII Corps continued its attack on Brest. The Central Group of Armies became officially 12th Army Group.

Week 6 (4–10 September)

VIII Corps moved to Ninth Army, but 83rd Inf and 6th Armd Divs were transferred to XV Corps, thus remaining in Third Army. Ninth Army prepared for action on the southern flank of Third Army. XX Corps was ordered to seize Metz, advance east of the Moselle, seize Mainz and secure a bridgehead over the Rhine. XII Corps was to seize Nancy and secure a bridgehead over the Moselle, protecting the southern flank until relieved by XV Corps. It was also to be ready to move swiftly to take Mannheim and seize a Rhine bridgehead. On 4 September XIX TAC flew 159 sorties, and on that same day gasoline supplies began to increase at long last. Lucky Forward moved into a bivouac area north of Marson, eight miles east of Châlons-sur-Marne and 319th Inf Div managed to force part of a battalion across the Moselle at Pont-à-Mousson. Fuel supplies continued to improve (on 7 September, receipts exceeded demands for the first time!), but a new crisis loomed – a shortage of artillery ammunition, which was alleviated by the end of the week for all natures except 105mm howitzer ammo. An increasingly large number of sorties was flown by XIX TAC – 389 on the 5th, 416 on the 6th, 238 on the 7th, 470 on the 8th, 308 on the 9th, then 377 on the 10th, destroying road and rail installations, countless enemy tanks and MT, attacking enemy airfields and gun installations.

Week 7 (11–17 September)

On 11–12 September, both XII Corps and XX Corps were fighting to maintain bridgeheads over the Moselle, XII Corps enlarging and expanding theirs to the north and south of Nancy, while XX Corps, on their left, pushed infantry across north of Bayon. In the south XV Corps had 79th Inf Div fighting forward, their infantry reaching Neufchâteau, Mirecourt and Charmes on the 12th. There were still some fuel shortages, but with PLUTO[2] reaching Chartres, these should soon be obviated. In the middle of the week, there were critical shortages of Class 1 supplies (rations), so captured German rations had to be issued. A Third Army air evacuation holding unit opened at Etain on 12 September, and a request was made by Lucky that the entire available airlift be used to bring forward priority ammunition. XV Corps continued to push eastwards, 79th Inf Div reaching Ramecourt on 14 September, while French

2nd Armd Div took Mattaincourt and made contact with elements of Seventh Army at Chaumont. Heavy counter-attacks against 80th Inf Div's bridgehead over the Moselle were broken up on the 15th, the same day that Lucky Forward moved to Braquis, eleven miles east of Verdun. G-2 reported that German strength on the western front was currently estimated at some 54 infantry and 16 panzer divisions, and that Field Marshal von Rundstedt had been reinstated as supreme commander only two months after his dismissal by Hitler. On the 17th, XV Corps was ordered to advance north-east, its missions being to protect Lucky's southern flank, to maintain contact with Seventh Army, to be prepared to seize Mannheim and then secure a bridgehead over the Rhine in its area (or move through bridgeheads secured by XII or XX Corps). On this day too XX Corps launched a co-ordinated attack on the heavily fortified city of Metz, with 5th Inf Div assaulting from the south and 90th from the west. There was a growing refugee problem in all areas, as many as 30 different nationalities being encountered. Civil Affairs detachments came forward to deal with them and a large centre was opened at Verdun, immediately housing more than 2,000. Throughout the week XIX TAC kept up its sorties, flying more than 1,600 missions and destroying a vast range of enemy road and rail transport, and military installations.

Week 8 (18–24 September)

On the 18th, XV Corps launched an assault to the north-east, 79th Inf Div crossing the Moselle near Bayon and advancing to Gerbéviller. The 6th Armd Div (less CCB) moved to Neufchâteau to relieve French 2nd Armd Div and protect the Army's southern flank. Metz was proving a tough nut to crack, even 240mm artillery was having little lasting effect on the forts. It was estimated by G-2 that the Germans would pivot at Metz, establishing a defensive line parallel to the Siegfried Line, while launching armoured attacks from Thionville in the north to the Forêt de Parroy in the south. The 7th Armd Div was transferred to First Army on the 22nd. The XX Corps continued to assault Metz, but were also ordered to protect the left flank, including the city of Luxembourg and maintain contact with First Army. XV Corps continued to advance north-eastwards, strengthening its bridgehead over the Meurthe. Lucky Forward moved to Etain on the 22nd, the first time they had been in covered billets since arriving in France. XII Corps continued its attack, reaching the high ground some ten miles north-east of Nancy on the 23rd, with 35th Inf Div, while 80th Inf Div held the high ground between Montenoy and Jeandelaincourt. On the same day 4th Armd Div repulsed a strong counter-attack. XX Corps continued to pound Metz, but made little progress. On 24 September, the first patrols began probing the outer defences of the Siegfried Line, but were met with strong resistance from pillboxes and other fortifications. Unfortunately, the earlier lack of fuel had prevented Third Army from reaching Germany before the enemy had time to withdraw and consolidate his defences. XIX TAC continued to fly hundreds of sorties daily, including vital ground support on 24 September to 4th Armd Div against a strong armoured counter-attack, which they halted. The bad weather prevented them returning to their airfield near St-Dizier and they were forced to land at Etain, where GSP met them and personally thanked them for their invaluable help and courage.

Week 9 (25 September – 1 October)

Metz continued to hold out, despite heavy artillery fire being directed on to the forts (Fort Jeanne d'Arc had two casements and an ammo dump destroyed, but did not fall, nor did Fort Kellermann). Bad weather halted flying on 25 and 26 September, but XIX TAC were able to resume, and flew more than 500 missions daily on the 27th, 28th and 29th, before the weather closed in again on the 30th. Third Army was once again being kept short of supplies, so was hampered in its advance into Germany. At Metz XX Corps attacked Fort Driant on the 27th, but was forced to withdraw. On 28 September, XV Corps passed to Seventh Army control, with 79th and 90th Inf Divs and French 2nd Armd Div. On the 29 September, 35th Inf Div and 4th Armd Div repulsed more counter-attacks around Jallaucourt, thirteen miles north-east of Nancy. Infantry of XII Corps cleared the enemy out of the Forêt de Grémecey, while 6th Armd Div took the high ground in the Lemoncourt–Fresnes–Chambrey area and to the immediate north, the enemy withdrawing farther north. On 1 October 80th Inf Div took control of the Seille river near Port-sur-Seille. Elements of 83rd Inf Div made contact with Ninth Army on the north flank, near the outskirts of Grevenmacher, north-east of the city of Luxembourg. Fuel rationing had to be re-instituted as supplies were under 50 per cent of requirements (219,392 gallons requested on 1 October, 95,840 gallons received). October would see Third Army making preparations for a major offensive to drive the enemy back behind the Rhine. This involved building-up supplies, regrouping troops and the detailed planning of future operations. Fortunately, winter clothing had already begun to arrive. The troop strength of Third Army was now some 300,000 men, having lost XV Corps to Seventh Army on 29 September.

Week 10 (2–8 October)

On 2 October XX Corps and XIX TAC launched a heavy ground and aerial attack on Fort Driant (Metz) on the west bank of the Moselle, but still encountered heavy resistance when they entered the fort on the following day. This attack was supported by 23 FA battalions and preceded by their firing a 30-minute preparatory barrage. Heavy fire was also directed on to Forts Jeanne d'Arc and Verdun, Batteries Moselle and Marivall.

Despite temporary neutralisation, the forts appeared to be impregnable and all the artillery firepower did was to chip the concrete! Heavy fighting continued all week, a special 'Task Force Driant' being created on 5 October.[3] Clearly the enemy intended to hold Metz as long as possible to gain time for the preparation of the Rhine defences. Elsewhere XIX TAC had more success, cutting railway lines, destroying trains, marshalling yards and military installations as well as four small naval craft! Such attacks were isolating the enemy from their supplies and preventing reinforcement. Aircraft also dropped psychological warfare leaflets. Lucky's communications were boosted by the establishing of East and West Wire-head,[4] which began operating in a suburb of Nancy in early October. A fuel rationing board was created, initial allotments being on average: 5,000 gals/Inf Div, 25,000 gals/Armd Div, 10,000 gals/Corps troops and 84,000 gals/Army troops (reserve stocks stood at 300,000 gallons on 3 October). On the 7th, in an attempt to enlarge its bridgehead, XII Corps attacked to the north-east, 35th Inf Div capturing Fossieux and the high ground around it. Moivrons was occupied by 6th Armd Div, and 80th Inf Div advanced towards Lixières. After a 45-minute barrage, XII Corps troops began to clear the northern half of the corps sector, up to the Seille. On 7 October General George C. Marshall (COS US Army) visited Lucky Forward, with his deputy (Lieutenant General Handy) and General Bradley. On 8 October XIX TAC not only flew 311 sorties but destroyed or damaged some 45 aircraft on the ground.

Week 11 (9–15 October)

On 9 October, CCA 6th Armd Div cleared Chenicourt and pushed on to Aulnois-sur-Seine, where they were relieved by 317th Infantry (80th Inf Div) and moved into mobile reserve at Leyr. At Metz, Task Force Driant was replaced by Task Force Warnock (Brigadier General Alva C. Warnock) prior to continuing operations in the tunnels, but the German defences remained firm. Elements of 90th Inf Div were engaged in fierce house-to-house fighting in Maizières-les-Metz on 9 and 10 October. HQ III Corps (Major General John Millikin) and 95th Inf Div were transferred from Ninth Army to Third Army, while 83rd Inf Div was transferred to the Ninth. After two days (9 and 10 October) of non-flying weather, conditions improved and XIX TAC began flying again. TAC recce reported that the Germans were constructing defensive positions on the high ground east of the Seille around Clémery. On 12 October, XX Corps decided to withdraw its forces and contain the enemy with newly assigned divisions. Twelfth Army Group drastically reduced FA ammo supplies by 95 per cent (from 12 October to 7 November), but there was no restrictions on tanks, TDs or AAA, so these weapons were used very effectively as secondary artillery, while maximum use was also made of captured enemy weapons. Both Lucky Forward HQs (front and rear echelons), plus HQ XIX TAC, moved to Nancy, on 11 October, all being located in adjoining buildings in the town by the 12th. Considerable German troop movement was noted in the XII Corps area, TAC recce locating large concentrations at Moussey and Héming, while heavy rail and road movement was observed in the XX Corps zone, with all types of vehicles moving to and from Metz. Third Army remained virtually on the defensive as 12th Army Group required. Only XIX TAC continued its sorties, destroying railway lines and rolling stock, as well as many other targets.

Week 12 (16–22 October)

Bad weather was now preventing flying, and lack of fuel prevented movement (on 16 October Third Army received no fuel, having requested more than 334,000 gallons). Ammunition was also severely restricted. Elements of 90th Inf Div were still engaged in hand-to-hand fighting in Maizières-les-Metz. Eisenhower and Devers (CG 6th Army Group) visited Lucky Forward on the 17th to review plans for a resumption of the Allied offensive. Front lines remained unchanged for the entire week, except for a minor advance on XII Corps front, when, on 21 October, 26th Inf Div launched a small attack towards Moncourt but only gained 2,000 yards. On 22 October 12th Army Group issued a letter of instruction to the effect that '12th Army Group will regroup and prepare for an advance by all three Armies to the Rhine River.... Third Army will advance in zone to the Rhine in the Mainz–Worms area and seize a bridgehead immediately if the situation permits. If it is impracticable to seize a bridgehead, Third Army will attack to the north and clear the area to the Moselle.' Bradley arrived on the 22nd to discuss the coming offensive with GSP. It was decided that the date for the attack would depend upon the weather.

Week 13 (23–29 October)

Bad weather still prevented much flying for most of the week, and there was so little ground action that some divisions instituted rigorous training programmes to keep troops on their toes. Twelfth Army Group stressed strict supply discipline. On 24 October, three 280mm shells landed on Lucky's HQ, narrowly missing Patton's personal quarters. GSP informed SHAEF that since 1 October he had received 2.1 million gallons less fuel than had been requested, pointing out that less than two more operational days' fuel remained. Supplies of 'B' rations were also critical. Front-line positions remained unchanged in XII Corps area, but aggressive patrolling took place. On the 28th, elements of 90th Inf Div resumed their attack on Maizières-les-Metz which, with the exception of the town hall, was captured the following day. The 29th was by far the best flying day, XIX TAC carrying out 419 sorties, during which 100 German fighters were engaged in the air and 26 shot down for the loss of six US aircraft.

Week 14 (30 October – 5 November)

At 1400 hrs on 30 October the town hall in Maizières-les-Metz was taken by 90th Inf Div. Twelfth Army Group was asked to send all available fuel to Third Army, so as to build up reserves, because currently Third Army was incapable of sustaining any offensive. A certain amount of rotation and regrouping took place so as to rest troops in contact and keep the enemy guessing. Fuel supplies, especially diesel, were still in short supply, Third and Seventh Armies doing a 'deal' and exchanging oil for diesel. The new month began with Third Army still acutely short of supplies and having to go on to the defensive, but this was not to Patton's liking so he began aggressive patrolling. Extreme weather conditions did not help, trench foot becoming a great problem. Nevertheless, during the month Metz would fall and Third Army would drive the enemy back behind the Siegfried Line. On 3 November, Third Army was ordered to (i) envelop Metz from north and south, also to destroy any enemy trying to withdraw from the Metz area; (ii) advance to seize the Mainz–Frankfurt–Darmstadt area; (iii) be prepared for further offensive action to the north-east. Patton ordered XII Corps to advance to Falkenberg and destroy enemy withdrawing from Metz; it was also to advance north-eastwards, establish a bridgehead in the Darmstadt area and be ready for further advances. XX Corps was to contain Metz with part of its forces, while using 80th and 83rd Inf Divs to advance east of the Rhine to seize the Mainz-Frankfurt area and also be prepared for further advances. By the end of the week, there was sufficient fuel for the coming offensive, while the ComZ was told to bring all US armies up to a five-day supply level. Seven new railheads were established, primarily for Third Army.[5]

Week 15 (6–12 November)

The week opened with 12th Army Group sending out revised dates for the coming offensive to all three Armies – Third Army's being 5 November (though the amendment didn't arrive until the 6th!). Further delay followed, but they were eventually allowed to begin the 'Battle of Germany' at 0600 hrs, 7 November. There was no preparatory aerial bombardment so tactical surprise was complete. The enemy high command had reckoned that the current conditions of extreme flooding would prevent any Allied offensive. XII Corps launched the attack with 26th, 35th and 80th Inf Divs advancing in the south, centre and north respectively, between Moncourt in the south and Clémery in the north. All were given heavy field artillery support, which not only dealt with enemy artillery batteries, but also caused serious disruption to their communications. Jallaucourt, Malaucourt and Rouves were all captured on the 7th as the divisions raced towards the Rhine. Simultaneously, XX Corps was preparing to launch a massive assault on Metz, which began on the 8th, but was handicapped by severe flooding in the area of the

Moselle. Nevertheless, 5th Inf Div reached Cheminot (south of Metz) having 'jumped off' first, while 90th Inf Div crossed the river using DUKWs[6] and established bridgeheads near Thionville. On 8 November 6th Armd Div crossed the Seille and prepared for a further advance, while 10th Armd Div concentrated ready to use established bridgeheads, and 95th Inf Div captured even more at Uckange. In the far north 83rd Inf Div came back to XX Corps from First Army. After a bad start to the week, the weather improved on the 8th and XIX TAC was able to fly 471 sorties. On the 9th thick minefields and floods hampered XX Corps' advance, but XII Corps made good progress. To break the Metz deadlock, the US Eighth Air Force sent 1,476 heavy bombers to blast all the fortified towns east of the bridgehead area: Metz, Verny, Orny, Pommérieux and Saarbrücken, with XIX TAC flying in support. Progress continued on the 10th and 11th, the enemy fighting delaying actions in suitable defensive positions (mainly villages and forests). Engineers began building their longest Bailey bridge to date (200ft) at Thionville, and two others at Malling, over which poured 10th Armd Div.

Unfortunately on 11 November, 83rd Inf Div reverted to First Army on General Bradley's verbal order, which prevented Saarburg being taken.[7] On the 12th, XII Corps met stubborn resistance in Bazoncourt, but fought hard and consolidated its positions. Bridgeheads were being enlarged and the armour (6th and 10th Armd Divs) began to play a major role. As a consequence of the cold, wet weather there were many cases of trench foot and GSP immediately instituted remedial action ('It's more important in war to keep your feet in good condition than it is to brush your teeth,' he told his younger staff officers).

Week 16 (13–19 November)

The enemy were continuing to impose delay, using counter-attacks, extensive minefields, roadblocks, increased artillery fire and all manner of obstacles. Nevertheless, both XX and XII Corps continued to push eastwards and to the north-east. On the 14th in the XII Corps area, leading elements of 26th Inf Div took Haraucourt and Marsal. 4th Armd Div and other elements of 26th Inf Div were close by taking Guébling and Zarbeling, while to the north, 6th Armd Div seized Landroff. In the XX Corps area, 95th Inf Div captured Ouvr St-Hubert, Fèves and Fort d'Illange that day, while 10th Armd Div began crossing the Moselle near Thionville and Malling, using a smoke-screen. Farther south, 5th Inf Div took Mécleuves in its flanking drive towards Metz. As the week progressed, the weather improved and XIX TAC was able to fly more and more sorties. The 18th saw a major breaching of the Metz defences and, with it enemy resistance in the XX Corps area visibly weakened, a general withdrawal began. Metz was now completely encircled, with only some six major strong-points still holding out. CCA of 4th Armd Div took Virming on the 19th, then joined 26th Inf Div to assault Dieuze, while, to its immediate north, 6th Armd Div and 35th Inf Div attacked eastwards. On 19 November 5th and 95th Inf Divs entered Metz, by which time XIX TAC aircraft were having a field-day, attacking the withdrawing enemy columns, flying 403 sorties on the 19th alone (armed recce, ground support and bomber escort).

Week 17 (20–26 November)

There was now only a skeleton German force in front of XII Corps, but with the aid of many roadblocks, blown bridges, and mines, the enemy continued to impose delay. In addition, certain forts around Metz were still holding out and had to be contained. On 20 November Metz was reported clear, but mopping-up continued for some days and the city, once called 'The Bastion of the East', was not officially reported subdued by XX Corps until 22 November, after a two-month siege, hampered by the worst flooding for twenty years and continual impossible flying weather. This opened up a new route to the German frontier and the Siegfried Line. Bad weather continued to hamper XIX TAC, but both XII and XX Corps made steady progress, east and north-east, 4th Armd Div crossing the Saar on 24 November and 10th Armd Div crossing the German border on the 25th to capture Bethingen. Reinforcements were now arriving at the rate of 5,600 daily, while a major request was sent in to 12th Army Group for large quantities of winter supplies – groundsheets, overshoes, trousers and jackets, sleeping-bags, sweaters and combat boots – more than a million and a half items in total! Emergency supplies of foodstuffs were sent into Metz on 26 November to help alleviate the suffering of the civilian population. TAC Air reported signs of heavy enemy rail movement into the Third Army zone of advance towards the end of the week, but XII Corps continued to attack on all its fronts, while XX Corps mainly continued to contain the forts and strong-points remaining around Metz.

Week 18 (27 November – 4 December)

The enemy continued to offer varied resistance all along Third Army's front, from Tettingen in the north to Sarre-Union in the south, as he withdrew towards his Siegfried Line positions, making use, for example, of the Maginot Line forts. Both XII and XX Corps continued to make steady progress in their attack on the German 'West Wall', despite the bad weather which not only restricted flying, but also meant that heavy AFVs, such as tanks and TDs, were confined to roads by the bad going. Some 46 towns and villages were captured on the two corps fronts during the week, which was about average for the month of November. In preparation for their continued advance, XII Corps regrouped on the 29th, more and more probes reached the Saar and 4th and 6th Armd Divs occupied high ground in the front of the corps area. To their north, in the XX Corps sector, 10th Armd and 95th Inf Divs were now within the borders of Germany, making successful progress. Meanwhile, III Corps remained non-operational at Etain. On 30 November Patton ordered 6th Cavalry Group to be formed, comprising 6th Cav Recon Sqn, 5th Ranger Bn, Coy 'C' of 602d TD Bn, Coy 'B' of 293d Engr Combat Bn and Troop 'E' of 28th Cav Recon Sqn. It would initially be attached to XX Corps. (See also Chapter 8 for more details of this Group which was soon known as 'Patton's Household Cavalry') There were clear indications of a definite build-up of troops and supplies opposite First Army's area. Major General Hugh Gaffey took over as CG 4th Armd Div from ' Tiger Jack' Wood on 3 December, while Brigadier General Gay became COS Third Army in his place. The week closed with the enemy making strong attacks to regain Sarre-Union and Lauterbach.

Week 19 (4–10 December)

On the 4th, it was decided that III Corps' 87th Inf Div should begin to relieve 5th Inf Div in the Metz area, but that those forts still holding out should be contained, not assaulted. This included Fort Jeanne d'Arc which continued to hold out all week. Sarre-Union was officially cleared on the 4th. Generally, on the XII Corps front, enemy resistance was stronger in the south, while farther north CCB of 4th Armd Div seized an intact bridge over the River Eichel at Vollerdingen and established a small bridgehead. The 6th Armd and 80th Inf Divs continued attacking, and in the XX Corps sector, 95th Inf Div encountered heavy street fighting in Saarlautern, but managed to establish a bridgehead at Lisdorf on 4 December and to enlarge it on the 5th. Also, on 5 December, 5th Inf Div advanced some 2–5 miles, north of Saarlautern, capturing Pachten. On the 6th III Corps moved its CP to Metz and on the 8th, 87th Inf Div completed the take-over from 5th Inf Div, following the surrender on 8 December of Fort Driant. On the 8th 35th Inf Div crossed the Saar in four places, using TDs in support. Bad weather reduced flying, but XIX TAC still managed a fair number of sorties, which included air recce, with more reports of an enemy build-up in the Eifel area. On 9 December Third Army G-2 sent a report to SHAEF indicating a probable enemy offensive in the Ardennes, but it was ignored.[8] Two groups of Allied military personnel were liberated from German POW camps at Denting and Kreuzwald, both suffering from hunger and lack of medical care – in contrast to German soldiers in American PoW camps.[9]

Week 20 (11–17 December)

An operational directive sent to CGs III, XII and XX Corps on 11 December stated that Third Army would continue its present mission of advancing north-eastwards within its zone, to seize the Mainz–Frankfurt–Darmstadt area. The corps were now disposed with XX Corps in the north, III Corps in the centre and XII Corps in the south. Grouping within corps would be: III Corps – 26 Inf Div, 6th Armd Div (from XII Corps), 6th Cav Gp and 42nd Inf Div (on arrival); XII Corps – 35th, 80th and 87th Inf Divs and 4th Armd Div; XX Corps – 5th, 90th and 95th Inf Divs and 10th Armd Div. On 12 December, Third Army G-2 sent yet another warning to SHAEF about the dangerous enemy build-up opposite First Army and the likelihood of a major offensive in the Ardennes area. Fort Jeanne d'Arc, last remaining strong-point in the Metz area, finally surrendered to 26 Inf Div on the 12th. Along the Third Army front enemy resistance remained patchy, as did the weather, although XIX TAC did manage a fair number of sorties on the 12th, 14th, 15th and 16th. In general, Third Army continued to improve its bridgeheads at Saarlautern and Ensdorf, while slowly advancing north-eastwards.

The Ardennes Offensive begins. On 16 December, spearheaded by elements of Sixth SS Panzer Army, the Germans unleashed their counter-offensive against US First Army. Some days earlier, Patton had instructed his staff to make a thorough study of the situation and be ready with plans which could be implemented quickly if and when Third Army was asked to assist. This would clearly involve a major 90-degree change of direction, from east to north.[10]

Week 21 (18–24 December)

By 18 December, in III Corps' area, 6th Armd Div, attacking to the north-east, was just south of Lixing. In the Metz area 26th Inf Div was regrouping, 6th Cav Sqn reinforced (known as Task Force Fickett) was patrolling aggressively. In XII Corps' area, 4th Armd Div and 87th Inf Div had made small advances, while 80th Inf Div was moving to an assembly area. On the southern flank of XX Corps, 5th Inf Div had made local gains around Saarlautern, as had 95th and 90th Inf Divs. Having been released from First Army, 10th Armd Div was concentrating, while Task Force Polk continued aggressive patrolling on the northern flank. From all this activity it can be seen that Third Army was still actively engaged all along its front. But to its north, the German Ardennes offensive into V and VIII Corps areas was by now some 40 miles deep and 30 miles wide (from St-Vith in the east to St-Hubert in the west, with flanks anchored in the south on Echternach, Diekirch and Ettelbruck, in the north on Monschau, Stavelot and Marche). Thanks to Colonel Oscar Koch's insistence that the Germans would launch an all-out offensive in the Ardennes and Patton's eminently sensible orders to plan for every emergency, Third Army was 'ready to roll' whenever it was finally given the green light.

GSP's plan was to allow the enemy to advance 40–50 miles into First Army's Ardennes salient, then to chop off this intrusion, thus allowing the Allies to surround and destroy the panzer forces. He had planned three possible lines of advance: one due north from Diekirch; the second towards Bastogne from Arlon; the third, on the

Neufchâteau–Bastogne road. General Eisenhower would opt for the second of these, with the limited aim of merely halting the German advance, then pushing them back without trying to destroy the bulk of their forces (GSP had wanted not only to 'cut 'em off', but also to 'chew 'em up'!). VIII Corps would come under Third Army's command for the operation.[11]

Patton immediately issued verbal orders, which were followed up in writing. In essence, these were:

1. XII Corps to relinquish control of its assigned zone to Seventh Army.
2. 80th Inf and 4th Armd Divs to go to III Corps and 87th Inf Div to Seventh Army.
3. III Corps to relinquish control of its zone to XX Corps, passing 6th Armd Div and TF Fickett to XX Corps. It would then move 26th Inf Div to Arlon and assume control of 4th Armd and 80th Inf Divs.
4. XX Corps would take over III Corps' zone, assume control of 6th Armd Div and TF Fickett, relieve 5th Inf Div and move it to Luxembourg.
5. Arty was to be extensively regrouped to support coming offensive operations.

To put this plan into action required maximum effort by both MP and Transportation Sections, to deal with the massive, complex troop movements, with nearly 12,000 vehicles moving over four major routes,[12] but III Corps swiftly got on with the job, while XII Corps had to deal with German counter-attacks launched against 35th Inf Div on 20 December. In outline the overall plan was:

1. First Army would attack south to restore the situation in the Malmédy area.
2. Third Army would change direction and attack north from Luxembourg to Arlon, then be prepared to move north-eastwards to seize crossings over the Rhine.
3. Under Army orders, III Corps would attack north towards St-Vith, destroying all enemy forces, maintaining contact with XII Corps to the east and VIII Corps to the west.
4. XII Corps would hold the west bank of the Moselle and patrol aggressively to the Sauer and Our Rivers.
5. VIII Corps would continue in defence, but be prepared to attack northwards.
6. XX Corps would defend Saarlautern bridgehead and be prepared (with 6th Armd Div) to counter-attack in any direction in Third or Seventh Army areas.

7. III Corps would attack on 21 December, XII and VIII Corps attacks would be when ordered, and all attacks would be in multiple columns composed of tanks and infantry.
8. Air support would be provided by heavy bombers from Eighth Air Force, medium bombers from Ninth Air Force and fighter-bombers, TAC recon and night-fighters from XIX TAC.

On 20 December, the tactical echelon of Lucky Forward moved to Luxembourg City, so as to be able to direct Third Army action in the break-through area. In the late afternoon of the 21st III Corps launched its attack, with 4th Armd, 26th Inf and 80th Inf Divs all making gains against heavy opposition. In VIII Corps' area 28th Inf Div continued to hold its defensive positions at Sibret (five miles south-west of Bastogne) and 101st Airborne Div held Bastogne, although completely surrounded. The assault had suffered from a lack of air support (see Chapter 6, Chaplain Section, for details of Patton's prayer for fine weather), but the weather cleared and many successful strikes took place on 21 and 22 December.

Week 22 (25–31 December)

Bitter, vicious fighting continued as III Corps, against determined opposition, pressed its advance in order to prevent further encroachment into the southern flank of the 'Bulge'. The formations of VIII Corps resisted all German attempts to capture such strong-points as Bastogne, the enemy launching two heavy attacks on the 25th. On the 26th, however, the leading elements of 4th Armd Div (under Major General Hugh Gaffey) reached the beleaguered garrison, despite snow, ice and bitter cold, as well as constant enemy action against their flanks. That day Patton issued the following amendment to his orders:

1. III Corps would pass control of 80th Inf Div to XII Corps at 2000 hrs on 26 December.
2. XII Corps would assume control of 80th Inf Div and move CCA 9th Armd Div to III Corps area immediately.
3. XII Corps would pass 35th Inf Div to III Corps and 10th Armd Div to XX Corps.
4. XX Corps would pass 6th Armd Div to XII Corps, assume control of 10th Armd Div and move 35 Inf Div to III Corps.

The 'Bastogne corridor' was under constant enemy attack, but with continuing assistance from XIX TAC, the enemy were repulsed, while both 26th and 35th Inf Divs made slow but steady progress. Enemy air activity dropped sharply. Requests for white paint and snow-suits poured in (the shortage of the former was overcome by the use of whitewash, while 10,000 snow-suits were made from mattress covers!) On 30

December, the enemy launched a major attack and recaptured Lautrebois, but failed everywhere else to make progress against Third Army. In VIII Corps' area, 11th Armd Div advanced to Redange on 30 December and 5th Inf Div took Riesdorf (seven miles north-west of Echternach). During this week, the remainder of Lucky Forward moved to Luxembourg City, to join the advanced detachment which had been there since 20 December.

Week 23 (1–7 January 1945)

The month of January would see the Germans still desperately trying to stop Third Army's northwards advance from the Bastogne area and, having failed, undertake a costly withdrawal to the Siegfried Line. Their much-vaunted Ardennes offensive gamble would have completely failed before the month ended. Initially, however, they still had a potentially powerful striking force on Third Army's front (G-2 estimate on 3 January was twelve divisions numbering some 93,000 troops and at least 290 tanks and assault guns). In the bitterly cold weather Third Army's four Corps (16 divisions) continued all-out activity in the III and VIII Corps zones, while XII Corps continued to patrol along the Sauer, Sure and Moselle Rivers. Twelfth Army Group ordered Third Army to seize Houffalize and effect a junction with First Army and to destroy the enemy trapped in its area. On the 4th, in an interesting, humanitarian agreement with the Germans in VIII Corps' area, Patton agreed to cease artillery fire on a certain cross-roads as it was close to an enemy hospital. XIX TAC flew many sorties at the beginning of the week (as did the Luftwaffe, 308 hostile aircraft attacking Third Army positions on 1 January). But on the 4th the weather closed in again and there was no more flying that week. A shortage of 'K' rations was alleviated by the receipt of nearly half a million at the Verdun depot which were rushed out to units. Fresh rations remained in short supply.

Week 24 (8–14 January)

Patton issued an operational directive to confirm previous verbal orders, the main points being:

1. 94th Inf Div assigned to XX Corps.
2. III Corps to assume control of 90th Inf Div, pass 4th Armd Div to VIII Corps, attack to the south-east of Bastogne on 9 January, and support VIII Corps in its attack on Noville and Houffalize.
3. VIII Corps was to continue to defend the River Meuse, assume control of 4th Armd Div and attack, on 9 January, to capture Noville and the high ground around Houffalize.
4. Under Army orders, XII Corps was to continue clearing all enemy west of the Moselle and Sauer rivers, then attack northwards.
5. XX Corps – no change to current mission.

III Corps' attack 'jumped off' at 1000 hrs on 9 January, supported by all the corps artillery. The 26th Inf Div captured the high ground overlooking Wiltz, while 90th Inf Div moved forward to attack and capture Berle and Trentelhof. The 35th Inf Div made a small advance and maintained contact with 6th Armd Div. In VIII Corps, 101st Ab Div advanced two miles and captured Recogne, 17th Ab Div maintained contact with 101st, while 87th Inf Div attacked around Tillet. The 4th and 11th Armd Divs made slight gains, being prepared to attack in any direction. By the 11th, III Corps had reached the Wiltz river and on the 14th VIII Corps made contact with British troops on the western tip of the salient. Spasmodic bad weather restricted XIX TAC to just three days' flying (9th, 10th and 13th), but it still flew nearly 1,000 sorties. Manufacture of snow-suits was now in full swing, 10,000 per week being made by local civilian firms. Approximately half a million troops were currently being fed by Third Army (368,000 Third Army, plus 31,500 ComZ troops, 42,000 Ninth Air Force, 3,000 French and 3,000 miscellaneous, plus some 52,000 PoWs, civil labour, etc.).

Week 25 (15–21 January)

On the 15th, VIII Corps units linked up with First Army troops at Houffalize and from then on were able to march eastwards abreast. A 'winter problem' which was becoming serious in the extremely cold weather was the firing of small arms wearing gloves, so Ordnance produced a trigger adaptor (a captured German device) and some 90,000 were manufactured locally. Local steel mills in Luxembourg and Esch were tasked to produce 1-inch steel cable for tank recovery vehicles. Another 'winter problem' was the virtual immobilising of AFVs because of ice and snow; this was overcome by welding manganese steel lugs to every fifth track block on steel tracks, or replacing every fifth track rubber block with a luge-equipped steel block on rubber tracks. German defence and delay tactics continued, but it was becoming obvious that the worst of the 'Battle of the Bulge' was now over, and on 17 January G-2 estimated that the Germans were now beginning the new campaign of retiring under pressure. SHAEF relieved Third Army of responsibility for the Meuse River line south of Givet and for any troops put under command for the Bastogne operation. By the 19th, Third Army's strength was listed at 350,296, some 34,000 under-strength, mainly in rifle companies. Third Army continued to advance, even though XIX TAC was grounded for most of the week.

Week 26 (22–28 January)

Fine weather on the 22nd at long last enabled XIX TAC to fly – 627 sorties in which they destroyed 1,177 motor vehicles and damaged 536 more. Similar success followed on the 23rd–26th. On 23 January numerous revisions of boundaries and re-organisations took place:

1. 87th and 4th Inf Divs from XII Corps to VIII Corps.
2. 76th Inf Div from VIII Corps to XII Corps.
3. 95th Inf Div from XX Corps to VIII Corps.
4. 17th Ab Div from VIII Corps to III Corps.
5. 26th Inf Div from III Corps to XX Corps.
6. 90th Inf Div from III Corps to VIII Corps.

So, VIII Corps on the left flank now had five divisions, XII Corps on the right flank four, while III and XX Corps had two each. The 35th Inf Div moved from Metz to join Seventh Army. Third Army's advance continued as the Germans fell back to their Siegfried Line positions, and severe weather continued to hamper progress more than enemy opposition. On the 24th, GSP attended a conference at Bradley's HQ with Lieutenant General Hodges (First Army), plus certain of their staff, to co-ordinate the coming attacks against the Siegfried Line. On the 24th, 94th Inf Div in the XX Corps area entered Berg and encountered both dragon's-teeth and minefields – they had reached the Siegfried Line. The Battle of the Bulge officially ended on 28 January, all the ground having been re-taken and severe casualties inflicted upon the enemy.

Week 27 (29 January – 4 February)

VIII Corps began a new phase of operations by crossing the River Our on the 29th, three infantry divisions up with 87th left, 4th centre and 90th right, capturing Hemmers, Elcherath, Lommersweiler and Setz. In the III Corps area, 17th Ab Div cleared Roder, while 6th Armd Div patrolled up and down the River Our. In XII Corps, Task Force Oboe was created from armoured infantry elements of 4th Armd Div and relieved 319th Inf Regt of 80th Inf Div. III and VIII Corps continued aggressively to push the enemy back, battling in the Siegfried Line emplacements by the end of January. Forces were generally on the line of the Moselle, Our and Clerf Rivers by the 31st. XII Corps experienced no heavy fighting this week, 5th, 76th and 80th Inf Divs all maintaining their positions and patrolling aggressively. After flying more than 500 sorties on the 29th, XIX TAC aircraft were shut in by bad weather for the rest of the week.

February would see Third Army having to come to grips with two major problems as well as the enemy, these being terrain and weather.[13] Combat engineers really came into their own, bridging swollen, swiftly flowing rivers, all units had to deal with frost-damaged roads that prohibited movement by heavy vehicles, and a sudden thaw on 2 February caused 50 per cent of reserve ammunition stacks to topple and have to be re-stacked. The 8th Armd and 95th Inf Divs were transferred to Ninth Army, the latter under the strictest secrecy. On 3 February, GSP and his four corps commanders decided that XII Corps would initiate a night attack on Bitburg on 6/7 February, while VIII Corps continued their drive towards Prüm. In III and XX Corps' areas aggressive patrolling continued. It appeared that the enemy were withdrawing panzer units to use on their Eastern front, while maintaining a defensive posture in the west, which involved using many low-grade troops, thousands of whom eventually surrendered or deserted.

Week 28 (5–11 February)

At 0100 hrs on 6 February, XII Corps began its attack, 5th Inf Div crossing the River Sauer and securing a 1,000-yard perimeter. It was followed two hours later by 80th Inf Div who also crossed the river, both divisions enlarging their bridgeheads during the week, so that they threatened Echternach to the east. In III Corps, a limited attack by part of 17th Ab Div supported by 6th Armd Div crossed the Our on the 6th. They managed to enlarge their bridgehead, but on 10 February, 17th Ab Div were relieved by 6th Armd Div, as III Corps passed to First Army and VIII Corps took over their zone. In VIII Corps, 11th Armd Div relieved 90th Inf Div who moved to a new zone and captured Habscheid. The 4th Inf Div took Brandscheid and Schlausenbach, while 87th Inf Div launched an attack on the Siegfried Line, using TDs firing direct to knock out several pillboxes and MG nests. At this time, cavalry reconnaissance squadrons started to receive the new M24 Chaffee light tanks (see Chapter 8), which greatly improved their capabilities. The 4th and 6th Armd Divs had received flame-throwers to mount in medium tanks, for use against pillboxes, etc. The VIII Corps continued its drive through the Siegfried Line fortifications towards Prüm, units of 4th Inf Div entering the western section of the town on the 11th, while 90th Inf Div took Watzerath and 11th Armd Div captured Harspelt and Sevenig. In XX Corps, both 94th and 26th Inf Divs were engaged in heavy fighting, the latter using artificial moonlight (from searchlights) for the first time, to support a 10 February night attack on Saarlautern, Roden and Fraulautern.

All this time, Third Army engineers and infantry battled against a long succession of rain-swollen, heavily defended streams which had become 100–200ft-wide raging torrents. The churning water overturned assault boats and floats, drowning many occupants who were never found. Nevertheless, the advance continued. XIX TAC flew on three days only but were still able to destroy many motor vehicles, tanks, cut railway lines and bomb marshalling yards and military installations. As a consequence of a rapid thaw, the roads became very muddy and some units were isolated, requiring air supply. Movement by rail and even by packhorse was used because the roads were so difficult.

Week 29 (12–18 February)

The successful crossing of the Sauer and Prüm Rivers by XII Corps, coupled with VIII Corps' attacks in the Prüm area, had forced the enemy back and created a bulge between these two points (known as the Vianden

Bulge), which Third Army was now fighting to clear. Prüm itself was cleared on the 12th by 4th Inf Div. Under continuing difficult weather conditions, Third Army continued to enlarge its bridgeheads, clear enemy pillboxes and strong-points in the Siegfried Line area and generally press forward, despite XIX TAC being unable to fly for most of the week, the 15th being the only really clear day when they flew 190 sorties.

Week 30 (19–25 February)
The 'Vianden Bulge' was finally cleared this week, thanks to the combined efforts of VIII and XII Corps. Just to give some idea of the size of the problem they had tackled, between 29 January and 21 February, VIII Corps units destroyed 936 enemy-held pillboxes. On the 21st, when CCA of 10th Armd Div had reached a point six miles from Trier, Patton ordered XX Corps to attack and seize this key German communications centre. Although there was no hard evidence of a German collapse at this time, there was definitely a notable loss of control and a general lowering of morale among enemy troops. On the 25th, XII Corps launched a major attack to the east towards Bitburg, led by 4th Armd Div. They gained seven miles, seized bridges (intact) over both the Prüm and Nims, driving to within two miles of the northern limits of Bitburg. They were followed by 80th Inf Div who mopped-up and captured Echtershausen, Mettendorf, Hamm and Mauel.

Week 31 (26 February – 4 March)
Twelfth Army Group ordered Third Army to hold 90th Inf Div in reserve for possible use by SHAEF and not to commit it without permission. The XII Corps attack was making rapid gains; for example, on 26 February, 2nd Cav Gp was fighting in Wasserbillig, 76th Inf Div was clearing the high ground overlooking the Nims, 5th Inf Div had captured an intact bridge and cleared Stahl. The 4th Armd Div captured two villages four miles north-east of Bitburg. To the north, 80th Inf Div moved forward six miles, relieving elements of 4th Armd Div along the Prüm, and clearing Maeul. Bitburg was taken on the 27th. In XX Corps, CCA 10th Armd Div crossed the Saar at Serrig on the 26th, while CCB took Zerf and CCR followed 94th Inf Div across at Saarburg. Trier was taken on 2 March, together with 28 other towns and villages. Poor flying weather was still hampering XIX TAC although they had more success in early March, flying more than 1,000 sorties on the 1st and 2nd. Third Army took 657 square miles of territory during February, but in March they would cross the Rhine and bring the war to the heart of the Fatherland. Strength of Third Army at the beginning of March was 304,690 troops.

Week 32 (5–11 March)
On the 5th, Third Army took its 200,000th PoW. According to G-2 reports, POW interrogations showed that the enemy was now having

to make up *ad hoc* combat commands, out of stragglers, convalescents and supply troops, to bolster the survivors of the Ardennes. Nevertheless, they were still unlikely to give up territory easily. It was estimated that the Germans had only about 45,000 combat effective troops and some 50 tanks facing Third Army – an ideal time, therefore, to strike at the heart of the Fatherland. The enemy had fallen back to the Kyll River in XII Corps' sector, but were fighting a strong delaying action against VIII Corps. Elements of eleven enemy divisions were caught between First and Third Armies' pincers and thoroughly mauled, only a fraction of their numbers escaping. By 9 March, the Rhine had been reached and the entire Eifel area cleared, except for a small area around Koblenz and in the Wittlich depression west of Cochem, where remnants of nine divisions were pocketed. In fact, on 9 March infantry units, following up the armour of both VIII and XX Corps, took over 266 square miles of territory that day alone, the largest territorial gain since the heady days of August–September 1944. The pace of the advance continued to increase as did the number of PoWs taken (more than 110,000 between 3 and 10 March), which began to create serious transportation problems. Operating under adverse weather conditions, XIX TAC co-operated fully with the advancing ground troops, attacking a variety of military targets where visibility allowed. On 10 March 11th Armd Div were clearing all enemy from the west bank of the Rhine within VIII Corps' zone, while only Koblenz remained uncaptured. In XII Corps' zone, 4th Armd Div cleared along the west bank of the Rhine and the northern bank of the Moselle, while XX Corps prepared for a major assault.

Week 33 (12–18 March)

Late on the 12th, XX Corps launched its attack with 26th, 80th and 94th Inf Divs, all gaining up to four miles by the end of the day. On 13 March, 12th Army Group issued orders covering all Armies, which told Third Army to defend the line of the Rhine in its zone and to attack in conjunction with Seventh Army in order to protect Seventh Army's flank and rear. This was obviously not to Patton's liking! Nevertheless Third Army continued its operations and by the 15th the enemy was caught in a triangle bounded by the Rhine, Moselle and Saar Rivers (cf: the Falaise pocket) and GSP was determined they would not escape. By fluid armoured operations, ably supported by a massive number of sorties from XIX TAC (643 on 15 March alone!), the enemy was harried remorselessly, more than 22,000 being taken prisoner between 11 and 17 March. By the 15th, Third Army troops were threatening the four major enemy communication centres on the Rhine within their area, namely, Koblenz, Bingen, Mainz and Worms. Koblenz and Bingen were both captured on the 18th. To the south of the Army area, the Seventh Army was breaking through the Siegfried Line.

Week 34 (19–25 March)

In VIII Corps' area, 4th Armd and 90th Inf Divs changed their direction of attack towards the south-east, to bring their forces to the Rhine in the Mainz–Worms area. In XX Corps, 10th Armd Div reached the outskirts of Kaiserslautern and cut off the city of Saarbrucken, while on 20 March XII Corps was clearing all along the Rhine south to Ludwigshafen. Worms and Kaiserslautern both fell on the 20th, Mainz and Landau on the 22nd.

Crossing the Rhine. On the night of 22/23 March, 1st and 3rd Bns of 11th Inf Regt, 5th Inf Div of XII Corps, used assault rafts to cross the Rhine at Nierstein and Oppenheim. By the end of the 23rd they had secured a bridgehead six miles deep and seven miles wide.[14] Other XII Corps units swiftly followed, enlarging the bridgehead and giving the enemy little chance to produce anything more than scattered, ineffectual resistance. They were unable to hold the Mainz–Frankfurt–Darmstadt triangle or prevent XII Corps from advancing eastwards, with the result that by the 25th crossings over the Main at Hanau and Aschaffenburg had been made. The second batch of Third Army crossings over the Rhine also came on the 25th, this time in the VIII Corps area, just south of Koblenz in the Rhine gorge, where there were both steep cliffs and a fast current to contend with as well as the enemy. At Rhens, the attempt by 347th Inf Regt failed initially, but further down at Boppard the 345th had more success. In all there were eventually four crossings in that area (Boppard, Rhens, St Goar and Oberwesel) on 25/26 March. There would be no stopping 'Georgie's Boys' now, especially after GSP, on the 14th, having walked across the pontoon bridge, built by his engineers at the Nierstein crossing, stopped in the middle, pissed into the river, then continued across and took up two handfuls of German soil, with the words 'Thus William the Conqueror'!

Week 35 (26 March – 1 April)

In an attempt to hold the River Main, the enemy again produced 'too little too late' and was unable to prevent another Third Army breakthrough. By 28 March, 4th Armd Div spearheads had driven 30 miles northwards, to link up with 9th Armd Div (First Army) near Giessen and trap thousands of enemy in the Wiesbaden-Bingen area. Thoroughly disorganised, the enemy could do little to halt Patton's armoured columns which, by the end of March, were some hundred miles to the east and threatening Kassel. Enemy resistance began to stiffen and they appeared to be establishing a new defensive line south-east of Kassel, between Fulda and the Werra-Weser river lines. Lucky Forward moved to Idar-Oberstein on 27 March, the first time it had been located on German soil. As at 29 March Third Army comprised the following:

VIII Corps	XII Corps	XX Corps
76th Inf Div	26th Inf Div	5th Inf Div
87th Inf Div	71st Inf Div	65th Inf Div
89th Inf Div	90th Inf Div	80th Inf Div
4th Armd Div	6th Armd Div	11th Armd Div

XIX TAC, who had been able to fly on most days (except on 29th and 30th) had destroyed a staggering number of enemy vehicles: 527 MT vehicles and 36 AFVs on the 25th, 361 MT vehicles on the 26th, 1,027 MT vehicles and 25 AFVs on the 27th, 649 MT vehicles and 21 AFVs on 28th, 685 MT vehicles and 47 AFVs on the 31st, not to mention numerous locomotives and rolling stock.

Week 36 (2–8 April)

At the beginning of the month 13th Armd and 70th Inf Divs were assigned to the Army. G-2 estimated that the German strength was now down to about the equivalent of two effective divisions, but that they still held good defensive ground south-east of Kassel, between the Rivers Fulda and Werra, and east of the Werra from Munden to Eisenach. On 2 April, 4th Armd Div established a bridgehead across the Werra, then advanced to Stregda and Goldbach, while 11th Armd Div did likewise at Ritschenhausen, then advanced fifteen miles. In XX Corps' zone, 80th Inf Div was clearing Kassel (captured on 4 April), while 6th Armd Div crossed the Wehre and advanced 20 miles, closely followed by 65th Inf Div. The 5th Inf Div was policing Frankfurt. Adjustment of Corps boundaries on the 3rd gave VIII Corps the central portion of Third Army's area, with XX Corps north and XII Corps south. Lucky Forward moved to Frankfurt-on-Main on 3 April. Third Army's continued rapid advance prevented the enemy from manning his proposed defences along the Eder, Fulda and Werra. Any possibility of a strong defence was nullified by the swift drive of the armoured columns down both sides of the Werra to Eisenach, across the Fulda and 20 miles beyond. Only in the north, near Kassel, did the enemy make any proper stand, still offering determined resistance to the east of the city after Kassel had fallen on the 4th. By that date, the armour had reached the general line Mulhausen–Gotha–Suhl, then paused while the infantry divisions mopped-up in the rear and First and Seventh Armies caught up and were able to protect the flanks. XIX TAC continued to cause havoc, knocking out hundreds of enemy vehicles and railway equipment and, on 7 April, 95 enemy aircraft. On 8 April, Third Army received 90 Pershing heavy tanks (see Chapter 8), 40 being issued to 11th Armd Div.

Week 37 (9–15 April)

On 10 April, Third Army resumed the advance, pushing the enemy towards the River Mulde. Having reached Coburg, the armour broke loose on the 11th, by-passing Erfurt, Weimar, Jena and Gera, crossing the Mulde and continuing for some 80 miles. On the fifth day, they halted on the outskirts of Chemnitz. The by-passed towns fell to the follow-up infantry, Weimar on the 11th, Erfurt on the 12th and Jena on the 13th. On 11 April, Lucky Forward moved to Hersfeld and the following day, Patton was visited by Generals Eisenhower and Bradley. He was given a verbal order to stop Third Army on the line from the Mulde River–Zwich–Mulde River–Plauen–Hoff–Bayreuth. On the 14th, GSP officially opened the Roosevelt Memorial Railway Bridge over the Rhine, near Mainz, next to the demolished Mainz–Gustavsburg bridge. Offered a pair of scissors to cut the tape he exclaimed: 'What do you take me for, a tailor? Goddamit! Give me a bayonet!' Administrative plans were being developed to advance Third Army's transfer point to the Mainz area, this being vital in view of the rate of advance, which was consuming vast quantities of fuel (during the period 8–14 April Third Army used nearly 4½ million gallons of petrol, an average of 618,727 gallons a day!). In the first fortnight of April XIX TAC had destroyed 117 enemy aircraft and damaged 49, for the loss of 23 aircraft. Military government estimated that at least 10 per cent of the people in the forward areas were displaced persons (DPs), the percentage being greatest in factory areas. More than 112,000 DPs had been placed in camps in Third Army's zone. On the 15 April, 120th Evacuation Hospital moved to Ettersburg to provide medical service for the inmates of Buchenwald, where there were 120,000 people in the camp, many of them needing immediate medical care.

Week 38 (16–22 April)

On the 17th, Third Army was ordered to change its path of advance to the south-east into Bavaria, to attack the German–Austrian Redoubt area, while maintaining patrols along the Czechoslovak border. The northern part of the Army area together with VIII Corps and its assigned units (4th and 6th Armd, 65th and 76th Inf Divs) passed to First Army, while III Corps came to Third Army and certain areas previously occupied by Seventh Army were taken over. At the same time as HQ III Corps was assigned to the Army, six more divisions came under command: 14th, 16th and 20th Armd Divs; 86th, 97th and 99th Inf Divs, although 20th Armd and 97th Inf Divs only remained for a few days. From 17 to 22 April, the Army re-deployed its units and prepared for the attack into the Austrian Redoubt area. III Corps began to occupy a new area on the southern flank with 86th and 99th Inf Divs. VIII Corps remained in its positions on the restraining line waiting for 'the off'. In XII Corps' advance to the south-east, 90th was in the north, 26th in the centre and 11th Armd Div in the south; all made gains of 12 to 15 miles on the 19th and 6th Armd Div captured Grafenwohr. XX Corps continued to attack with 71st Inf Div which advanced eight miles due south of Bayreuth and captured Pegnitz. It had become very evident that the enemy defences were merely a thin crust and were being swiftly penetrated. Local German civilian reaction seemed to be relief that the war was almost over, blaming everything (including the concentration camp horrors of which they denied all knowledge) on the Nazi leadership.

As Third Army got nearer to the Eastern front, specific recognition data about Russian vehicles and equipment was issued. The speed of advance gained momentum every day, while XIX TAC continued to fly whenever the weather allowed and to destroy masses of enemy vehicles of all types. On the 22nd, Lucky Forward moved 150 miles from Hersfeld to Erlangen.

Week 39 (23–29 April)

III Corps had now assumed XV Corps' former zone and was advancing with 86th and 99th Inf Divs abreast, preceded by 14th Armd Div and with 14th Cav Gp screening the left (east) flank. Losses on the 23rd were the smallest on any day in the history of Third Army operations up to that date (3 killed, 37 wounded, 5 missing). In XII Corps, 11th Armd Div preceded 26th, 90th and 97th Inf Divs and 2nd Cav Gp. All the units behind the armour were moving south in a long, continuous column and screening along the Czech border. Preceded by 3rd Cav Gp, 65th and 71st Inf Divs of XX Corps were in the centre, with 80th Inf Div (SHAEF reserve) and 13th Armd Div in the rear. On the 24th, in III Corps' area, 86th Inf Div crossed the Altmühl in three places, advanced 24 miles and cleared a number of small towns. The 14th Armd Div did likewise, keeping parallel with the two infantry divisions, while 14th Cav Gp reached the Danube by the end of the day. XII Corps was doing equally well, spearheaded by 11th Armd Div which advanced 28 miles, cleared Regen and reached Swiessel. The 26th Inf Div crossed the Regen and mopped-up behind the armour. The Corps' southern flank was protected by 90th and 97th Inf Divs, assisted by 2nd Cav Gp. In XX Corps' area, 65th Inf Div advanced twelve miles through Killersreid and Rechenberg, reaching the Danube to the west and south-west of Regensburg.

The advance continued throughout the week. Then a 12th Army Group directive of the 28th ordered Third Army to continue its drive to join the Russians in the Danube valley and to seize Salzburg, First Army having taken over responsibility for the Czech border on the 27th. Ingolstadt was taken on the 26th, and an enemy field order captured that day disclosed that the German First Army had intended to attack Third Army's exposed left flank with 11th Panzer Division on the 23rd. But the attack had failed to materialise and later the panzers were to surrender *en masse*. Advancing from their bridgeheads over the Danube, III and XX Corps swept south to the Isar which was reached on the 29th.

Concurrently, armoured elements of XII Corps had also crossed the Austrian border and were fifteen miles inside Austria, with enemy resistance apparently collapsing. XIX TAC had, as usual, contributed to all these successes, smashing ground installations and battering the remnants of the Luftwaffe – in April the Air Command destroyed or damaged 237 enemy aircraft in the air, plus a staggering 1,376 on the ground, for the loss of 46 of their own aircraft. Their 'bag' for the month included 9,165 MT vehicles, 545 AFVs, 1,505 locomotives, 9,238 items of rolling stock and 1,369 factory buildings.

Week 40 (30 April – 6 May)

Poor roads, roadblocks and rough terrain were now the only real defence offered against Third Army's advance. It improved its bridgeheads over the Isar and at the same time armoured spearheads drove to the Austrian border in the vicinity of Braunau on the Inn and ten miles down the Danube towards Linz. On 2 May Lucky Forward moved to Regensburg. On 4 May, 11th Panzer Division surrendered unconditionally and was moved to a designated assembly area. This was the first surrender of an entire division and coincided with V Corps' (attached from First Army) attack to the north-east in Czechoslovakia, which captured Pilsen, then on the 5th, Linz and Steyr, then swept on down the Danube twenty miles past Linz. The enemy continued to surrender in vast numbers, failing to obey Adolf Hitler's last orders to stand fast as they desperately tried to move westwards, away from the Russians, Third Army taking more than 90,000 prisoners in the first week of May. On the 5th, when Third Army units entered the city of Plze in Czechoslovakia, they found it to be controlled by Czech partisans, the German garrison having been confined to their barracks. That same day the entire German Army Group 'G' surrendered, and indeed it was clear that a total collapse of all central control of German forces was about to take place.

Week 41 (7–8 May)

A TWX received from General Eisenhower officially ended the War in Europe:

'1. A representative of the German High Command signed the unconditional surrender of all German land, sea and air forces in Europe to the Allied Expeditionary Force and simultaneously to the Soviet High Command at 0141 hours, Central European Time, 7 May, under which all forces will cease active operations at 0001 B hours, 9 May.

2. Effective immediately, all offensive operations by Allied Expeditionary Forces will cease and troops will remain in present positions. Moves involved in occupational duties will continue. Due to difficulties of communication there may be some delay in similar orders reaching troops, so full defensive precautions will be taken.

3. All informed down to and including divisions, tactical air command and groups, base sections and equivalent. No, repeat no, release will be made to the press pending an announcement by the heads of the three governments.'

Only a few, small fire-fights were encountered by Third Army units, the Germans continuing to surrender in large numbers. Contact was made with Soviet troops near Amstettin by Third Army patrols. The commander of German Army Group South surrendered all his troops to CG XX Corps. The 33rd Field Artillery Brigade was made responsible for collecting, supplying, administering and evacuating all Allied POWs and civilian internees within Third Army's area; also for collecting, guarding and protecting all DPs in the Army area, moving them into temporary camps where necessary, which would be guarded to ensure a 'stay put' policy.

General Patton held his last operational briefing for officers of the headquarters and talked with the assembled section chiefs. Some days previously he had recorded a speech to be broadcast on American radio stations during the coming VE Day celebrations, which read:

'Now that victory in Europe has been achieved, let us review the Third Army's part in this epic struggle.

'From Avranches to Brest, thence across France, Germany, and into Austria, the Third Army and its equally victorious comrades of the 19th Tactical Air Command have fought their way.

'The Seine, the Moselle, the Saar, Rhine and the Danube, not to mention twenty other lesser rivers have been successfully stormed.

'The Siegfried Line has been penetrated at will. Metz, Trier, Koblenz and Frankfurt and countless other cities and towns have been cleared of the enemy. More than 80,000 square miles of country have been liberated or conquered.

'You have demonstrated your irresistible powers in France, Belgium, Luxembourg, Germany, Czechoslovakia and Austria. You have captured more than three-quarters of a million Nazi soldiers and have killed and wounded at least half a million others.

'But, in thinking of the heritage of glory you have achieved, do not be unmindful of the price you have paid. Throughout your victorious advances, your line of march is marked with the graves of your heroic dead; while the hospitals are crowded with your wounded.

'Nor should we forget the efforts of those at home who have invariably provided us with the sinews of war, the means to Victory. To those at home we promise that, with their unremitting assistance, we shall continue so that with the help of Almighty God, and through the inspired leadership of our President and the High Command, we shall conquer not only Germany, but also Japan; until the last danger to life, liberty and the pursuit of happiness shall perish from the earth.'

Notes to Chapter 10

1. The subterfuge about the main landing taking place in the Pas de Calais was still being maintained. Sadly, Lieutenant General Lesley J. McNair, CG Army Ground Forces, who had come to the ETO to perpetuate this myth, was killed by American bombs dropped in error on their own troops at the start of Operation 'Cobra'.
2. PLUTO = Pipeline Under the Ocean, the revolutionary means of getting petrol across to Normandy, which had been laid between England and France, was extended behind the advancing armies as they progressed eastwards.
3. This comprised an infantry regiment, a tank company and an engineer company.
4. These wire-heads used the facilities of the *'Postes Téléphones et Télégraphes'*, the commercial telephone system in Nancy which was still in fairly good condition. They were also used as dispatch points for maintenance teams.
5. These were at Nancy, Chambley, Belleville, Dieulouard, Baroncourt, Trieux and Audun-le-Roman.
6. DUKW. This was the Truck Amphibious 2½-ton 6x6 DUKW, which used its normal drive on land, but in the water had a propeller and a rudder. More than 21,000 were built during the war.
7. Patton was to record that he considered this to be one of the major errors of the entire campaign. 'If Bradley had not welshed on his agreement,' he wrote in his diary, 'we would have taken Saarbrücken within 48hrs after we got Königsmacker. Once we had [Königsmacker], they couldn't have stopped us from taking Trier, and if we'd had Trier it would have been impossible for the Germans to have launched their Ardennes Offensive.... I'm firmly convinced that Bradley's refusal to allow me to use the 83rd, as he had promised, was one of the underlying causes of the Battle of the Bulge.' (Quoted in *Patton's Third Army* by Charles M. Province.)
8. G-2 Section report on significant enemy order of battle facts for the period 3-10 December 1944, contains the following: 'Overall the initiative rests with the Allies, but the massive Armored force the enemy has built up in reserve gives him the definite capability of launching a spoiling (diversionary) offensive to disrupt the Allies' drive.'
9. Ibid. GSP discovered that German PoWs were being fed almost twice as much food than was currently being issued to GIs in their daily rations. He ordered the Camp CO personally to weigh each portion and not to give any more than prescribed under the Geneva Convention.
10. It would be at Eisenhower's conference at Verdun, on 19 December, that Patton would calmly announce that he could attack the southern flank of the enemy 'bulge' with three divisions in just three days' time. No one really believed him, but it was thanks to this previous planning that he was able to speak with such confidence – and achieve it!
11. Not knowing how well GSP had prepared, Eisenhower had asked him whether he could hold von Rundstedt in the south. 'Hold von Rundstedt? I'll take von Rundstedt and shove him up Montgomery's ass!' Patton replied. (Quoted in *The Biography of General George S. Patton* by Ian V. Hogg).
12. Not only did they have to deal with landslides, weak bridges, enemy air attacks, breakdowns and accidents, but also, initially anyway, a serious

shortage of maps (during the month Third Army and its Corps issued 57 tons of maps!).

13. One somewhat bizarre, but no doubt useful feature, was the notification that Third Army would be receiving a number of dog sled teams by air from Labrador!
14. Later that morning Lucky's liaison officer at 12th Army Group HQ could not conceal his smile as he announced that 'Without benefit of aerial bombardment, ground smoke, artillery preparation or airborne assistance (a direct dig at Montgomery) the Third Army at 2200 hours Thursday evening 22 March crossed the Rhine River.' Patton timed his announcement to the world carefully. Just hours before Field Marshal Montgomery's crossing began, he phoned Bradley again: 'Brad,' he shouted, 'for God's sake tell the world we are across.... I want the world to know Third Army made it before Monty starts to cross!' (Quoted in *After the Battle*, Vol. 16, 1977, ed. Winston G. Ramsey.)

11
Operational Summary

From the Channel to the Alps

'In nine months and eight days of campaigning, Third US Army compiled a record of offensive operations that could only be measured in superlatives, for not only did the Army's achievements astonish the world but its deeds in terms of figures challenged the imagination. The Army's operations in France, Belgium, Luxembourg, Germany, Czechoslovakia and Austria gave a new and terrible meaning to fluid warfare, for the Army had only one general order – seek out the enemy, trap and destroy him. To this end, the Army mastered the swift exploitation of tactical opportunity to a degree that struck fear into the hearts of the enemy, who found it impossible to "G-2" Third US Army except to predict the worst. The enemy invariably realised his worst fears – his line was breached, his forces were trapped or all but enveloped and he was forced to flee to save what he could.' So reads the opening paragraph of the Summary contained in *Third Army's After Action Report*, which goes on to catalogue some of their remarkable achievements.

Reduced to cold, hard figures, the results are undoubtedly astounding. The extent of territory liberated or gained in terms of square mileage was enormous: 81,522 square miles in France, 1,010 in Luxembourg, 156 in Belgium, 29,940 in Germany, 3,485 in Czechoslovakia and 2,103 in Austria. During the greater part of the fighting, the Army maintained an average length of front of 75–100 miles as the crow flies, but at times it was much longer; on 20 April, for example, it measured 200 miles. An estimated 12,000 cities, towns and villages were liberated or captured, 27 of which contained more than 50,000 people.

In simple terms, Third Army went farther and faster than any Army had ever done in the history of warfare, thanks to their unique driving force namely, General George Smith Patton Jr, so let us examine some of the statistics which make up their amazing record.

Decorations

A total of 34,480 men of Third Army won decorations. These included nineteen Medals of Honor, 291 Distinguished Service Crosses, 44 Distinguished Service Medals, 4,990 Silver Stars, 1,159 Legion of Merit, 247 Soldier's Medals, 29,090 Bronze Stars. In addition, 1,817 were awarded battlefield promotions and 848 combat appointments.

Records of the Supporting Arms and Services

AAA. The Anti-aircraft Artillery claimed 1,084 enemy aircraft shot down and 564 probably destroyed, out of a total of 6,192 enemy aircraft that flew into Third Army air space – in other words, they destroyed some 26.6 per cent of all enemy aircraft entering their air space.

Artillery. When Third Army became operational they had 636 field pieces of 105mm calibre or larger, but by the time the war ended they had 1,464. With these guns they fired nearly six million rounds – 158,207 tons of ammunition. Their artillery observation aircraft flew 87,002 missions (totalling 93,933 flying hours).

Tank Destroyers. TDs knocked out 648 enemy tanks and 211 self-propelled guns. In addition, while operating as assault guns in support of infantry and armour, the TDs destroyed 349 anti-tank guns, 175 artillery pieces, 519 machine-guns and 1,556 vehicles. In the advances through the Maginot and Siegfried Lines, the TDs wiped out 801 pillboxes and bunkers.

Engineers. Third Army engineers assisted in 32 major river crossings. The Moselle was crossed five times in five different places; the Seille, Our and Saar were each crossed twice; other major crossings included the Altmühl, Blies, Danube, Isar, Inn, Kyll, Lahn, Main, Marne, Mayenne, Meurthe, Nahe, Nied, Prüm, Rhine, Sarthe, Sauer and the Yonne. Add to this all the smaller rivers, streams and canals and a staggering figure of 2,498 bridges emerges, to give a total of 255,250 feet – nearly 8.5 miles! They included 705 assault bridges and 1,793 Bailey bridges. In addition, they averaged 2,240 miles of road maintenance during operations. Third Army engineers reconstructed 2,092 miles of railway track from St-Germain in France to the National Redoubt Area. Some 496 rail-heads were surveyed and two-thirds of them put back into use by the supply services. Supplies received were 774,541 long tons.

Signals. In order to provide good, continuous communications, Third Army Signal Corps personnel laid 3,747 miles of open wire, recovering nearly 75 per cent (3,115 miles) for further use. They also rehabilitated 3,965 circuit miles of French and German open telephone wire and 36,338 miles of underground cable. Third Army Message Centre handled a total of 7,220,261 code groups, while both Forward and Rear Echelons switchboard operators handled an estimated average of 13,986 telephone calls daily.

CWS. The nine Chemical Warfare Companies (including four Chemical Smoke Generator Coys) assigned to Third Army fired 349,997 rounds of 4.2in chemical mortar shells, including 160,002 rounds of white phosphorus and 189,095 rounds of high-explosive. Among the CWS supplies were 32,454 gallons of flame-thrower fuel and 335,944 grenades of all types.

QMC. All supplies brought into the Third Army area, by every means of transportation, totalled a staggering 1,234,529 long tons, which included 741,201 long tons by rail and truck, and 33,340 by air. Within Third Army's boundaries, 2,186,792 tons of supplies were transported a total distance of 141,081,336 miles. Some 264,606 trucks were in convoys issued with 2,242 highway clearances. A total of 3,655,322 vehicles, carrying supplies for the troops, were clocked through 109 traffic regulating points.

Ordnance. 533,825 tons of all types of ammunition were received during the 281 days of combat, 482,345 tons of which were issued to divisions, the remainder going to Third Army headquarters units. The trucks of Third Army travelled 14,101,977 miles, hauling 1,549,993 long tons of ammunition.

Large items of equipment issued to Third Army units included

Combat vehicles:	7,581
Artillery pieces:	4,482
General-purpose vehicles:	26,905
Small arms:	193,910
Spare parts:	47,611

Large items of equipment repaired by Third Army Ordnance included

Combat vehicles:	21,761
Artillery pieces:	11,613
General-purpose vehicles:	99,114
Small arms:	125,083
Instruments:	32,740

Medical. Third Army ambulances carried 269,187 patients from divisional casualty clearing stations, etc., to Third Army hospitals. A total of 168,801 were evacuated from the Army's area: 28,826 by air, 91,005 by road, 43,815 by rail and 1,164 by ship. The mortality rate in Third Army hospitals was 2.78 per cent, the percentage of deaths from all causes was 1.4 per cent, and 43.5 per cent (114,024) men were returned to duty without having been evacuated from the Army area.

Civil Affairs. The Third Army provided administration in Belgium, Czechoslovakia, France and Luxembourg. They also provided military government administration in Germany and Austria, to control some 30 million people. The military government courts tried 1,015 cases, involving 1,323 people, of whom 129 were found innocent, the remainder guilty. 116,405 Reichsmarks were collected in total fines and 17,817 days of imprisonment were imposed. The military government took charge of five concentration camps formerly operated by the Nazis, which contained 47,645 political prisoners. A total of 875,000 DPs were cared for and had been repatriated by 9 May 1945.

Judge Advocate. There were 325 general courts-martial, 1,205 special and 6,474 summary, tried and reviewed.

Chaplains. On average there were 320 chaplains, representing 25 different denominations. Seven chaplains were killed in action, five were missing in action, three captured, three more captured and immediately released and 45 wounded in action.

Special Services. Attendance at entertainment was as follows: 11,230,000 at films, 650,000 at USO shows and 625,000 at soldiers' talent shows.

News correspondents. A total of 30,326 stories, more than seven million words, were written by news correspondents about Third Army soldiers and 7,129 photographs submitted to Third Army censors.

Psywar. Both aircraft and artillery bombarded the Germans with more than 31½ million psychological warfare leaflets. A total of 722 combat and military government loudspeaker missions were completed in an attempt to get enemy soldiers to surrender.

Strength of Third Army. Details of all six Corps and forty-two Divisions which served under Third Army are given in Annex 'A' to this chapter. They were not all under command throughout the entire 281 days of campaigning, so the Army's strength fluctuated, being at its greatest during the final campaign which ended on 8 May 45 when 437,860 personnel were assigned. Strength at other times was: 1 August 1944 – 92,187; 31 August – 220,169; 30 September – 138,639; 31 October – 252,514; 30 November – 247,150; 31 December – 347,660; 31 January 1945 – 353,981; 28 February – 304,542; 31 March – 312,205; 30 April – 346,839. Reinforcements received during the period numbered 258,924.

Promotions. There were 6,474 normal promotions, 1,817 battlefield promotions and 848 combat appointments, during the operational period.

Pay. Military personnel were paid a total of $240,539,569 from 1 August 1944 to 30 April 1945, 43.83 per cent going to family or individual allotments, 7.13 per cent to government insurance, 6.56 per cent to war bonds, 1.9 per cent to soldiers' deposits, 23.99 per cent to personal transfers, 5.49 per cent to other collections and 11.1 per cent was retained.

Prisoners of War. Third Army captured 1,280,688 PoW from 1 August 1944 to 13 May 1945, including 485,405 who were processed in Corps and Division cages from 9 to 13 May 1945 inclusive. The enemy lost 47,500 killed and 115,700 wounded by Third Army, for a total of 1,443,888.

Campaign	*PoW captured*	*Daily average*
The Campaign in France, Avranches–Brest to the Moselle(1 Aug to 24 Sep 1944)	94,199	1,713
Forcing the line of the Moselle (24 Sep to 7 Nov 1944)	8,481	193
The capture of Metz and the Saar Campaign (8 Nov to 18 Dec 1944)	36,489	890
The Bastogne–St-Vith Campaign (19 Dec 1944 to 28 Jan 1945)	23,218	566
The Eifel to the Rhine and the capture of Trier (29 Jan to 12 Mar 1945)	58,781	1,367
The capture of Koblenz and the Palatinate campaign (13–21 Mar 1945)	81,692	8,169
Forcing the Rhine – Frankfurt and across the Mulde (22 Mar to 21 April 1945)	240,661	8,022
Crossing the Danube, entering Czechoslovakia and Austria (22 April to 8 May 1945)	221,962	13,057
TOTAL	765,483	2,724
Plus total for period 9–13 May 1945	515,205	
GRAND TOTAL	1,280,688	

Spies and Saboteurs. G-2 intelligence troops apprehended 42 enemy agents/saboteurs, having investigated 337 reports and interrogated 2,500 civilians.

Casualties. Third Army suffered 160,692 casualties, including 27,104 killed, 86,267 wounded, 18,957 injured, 28,237 missing in action, of whom many later were reported captured and 127 captured by the enemy. The Army's casualties included 8,372 officers and 152,324 enlisted men (approximately one officer to eighteen enlisted men). Of the total casualties, 33,004 were returned to duty.

XIX TAC. Third Army's air support arm flew 7,326 missions and 74,447 sorties in the 281-day campaign. They dropped 17,486 tons of bombs, 3,205 Napalm tanks and launched 4,599 rockets. They destroyed 1,640 enemy aircraft and lost 582 of their own aircraft from all causes. August 1944, was the busiest month when 12,229 sorties were flown, but more bombs (2,134 tons) were dropped in December 1944. Targets destroyed or damaged included:

Tanks and armoured cars	3,833
Motor vehicles	38,541
Locomotives	4,337
Railway lines cut	2,585
Marshalling yards	974
Towns and villages	816
Factories	3,664
Supply dumps	220

Military installations	1,730
Gun installations	2,809
Highway and road bridges	285
Miscellaneous naval targets	654
Miscellaneous targets	3,010

XIX TAC also completed 1,767 tactical reconnaissance missions and 77 photographic reconnaissance missions on behalf of Third Army intelligence units, the latter resulting in the distribution of more than 3 million aerial photographs.

Annex 'A' to Chapter 11
The six corps and the divisions that served with US Third Army in combat (Operational period 1 Aug 1944 – 8 May 1945).

Corps	*Period under command*	*No of days*
XII	1 Aug 1944 to 8 May 1945	281
XX	1 Aug 1944 to 8 May 1945	281
VIII	1 Aug to 5 Sept 1944	
	21 Dec 1944 to 22 April 1945	160
III	10 Oct 1944 to 11 Feb 1945	
	18 April 1945 to 8 May 1945	145
XV	1–24 Aug 1944	
	26 Aug 1944 to 29 Sep 1944	61
V	6–8 May 1945	3

A total of 42 divisions served under Third Army control (26 inf, 14 armd, 2 ab) during their operations in ETO. Those that served longest were:

Divisions	*Period under command*	*No of days*
4th Armd	1 Aug 1944 to 22 April 1945	
	24 April 1945 to 8 May 1945	280
5th Inf	4 Aug 1944 to 8 May 1945	276
80th Inf	1–16 Aug 1944	
	24 Aug 1944 to 8 May 1945	274
90th Inf	1–16 Aug 1944	
	26 Aug 1944 to 8 May 1945	272
6th Armd	1 Aug 1944 to 4 Sep 1944	
	17 Sep 1944 to 22 Apr 1945	252

DIVISIONS UNDER COMMAND

Infantry: 1st Inf, 2nd Inf, 4th Inf, 5th Inf, 8th Inf, 26th Inf, 28th Inf, 29th Inf, 30th Inf, 35th Inf, 42nd Inf, 65th Inf, 69th Inf, 70th Inf, 71st Inf, 76th Inf, 79th Inf, 80th Inf, 83rd Inf, 86th Inf, 87th Inf, 90th Inf, 94th Inf, 95th Inf, 97th Inf, 99th Inf (total 26)

Armoured: 2nd Fr Armd, 4th Armd, 5th Armd, 6th Armd, 7th Armd, 8th Armd, 9th Armd, 10th Armd, 11th Armd, 12th Armd, 13th Armd, 14th Armd, 16th Armd, 20th Armd (total 14)

Airborne: 17th Ab, 101st Ab (total 2)

TOTAL 42 all types.

Source: Order of Battle of the US Army WWII European Theater of Operations, Divisions, prepared in the Office of the Theater Historian, European Theater, published in Paris in December 1945

Notes to Chapter 11

1. All facts and figures contained in this chapter were taken from the two volumes of *Third Army's After Action Report.*

Part IV

End of an Old Campaigner, Birth of a Legend

12
New Challenges

Section 1 The Traumas of Peace

Lucky's Last Operational Briefing

Third Army Headquarters held its last operational briefing on Wednesday, 9 May, in an improvised War Room located on the second floor of a bombed German barracks on the outskirts of Regensburg. It was a perfect spring day. Colonel Robert S. Allen comments in his book *Lucky Forward* that the War Room was a far cry from the magnificent premises they had occupied in the city of Luxembourg a few months previously, with no vaulted ceilings or panelled walls, instead: 'The cracked rain-soaked ceiling sagged in many places, the walls were scarred by bullets and shell fragments and the windows paneless.' The briefing followed its normal form and was, as usual, '... smart and thorough'. When all section heads had given their briefings, the Chief of Staff started to get up to say his piece, but GSP stopped him, sat quietly for a few moments as the room tensed, then got up, walked to the War Map, turned and faced his Staff. 'He stood there tall, straight as an arrow, in his tight-fitting tailored battle jacket with gleaming brass buttons and 16 silver stars, eight each on his shoulders and shirt collar, knife-creased trousers and high-polished battle boots. Around his waist was the hand-tooled leather belt with ornate brass buckles and an open holster with a .38-caliber automatic, its black plastic butt inlaid on each side with three white stars.'

Patton didn't start speaking immediately, but rather looked intently at, to quote Allen again, 'his matchless team of great courage, great skill, great endurance and great loyalty'. Then he spoke in his slightly squeaky voice: 'This will be our last operational briefing in Europe. I hope and pray that it will be our privilege to resume these briefings in another Theater that still is unfinished business in this war. I know you are as eager to go there as I am. But you know the situation. However, one thing I can promise you. If I go, you will go.

'I say that because the unsurpassed record of this Headquarters is your work. It has been a magnificent and historic job from start to finish. You made history in a manner that is a glory to you and to our country. There probably is no Army commander who did less work than I did. You did it all, and the imperishable record of Third Army is due largely to your unstinting and outstanding efforts. I thank you from the depths of my heart for all you have done.'

That was all he said. After a few moments of silence, he nodded to 'Hap' Gay, snapped his fingers at Willie and started to walk to the door at the end of the long room. The Staff began to rise but GSP told them to stay seated as the COS made the day's announcements, starting by saying that from the following day Lucky would stop wearing steel helmets, and wear only the fibre liner. Patton broke in from the doorway: 'And make damn sure those liners are painted and smart-looking. I don't want any sloppy headgear around here.' Everyone smiled. That was 'Georgie'!

Patton's General Order for VE-Day

As well as thanking his staff, General Patton wrote and then issued on 10 May General Orders No 98, writing in his diary that this was the order: 'terminating the war'. It was sent to all units and contained the following stirring paragraphs: 'During the 281 days of incessant and victorious combat, your penetrations have advanced farther in less time than any other army in history. You have fought your way across 24 major rivers and innumerable lesser streams. You have conquered more than 82,000 square miles of territory, including 1,500 cities and towns, and some 12,000 inhabited places. Prior to the termination of active hostilities, you had captured in battle 956,000 enemy soldiers and killed and wounded at least 500,000 others. France, Belgium, Luxembourg, Germany, Austria and Czechoslovakia bear witness of your exploits.

'All men and women of the six corps and thirty-nine[1] divisions that have at different times been members of this Army have done their duty. Each deserves credit. The enduring valor of the combat troops has been paralleled and made possible by the often unpublished activities of the supply,[2] administrative and medical services of this Army and of the Communications Zone troops supporting it. Nor should we forget our comrades of the other armies and of the Air Force, particularly the XIX Tactical Air Command, by whose side or under whose wings we have had the honor to fight.

'In proudly contemplating our achievements, let us never forget our heroic dead whose graves mark the course of our victorious advances, nor our wounded whose sacrifices added so much to our success.

'During the course of this war I have received promotion and decorations far above and beyond my individual merit. You have won them: I as your representative wear them. The one honor which is mine and mine alone is that of having commanded such an incomparable group of Americans, the record of whose fortitude, audacity and valor will endure as long as history lasts.'

Towards the end of the General Orders, GSP included a paragraph about possible combat against the Japs: 'The termination of fighting in Europe does not remove the "opportunities" for other outstanding and equally difficult achievements in the days which are to come ...' XII Corps' history, which included extracts from the Orders, comments that some people would take a 'dim view' of having additional 'opportunities' for combat until they had first had the opportunity to pay a visit to the USA! GSP personally had no such inhibitions: 'Please don't forget I still am very anxious to fight in China,' he wrote to General Thomas T. Handy, who had been the commander of an artillery unit in Patton's 2nd Armd Div but was then transferred to General Marshall's office in Washington and had risen to become a four-star general. However, for the immediate future GSP was finished with war and would have to get to grips with the 'peace' that followed.

Occupation Problems for Patton

A non-existent civil government, an economy in ruins, a population near to starvation, thousands of PoWs filling hastily established cages, equally vast numbers of DPs from all over Europe to be looked after then got home – if their homes still existed. All these and many other problems made for a totally chaotic situation with which GSP and his Third Army soldiers had to deal. Clearly this was not the type of environment which Patton enjoyed. Always the man of action rather than the politician, GSP tried to do his best in his usual forthright manner. He saw his first priority as being to get his portion of Germany sufficiently well organised in time to cope with the coming winter, so that the people would have enough food, shelter, medicines, etc., in other words, the basic necessities of life in order to prevent yet another major human disaster occurring. And all this had to be achieved against a background of de-Nazification and de-militarisation, which indirectly helped to destroy the only order that remained in the broken country. Add to this the extremely strong, vocal, Jewish lobby in the United States, plus a hostile press breathing down his neck and it was inevitable that he would lose his temper. He was accused of keeping known Nazis in public office, goaded into making some incautious and ill-timed remarks, then branded as a Nazi sympathiser. 'The more I see of people the more I regret that I survived the war,' he wrote bitterly in his diary.

The inevitable result of all of this was that he would lose command of Third Army and the government of Bavaria. This was done 'humanely' by 'kicking him upstairs to Fifteenth Army' as GSP himself put it. Although he was desperately sad about having to give up his beloved Third Army, I believe that even Patton, much-maligned and misunderstood though he was, realised that it was the only way out if he were to retain his honour and dignity. It was of course a scandalous way for America to treat 'the greatest soldier of this terrible war' – but the press would not refer to him in such glowing terms until he was safely dead and buried. 'In a sense I am glad to get out,' he wrote to Beatrice, 'as I hate the role we are forced to play and the unethical means we are required to use.... All military governments are going to be targets from now on for every sort of Jewish and Communistic attack from the press.'

All Good Things Must Come to an End

At midday on 7 October 1945, in a simple ceremony, General Patton handed over to General Lucian K. Truscott. 'All good things must come to an end,' he said in a short, but moving speech, which continued: 'The best thing that has ever come to me thus far is the honor and privilege of having commanded the Third Army. The great successes we have had together have been due primarily to the fighting heart of America, but without the co-ordinating and supply activities of the General and Special Staffs, even American valor would have been impotent. You officers and men here represent the fighting, the administrative and the supply elements of this Army. Please accept my heartfelt congratulations on your valor and devotion to duty, and my fervent gratitude for your unswerving loyalty. When I said that all good things must come to an end, I was referring to myself and not to you because you will find in General Truscott every characteristic which will inspire in you the same loyalty and devotion which you have so generously afforded me. A man of General Truscott's achievements needs no introduction. His deeds speak for themselves. I know that you will not fail him. Good-bye and God Bless you.'

'Auld Lang Syne' was played and GSP formally handed over Third Army colours to Truscott, who then made a short, emotional speech, obviously very perturbed at taking over the command, because it meant replacing Patton. The band then played the Third Army March, followed by 'For He's a Jolly Good Fellow' as they left to repair to the officers' dining-room, where there were cocktails, more speeches and luncheon. Patton left at about 2.30 p.m. to go to the station, accompanied by General Truscott, to catch the Third Army train which was to take him to Bad Nauheim, north of Frankfurt.

Fifteenth Army

Fifteenth Army[3] could not have been more different from Third Army. It was now just a 'paper organisation', controlling only those units it needed for its own housekeeping. Charles Whiting, in *Patton's Last Battle,* describes it as being made up of 'little more than clerks and cooks and historians', its main mission being to prepare historical and analytical studies on the tactics, techniques, organisation and administration of the war in Europe. As GSP wrote to Beatrice: 'Committees of officers wrote Theater or General Board reports, as they were known, on a variety of subjects. Some were excellent. But the typed and mimeographed pages inevitably grew into mountains of paper.'[4] These paper mountains had been constructed not just by American soldier historians, but also by a large number of senior German officers who were in Bad Nauheim on parole – PoWs in minimum-security custody – to assist Fifteenth Army in their mammoth task by supplying the German side. Ladislas Farago in his book, *The Last Days of Patton*, says that Fifteenth Army's historical mission and the German assistance, was one of General Eisenhower's 'most significant but least known contributions as Supreme Commander. Not only did he conceive this monumental enterprise of scholarship to write the history of the war while the facts were still fresh in the minds, but he insisted absolutely that it be devoid of partisanship, chauvinism, or considerations for any personal sensitivities, including his own.' In other words it would be an honest, truthful account 'warts and all'. Fifteenth Army staff had been hand-picked with this in mind, and a search had been undertaken at the same time for German senior officers who could supplement them. I wonder what they thought when they heard that General Patton was to take over as their Commanding General!

Undoubtedly GSP was interested in his new task, but decided, in his own inimitable way, to inject more speed into the process of producing the history than his predecessor General Gerow, who had allowed his polyglot assembly of history scribes to work at a leisurely pace and in a casual atmosphere. John Eisenhower told his father that since GSP had taken over the Fifteenth Army 'people had begun to work!' Patton set a deadline of 26 December 1945 for the completion of the Board Reports, because everyone, including himself, was now eager to get home – except perhaps for the German officers, whom Patton discounted anyway, treating them exactly as they should have been treated, namely as PoWs and not a privileged and chosen 'few'.

In addition, he seems to have spent a fair amount of time visiting old friends, units, touring Germany and going to other European countries, receiving a 'caseful of medals and honorary citizenships'[5] from France, Belgium and Denmark. He also visited Sweden, where he was re-united with the Swedish 1912 Olympic Pentathlon team in a re-run of the pistol shooting competition. GSP got the second highest score, thus beating his original Olympic result. His aide, Major Merle-Smith, described him as being 'just as delighted with himself as a small boy with a silver cup won for bow-and-arrow shooting at a summer camp'.[6]

Patton celebrated his sixtieth birthday on 11 November, writing to Beatrice that he felt fine and that everyone said that he looked the same way. However, that was his outward appearance, inside he was boiling with mounting rage at the way he had been treated. And there were plenty of people who considered that he had been given a raw deal. Some perhaps he could have done without – such as John O'Donnell of the New York *Daily Times*, who had earlier really 'stirred the pot' by resurrecting the Sicilian 'slapping incident' and trying to link it in with GSP's current treatment by sections of the US media, blaming once again the Jewish lobby (he later had to retract and apologise). General Otto Weyland (Commander, XIX TAC), on the other hand, wrote privately to Patton in late November, simply saying what must have been obvious to everyone, that since GSP had left Lucky, the Third Army had died – 'when you left it ceased to be a thing alive', while General Giraud told him that France was 'shocked to the heart at the treatment accorded the greatest soldier since Napoleon'. In the USA, many appeared worried that Patton might decide to retire from the Army so that he could speak out in his own defence and were disturbed about what he might say. GSP certainly had little respect for the senior commanders who had now arrived to replace the wartime ones: 'General Smith[7] gave a luncheon for General McNarney, the new Theater Commander,' he wrote in his diary on 3 December, 'at which were present all the youth and beauty of the ETO. With the exception of Generals Keyes, Truscott, Allen, Gay and myself, and a limited number of others, I have rarely seen assembled a greater bunch of sons-of-bitches....' He was not to know that this would be his last diary entry. He was due to leave Germany on the 12th for Southampton, there to board the battleship USS *New York* for a month's leave. He did not intend to return to Germany, telling Beatrice, in a final letter dated 5 December, that if he got a really good job he would stay in the Army, otherwise he would retire.[8]

SECTION 2. THE ACCIDENT

On 9 December 1945, General Patton was travelling in his big black Cadillac 75 Special staff car along the Frankfurt–Mannheim road. The car was being driven by 20-year-old Private First Class Horace L. Woodring, who had been with GSP for a only few months. Patton was accompanied by his Chief of Staff, Major General 'Hap' Gay, and the object of their journey was a hunting trip. Gay had arranged it on the spur of the moment the day before, in order to try to cheer up his general, who had become increasingly tense and nervous as the days passed, smoking too many cigars, pacing his office, taking long, solitary drives, in fact almost becoming a recluse instead of his usual outgoing 'life and soul of the party' self. Patton had really perked up at the idea. 'Yes, let's do it,' he said. 'You've got something there Hap. Doing a little bird-shooting would be good. You're right. I haven't been out much of late and before I leave I ought to see how good that gun is and whether my hunting eye is as sharp as it used to be. Yes, let's do it. You arrange to have the car and the guns on hand early tomorrow and we'll see how many birds we can bag.'[9] Following the staff car was a jeep, with Sergeant Joe Spruce and GSP's hunting-dog.

For part of the journey Patton had been sitting in the front, talking to Gay through the opened glass panel which separated the front seats from the rear of the car. As they approached Mannheim, he changed to the rear of the car with Gay on his left. He had also brought the dog into the car to stop him getting too cold, and Sergeant Spruce's jeep had taken the lead, travelling at a sensible 30mph, as it was a cold, frosty day. At about 1145 hrs, they were passing a QMC depot, crowded with wrecked vehicles which had been towed in. GSP made a remark about the wrecks and how awful war was, while all glanced at the derelicts. Coming in the opposite direction were two 'Jimmys', the front one being driven by T/5 Robert Thompson. He said that he signalled that he was going to turn across the road into the QMC depot, in front of the oncoming staff car. Woodring, for his part, stated that the oncoming vehicle did not signal but merely turned into the car: 'I saw him in time to hit my brakes but not in time to do anything. I was approximately not more than twenty feet away from him. The GMC barely hit with its right front fender and hit us solid with the right side of the bed.'[10]

There wasn't much damage to the GMC, but the left front of the Cadillac was crushed and the headlights smashed. The accident had occurred at relatively slow speed (the GMC was travelling at about 10mph and the car at about 30mph) and no charges were ever brought against either driver by the MPs who arrived on the spot within five minutes. All concerned had been shaken, but no one had apparently been badly injured, the worst being General Patton, who had been thrown forward by the impact and hit his head on the rail[11] above the rear of the driver's seat (the glass partition being in the lowered position at the time), then in the next instant had been jerked backwards, ending up in Gay's arms, his head hanging limply to the left. The driver remembered that the general had been conscious and that he had sworn a little.

Then 'Hap' Gay, as he recovered from the shock of the accident, realised that Patton was more seriously injured than he had thought. He had lost all the skin off his forehead, about three inches above his eyebrows and was bleeding profusely. Worse still, he could not move, but lay helpless in Gay's arms. Having asked Gay if he was hurt, and having received the answer 'Not a bit, Sir,' he then told Gay that he thought he was paralysed. This became more evident as the Chief of Staff tried desperately to get some reaction from Patton's limbs. Lieutenant Peter Babalas, of the 8081st MP Company, had by now arrived and taken charge. It was decided that GSP must be moved immediately, an ambulance was summoned and he was driven off at high speed, to the 130th Station Hospital in Heidelberg, some 25 miles away. General Patton was conscious when admitted, in mild shock, but fully aware that he had been seriously injured. He was now unable to move his arms or legs and had no sensation below his neck except at the tips of his shoulders. In outpatients, they cut away his clothing, gave him blood plasma, a tetanus shot and penicillin. 'Relax, gentlemen,' GSP told the anxious hospital staff, 'I'm in no condition to be a terror now.'

Heidelberg was in the Seventh Army area, now commanded by Patton's old friend General Geoffrey Keyes. He visited the hospital as soon as he heard about the accident and spent the rest of the day there. Within two hours eleven generals had come to the hospital, including another old friend, Major General Albert W. Kenner, now chief surgeon in the Theatre. In addition, there were Colonels Earl E. Lowry, chief Theatre surgical consultant, and Duane, chief of neuro-surgery at a nearby hospital. Kenner quickly realised the gravity of GSP's injury and spoke on the telephone to Washington. This resulted in the Surgeon General advising that Brigadier Hugh Cairns, Professor of Neuro-surgery at the School of Medicine, Oxford University, should be approached. He agreed to come to Heidelberg and Kenner sent an aircraft to fetch him. Beatrice Patton was also notified, General Eisenhower (now Army Chief of Staff) laid on an aircraft, while the State Department dealt swiftly with passport regulations. She arrived on the 11th, and by the 13th Patton was showing such improvement that his doctors began to consider flying him back to the States. But it was not to be. On the 19th a crisis suddenly developed and he had great difficulty breathing as the pressure on his spinal cord increased. For two days he struggled for survival, but at 1730 hrs on 21 December he died of acute heart failure, having confided to his brother-in-law, Fred Ayer, that this was 'a hell of a way for a soldier to die'.

'Seventh Army General Orders 635, December 22, 1945, signed Keyes.

'With deep regret, announcement is made of the death of General George S. Patton, Jr....

'Probably no soldier has had a greater compliment paid him than that given to General Patton by his most powerful and skilful opponents. He was termed the ablest American field commander faced by the German Army on any front.

'The entire Allied World now plays tribute to the man who deserves more than a lion's share of the credit for the victories of our arms in the bitter European struggle just ended.

'Seventh Army has lost a great friend, a gallant warrior and inspiring leader. Our country has lost a great and fearless citizen. May we comfort ourselves with the thought that he died as he loved to live – ever fighting!'

General Patton was buried at the Military Cemetery, Hamm, just outside Luxembourg, on 24 December 1945, after a funeral service in Heidelberg the day before. There had been proposals to take him back to the United

States for burial and certainly that is what Beatrice would have secretly wished for, so that they could have eventually lain side by side. But no deceased American soldier had been sent home since the beginning of the war, and GSP had specifically asked to be buried 'over there', with the rest of the war dead. 'Of course he must be buried here,' said Beatrice, 'why didn't I think of it? Furthermore, I know George would want to lie beside the men of his Army who have fallen.' Mrs Patton would die nine years later, breaking her neck in a riding accident. I have found more than one reputable historian postulating that her ashes were then secretly shipped over to Luxembourg so that she could have her final wish, but that is pure hearsay. Patton's grave was moved in 1948 to a more central location within the cemetery, the five surrounding graves being left vacant, so that the thousands of visitors who came to visit him could approach his grave more easily.

SECTION 3. PATTON, THE MAN AND THE LEGEND

A change of heart. The accident, the thirteen days in hospital and his eventual death, all served to focus public attention in America on the fact that one of their greatest – in many eyes the greatest – military leaders had died tragically and, worst of all, that he had been scurrilously treated by the nation's press, despite all that he had achieved for his country on the battlefield. No one but GSP could have turned American fortunes around in North Africa, whipping II Corps into fighting shape, then restoring the nation's pride in its army with his whirlwind campaign in Sicily. He had followed this with an equally breathtaking campaign all the way across France, driving the enemy before him, until he was held up, not by enemy action but by a shortage of petrol. This was followed by success of a very different kind in the 'hard pounding' which resulted in the capture of the fortress of Metz. Third Army's amazingly swift 90-degree turn and their relief of Bastogne effectively put an end to Hitler's last despairing hope of a counter-thrust, which undoubtedly hastened the end of the Third Reich. Patton then had capped it all by crossing the Rhine and pressing on deep into the Fatherland, ending the campaign as victoriously as he had begun it. All this he and his great Third Army had achieved, and what had he received in return?

Public conscience, and in particular the press who had been so strident in their condemnation of him just a few short weeks ago, now could not find sufficiently flowery words to praise him. 'Our most gallant soldier', 'The greatest general of all times', 'Essential to the nation', 'There will never be another like him', the headlines went on and on. 'No doubt he smiled cynically' is how Martin Blumenson describes GSP's probable reaction as he observed the scene from 'some unearthly place'. Mrs Patton received an almost unending stream of condolences and letters of genuine grief at his untimely death from ordinary men and women all over America. The hold which his devil-may-care 'Old Blood and Guts' image had gained over soldier and civilian alike was clear for all to see. However, much more importantly, and just as clear, was the undoubted love which so many of his soldiers felt for him. Martin Blumenson tells of one staff sergeant, so at a loss for words, having written a hopelessly inarticulate letter, 'signed his name and added quite simply, "I love him"'. There came a flood of tributes from all over the world which continued long after his death. There were Bills in Congress to award him, posthumously, America's highest military decoration, the Congressional Medal of Honor; to promote him to five-star rank; to provide a wealth of monuments and memorials, which included naming buildings, streets, etc., after him. And in 1972, of course, came the opening of the Patton Museum of Cavalry and Armor at Fort Knox.

'Not to be beaten.' Like all truly great men, especially great military commanders, General George Smith Patton, Jr, was a complex character, certainly not just the swashbuckling, fire-eating, gun-toting 'superman', which was how the press liked to portray him. This book is certainly not the place to dissect his character as it is primarily intended as an *aide mémoire* on the armies which he commanded during his military career. But bearing in mind that his career in armour spanned a longer period than any other armour commander who served in the Second World War, it is his success or failure on the battlefield that really counts and not the gaffes he made off it. When Patton was interviewed by the Swiss writer and biographer of Napoleon, Emil Ludwig, not long before his fatal accident, Ludwig asked him the simple question: 'What makes a great general?' GSP answered equally simply: 'Not to be beaten.' And he never was!

Notes to Chapter 12

1. This is as per the quote from GO 98 which appears in the XII Corps history, but of course the Third Army After Action Report lists 42.
2. 'The 2½-ton truck is our most valuable weapon,' GSP told various QM Groups during the operational period.
3. From the outset, Fifteenth Army had been destined to serve primarily as an occupation force as the Allies swept across Germany. It had been part of General Bradley's 12th Army Group, commanded by General Leonard T. Gerow, which had handled only rear echelon assignments, and became operational in January 1945 with two corps and six divisions. It then assumed a holding mission along the Rhine, facing the Ruhr, then later relieved the other armies of 12th Army Group of occupation duties as they drove deep into Germany – see *The Last Offensive* by Charles B. MacDonald.
4. Patton had just completed *War as I Knew it* (originally entitled 'War as I Saw it') in September/October, which Mrs Patton would see published after his death.

5. As his then aide, Major Merle-Smith, put it: 'sufficient certificates of honorary citizenship to paper the walls of a room'.
6. As quoted in *Patton's Last Battle* by Charles Whiting.
7. General Walter Bedell Smith was Eisenhower's Chief of Staff with whom GSP had had a 'love-hate' relationship over the years. He expressed a liking for him in 1943 during the Sicilian campaign, but this had deteriorated to a point where, in October 1945, Patton told Eisenhower, during dinner on the 13th, that he could not thereafter eat at the same table as General Bedell Smith.
8. In fact USFET Order dated 7 December 1945 directed Patton to proceed to Paris on or about 14 December, to travel to the USA by air.
9. Quoted in *Patton's Last Battle*, as having been taken from an article by Colonel Robert Allen in *Army Magazine*, June 1971.
10. Quoted in *The Patton Papers*.
11. Gay thought that Patton's head had hit the partition, while the MO who examined him concluded that he had hit the strut of the car roof. Whatever it was, it had been a severe blow and had severely damaged the spinal cord.

Bibliography

Published Works

Allen, Colonel Robert S. *Lucky Forward*, Vanguard Press Inc., 1947

Bell, William Gardner. *Commanding Generals and Chiefs of Staff 1775-1983*, Center of Military History, Washington, DC, 1983

Blumenson, Martin. *The Patton Papers*, 2 vols. Houghton Mifflin, 1974

Crismon, Fred W. *US Military Wheeled Vehicles*, Crestline Publishing Co. Inc., 1983

Dyer, Lieutenant Colonel George. *XII Corps, Spearhead of Patton's Third Army*, The XII Corps History Association, 1947

Essame, Major General H. *Patton, the Commander*, Batsford Ltd.

Farago, Ladislas. *The Last Days of Patton*, McGraw-Hill Co., 1981

Forty, George. *Tank Commanders, Knights of the Modern Age*, Firebird Books, 1993

– *US Army Handbook*, Ian Allan Ltd, 1979

– *Patton's Third Army at War*, Ian Allan Ltd., 1978 (rep. Arms & Armour Press, 1990, and in paperback, 1992).

Garland, Lieutenant Colonel Albert N., and McGaw Smyth, Howard, assisted by Martin Blumenson. *Sicily and the Surrender of Italy*, Office of the Chief of Military History of the Army, 1965

Georgano, G. N. *World War Two Military Vehicles, Transport and Half-tracks*, Osprey, 1994

Hatch, Alden. *George Patton, General in Spurs*, Simon & Schuster Inc., 1950

Hogg, Ian V. *The Biography of General George S. Patton*, Bison Books, 1982

Houston, Donald E. *Hell on Wheels, the 2nd Armored Division*, Presidio Press, 1977

Howe, George F. *The Battle History of 1st Armored Division, Combat Forces Press*, 1954

Katcher Philip. *The US Army 1941-45*, Osprey, 1977

Mosley, Leonard. *Marshall, Organiser of Victory*, Methuen, 1982

Pack, S. W. C. *Invasion North Africa 1942*, Ian Allan Ltd., 1978

– *Operation Husky, The Allied Invasion of Sicily*, David & Charles, 1977

Patton, General George S. Jr. *War as I Knew it*, Houghton Mifflin, Boston, 1975

Perkins, Major Norris H, and Rogers, Michael E. *Roll Again Second Armored*, Kristall Productions Ltd., 1988

Province, Charles M. *The Unknown Patton*, Hippocrene Books Inc., 1983

– *Patton's Third Army*, Hippocrene Books Inc., 1992
Wallace, Brigadier General Brenton G. *Patton and His Third Army*, Military Service Publishing Co., 1946
Weigley, Russell F. *Eisenhower's Lieutenants*, Sidgwick & Jackson, 1981
Whiting, Charles. *Patton's Last Battle*, Stein & Day, 1987
Wilson, Dale E. *Treat 'em Rough!*, Presidio Press, 1989
Marquis Who's Who. *Who Was Who in America*, vol. V, Marquis Who's Who Inc., 1974
– *Who Was Who in American History – The Military*, Marquis Who's Who Inc., 1974

Unpublished or Privately Published Works

Third US Army's After Action Report (two vols.), covering the period 1 August 1944 to 9 May 1945. Reproduced jointly by 652nd Engineer (Topo) Bn, Co 'B' 942nd Engineer Avn (Topo) Bn, 15 May 1945. Original graded SECRET, but regraded as UNCLASSIFIED by Executive Order 11-652, Section III(E) and 5(D) or (E)
Military Essays and Articles by George S. Patton, Jr, 1885–1945, edited by Charles M. Province and published by the George S. Patton, Jr. Historical Society, 1993
We Ripened Fast. The unofficial history of the 76th Infantry Division. Published in Frankfurt by the Board of the Directors of the 76th Infantry Division Officers' Association.
Miscellaneous Patton archives, held at the Patton Museum of Cavalry and Armor and quoted here with kind permission of the Museum Librarian.

Index

Scope of the Index: This index has been used mainly for 'people and places', rather than including the location of every single facet of the various armies that General Patton commanded, in particular US Third Army. This is because the general layout and subdivisions within chapters already makes finding such information both logical and easy, so it is not felt necessary to repeat it here.